Professional Reference for the Office

PROFESSIONAL REFERENCE FOR THE OFFICE

Rosemarie McCauley, Ed.D.
Department of Business Education and Office
Systems Administration
Montclair State College

GLENCOE/McGRAW-HILL
A Macmillan/McGraw-Hill Company
Mission Hills, California

Copyright © 1987 by Glencoe Publishing Company, a division of Macmillan, Inc.

Adapted from the *Pitman Office Handbook*, copyright © 1982, Copp Clark Pitman Ltd., Toronto, Ontario

All rights reserved. No part of this book shall be reproduced or transmitted in any form or by any means, electronic or mechanical, including photocopying, recording, or by any information retrieval system, without written permission from the Publisher.

Send all inquiries to:
Glencoe/McGraw-Hill
15319 Chatsworth Street
P.O. Box 9609
Mission Hills, CA 91346-9609
Printed in the United States of America

Library of Congress Cataloging-in-Publication Data

McCauley, Rosemarie
Professional reference for the office

    Includes index
    1. Office practice.   2. Office management.   I. Title.
HF5547.5.M293 1987   651   86-9771
ISBN 0-02-683010-8 (Student Text)
ISBN 0-02-683030-2 (Student Working Papers)
ISBN 0-02-683020-5 (Instructor's Guide)
    3 4 5 6 7 8 9 92 91 90

Contents

Introduction   xi

How to Use This Manual   xi

Unit 1   **Airline and Other Travel Arrangements**   1
            A1 Using a Travel Agent   3
            A2 Air Travel   3
            A11 Automobile Travel   7
            A15 Bus Travel   8
            A16 Train Travel   8
            A20 Sea Travel   9
            A21 Hotel/Motel Accommodations   10
            A25 The Itinerary   12
            A26 Travel Funds   12
            A27 Travel Insurance   14
            A30 International Travel   14
            A36 Travel Expense Reports   16
            A37 Planning Wisely for Travel   16
            A38 Office Worker's Role in Executive's Absence   18
            A39 Itinerary Form   19
            A40 Expense Report Form   20

Unit 2   **Banking and Financial Management**   21
            B1 Using Banking Services   23
            B55 Operating a Petty Cash Fund   42
            B56 Handling the Payroll   44
            B75 Understanding Basic Accounting Records   51
            B84 Related Vocabulary   59
            B85 Final Reminders   64
            B86 Sample Petty Cash Record   65
            B87 Sample Balance Sheet   66

v

Contents

Unit 3	**Communication in Business**	67
	C1 The Communication Process 68	
	C4 Written Business Correspondence 71	
	C27 Preparing Other Prevalent Written Communications 88	
	C41 Checklist for Writing Effective Communications 99	
	C42 Oral Communication in Business 100	
Unit 4	**Delivery and Shipping Services**	107
	D1 Alternatives to Postal Delivery Services 108	
	D9 Shipping Goods Within the United States 112	
	D12 Exporting Goods 113	
	D24 Importing Goods 115	
	D33 Transportation Terms 116	
	D34 Delivery and Shipping Log 117	
Unit 5	**Editing, Formatting, and Word Processing**	118
	E1 Typewriting Operations 120	
	E20 Categories of Keyboarding Equipment 134	
	E26 Corrections, Revisions, and Text Editing 137	
	E38 Style Practices 146	
	E39 Typing Metric Expressions 146	
	E42 Spacing Rules 148	
	E43 Typed Communications 149	
	E94 Reports, Essays, and Manuscripts 181	
	E137 Word Processing Configurations 201	
	E142 The Word Processing Cycle 202	
	E143 Dictation Equipment 203	
	E146 Word Processing Terms 204	
Unit 6	**Filing Systems and Records Control**	208
	F1 Data Versus Information 210	
	F2 The Records Cycle 210	
	F3 Creation 212	
	F4 Maintenance and Use 212	
	F17 Alphabetic Indexing 220	
	F42 Filing Systems 230	
	F51 Retention 238	
	F52 Transfer 240	

Contents

F53 Destruction 241
F54 Records Storage Equipment 242
F62 Systems Control 247
F69 Elements of a Comprehensive Records Management Program 252
F70 A Summary of Factors to be Considered When Evaluating a Records System 252
F71 Micrographic Storage 253
F74 Electronic Filing 257
F80 Insurance Record Maintenance 260
F81 Related Vocabulary 261

Unit 7 Grammar, Usage, and Style 263
G1 Grammatical Terms 265
G2 Correct Sentence Structure 268
G5 Punctuation 272
G43 Selecting the Right Words 283
G49 Spelling 295
G53 Style Mechanics 299
G91 Additional Reference Sources 316

Unit 8 Handling Forms 317
H1 System Flowcharts 318
H2 Forms 319
H3 Forms Used in Basic Business Activities 319
H28 Rubber Stamps and Die Plate Stamps 330
H29 Principles of Forms Design 331

Unit 9 Information Processing 333
I1 The Automated Office 335
I4 The Computer's Role in Information Processing 338
I12 Information Processing Devices 344
I13 Input Devices 344
I32 Storage Devices 348
I39 Processing Devices 350
I40 Output Devices 350
I53 Distribution Devices 353
I61 Technological Subsystems in the Integrated Office 354
I62 Computer-Related Terms 355

VII

Contents

Unit 10	**Job Search and Application**	362
	J1 The Search 363	
	J3 The Application 364	
	J12 The Application Form 370	
	J13 The Interview 370	
	J16 Follow-Up 375	
	J17 Resume Log 375	
	J18 Final Thoughts 376	
Unit 11	**Letter and Message Delivery**	377
	L1 Mail Techniques 378	
	L5 Mailroom Facilities and Equipment 382	
	L11 Ways to Ensure Efficient Mail-Handling 385	
	L12 Services and Products of the United States Postal Service 386	
	L49 Alternatives to Postal Services 395	
	L50 Checklist for Controlling Mailing Costs 396	
	L51 Stay Current 396	
Unit 12	**Mathematics in Business**	397
	M1 Fractions 398	
	M2 Decimals 400	
	M3 Percentages 402	
	M4 Common Equivalents 404	
	M5 Algebraic Equations 405	
	M6 Business Formulas 407	
	M13 Pricing Goods for Sale 408	
	M19 Statistical Data 411	
	M24 Foreign Currency Exchange 413	
	M25 Electronic Calculators 414	
Unit 13	**Organizing Meetings and Conferences**	420
	O1 Planning the Meeting 421	
	O6 Conducting the Meeting 425	
	O12 Minutes (Record) of the Meeting 428	
	O17 Follow-Up After the Meeting 431	

Unit 14	**Personnel Planning: Staffing The Office**	432
	P1 Personnel Planning 434	
	P2 Job Analysis 434	
	P3 Recruitment 435	
	P13 Orientation of New Employees 441	
	P14 Evaluation of Employees 442	
	P17 Promotion Policy 444	
	P18 Leaving a Job 444	
	P21 Records 445	
	P22 Payment Policy 446	
	P25 Temporary Help 447	
	P29 Channeling Employee Motivation 449	
Unit 15	**Queries: Locating Information**	450
	Q1 Almanacs and Yearbooks 452	
	Q2 Atlases 452	
	Q3 Biographical Dictionaries (Who's Who) 453	
	Q4 Dictionaries 454	
	Q6 Encyclopedias 455	
	Q7 English Usage Books 456	
	Q8 Form and Style Books 456	
	Q9 Government References 457	
	Q10 Indexes to Periodicals 458	
	Q13 Information About Business Organizations 459	
	Q18 Postal Information 462	
	Q19 Specialized References 462	
	Q20 How to Use a Library 463	
	Q24 Computerized Reference Searches 465	
	Q25 Company Library 466	
	Q26 Related Vocabulary 466	
Unit 16	**Reprographics**	469
	R1 Definition of Terms 470	
	R2 The Reprographic Process 471	
	R3 Reprographic Options 472	
	R4 Considerations in Selecting a Copying or Duplicating Process 473	

Contents

R5 Copying Processes 473
R21 The Duplicating Processes 482
R24 Choosing Reprographic Equipment 484
R28 Auxiliary Reprographic Equipment 487
R29 Photocomposition 488
R30 Photocomposition Terms 488
R31 Computer Graphics 489
R32 Intelligent Copiers 490
R33 Paper Terms 490
R34 Controlling Reprographic Costs 491

Unit 17 **Telephone and Telecommunication Systems** 493
T1 The Telephone 494
T35 Telecommunication Systems 508
T48 Controlling Telecommunication Costs 514

Unit 18 **Workstation and Personal Organization** 515
W1 Workstation Organization 516
W16 Personal Organization 526

Appendix A1
Abbreviations A2
Commonly Used Foreign Words and Phrases A2
Holidays A3
Metric System A4
Roman Numerals A7
Time Zones A8
Weights and Measures A9
Other A11

Index I1

Introduction

Professional Reference for the Office is a practical, authoritative reference manual for the contemporary business student and office worker. It is designed as a handy, easy-to-use source of information that answers the "How do I *do/write/format* this?" questions encountered daily in the classroom and on the job.

PRO provides a unique alternative to existing office reference manuals because it is more comprehensive in the range of topics covered. As in other office handbooks, PRO covers English skills and document formatting, but also includes discussions of many other areas of office operation. Up-to-date information is provided on financial and banking matters, math operations, time management, the electronic office, information processing, telecommunications, records manaagement, reprographics, personnel policies, and resume preparation. The topics discussed in *Professional Reference for the Office* cover most of the practical and applied aspects of the Certified Professional Secretary examination.

In certain units you will find handy checklists and blank sample forms that provide quick reference and practical suggestions for some common procedures. The sample forms may be used as a guide for implementation in actual office situations if desired.

Working Papers to accompany this manual are available from the publisher. They provide a three-part language skills exercise, a calcuation skills exercise, and an on-the-job application activity for 15 of the 18 units in the book. (The Communication, Grammar, and Mathematics units are treated throughout the Working Papers.) The Instructor's Resource Guide contains objectives for each unit, suggested questions for testing content knowledge, discussion topics, chapter exams, a final exam, and answers to the Working Papers exercises.

How to Use This Manual

PRO is arranged in a concise, *alphabetic* presentation with many cross-references, main headings, and subheadings to make locating information quick and easy for the user. The entry numbers are based upon the first letter of the first word in each unit title. This letter is the control for the system and will make locating information easier as you become familiar with the book's organization and content. For example, the sections in Unit 2, "Banking and Financial Management," are numbered B1, B2, B3, and so on.

Introduction

There are three ways to find information in this manual. To find a particular topic that you are interested in, locate it in the alphabetic index at the back of the book. Beside the index entry is an entry number in boldface type and a page number. You will find the entry number in the left margin of the indicated page.

Consult the main table of contents for the primary topics covered in each unit and the unit table of contents for a series of subtopics within a particular unit.

A thumb tab showing the initial letter of the unit title is provided in the outside margin of each page to assist you in locating individual units in the manual. Each unit's tabs correspond to those on the left edge of the back cover. To turn to a particular unit, find its title initial in the table of contents on the back cover and use the appropriate tab.

UNIT 1

A

AIRLINE AND OTHER TRAVEL ARRANGEMENTS

Using a Travel Agent	A1
Air Travel	A2-A10
Official Airline Guide (OAG)	
Confirmation and Cancellation	
Fares	
Special Fares	
Types of Flights	
Baggage	
Getting to and from the Airport	
Automobile Travel	A11-A14
Recording Mileage	
Rental Cars	
Travel Aids	
Bus Travel	A15
Train Travel	A16-A19
Fares	
Classes of Accommodations	
Luggage	
Sea Travel	A20
Hotel/Motel Accommodations	A21-A24
Requesting Accommodations	
Hotel and Restaurant Terms	
The Itinerary	A25

1

Airline and Other Travel Arrangements

Travel Funds	A26
Travel Insurance	A27-A29
Life and Baggage Insurance	
Other Insurance	
International Travel	A30-A35
Required Documents	
Health Requirements	
Customs	
Travel Expense Reports	A36
Planning Wisely for Travel	A37
Office Worker's Role in Employer's Absence	A38
Itinerary Form	A39
Expense Report Form	A40

A1-A2 Using a Travel Agent

Travel plans can include deciding on a method of transportation, reserving hotel accommodations, booking rental cars, obtaining international travel documents, and many other details. Some organizations have a department that makes all travel arrangements, but more often the office worker will use a travel agent or do the work alone. In any case, a knowledge of travel methods and regulations can be very useful whether arranging for your own travel or making travel plans for someone else. This unit provides you with an overview of the details you need to consider when handling travel arrangements.

A1 Using a Travel Agent

Travel agents are paid by carriers and hotels; there is no charge to the traveler. Travel agencies can offer excellent advice on accommodations, package tours, travel documents, car rentals, and overseas travel. In addition, they can be helpful about currency exchange rates, suitable clothing, customs arrangements, special events, and places of interest. However, an incompetent or unscrupulous agent can be a costly one. Before any agency is employed, check its reputation with the Better Business Bureau or the local Chamber of Commerce.

A2 Air Travel

Reservations may be made either by phone or in person at the airport, at airline ticket offices, or at a travel agency. Tickets will be issued when payment is made or credit is established. Some companies maintain monthly accounts with travel agencies; other companies provide key employees with credit cards for charging their travel arrangements.

When making air travel arrangements, the necessary reservation information includes:

- name(s) of traveler(s)
- departing airport/arrival airport
- date of travel and preferred times of departure/arrival
- class of service desired
- credit card or account numbers
- seating preference if advanced seating assignment is available
- contact telephone number(s) of the traveler(s)

Airline and Other Travel Arrangements

A3 The Official Airline Guide

Official Airline Guides, Inc. publishes a reference book that can be very helpful in booking flights when a travel agent is not used. The *Official Airline Guide* provides a listing of direct flights between cities, ground transportation information, and instructions on how to arrange connecting flights when direct flights are unavailable. An electronic edition of the OAG is available (for a subscription fee) for use with your home or office personal computer. To use it, your computer terminal must have telecommunicating capability. The sample listing in Figure 1.1 shows how to read the OAG.

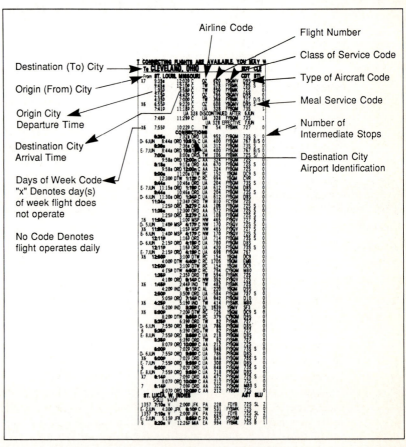

Figure 1.1 A sample listing from the Official Airline Guide
Reprinted by special permission from the June 1, 1985 edition of the *Official Airline Guide* NORTH AMERICAN EDITION. Copyright© 1986, Official Airline Guides, Inc. All rights reserved.

A4 Confirmation and Cancellation

It is important to confirm and cancel flights in a timely manner. When arriving at your destination, reconfirm your return reservation and leave a local contact number. If your travel plans change, call the airline and cancel your reservation. Failure to cancel may result in penalties.

A5 Fares

A6 First Class and Economy

First class air travel is the most expensive. First class passengers can expect more room, more comfortable seats, a more extravagant meal, complimentary bar service, and more personal services than can economy class passengers. There are only a few first class seats on each flight.

Economy, or coach class, is the least expensive class of service. Most special discounts apply to economy fares. The economy section may be more crowded and may not include complimentary food and beverage service.

Some airlines offer special business class sections for travelers who pay full economy fares. Passengers in this category generally can expect special check-in counters, complimentary bar service, first choice of meals and literature, and an adjacent vacant seat. Full fare tickets usually provide flexibility and alternate booking if your plans change.

A7 Special Fares

Super Saver, Tourist, and *Advance Purchase Excursion (APEX) fares:* Many airlines offer a limited number of special discount fares on many flights. These special bargain fares often have restrictions such as length of stay, lengthy advance purchase requirements, or required round-trip purchase. Some discounts may apply only to certain flights at specific times of the day. Under certain conditions, there may be a penalty fee charged for canceling an already purchased special fare ticket. The many restrictions on special fare tickets often make travel very inflexible. Be certain to ask the airline or travel agency for the availability of special fares, and about any restrictions or possible penalty payments.

A8 Types of Flights

Nonstop flight: no stops are made between the departure and destination points.

Airline and Other Travel Arrangements

Direct flight: a stop or stops along the way will be made, but there will be no need to change planes.

Connecting flight: passengers must get off one plane along the route and transfer to another plane on the same or another airline.

For business travel, where tight schedules often exist, it is best to book a nonstop or direct flight. Even if the flight departs late, the traveler usually gets to the final destination with little inconvenience. If the originating flight scheduled for a connecting flight is late, the traveler may miss the connection. Extensive rebooking may then be necessary and there is a risk of baggage delay.

Scheduled flight: a regular flight established by an airline that departs according to a regular schedule regardless of the number of seats sold.

Charter flight: a flight booked exclusively for group travel. This is among the least expensive forms of air travel, but you should anticipate crowded planes, a penalty for canceling, and inflexibility in changing dates. The charter agent may also cancel a proposed charter flight if enough seats are not sold prior to the departure date.

Private charter flight: In many areas it is possible to charter private airplanes. Charter companies are listed in the Yellow Pages. Although the cost may be higher than scheduled airlines, private charters offer the convenience of leaving according to your schedule and providing service to destinations not served by scheduled airlines. Before engaging a private charter, be sure to check on the company's reliability and the quality of service offered.

A9 Baggage

Individual airlines have their own regulations for free baggage allowances. This allowance could depend on total number of pieces, size, weight, or a combination of all of these elements. Generally, up to two pieces of luggage can be checked as baggage, but international flights may have different regulations. If in doubt about baggage allowance, check with the airline.

Most commercial airlines allow each passenger one piece of carry-on luggage. It must fit under the passenger's seat. Carry-on luggage normally does not count as part of a passenger's baggage allowance, and it provides an efficient way to pack for an overnight or short trip. Any excess baggage beyond free allowance will incur an additional charge.

Airline liability for delayed or missing baggage is limited. The exact limit can be verified at any airline ticket office. Excess value insurance can be purchased for additional fees. The airline accepts no liability for loss or damage to fragile or perishable items, money, jewelry, or negotiable securities. Be sure to identify all luggage with a tag on the outside and identification on the inside.

A10 Getting To and From the Airport

Crowded conditions often discourage parking your personal car at an airport. Large airports offer limousine, taxi, bus, and even helicopter service to and from all terminals. Compare the costs and time involved to determine the most efficient ground transportation. Many hotels provide complimentary airport limousines or vans.

A11 Automobile Travel

More and more, whether for business or vacation trips, the automobile is a popular way to travel. It offers convenience, privacy, and is generally less expensive than other means of transportation.

A12 Recording Mileage

Often, the businessperson is called upon to travel by car to attend a meeting, or to call on customers or clients. In such situations, a company-owned car may be used if one is available; otherwise, an individual's own car must be used. In any case, it is important to keep an accurate record of the trip because reimbursement will be based on the documented expenses. Similarly, self-employed individuals must maintain accurate and well-documented travel records if they are to be submitted for income tax purposes. Some of the items to record are:

- the dates
- the destination—to and from
- the reason for the trip
- the exact mileage (from odometer readings)
- tolls paid (with receipts, if possible)
- parking fees incurred
- receipts for the purchase of fuel

Most companies reimburse personal automobile use on a fixed mileage rate which varies from company to company. To determine reimbursement due, simply multiply the total business mileage by the fixed rate. For example:

Odometer Reading at End of Trip	24,200
Odometer Reading at Beginning of Trip	24,011
Round-trip Miles	189

Company mileage allowance is 22¢; therefore,
$$189 \times .22 = \$41.58$$

At the end of a trip, a business expense report is filed to request reimbursement for all travel expenses (see A36).

Airline and Other Travel Arrangements

A13 Rental Cars

Travelers wanting to rent cars can do so at airports, bus and train stations, hotels, through travel agents or airlines, or directly from the leasing companies. Advance reservations are essential, and comparison shopping is recommended. Some companies quote unlimited distance rates and others quote a flat fee plus a charge per mile. Compare the insurance coverage provided in the rental arrangement, the amount of liability (deductible amount) in the event of an accident, and the amount to be paid if the car is dropped off at another location. A valid driver's license and a credit card are usually mandatory before a car may be rented; otherwise, a cash deposit and verification of employment are necessary.

A14 Travel Aids

Road, county, and city maps are handy resources for the car traveler. The frequent traveler often subscribes to some type of road aid plan that provides for assistance in the case of auto breakdowns on the road. A service often available through companies providing road aid service is *personal trip planning*, which can be requested by the traveler prior to the trip. Personal trip planning services supply all maps needed to take a specific trip, and the most direct or scenic routes can be requested. Often, the plan will indicate areas where there will be construction delays and alternate routes will be suggested.

A15 Bus Travel

Buses provide economic, efficient, and reasonably comfortable travel. Most over the road buses are air-conditioned and many have washrooms. The disadvantages of bus travel are lack of advance reservations on short trips, schedules that may be interrupted by weather, lack of sleeping accommodations, and no food service. Bus travel is most suitable for travel to locations not served by air or rail lines. Baggage regulations are determined by individual carriers, and these need to be checked on an individual basis.

A16 Train Travel

In many parts of the country, train travel is the most economical and convenient form of transportation. Most trains run on a regular schedule. Reservations may be made directly with the railroad company via a

A13-A20   Rental Cars

toll-free number or through a travel agent. Reservations are required for sleeping accommodations, club car, and coach travel. Necessary reservation information includes:

- destination
- desired departure and arrival times
- type of accommodation

A17   Fares

Uniform fares operate all year round, although prices are slightly higher during the summer and holiday travel periods. Credit cards are accepted for payment of fares.

A18   Classes of Accommodations

Long distance trains offer a variety of accomodations which include:

- *Coach:* slightly reclining seat only.
- *Daynighter:* reclining seat with footrest.
- *Compartment:* a private section with bed and bath facilities.
- *Club Car:* offers a reclining seat with footrest. A free meal is served and bar service is available.
- *Sleeping Berth:* a compartment with a bed for long or overnight trips.

A19   Luggage

Three pieces of luggage may be checked, not to exceed 75 pounds each, and two bags may be carried on.

Arrangements may be made to transport animals in the baggage car only. Feeding and other pet care is the responsiblity of the owner.

A20   Sea Travel

Once the major international carrier, ships tend now to be used mainly for holiday cruise travel. Travel agents and the shipping lines will provide information and make arrangements.

Airline and Other Travel Arrangements

A21 Hotel/Motel Accommodations

A22 Requesting Accommodations

There are many ways of reserving hotel or motel accommodations. Some of these are:

- through central reservation service for large chains via toll-free telephone numbers
- through local offices of large hotel chains that have Telex or telephone tielines with their branches
- directly with the hotel by letter, telegram, telephone, Telex, or the *Hotel & Motel Red Book* (see A23)
- through a travel agent (but possible room rate discounts might be forfeited)

When requesting accommodations, state the type and size of room required, length of occupancy, and arrival and departure times. Rates are generally based on single occupancy of the room; a small additional charge is made for accommodating more people. Be sure to take advantage of any commercial room rate (corporate rate) discounts possible (e.g., to members of the Commercial Travelers Association, other registered associations, and travelers for large companies that give hotels regular business). Room rates do not usually include meals or taxes.

Hotels will generally not hold a reservation past 6 p.m. unless a guaranteed reservation is requested. To guarantee arrival, use a credit card number or deposit one night's room rate. If you arrive later than expected, your room will be held for you. If you do not claim or cancel a guaranteed reservation, you will be charged for the room even though not used.

A23 The Hotel & Motel Red Book

The American Hotel & Motel Association publishes an annual directory that lists hotels, motels, resorts, and meeting facilities in the United States and other countries. The *Red Book* (Figure 1.2) lists U.S. hotels and motels alphabetically by state and city, and international hotels and motels alphabetically by country, then by city. Information is provided on room rates, locations, and credit cards accepted.

A21-A23 Hotel/Motel Accommodations

NEW OTANI HOTEL & GARDEN 120 S Los Angeles St 90012 Location: Downtown Credit Cards: AE, CB, DC, MC, VS	Tel: (213) 629-1200	(800) 421-8795
	Rooms: 448	Meal Plan: E
	Single: $94–114	
	Double: $109–129	
	Telex: 677022	
PARK PLAZA HOTEL 607 S Park View St 90057	Tel: (213) 384-5281	
	Rooms: 150	Meal Plan: E
	Rates: $25–45	
PARK SUNSET HOTEL 8462 Sunset Blvd 90069	Tel: (213) 654-6470	
	Rms.: 100	Rts.: $49–57
QUALITY INN—INTERNATIONAL AIRPORT 5249 W Century Blvd 90045 Location: Airport Credit Cards: AE, CB, DC, MC, VS	Tel: (213) 645-2200	(800) 228-5151
	Rooms: 265	Meal Plan: E
	Rates: $42–145	
	Telex: 910 328 7249	
RAMADA HOTEL—BEVERLY HILLS 1150 S Beverly Dr 90035 Location: Suburban Credit Cards: AE, CB, DC, MC, VS	Tel: (213) 553-6561	(800) 228-2828
	Rooms: 260	Meal Plan: E
	Single: $88–97	
	Double: $100–124	
	Telex: 696156	
RAMADA INN—INTERNATIONAL AIRPORT 9620 Airport Blvd 90045 Location: Airport Credit Cards: AE, CB, DC, MC, VS	Tel: (213) 670-1600	(800) 2RA-MADA
	Rooms: 149	Meal Plan: E
	Single: $58–64	
	Double: $68–74	
ROYAL PALACE WESTWOOD 1052 Tiverton Ave 90024 Credit Cards: AE, CB, DC, MC, VS	Tel: (213) 208-6677	
	CA: (800) 248-6955	(800) 631-0100
	Rooms: 35	Meal Plan: E
SHERATON GRANDE HOTEL 333 S Figueroa St 90071 Location: Downtown Credit Cards: AE, CB, DC, MC, VS	Tel: (213) 617-1133	(800) 325-3535
	Rooms: 470	Meal Plan: E
	Single: $135–195	
	Double: $155–215	
	Telex: 677003	

Figure 1.2 A sample listing from the Hotel & Motel Red Book
Reprinted from the Hotel & Motel Red Book, 100th Anniversary edition, © 1986. Courtesy of Pac Tel Publishing.

Airline and Other Travel Arrangements

A24 Hotel and Restaurant Terms

If you are considering a package travel plan, the following definitions may be helpful:

Concierge: hotel employee to contact for help with any problem or concern.

European Plan (EP): no meals included.

American Plan (AP): room and meals included.

Modified American Plan (MAP): room, breakfast, and dinner.

Continental Plan: room and breakfast.

Table d'hôte: fixed charge for the meal.

À la carte: each dish on the menu is priced separately.

A25 The Itinerary

An *itinerary* (Figure 1.3) is a detailed list of travel arrangements, accommodations, appointments to be kept, and essential reminders. If arrangements are made through a travel agent, the agent will usually provide a travel itinerary as part of the service.

When establishing a personal itinerary, be sure that sufficient time is provided for transportation to and checking in at airports, that arrival and departure times are *local* times, and that sufficient travel recovery time is allowed before meetings are scheduled. (See A39 for a blank itinerary form.)

A26 Travel Funds

To avoid the need for large sums of cash, funds may be taken in one of these forms:

- Credit cards: Bank credit cards such as Visa and Mastercard, and travel and entertainment cards such as American Express and Diner's Club are acceptable for most purchases in and out of the United States (see Unit 2, B40).
- Traveler's Checks: (See Unit 2, B52.) Traveler's Checks are easily replaced if lost or stolen, and widely accepted. They are available in varying denominations. It is usually a good idea to

```
                    ITINERARY FOR MS. PATRICIA WORTH
                     April 24, 19-- to April 26, 19--

Monday, April 24

10:55 a.m.      Leave Newark Airport
                Flight 26, United

2:25 p.m.       Arrive Las Vegas, Nevada
                Ground transportation to The Algonquin Hotel
                Single room confirmed

5 p.m.          Dinner Meeting with Ms. Pam Merriweather and Mr. Frank Sitta,
                Crest Corporation; Meet in the hotel lobby

Tuesday, April 25

9 a.m.          Registration for ABCA Conference, Mezzanine, Algonquin Hotel

12 noon         Lunch Meeting with Ms. Jody Albright, ABCA Vice President
                Meet in hotel lobby

3 p.m.          Presentation, Midway Room, 3rd Floor
                Bring handouts and visuals

8 p.m.          Reception, Grand Ballroom, Lower Level

Wednesday, April 26

8 a.m.          Breakfast Meeting with Ms. Pam Merriweather
                Coffee Shop, Algonquin Hotel

10 a.m.         Presentation, Forsgate Room, 2nd Floor

1 p.m.          Van Service available from hotel to airport

2:35 p.m.       Leave Las Vegas, Nevada, Airport
                Flight 22, Delta

6 p.m.          Arrive O'Hare Airport, Chicago
                Change planes

8 p.m.          Leave O'Hare Airport, Chicago
                Flight 113, United for Newark Airport

11:05 p.m.      Arrive Newark Airport
                Call for airport pickup:   787-3389
```

Figure 1.3 Sample Itinerary

get them in the currency of the country to be visited if international travel is planned.

- Letters of credit: (See Unit 2, B46.) With letters of credit, the holder may obtain amounts of cash up to the stated limit in any branch of the bank that issued the letters.

If the need for an emergency supply of money arises, funds can be telegraphed to the traveler (see Unit 2, B54 and Unit 18, T39).

Airline and Other Travel Arrangements

A27 Travel Insurance

A28 Life and Baggage Insurance

Life and baggage insurance additional to that provided by carriers is available from travel agents or insurance company booths at airports and railway stations.

A29 Other Insurance

Additional health insurance for international travelers may be purchased directly through major insurance companies. Trip cancellation insurance for charter flights can be purchased for both pre-departure or post-departure coverage. Travel accident and emergency medical plans, as well as a number of other special plans are available to the traveler. Check with the airline or your travel agent.

A30 International Travel

Making arrangements for international travel is no different from making domestic bookings. You may prefer, however, to rely more on the travel agent's specialized knowledge.

For regular international travel, APEX fare is the most economical. It carries its own rules and requirements regarding cancellation charges; however, it must be booked and ticketed 21 days prior to departure.

A31 Required Documents
A32 Passport

A passport is required for travel to all overseas destinations. It is usually available from your local county court house and serves as a verification of your citizenship. With the application form, you must present a birth certificate or previous passport, two recent (within the last six months) photographs, and the appropriate fee. A new passport costs approximately $45 for persons over the age of 18 and about $35 for children (fees may vary from state to state). A U.S. passport is valid for ten years. The fee to renew a passport is $35. Allow sufficient time for the processing of the application—usually from four to six weeks depending on the season.

A33 Visa

A visa is a special permit required for visits to certain countries overseas. Travel agents have information on these countries, the documents required when traveling to them, and the visa fee. Visas are obtained at the respective consulate offices of the countries requiring them, and must be secured *before* entering these countries. You must obtain your passport first because this will be required as part of your application for the visa. Allow plenty of time for obtaining visas.

A34 Health Requirements

Vaccinations and immunizations are required for travel to some countries. Travel agents or local health officers can provide full details as to the requirements and the documentation needed. Do not wait until the last minute because certain vaccinations consist of a series of injections given over a three-week period.

A35 Customs

The amount of duty-free (tax-free) purchases that travelers may bring back into the United States varies according to the country visited and the length of the stay. Check with your local customs office for the duty-free regulations applicable to your destination and the length of your stay.

Travelers may, of course, bring back additional items beyond the duty-free allowance, but they must be prepared to pay the tax on any amount in excess of the regulations. Some items, such as food and plants, may not be brought into the country. Check with the local customs office if in doubt about a planned purchase.

It is wise to register with the customs office any valuables (e.g., camera, jewelry) being taken out of the country so that there is no problem in bringing them back into the United States.

Airline and Other Travel Arrangements

A36 Travel Expense Reports

Travel Expense Reports (Figure 1.4) may need to be filed for day trips, for overnight trips, and for trips that extend into several days. The steps in reporting travel expenses are:

1. Expenses are noted in a diary or log as they are incurred.
2. At periodic intervals, expenses are transferred to an expense report.
3. Expense reports are submitted to a designated company official for approval.
4. Expense reports go to the accounting department for processing.
5. Reimbursement is made to you.

Guidelines for preparing travel expense reports are:

- Know the company's policies.
- Estimate cash needs before traveling and determine how your company prefers to have payments made.
- Update your expense record daily.
- Collect and retain all required receipts and forms.
- Record automobile mileage accurately.
- Verify each item that you place on the expense report.
- Verify the calculations on the expense report.
- Make a copy of the report and all receipts for your records *before* officially submitting the report. (See A40 for a blank expense report form.)

A37 Planning Wisely for Travel

Whether you are planning a business trip for yourself or for someone else, the following suggestions should be helpful:

- Recognize that no means of travel is best at all times for all people. To decide which method of travel to select, consider the purpose of the trip, the time available, the budget restrictions, and the time of the day, month, or year that the travel is to take place.
- Consider the effect of the loss or gain of time as you travel through the time zones on cross country or international trips (see Appendix, page A8).

A36-A37 Travel Expense Reports

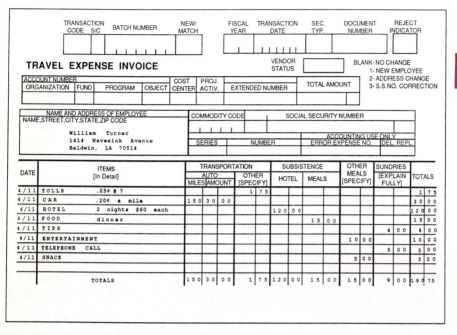

Figure 1.4 Completed Travel Expense Report

- Determine the ideal time to arrive at the destination, considering possible weather delays, traffic slowdowns, or other possible problems.
- Make air, railroad, and bus reservations well ahead of time —especially for holiday travel periods.
- Use toll-free numbers whenever possible to make advance reservations at hotels and motels and to confirm flights.
- If an overnight stay is necessary, determine what type of accommodations would be best. You may wish to compare hotel rates and distances to places where you will be conducting business.
- Estimate how much money you will need for the trip. Do not take along large sums of cash; plan to use credit cards or traveler's checks to cover expenses.
- Confirm all flights ahead of time, including connecting flights.
- Have important documents with you. Pick up airline tickets, arrange to get a passport or visa, if needed, and bring all business-related material and files with you.

17

Airline and Other Travel Arrangements

- Clearly label all folders containing important papers to be used on the trip.
- Label envelopes and packages clearly with the office address so they may be easily returned if lost.
- Keep a record of all files being taken out of the office and check them off when they are returned.
- Include a packet of supplies—stationery, envelopes, stamps, pens, pencils, etc.
- Forward any bulky envelopes or packages and mark them *Hold for Arrival* with the appropriate arrival date indicated.
- If a speech or presentation is being given, mail an extra copy of the materials to the hotel in the event of a lost or misplaced briefcase.
- Gather any personal items that you will need while away to make you comfortable. Take along prescriptions, air sickness medicine, a second pair of eyeglasses or set of keys, road maps, lodging guides, and lists of recommended restaurants and places to visit.
- Prepare an itinerary and leave copies of it at the office and at home.

A38 Office Worker's Role in Executive's Absence

If you are left in charge while your employer is away on a business trip, vacation, or for any other reason, you must be prepared to function effectively in that role. The following list suggests ways to help you maintain an efficient operation while your employer is away:

1. Discuss with your employer how to handle routine matters effectively.
2. Determine when and how correspondence is to be forwarded.
3. Know how to handle routine mail.
4. Assist your employer by establishing priorities for his or her return. Sort mail and place into folders labeled, for example, *For Signature, For Immediate Action, Action Required, To Be Read—No Action Required, Reading Material*, etc.
5. Keep a log of calls, messages, visitors, and any important activities that take place during your employer's absence.

A38-A39 Office Worker's Role in Executive's Absence

6. Know how and when to communicate with your employer.
   a. Have phone numbers where he or she may be reached.
   b. Anticipate any needed information and questions your employer may ask before placing a long-distance call.
   c. Determine which items are crucial and which items can await your employer's return; do not bother the executive with unimportant matters while he or she is away.

A39 Itinerary Form

Itineraries may be prepared in many different formats. Figure 1.5 illustrates a form that is merely suggestive of one of those ways.

```
                    ITINERARY FOR _____

                          _/_/_-_/_/_

Day     Date    From    To    Via    Leave    Arrive    Hotel
```

COMMENTS (appointments, contacts, telephone numbers, reminders, etc.)

Figure 1.5 Itinerary Form

Airline and Other Travel Arrangements

A40 Expense Report Form

Expense report forms vary from company to company depending upon particular needs, accounting procedures, and information required. Figure 1.6 illustrates one example of an expense report form.

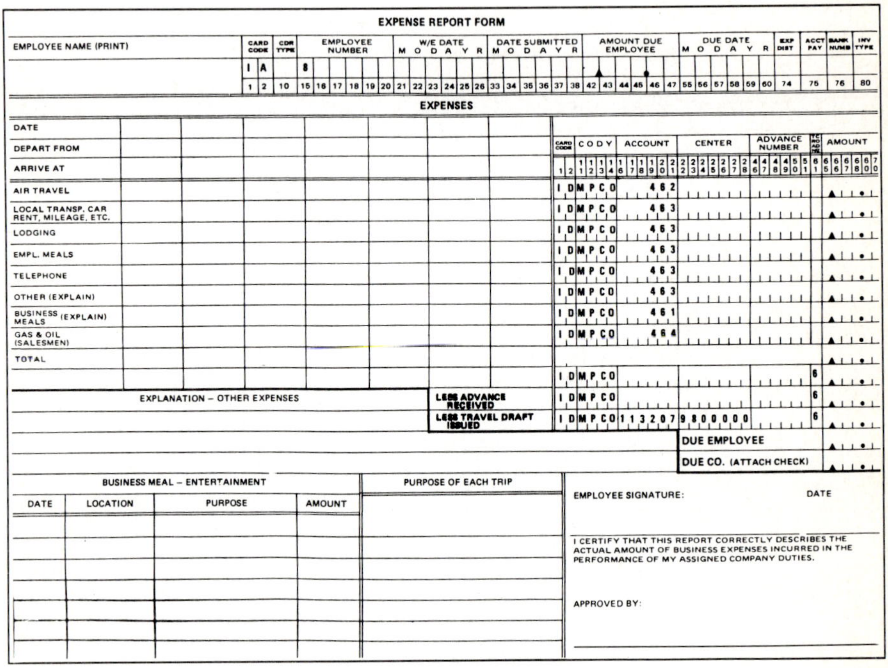

Figure 1.6 Expense Report Form

UNIT 2

Banking and Financial Management

Using Banking Services — B1-B54
  Types of Accounts
  Certificates of Deposit
  Money Market Accounts
  Tax-Sheltered Pension Trust Accounts
  Making Deposits
  Preparing a Deposit Slip
  Making Withdrawals
  Parts of a Check
  Making Entries for Checkbook Withdrawals
  Preparing Checks
  Endorsing Checks
  Special Types of Checks
  Reconciling the Bank Statement
  Other Banking Services

Operating a Petty Cash Fund — B55
Handling the Payroll — B56-B74
  Calculating of Gross Earnings
  Preparing the Payroll
  The Employee Earnings Record
  Payroll Deductions
  Vacation, Holiday and Severance Pay
  Methods of Payroll Payment
  Employers' Legal Obligations

Banking and Financial Management

Understanding Basic Accounting Records	**B75-B83**
Source Documents	
Journals	
The Ledger	
An Account	
Trial Balance	
Financial Statements	
Related Vocabulary	**B84**
Final Reminders	**B85**
Sample Petty Cash Record	**B86**
Sample Balance Sheet	**B87**

Since money plays a significant role in most business activities, the efficient office worker must understand and be able to perform routine tasks associated with money management. This unit presents information that will help you use outside financial services (banks and similar institutions), and help you organize and maintain internal financial records such as petty cash funds, payroll for a small business, and basic accounting procedures.

B1 Using Banking Services

Banks are businesses that hold, loan, exchange, and issue money. They usually offer a wide variety of services. Legally, banks and similar institutions must be chartered by the federal government or the governments of the states in which they operate. The chartering agency regulates and monitors banking activities by imposing rules, regulations, and legislation that govern virtually all aspects of banking practices.

Financial institutions may be chartered as trust companies, commercial banks, savings banks, savings and loan associations, and credit unions. The maximum insured amount for a deposit is $100,000 by most financial institutions. Deposits maintained in different rights or capacities are separately insured up to $100,000; thus, a person may hold or have an interest in more than one separately insured account in the same insured bank.

The information provided in this unit outlines some of the characteristics of the major services typically provided by chartered financial institutions.

B2 Types of Accounts

A bank account is a contract between the bank and the depositor. Accounts may be opened by individuals or by businesses and organizations. *Joint accounts* may be opened by two or more individuals. They provide that each person may use the account on his or her own signature, unless arrangements with the bank specify that two or more signatures are necessary for transactions. Interest rates, minimum balances for initial deposits, terms and methods of computing interest, minimum balances that must be maintained, and service charges are just some of the conditions that must be considered when opening an account. These conditions vary from account to account as well as from institution to institution. It is important to recognize that banks act only as collection agents in processing checks deposited in your account.

B3 Passbook Savings Accounts

An account opened by individuals or businesses wishing to earn interest on deposits is a *passbook savings account*.

- Interest may be compounded daily, monthly, or quarterly.
- A savings passbook is issued in which all transactions are recorded.
- Withdrawals may be made by completing a withdrawal slip and presenting the passbook for the account.
- Accounts usually have a minimum monthly balance requirement in order to earn interest.
- The account can usually accept the direct deposit (see B41) of social security checks, payroll checks, and recurring payment checks.

B4 Statement Savings Accounts

An account opened by individuals or businesses wishing to earn interest on deposits is a *statement savings account*.

All the features of passbook savings accounts apply to statement savings accounts *except:*

- A receipt is issued for deposits and withdrawals when they are made at the bank instead of an entry made in a passbook.
- Once a month, or quarterly, you receive a statement from the bank summarizing your transactions in the month or quarter, and showing your current balance and interest earned.
- If a minimum balance is not maintained, a service charge may be imposed.

B5 Checking Accounts

Checking accounts are used by individuals, associations, estates, and businesses for making deposits and payments. Written documents, called *checks*, direct the bank to pay money as instructed.

B6 Noninterest-Bearing Checking Accounts

- A minimum balance must be maintained; if balances fall below the minimum balance, service charges are usually imposed.
- Withdrawals are made by check (see B15).

- Regular statements plus canceled checks and explanations of deposits (credit) or withdrawals and service fees (debits) are supplied monthly to the account holder.
- An unlimited number of checks may be written, provided that the debits do not exceed the account balance.
- Usually there is no service charge if a minimum balance is maintained; however, some banks charge a per check or per transaction fee.

B7 Interest-Bearing Checking Accounts

- Essentially the same features as the noninterest-bearing checking account *except:*

    Usually a higher minimum balance is required than with a noninterest-bearing checking account.

    The minimum deposit required to open the account is usually higher than that required by the noninterest-bearing checking account.
- Sometimes canceled checks are not returned with the monthly statement unless a service charge for processing and handling is paid.
- Interest paid is usually about the same as that paid on passbook savings accounts.

B8 Certificates of Deposit

Certificates of deposit are high-yielding certificates that offer a unique combination of guaranteed interest rates and flexible terms. Minimum deposit requirements must be considered at the time of purchase.

- A variety of interest-bearing plans are often available.
- Shorter term certificates usually require higher minimum deposits; here are some examples:

Term	Minimum Balance Ranges*
7 to 31 days	$1,000 - $2,500)
91 days	$1,000 - $2,500) *Variable
6 months	$1,000 - $2,500) from bank
30 months	$500) to bank
5 to 10 years	$500)

Banking and Financial Management

- Interest rates fluctuate from week to week.
- Once a certificate is purchased, the interest rate is fixed for the term of the certificate.
- Penalties for early withdrawal and bank service charges are imposed.
- A variety of interest-earning plans are available. These may include interest compounded and received at maturity, interest paid monthly or quarterly, and interest deposited into one's savings account.
- Some certificates may be automatically *rolled over*—that is, renewed—at the interest rate being given on the renewal date.

B9 Money Market Accounts

Money market accounts are used by individuals or businesses to obtain higher interest rates than passbook savings accounts, plus the advantage of demand withdrawals without penalty.

- Requires a large deposit to open an account—often between $2,500 and $5,000, but amount varies from bank to bank.
- Usually balances under $2,500 earn passbook interest rate only. However, if the balance is over $2,500, the higher money market rates (which fluctuate weekly and which run from 3 to 5 percent higher than passbook savings) will be earned for the full amount of the deposit.
- Insured up to $100,000.
- Provides a monthly statement describing transactions and interest rates paid.
- A limited number of third party checks is permitted per month without a service charge.
- Unlimited over-the-counter withdrawals by use of special forms.
- A service charge is levied if the minimum number of checks is exceeded (often 3 to 6 per month).
- Monthly fees are often levied if balances fall below a certain minimum amount.

B10 Tax-Sheltered Pension Trust Accounts

B11 IRA (Individual Retirement Accounts)

- Can be opened by any wage earner.
- Penalty for early withdrawal imposed by bank and Internal Revenue Service.
- Minimum deposit $100.

B9-B14   Money Market Accounts

- Maximum annual deposit fixed by federal law:

    $2,000 may be deposited annually by an individual

    $4,000 may be deposited annually by a couple, both working

    $2,500 may be deposited annually by a couple, one working

    Note: These amounts were current at the time of this writing. Because of frequently changing laws, however, they cannot be considered constant.
- Trust plan can be selected from a variety of high-yielding certificates of deposit or investment plans.
- Tax-free interest until withdrawal at retirement (subject to legislative decisions).
- Withdrawals may begin at age 59 1/2.

B12   Keogh Plan

- A tax-deferred retirement plan for self-employed, non-incorporated individuals.
- Effective January 1984, an individual may deduct the lesser of 25 percent of income, or $30,000. **Note:** These amounts were current at the time of this writing. Because of frequently changing laws, however, they cannot be considered constant.
- Tax-free interest until withdrawal at age 59 1/2 (subject to legislative decisions).
- A variety of savings or investment plans may be selected.
- Penalty for early withdrawal imposed by bank and Internal Revenue Service. Amount varies.

B13   Making Deposits

Deposit slips are completed when adding money to savings or checking accounts. You must present your passbook, as well as your deposit slip, when placing funds in a passbook savings account.

Deposit slips vary in format but contain similar information. They indicate which account should be credited by name and account number, the amount of the deposit, and the date of the deposit. Statement savings accounts do not require a passbook.

B14   Preparing a Deposit Slip

If you make regular deposits, you will have pre-printed deposit slips that include the appropriate account number (Figure 2.1). Sometimes, however, you must provide the account number on a bank deposit slip. To

Banking and Financial Management

speed the processing of a deposit slip:

- Fill out the deposit slip neatly and accurately.
- Arrange bills with the smallest denomination on top. Use money wrappers for large deposits of bills and coins. (These money wrappers are often available free of charge from banks.)
- Be certain that all checks are properly endorsed (see B19).
- List checks *separately* on the deposit slip.
- Verify the total deposit by re-adding the total—preferably on a calculating machine with a paper tape.

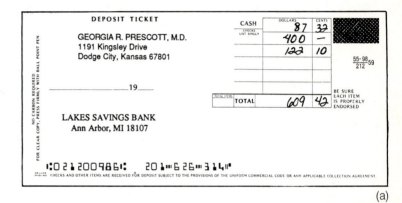

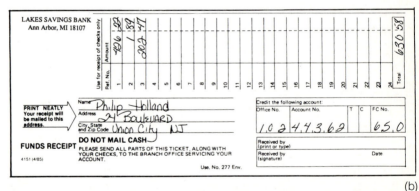

Figure 2.1 (a) Pre-printed Deposit Slip (b) Bank Deposit Slip

B15 Making Withdrawals

Withdrawal slips (available at the bank) are used to withdraw funds from passbook savings accounts and money market accounts. Withdrawals from checking accounts are made by check.

B15-B17 Making Withdrawals

B16 Parts of a Check

The parts of a check are illustrated in Figure 2.2.

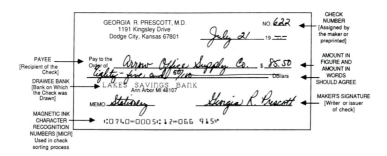

Figure 2.2 Completed Bank Check

B17 Making Entries for Checkbook Withdrawals

The check stub or check register entry should be made before the check is actually written to ensure that every deduction will be included. Two basic check payment records are commonly used: the checkbook (Figure 2.3) and the check register (Figure 2.4).

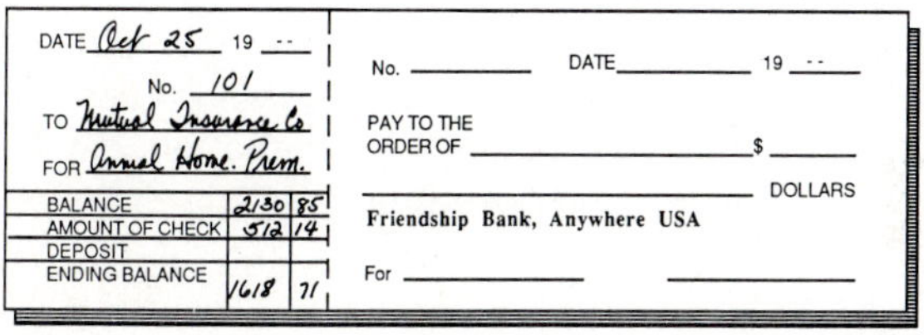

Figure 2.3 Checkbook

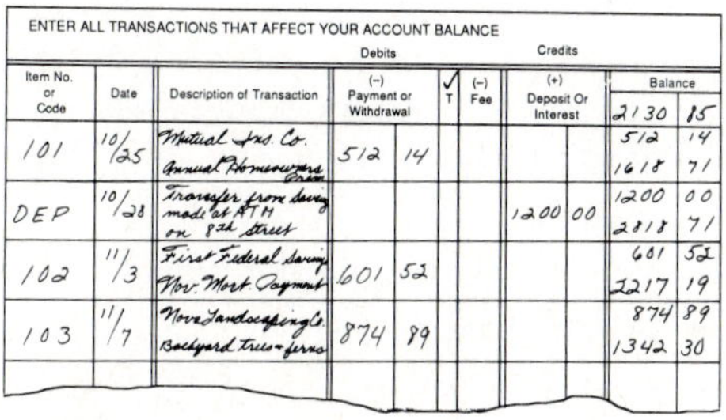

Figure 2.4 Check Register

Banking and Financial Management

B18 Preparing Checks

Checks may be written for any amount up to the amount held in deposit in the account. Checks may be prepared by hand, typewriter, check protector, or computer.

When preparing checks by hand:

- Complete the check stub or check register first.
- Use indelible ink.
- Be sure to insert the correct date.
- Spell the name of the payee correctly (see B16). Omit courtesy titles such as Mr., Mrs., Ms., Miss, Dr., and Reverend. Never make a check payable to *Cash, Self,* or *Bearer.* If lost, it belongs to anyone!
- Write the amount in figures close enough to the printed dollar sign so that it cannot be altered.
- Write the amount in words, making sure it is the same amount as that expressed in figures. Begin at the extreme left and fill in any unused part of the line so that there is no space for changes.
- Express cents as fractions of a dollar (25/100 for twenty-five cents).
- Do not erase. Either prepare a new check or correct and initial at the point of error. Do not destroy an unused check. Instead, write *VOID* in large letters across the face of it and the stub and retain them in your files. Tearing off the magnetic code information and signature line at the bottom of a check is also an effective precautionary measure.
- Be certain the check is properly signed. Sometimes two or more signatures are needed for businesses and other organizations.

When typing checks:

- Follow the steps for writing checks.
- Take care to align the typing so that it is close to the preprinted lines.
- Type carefully to avoid mistakes.
- In case of error, do not strike over or use any type of cover-up correction medium. The check must be voided and retyped.
- Businesses often use *Voucher Checks* that have an explanatory stub attached, as shown in Figure 2.5.

B18-B20 Preparing Checks

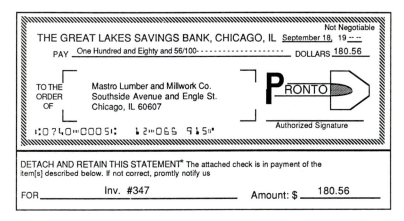

Figure 2.5 Voucher Check

B19 Endorsing Checks

Before a check can be cashed or deposited, it must be properly endorsed. This means that the payee *signs* his or her name on the reverse side of the check. The endorsement does three things.

- It relieves the bank of responsibility should the check be dishonored (see B31).
- It acts as a receipt for the cash.
- It serves as identification of the payee.

There are three types of endorsements.

B20 Blank Endorsement

The *blank endorsement* (Figure 2.6) is used if the payee cashes or deposits the check. It is used by businesses or individuals for making deposits and payments.

- Hold the check so that the front of the check is in reading position before you; then turn the check over and place the endorsement at the left side of the check.
- Endorse (sign) the check exactly as the name appears on the face of the check.
- Place a blank endorsement on a check only at a bank, just before cashing or depositing it. The blank endorsement enables anyone presenting the check to cash it.

31

Banking and Financial Management

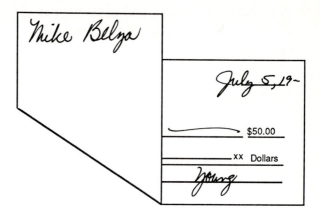

Figure 2.6 Blank Endorsement

Figure 2.7 Double Endorsement

Note: If the payee's name is incorrectly spelled on the face of the check, endorse the check twice—once as it is shown on the check and then correctly (Figure 2.7). This is called a *double endorsement*.

B21 Full Endorsement

The *full endorsement*, or *second party check*, is used if the payee wishes to transfer ownership of the check to another person. Endorse the check with the wording *Pay to the order of (new payee)* and sign it as shown on the face of the check (Figure 2.8). The new payee may then cash, deposit, or transfer ownership of the check again.

Note: Many banks will not accept or cash second endorsed checks since they cannot vouch for the first signature.

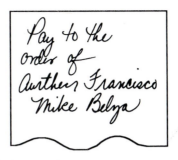

Figure 2.8 Full Endorsement

B22 Restrictive Endorsement

The *restrictive endorsement* is used when it is necessary to protect a check against loss or theft. Any check for deposit sent through the mail should include a restrictive endorsement. Endorse the check with the wording *For deposit only*, or *For deposit to the account of*... and sign it as shown on the face of the check (Figure 2.9). The endorsement may either be written or rubber stamped. This type of endorsement is recommended by bankers.

Figure 2.9 Restrictive Endorsement

B23 Special Types of Checks

B24 Bank Checks

Bank checks are also called *Cashier's Checks* or *Treasurer's Checks*.

- Issued primarily to bank customers for large withdrawals from savings accounts or other forms of accounts, or for loan payments.

Banking and Financial Management

- The drawee and the maker (the bank from which the funds are being withdrawn) are the same.

B25 Certified Checks

Certified checks are used when personal checks are not acceptable (for instance, when the payee desires immediate payment). This is the normal procedure for obtaining a certified check.

- Prepare a check in the regular way and present it to the drawer bank.
- The bank will immediately deduct the amount of the check from the account and transfer it to a special account so that payment is assured when the check is presented for payment. This can only occur, of course, when the funds in the account are clear (not out for collection).
- The teller will stamp *Certified* on the face of the check and return it to you for presentation to the payee.
- A service charge is usually imposed.

B26 Stopped Checks

Stopping checks involves a bank service that is used when for some reason— theft, loss, error in preparation—you do not want the bank to make payment on a check you have issued. Follow these procedures when you wish to stop payment on a check.

- Phone the bank immediately to explain why stopping payment is necessary, and give complete details of the check, the amount, the name of the payee, the date and the maker's name.
- Write a confirming letter to the bank or complete a stop payment form. This must usually be done within ten days of the original notification.
- Do not issue a replacement check until the bank confirms that payment has been stopped on the first one. Thanks to the use of computerized systems in most banks, stopping payment can be done in as little as one day.
- A service charge is usually imposed.

B27 Post-Dated Checks

Checks issued for some date in the future are called *post-dated checks*. For example, two checks may be issued as payment for an amount due. One check for half the amount is dated with the current date. A second check for the balance is dated 30 days in the future. Banks recommend that post-dated checks not be used because they are easily forgotten, and the money may not be available in the account when they are eventually presented for payment.

B28 Stale-Dated Checks

Banks concede that checks have a life span of six months. *Stale-dated checks* are over six months old and will most likely *not* be accepted for payment.

B29 N.S.F. Checks

N.S.F. means *not sufficient funds.* Checks stamped with these letters are returned to the payee when the maker's account lacks enough money to meet the amount of the check. It is up to the payee, not the bank, to follow up on the problem. The payee must contact the maker of the check to obtain the money due.

B30 Canceled Checks

Canceled checks are checks on which all transactions have been completed. They are usually returned to the maker with his or her regular checking account statement and serve as receipts of payment. **Note:** Some banks no longer return canceled checks with the monthly statement, but rather retain them in microfiche or computerized form if needed for later reference. Each check is listed on the maker's monthly statement.

All checks processed by a bank are stamped *Paid* as they are microfilmed for future reference; therefore, a check can be returned to a payee as dishonored even though stamped *Paid*.

B31 Dishonored Checks

A *dishonored check* is a check that the bank will not accept. For example, if amounts in words and figures do not agree, if the check is not dated, or if it is unsigned.

Banking and Financial Management

B32 Reconciling the Bank Statement

Once a month, a checking account holder will receive a statement from the bank explaining the debits and credits to the account caused by deposits, checks, or other related transactions (Figure 2.10). The amount on the bank statement will usually differ from the balance shown on the check register or last check stub for several reasons.

- The bank may not yet have recorded all deposits made.
- All checks issued may not yet have been cleared by the bank for payment at the time the statement is prepared. The checks that have been written but not yet deducted from the maker's account are known as *outstanding checks*.
- The bank may have added interest or other payments.
- The bank may have deducted service charges.
- An error has been made by the account holder or by the bank.

Follow these steps to prepare a *Bank Reconciliation Statement*, which will verify the accuracy of the monthly bank statement balance and your current checkbook balance (Figure 2.11).

DIRECT INQUIRIES TO: Friendship Bank
Anywhere, USA

CUSTOMER NO. 09-88-122342
DATE 07-23-85

CUSTOMER: J.R. WILSON
11 PATRICK DR.
LITTLE ROCK, AR 72204

NO. OF ENCLOSURES 08

DATE	WITHDRAWALS	WITHDRAWALS	DEPOSITS	BALANCE	DESCRIPTION
06/25				1,711.35	BEGINNING BALANCE
07/01	30.00			1,581.35	CHECK PAID #109,115
07/02	3.75	100.00		1,577.60	CHECK PAID #108
07/09	30.00			1,473.41	CHECK PAID #119,116
07/16	75.00	74.19		1,398.41	CHECK PAID #107
07/22	10.00		41.00	1,429.41	NSF CHECK, DEPOSIT
07/22	387.41			1,402.00	CHECK PAID #106
				1,402.00	ENDING BALANCE

Figure 2.10 Monthly Checking Account Statement

B33 Preliminary Steps

- Take the canceled checks returned by the bank with the statement (or just the statement itself if canceled checks are not returned) and— one at a time—locate the check stub or the line in the check register for each check or listed check amount. Circle the amount in the checkbook or place a checkmark in the column provided in the register as you proceed.
- When you complete the procedure just described, the check amounts that are *not* circled or checked represent the outstanding checks.
- Compare the deposits shown on the bank statement with the deposits listed in your checkbook record.
- List any deposits shown in your checkbook balance but not shown on the bank statement. These are *late deposits.*

B34 Preparing the Reconciliation Statement

- Arrange your data in the format shown in Figure 2.11.
- Enter the bank statement balance.

```
                    J.R. Wilson
              Bank Reconciliation Statement
                   July 23, 19- -

    Bank Statement Balance              $1,042.00
    Plus Late Deposit                      350.00
                                        $1,392.00
    Less Outstanding Checks
          #110    $   5.10
          #114       24.80
          #120      161.07                 191.43

       Adjusted Bank Balance            $1,200.57

    Checkbook Balance                   $1,169.57
       Plus Credit - -Interest              41.00
       Less Bank Service
          NSF Check                         10.00

    Adjusted Checkbook Balance          $1,200.57
```

Figure 2.11 Bank Reconciliation Statement

Banking and Financial Management

> *Add* the total of late deposits.
>
> *Subtract* the total of outstanding checks.

- Enter the amount representing the ending balance of the checkbook record.

  Add any interest or other items credited by the bank.

  Subtract any debit memos or finance charges shown on the bank statement—provided you agree that the charges are justified.

- Compare the adjusted bank balance and the adjusted checkbook balance. They should be the same.
- Contact your bank if discrepancies remain after you have double-checked your calculations.

B35 Other Banking Services

B36 Cash Dispensers (Automatic/Electronic Tellers)

Automatic banking machines permit withdrawals and deposits 24 hours a day, 7 days a week. They can also be used to transfer money between accounts, to make loan or utility payments, and to check a bank balance. The user is issued a special card and a confidential code number. Some automatic bank machines are now capable of providing the user access to his or her account via bank machines in out of state localities.

B37 Collections

Banks offer collection services for businesses in a variety of ways. Commercial drafts and discounted promissory notes are examples.

B38 Commercial Drafts

Once the buyer and the seller have come to a financial agreement, the creditor originates the draft, indicating that presentation of the draft will be made on a particular date. On that date, collection is made from the debtor's bank and the amount (less collection charges) is added to the creditor's bank account.

B39 Discounted Notes

If the holder of a promissory note needs the funds before the date specified on the note, the bank may discount the note—that is, give the creditor the value of the note, less a discount (the bank charge for redeeming the note earlier than the due date). The bank then collects the proceeds of the promissory note from the debtor.

B40 Credit Cards

Participating banks issue Visa, Master Charge, American Express *Gold*, or other similar cards. These cards may be used to purchase goods and services or to obtain cash advances. Such cash advances are treated as loans and interest is charged on a daily basis from the date of the advance. Accounts may be paid in full at one time, or in installments. If payment is made in installments, the unpaid balance is automatically carried to the next statement and further interest is charged.

Credit card checks may also be drawn on the holder's credit card account. The money drawn against this account is treated as a loan on which daily interest is charged from the day of posting.

B41 Direct Deposit

Direct deposit is a service that prevents the loss of Social Security, Civil Service, Railroad Retirement, Veterans Administration, other government checks, and payroll checks, by having them deposited directly into existing accounts. Interest begins as soon as the check is deposited.

B42 Drafts

Drafts are documents issued by one bank that instruct another bank to pay a specified sum to the person or company named (see Commercial Drafts, B38).

B43 Financial Advice

The bank will give financial advice on such matters as savings and investment programs, pension and annuity plans, home ownership plans, and trust fund arrangements.

B44 Foreign Currency

Foreign currency may be bought and sold at most branches of banks. Fees are charged for the conversion and convenience of the service, and there may be a waiting period. Trip paks containing about $25 in varying denominations of a country's currency are available for a traveler's convenience.

B45 Gift Checks

A specialized money order service enabling customers to purchase wedding, birthday, graduation, and other types of money order greetings for a fee.

B46 Letters of Credit

A letter of credit gives instructions from one bank to another to pay up to a specified amount of money to the holder. Satisfactory identification is needed. Letters of credit may be used in the United States, Canada, and abroad.

B47 Loans

Loans are available for both business and personal use. Interest rates vary from institution to institution at any given time. Loans can be short-term, for the purchase of cars, boats, supplies, and home or office improvement; or long-term, for tuition, mortgages, and/or capital improvements. Businesses sometimes borrow from banks to meet payments on outstanding liabilities during periods of slow sales, or for the purchase of equipment or merchandise. A contractual agreement to repay the loan is the *promissory note*, which shows the amount borrowed, the interest, and the due date. Loan payments are usually due monthly and are often accompanied by a preprinted payment stub covering the length of the loan. Loans are usually recorded in a firm's cash receipts journal as *cash debits*, with the interest paid for the use of the money recorded as a debit in a special *Interest Expense* column.

B48 Money Orders

For a fee, domestic money orders may be purchased in American dollars for amounts up to $1,000. They are redeemable by the payee or may be transferred by endorsement.

B49 Notary Service

Bank officers often have the power of notary publics and will notarize documents for bank customers. Notarizing means that bank officers (or other qualified persons) are authorized to place a special seal on a document certifying its validity.

B50 Pay by Phone

Payment by phone eliminates check writing and postage costs, and offers the convenience of paying bills through the electronic transfer of funds from an existing account. A touchtone telephone is required, and periodic statements summarize the transactions. There is some charge for the service but the cost will probably be less than traditional ways of paying.

B51 Safety Deposit Boxes

Safety deposit boxes are available in a variety of sizes and may be rented for the safekeeping of valuables such as jewelry or documents. They usually can be accessed only during regular banking hours. To gain access to a safety deposit box, the renter must sign a form and present a special key. The renter must pay for insurance coverage for valuables in the box if the coverage is desired. Businesses use safety deposit boxes for the safekeeping of agreements, contracts, special files, and other important and/or irreplaceable documents.

B52 Traveler's Checks

Traveler's checks provide a safe method of carrying currency when traveling. If they are stolen, the money is replaced. The purchaser signs each check at the time of purchase; the checks are countersigned (signed again by the purchaser in the presence of the recipient) when used. A small fee is charged by the bank, and the checks are available in denominations from $10 to $500.

B53 U.S. Savings Bonds

When you purchase a savings bond, you essentially lend money to the U.S. Government and the government pays you interest for the use of your money. United States Savings Bonds, Series EE, may be purchased or cashed at all banks. The purchase price is 50 percent of the face value of the bonds, and Series EE bonds are redeemable after six months. In order to verify the social security number, Series EE bonds can usually be cashed by bank customers only. If interest received is over $10, the person redeeming the bond will receive an A1099 Form from the Internal Revenue Service on which to report the interest.

Banking and Financial Management

B54 Wire Transfers

Wire transfers are a special service offered to customers who must send money to a correspondent bank within 24 hours. Usually a minimum wire amount is set, such as $250. There are often incoming and outgoing wire charges (see T39).

B55 Operating a Petty Cash Fund

Petty cash is a small amount of cash kept in the office to pay for small or emergency purchases or expenses. Follow these practices to operate a petty cash fund successfully. Figure 2.12 illustrates the entire procedure.

- Determine which expenses can be covered with the fund. The most usual are emergency postage, miscellaneous office supplies, emergency transportation funds, minor office repairs and maintenance, and refreshments for visitors.
- Decide on a starting sum for the fund (usually enough to cover the projected expenses for approximately one month).
- Give *one person* responsibility for operating the fund.
- Keep the cash and supporting records in a locked cash box or drawer during the day and in the vault or safe overnight.
- Fill out a *Petty Cash Voucher* (showing the amount paid, date, purpose of expenditure, and signature of spender) for each amount paid from the fund. Obtain receipts (invoices, sales slips) whenever possible and attach them to the voucher.
- Record each transaction in a *Petty Cash Book* or bound journal to sort and summarize the voucher payments.
- Replenish the fund before it becomes depleted. (The amount required to restore the fund to its original amount should be the sum of the vouchers.)
- Prepare a *Petty Cash Replenishment Request* to summarize the information in the Petty Cash Book by accounts to be charged.
- Prepare a *Cash Requisition Form* to specify the denominations of cash requested.
- The cash box should always contain cash and/or vouchers equaling the exact amount of the fund.
- Periodically review the petty cash flow. If the fund is being replenished too frequently, there may be a need to increase the fund or transfer certain items to regular budget expenses. (See Figure 2.23 for a blank petty cash record.)

B54-B55 Wire Transfers

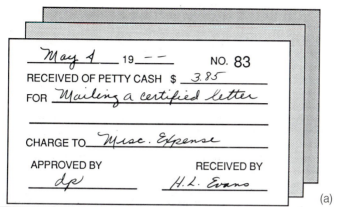

Figure 2.12 (a) Petty Cash Vouchers (b) Petty Cash Book (c) Petty Cash Replenishment Request (d) Cash Requisition Form

Banking and Financial Management

B56 Handling the Payroll

Every business has a payroll—a listing of all employees receiving compensation and the amount due each. Keeping payroll records requires working with a number of independent yet interrelated forms and transactions needed to pay the salary or wages of employees. The methods for handling payroll records differ widely, often depending on the number of employees, the type of office equipment available, the length of the pay period, and whether hourly wages, weekly salaries or commission rates are paid.

In larger organizations, payroll transactions are often automated and handled by a specialized department. Some businesses even prefer to have an outside service prepare the payroll. In smaller firms, payroll-related transactions may be performed manually as part of an office worker's regular duties. Many procedures are basic, however, regardless of the size of the payroll.

Some of the fundamentals of successful payroll operation—regardless of size or extent of automation—are:

- Every employee should be paid on time.
- Payment must be accompanied by a statement explaining gross earnings, deductions, and net payment.
- Federal and state laws concerning payroll records and payment of collected funds must be followed.
- All payroll information must be kept confidential.

B57 Calculating of Gross Earnings

Earnings are usually calculated in one of the following ways:

- **Wages.** Wages represent earnings based on an hourly rate. When a position pays $5 per hour, the gross pay at the end of a pay period is equal to $5 multiplied by the number of hours worked.
- **Salaries.** Salaries represent incomes quoted for a specific period of time (weekly, biweekly, monthly, or yearly) with equal payments being made each pay period. For example, a yearly salary of $24,000 paid monthly would yield a monthly gross pay of $2,000.

- **Commissions**. Commissions are frequently paid to salespeople. The rate payable is usually stated as a percentage of the dollar amount of sales; for example, 8 percent of net sales each week. Employees may receive straight commission or a combination of salary and commission. The amount due may vary from pay period to pay period.
- **Piecework rates**. Piecework rates base earnings on the number of units produced. For example, each unit produced may earn the worker 25¢. For convenience, the amount earned is paid on a periodic basis—daily, weekly, or monthly. Thus, a person producing 1000 units in a time period would earn $250.

Under an hourly salary or wage system, employers are required by law to keep a record of the hours worked by employees. In most cases, this work attendance record is in the form of a time card or time sheet that reports a record of the employee's arrival and departure times, or the time spent on a particular job. The employee's gross earnings are based on the total hours shown on the time card. In most cases, there are federal, state, or union contract guidelines for computing overtime pay at a rate greater than the stated hourly wage. Most companies also have rules for penalties or deductions for lateness or excessive absence.

With a commission or piecework system, the employer must keep records on the amount earned based upon the method of compensation. Time records are seldom used for compensation purposes, but are important for controlling attendance or number of hours worked.

B58 Preparing the Payroll

B59 The Payroll Register

The information collected on time cards or time sheets is summarized in the *Payroll Register*. The payroll register becomes the permanent record of all employees' hours, gross pay, deductions, and net pay. This form must be completed for each pay period.

The following data in the payroll register must balance:

- The sum of the regular and overtime earnings columns must equal the sum of the gross earnings column.
- The sum of the total deductions column must equal the total of all the separate deductions columns.
- The sum of the net pay column must equal the sum of the gross pay column minus the total deductions column.

Banking and Financial Management

B60 The Employee Earnings Record

Federal and state laws mandate that an *Employee Earnings Record* be kept for each employee. This is a cumulative record of the employee's earnings and deductions for an entire year. Figure 2.13 illustrates the wage system described above.

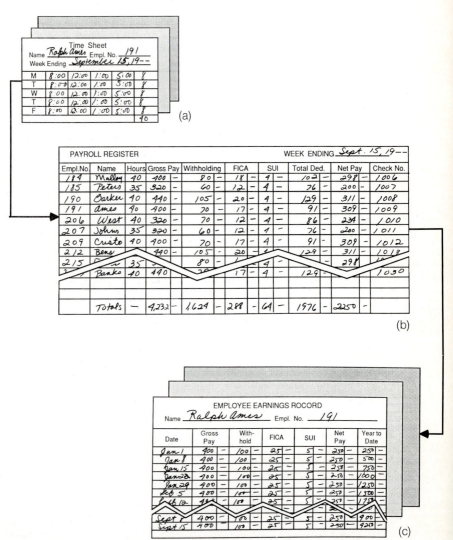

Figure 2.13 (a) Time Sheets (b) Payroll Register (c) Employee Earnings Record

B61 Payroll Deductions

Under most circumstances, employers are required by federal and state laws to withhold a portion of an employee's wages in each pay period. Employees may also instruct employers to make periodic payroll deductions for special purposes.

B62 Compulsory Deductions

Federal laws mandate that a portion of an employee's pay be withheld toward the payment of federal income tax and FICA (Federal Insurance Contributions Act) or Social Security taxes. State laws vary, but some also stipulate payroll deductions toward income and/or unemployment taxes. (Additional *voluntary* deductions are discussed in section B65.)

B63 Federal Taxes

In each pay period, an amount must be withheld and applied toward the employee's income tax liability (the amount of federal taxes due each year). The amount withheld depends on the gross earnings and the number of qualified dependents of the employee. Upon employment, each employee must complete the IRS form *W-4*. This form classifies the employee as single or married and indicates the number of qualified dependents. Generally, the greater the number of dependents, the lower the amount of taxes withheld. FICA (Social Security—see B72) taxes are withheld for all employees at a rate established by Congress. Tax tables, available from the Internal Revenue Service, list amounts to be withheld under various categories and ease tax computations. Money withheld from employee wages for federal tax purposes must be sent on a regular schedule to district Internal Revenue Service centers or banks authorized to receive such funds for the government.

B64 State Taxes

In some states, employers are required to withhold state or city income taxes and/or state unemployment taxes from employee salaries. Amounts withheld vary according to the laws and rates of individual states. Like withheld federal taxes, withheld state taxes must be sent by employers to state tax agencies on a regular basis (see B73).

B65 Voluntary Deductions

In addition to deductions required by law, most businesses offer employee benefits that are paid, in part, through money withheld from the employee's paycheck. Since not all employees are required to accept these deductions, they are referred to as *voluntary*. The employer must have the employee's permission to withhold voluntary deductions. Amounts withheld are paid periodically to the account that provides the benefit. The following list suggests the most frequent voluntary deductions, but remember that deductions vary from business to business.

Private pension plan contributions

Extended health care

Dental health care

Professional association fees or union dues deductions

Group life insurance premiums

Bond purchases

Charitable contributions

Stock purchases

Credit union savings or loan repayments

Employee savings plans

B66 Vacation, Holiday, and Severance Pay

Many businesses provide pay for legal holidays and vacation periods. This pay does not show on time forms, but must be accounted for in the payroll report. The usual method is to credit the average daily regular time pay for each holiday or vacation day.

There are no federal laws mandating vacation pay and holiday pay requirements. Policies are determined by individual firms and/or union contracts.

Many businesses offer special compensation for employees whose job is terminated. This *severance pay* is calculated according to company policy and/or union contracts. Severance pay is treated as regular income and is subject to appropriate deductions. As with holiday and vacation pay, there are no federal laws that mandate the amount to be paid.

B67 Methods of Payroll Payment

Payroll payments may be made in cash, by check, or by transferring the net earnings to a particular bank or the employee's bank. Payment by check or transfer of funds eliminates handling large sums of cash and cuts down on the danger of theft.

B68 Paying by Check

Payroll checks are usually issued through a special bank account that is separate from other business accounts. To transfer funds to this account, a check for the amount of the total payroll is issued and deposited in the special payroll account. This account is easy to reconcile because when all the checks are cashed, the balance will be zero. Attached to each employee's check is a voucher indicating gross pay, deductions, and net pay. It is called an *Earnings Statement* (Figure 2.14). Often, the voucher also shows cumulative earnings and deductions up to the date of the check.

DEPT.	EMPL. NO.		EMPLOYEE NAME		EXEMP.	MAR ST	SOCIAL SECURITY NO.	PERIOD ENDING
0001	0016-	.			01	S	187-52-8645	6/06/86

HOURS			EARNINGS				GROSS PAY
REGULAR	OVERTIME	RATE	REGULAR	OVERTIME	COMMISSION	BONUS	
			315.00				315.00

22.52	42.20	6.51		32			
FICA TAX	FEDERAL TAX	STATE TAX	LOCAL TAX	DIS. ABILITY INSUR-ANCE			

YEAR TO DATE							
6575.00 GROSS	470.12 FICA	942.35 FEDERAL	134.99 STATE	LOCAL DISABILITY		MEMO NUMBER	243.45

Figure 2.14 Employee Earnings Statement

B69 Paying in Cash

Payment by cash requires that a check be issued on the firm's regular bank account for the total of the net earnings column on the payroll register. The bank is also supplied with a *Payroll Currency Requisition* form. This is a breakdown of each employee's earnings according to the denominations of both bills and coins.

Banking and Financial Management

On payday, each employee receives a pay envelope containing a statement similar to a check voucher and the exact cash that is due. When the envelopes are distributed each employee signs a voucher as proof of payment.

B70 Transferring Payroll Funds

Transferring payroll funds directly to a particular bank can be done by an internal transfer of funds if the firm is a depositor in the bank to which the funds are being transferred. Otherwise, one of the firm's checks will be issued to the bank or banks involved in the fund transfer. Employees receive confirmation of the deposit on monthly bank statements. At the end of each pay period, employees receive a voucher summarizing the earnings, deductions, and net pay.

B71 Employers' Legal Obligations
B72 Payment of Federal/State Mandated Taxes

Every employer must pay to the federal government a FICA (Federal Insurance Contributions Act) tax equal to that withheld from employees. These funds are credited to each employee's FICA account and provide for old-age and survivor insurance benefits to qualified employees and members of their families.

Provisions of federal and state unemployment insurance laws require employers to pay taxes into a fund used for unemployment compensation (FUTA or Federal Unemployment Insurance Tax Act). The amount of unemployment taxes paid by the employer is based on the taxable amounts of the total salaries, and the payments are credited to a general fund rather than to an individual account. Unemployment tax rates vary from state to state. Federal rates may vary based on the business' eligibility for tax credits. In most cases, federal and state unemployment taxes are paid solely by the employer. There are no deductions taken from an employee's earnings.

B73 Remittance of Employee Tax Deductions

Either quarterly or monthly, depending on the amount of money withheld from employee payroll checks, employers must send to appropriate federal and state agencies those funds that have been withheld from employee salaries as payroll deductions. Special filing forms must be used and the filing must be completed within time frames specified by federal and/or state laws.

B70-B75 Transferring Payroll Funds

1 Control number					
		OMB No. 1545-0008			
2 Employer's name, address, and ZIP code		3 Employer's identification number		4 Employer's State number 090-46-1234	
		5 Statutory employee / Deceased / Legal rep ☐ ☐ ☐		942 emp / Subtotal / Void ☐ ☐ ☐	
		6 Allocated tips		7 Advance EIC payment	
8 Employee's social security number 22-33-4330	9 Federal income tax withheld 970.00	10 Wages, tips, other compensation 9,440.00		11 Social security tax withheld 533.11	
12 Employee's name, address, and ZIP code Michael Gallagher 22 Park Avenue Avon, NJ 07058		13 Social security wages		14 Social security tips	
		16			
		17 State income tax	18 State wages, tips, etc	19 Name of State	
		20 Local income tax	21 Local wages, tips, etc.	22 Name of locality	

Form W-2 Wage and Tax Statement 1985   Copy D for employer   Department of the Treasury Internal Revenue Service

Figure 2.15 W-2 Form

B74 W-2 Form (Withholding Statement)

By January 31 of each year, employers must provide each employee with an IRS *W-2 form*. This form shows the employee's gross earnings, any taxable benefits received by the employee for the preceding year, amounts withheld for federal and state income tax, FICA tax, and any other tax-related deductions. An employee usually gets 4 copies of the W-2 form—one to file with the federal income tax return, one to file with the state income tax return, one to file with the county or local tax return (where applicable), and one to keep as a personal record. Information summarized on the W-2 form (Figure 2.15) comes from the employee's yearly cumulative earnings record (see B60).

B75 Understanding Basic Accounting Records

Accounting in a business involves the recording of all financial transactions (purchases, sales, returns, money received, money spent) and the preparation of financial statements. All accounting is based on the basic accounting formula:

Assets = Liabilities + Owner's Equity.

While the accounting function in most organizations is automated and is the concern of specialists in the field, *every* office worker should at least be familiar with the terms and processes involved.

B76 Source Documents

The accounting process starts with a basic business record known as a *source document*. Invoices, credit slips, checks, purchase orders, cash register tapes, and time cards are all examples of source documents. Where an automated accounting system is involved, the source document information must be translated into a form that can be used by automated and/or electronic equipment. The information is usually keyboarded on a data-entry terminal or scanned by optical character recognition equipment so that the data base (electronic filing cabinet) of the automated equipment is updated. The data base may be in the form of electronic computer storage, magnetic tapes or disks, floppy diskettes, or hard drum storage (see Unit 9, *Information Processing*).

B77 Journals

Information drawn from source documents is recorded in a journal (a daily record) that may be in the form of a loose leaf book, a bound book, or a card. Each journal entry shows the accounts affected by the transaction and provides a brief explanation of the transaction. Small businesses may use only one general journal; larger ones may use some or all of the following:

Cash Receipts Journal: to record cash received in currency, checks, money orders, or other cash substitutes

Cash Payments (or Disbursements) Journal: to record payments made by cash or check

Purchases Journal: to record purchases made on credit

Sales Journal: to record sales made on credit

General Journal: to record transactions not already recorded in one of the other journals (Figure 2.16 illustrates a general journal entry.)

Some businesses consolidate these journals into one *combination journal*.

B78 The Ledger

The information recorded in a journal is *posted* (transferred) to separate, individual accounts. A group of related accounts (e.g., accounts payable, accounts receivable) is referred to as a *ledger*. Figures 2.17, 2.18, and 2.19 are examples of ledger accounts.

B76-B78 Source Documents

| \multicolumn{5}{c}{**GENERAL JOURNAL**} Page 64 |

Date		Description	Post Ref.	Debit	Credit
July	5	Cash 　　Service Fee Revenues To record services performed in exchange for cash		14,000	14,000
	10	Office Equipment 　　Cash 　　Notes Payable Purchased equipment for cash and issued a short- term note		62,000	22,000 40,000

Figure 2.16 General Journal

Account - Cash   Account No. 100

Date	Item	Post Ref.	Debit	Credit	Balance Debit	Balance Credit
19--						
June 1		1	60,000		60,000	
2		1		12,000	48,000	
3		1		960	47,040	
5		1		5,000	42,040	
6		1		120	41,920	
22		2		1,800	40,120	
23		2	250		40,370	
23		2		600	39,770	
27		2		620	39,150	
29		2	280		39,430	
30		2		72	39,358	
30		2	4,200		43,558	

Account - Accounts Receivable   Account No. 104

Date	Item	Post Ref.	Debit	Credit	Balance Debit	Balance Credit
19--						
June 15		1	4,200		4,200	
19		2	5,400		9,600	
30		2		4,200	5,400	

Figure 2.17 General Ledger

Banking and Financial Management

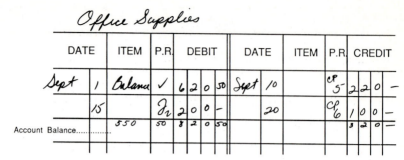

Figure 2.18 Asset Account in the General Ledger

Figure 2.19 Creditor's Account in the Accounts Payable Ledger

B79 An Account

An account is a record of all transactions in a firm's financial statements that affect revenue; a particular client; or a specific asset, expense, or liability. Each account may have three columns—debit, credit, and balance.

There are six basic account types:

Assets: items owned that have value such as cash or anything that can be converted to cash

Liabilities: amounts that are owed

Proprietorship: the difference between assets and liabilities, or the *owner's equity* in the business

Income: earnings gained by producing a service or selling goods

Cost: the amount paid for the purchase of goods to be sold or raw materials to be manufactured

Expense: amounts incurred in doing business such as rent, salaries, advertising, etc.

Increases in asset, cost, and expense accounts are recorded in the debit column, and decreases are recorded in the credit column. Increases in liability, income, and proprietorship accounts are recorded in the credit column, and decreases are recorded in the debit column. The difference between the total debits and total credits in an account is the account *balance*.

Some organizations use an accounting system without journals or ledgers. In this case, documents related to a particular customer are simply filed and used to produce a statement of account on a particular day of the month. In a computerized accounting system, too, statements may be compiled and printed by the computer directly from information stored in its internal or external data base.

Monthly *Statements of Account* are sent to customers who owe money. The statement shows the opening balance, purchases, returns, payments, interest charges, and the closing balance for the month (see B32).

B80 Trial Balance

A trial balance is prepared as a check on the mathematical accuracy of the ledger. On the trial balance, the balances of the separate accounts are listed under the headings *debit* and *credit*. The totals of the two columns must be identical. The information provided on the trial balance is used in the preparation of the *Income Statement* and the *Balance Sheet*. Figure 2.20 illustrates a trial balance.

Banking and Financial Management

BARNES ELECTRICAL SERVICE Trial Balance June 30, 19- -		
Account Title	Debit	Credit
Cash	$ 43,558	
Accounts Receivable	5,400	
Prepaid Insurance	960	
Office Supplies Inventory	620	
Land	10,000	
Building	62,000	
Office Equipment	9,600	
Accounts Payable		$ 4,600
Unearned Appraisal Fees		280
Mortgage Notes Payable		60,000
Mike Starbuck, Capital		60,000
Mike Starbuck, Drawing	600	
Commision Revenue		9,600
Appraisal Fee Revenue		250
Salary Expense	1,800	
Utilities Expense	72	
Advertising Expense	120	
Totals	$134,730	$134,730

Figure 2.20 Trial Balance

B81 Financial Statements

The operating results and financial standing of a business are reported to shareholders, management, government agencies, and others by means of financial statements. The two key statements are the *Income Statement* and the *Balance Sheet*.

B82 The Income Statement

A summary of the revenue, expenses, and net income earned or net loss suffered over a given period of time is called an *Income Statement*, *Profit and Loss Statement*, or *Earnings Statement*. Each income statement must specify the fiscal period (month, quarter, year, or other period of time) covered by that statement. Its purpose is to provide a brief summary of how well the business is doing in terms of profit or *net income*, sometimes called *the bottom line*.

```
                        J. Savage Services
                         Income Statement
                 For the Month Ended December 31, 19--
                         Current Year                    Previous Year
   Income

   Gross Sales............      $103, 000
        Less Returns.......        3, 000

   Net Sales..............                    $100, 000 (100%)    $85, 000 (100%)

   Cost of Goods Sold

   Opening Inventory, Dec. 1...  $ 16, 000
   Purchases..................     54, 000

   Cost of Goods for Sale.....     70, 000
        Less Ending Inv., Dec. 31  10, 000

   Cost of Goods Sold.........                    60, 000
   Gross Profit...............                 $ 40, 000 (40%)    $35, 000 (41.2%)

   Expenses:

   Salaries Expense...........   $ 20, 000
   Advertising Expense........      5, 000
   Depreciation Expense.......      2, 000
   Miscellaneous Expense......      2, 000
        Total Operating Expenses                   29, 000

   Net Income.................                 $ 11, 000 (11%)    $12, 000 (14.1%)
```

Figure 2.21 Income Statement (comparative)

Figure 2.21 illustrates an income statement for a business involved with the sale of goods either as a manufacturer or as a retailer. This example is called a *comparative* statement since it includes financial information from the same time period for the previous year. In this way, a business can quickly compare results of the present time period with a similar previous period.

Ratios that exist between the separate elements of the income statement provide worthwhile comparisons with previous years' performances and with competitors' prices. (See illustration.) Some firms have standard ratios that they aim to achieve each year. The standard ratio also proves useful in establishing prices for items where competitive prices are not significant factors.

Key Terms:

Net Sales: the total sales (or revenue) minus returns and discounts.

Cost of Goods Sold: calculated by adding the beginning inventory and purchases made during the period and then deducting the ending inventory.

Gross Profit: the difference between the cost price and the selling price. If this difference is not large enough to cover the expenses of the business, a loss will result.

Operating Expenses: the expenses incurred in running the business.

B83 The Balance Sheet

The *Balance Sheet* (Figure 2.22) is a picture of the financial standing of a business at a specific time. It summarizes the assets, liabilities, and owners' equity, which is the owner's share of the assets. The *balance* in the title of the statement indicates that assets should equal liabilities *plus* the owner's equity.

The balance sheet reflects how much a business is worth. It is usually needed for all legal matters, and for financial matters, such as borrowing money from a bank. (See Figure 2.24 for a blank balance sheet.)

Key Terms:

Current Assets: assets used up or converted into cash within one year

Accounts Receivable: the amount not yet received by a company from customers supplied with goods or services purchased on credit

Notes Receivable: outstanding promissory notes (promises to repay a debt)

Fixed Assets: virtually permanent assets of a firm

Current Liabilities: the debts that will be paid within one year

Accounts Payable: the amount of money to be paid by a business to its creditors

Owner's Equity: the owner's claim against the assets of a company

B83-B84 The Balance Sheet

```
                    J. Savage Services
                      Balance Sheet
                   as of December 31, 19--
                         Assets

Current Assets
  Cash..................................  $12,000
  Accounts Receivable...................   45,000
  Notes Receivable......................    3,000
  Inventory.............................   10,000
                                                     $ 70,000

Fixed Assets
  Land..................................  $45,000
  Buildings................  $60,000
       Less Depreciation ....  10,000
                                           50,000
                                                       95,000
  Total Assets...........................             $165,000
                         Liabilities

Current Liabilities
  Accounts Payable......................  $52,000

Fixed Liabilities
  Long-term Debt........................   10,000
  Total Liabilities.....................             $ 62,000
                        Owner's Equity

  J. Savage, Capital....................  $92,000
  Net Income............................   11,000
                                                      103,000

  Total Liabilities and Owner's Equity...              $165,000
```

Figure 2.22   Balance Sheet

B84 Related Vocabulary

Account (See B2 and B79).

Accrued Interest Interest earned but not yet paid or collected.

Altered Check A check on which the date, payee, amount or other portion has been changed.

Banking and Financial Management

Assets Items owned that have value, such as cash or anything that can be converted to cash (see B79).

Audit An official examination of the accuracy of account records and activities of a business or institution.

Balance The difference between the debits and credits in an account (see B79).

Balance Sheet A financial statement summarizing the assets, liabilities, and owner's equity on a particular date (see B83).

Bank Check Also Cashier's Check, Teller's Check (see B24).

Bank Endorsement An endorsement by a bank on the back of a check; usually stamped.

Bearer Check A check payable to cash or to the bearer rather than to a specific party. (This is not a good practice.)

Beneficiary The person designated to receive principal or interest from an insurance policy, annuity, or estate.

Canceled Checks (See B30).

Certificate of Deposit (See B8).

Certified Check (See B25).

Checking Account (See B5).

Clearinghouse An institution used by banks to clear checks. The institution acts as a collection point from which the check is routed to the drawee bank.

Collateral Loan A loan for which the borrower pledges a savings account, a certificate of deposit, or some property such as a car, boat, or house as security. If the borrower defaults on the loan repayment, the lender takes possession of the collateral and lays claim to the cash value.

Collection Item An item accepted by a bank (certificate of deposit, passbook, etc.) that must be forwarded to another bank for payment.

Compound Interest Calculating interest at periodic intervals based on the principal plus interest already earned to date. The more frequently the interest is compounded, the greater the return. Daily compounding provides the best overall return for the investor. (See also *simple interest*.)

Corporation/Business Account An account established by a business in accordance with a resolution adopted by its Board of Directors.

Counterfeit Currency Imitation coins or paper money used with the intent to defraud.

Credit A transaction adding to the balance of a depositor's account; posting to the right-hand side of a general ledger account.

Debit A transaction decreasing the balance of a bank depositor's account (withdrawal, service charge); posting to the left-hand side of a general ledger account.

Decedent An account holder who has died.

Deposit The placement of funds in a bank subject to terms by the depositor and the institution.

Dishonored Check (See B31).

Dividend The portion of a corporation's profits paid to each stockholder or bondholder as a return on investments.

Dormant Account An account that has shown no activity, either by an increase through deposits or a decrease through withdrawals, for a specified period of time.

Drawee The bank on whose paper a check or other negotiable document is written (see B16).

Drawer The person who signs a check or other negotiable document. Also *Maker* or *Payer* (see B16).

Employee Earnings Record (See B60).

Endorsee The person or entity to whom a bill or exchange, promissory note, check, or other negotiable document is endorsed.

Endorsement (See B19).

Endorser The person or entity who endorses a negotiable document.

Escheat After an account is inactive for a certain number of years, the bank will advertise for the owner and if there is no response, the money will revert to the state.

Federal Deposit Insurance Corporation (FDIC) An agency of the federal government that insures savings accounts in member banks up to $100,000 per depositor.

Gross Earnings An individual's total earnings prior to deductions.

Income Statement Also Profit and Loss Statement (see B82).

Individual Account A bank account owned and controlled by one individual.

Banking and Financial Management

Interest The sum paid by a bank or other financial institution for the use of money or credit.

Individual Retirement Account (IRA) (See B11).

Joint Account (See B2).

Journal (See B77).

Keogh Plan (See B12).

Late Charge A penalty imposed by the lender for delinquent repayment.

Ledger (See B78).

Liabilities (See B79).

Magnetic Ink Character Recognition (MICR) The electronic scanning of numbers printed in magnetic ink such as those found in the lower left-hand corner of checks. These numbers are used by the clearinghouse for sorting.

Maturity Date The date on which a certificate of deposit, promissory note, or loan becomes due for payment.

Minimum Balance The lowest possible amount that may be maintained in a bank account to qualify for interest.

Minimum Deposit The lowest possible amount that may be deposited to open a checking account, savings account, or certificate of deposit.

Money Market Account (See B9).

Mortgage A legal document by which real property is pledged as security for repayment of a loan; the pledge ends when the debt is settled.

Net Pay An individual's earnings after deductions have been subtracted; often referred to as *take home pay*.

Notary Public An individual with the legal permission (usually certified by the state government) to witness and authorize a signature on official documents, often for a fee.

N.S.F. Check (See B29).

Outstanding Checks (See B32).

Passbook Evidence of ownership of a savings or certificate account. The book is used to record deposits, withdrawals, and interest earned. This type of account is being phased out in favor of statement savings accounts.

Payee The person who receives a check or other negotiable document (see B16).

Payroll Register (See B59).

Personal Check A check drawn on a bank by an individual against his or her own account.

Petty Cash Fund (See B55).

Post-Dated Checks (See B27).

Power of Attorney A written document authorizing a named individual to act in place of the signer on specific matters. It can be revoked by the signer at any time and it becomes null and void upon the signer's death.

Premature Withdrawal Money that is withdrawn from an account before the maturity date has been reached.

Proprietorship Equity or net worth (see B79); also a form of business organization.

Reconciliation Statement (See B32).

Rollover The arrangement by which a certificate of deposit automatically renews at the going rate of interest at maturity; also a way to reinvest money from one account into a new account without penalty.

Savings Account (See B3 and B4).

Series EE Bonds A U.S. Treasury certificate issued at a discount and redeemable at face value upon maturity.

Service Charges Fees imposed by a bank for services rendered, such as collecting payments, imprinting checks, and certifying checks.

Signature Card A form signed by a bank depositor when an account is opened.

Simple Interest A fixed rate of interest paid only on the principal amount invested.

Stale-Dated Check (See B28).

Stop Payment (See B26).

Tax ID Number A depositor's social security number (or other number if a business or corporation) used by the bank to report interest to the federal and state government.

Banking and Financial Management

Teller Terminal A computer terminal used by a teller to input transactions and retrieve information.

Term A period of time agreed to by the depositor and the bank during which interest will accrue but withdrawals cannot be made.

Trust Account An account in which funds are held by a trustee for the benefit of another individual.

Uncollected Funds Funds that have been deposited in an account in the form of a check that has not yet been paid by the drawee bank.

Void (See B18).

Voucher Check (See B18).

Withdrawal Taking money from a bank account by writing a check or filling out a withdrawal form.

B85 Final Reminders

- Never write a check made payable to *Cash* or *Bearer*.
- Use the restrictive endorsement recommended by bankers: *For deposit only, your name*).
- Shop around before you open any bank account because interest rates, charges, and required minimum balances vary substantially from bank to bank.
- When possible, use more than one bank to handle your banking needs.
- Look for bank interest plans that compound interest daily because the amount of interest earned will be greatest.
- Save deposit and withdrawal slips from statement savings accounts and verify the account balance as soon as a monthly statement is received.
- Keep your check stub balance and register up to date. Never write a check without making an appropriate entry on the stub or register first.

B85-B86 Final Reminders

- Handle *Void* checks properly (see B18).
- Be aware of minimum balances so that you can avoid unnecessary service charges.
- Write checks carefully to prevent alteration.

B86 Sample Petty Cash Record

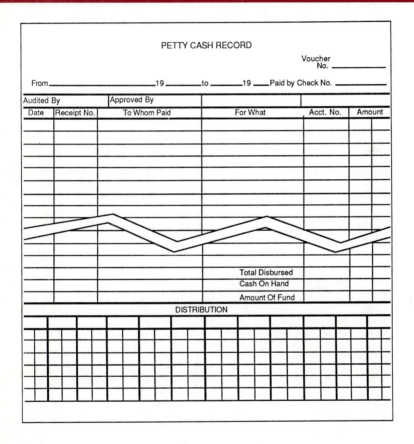

Figure 2.23 Sample Petty Cash Record

Banking and Financial Management

B87 Sample Balance Sheet

Balance Sheet
Year 19____

Assets and Liabilities at Beginning of Year
Assets

Current Assets:
- Cash on Hand....................
- Cash in Bank.....................
- Notes Receivable................
- Accounts Receivable............
- Inventory Stock on Hand........
- **Total**..........................

Fixed Assets:
- Land................................
- Buildings..........................
- Equipment........................
- Furniture and Furnishings.......
- **Total**..........................

Other Assets:
- _____
- _____

Total..
Total Assets..

Liabilities

Current Liabilities:
- Notes Payable....................
- Accounts Payable................
- _____

Total..........................

Fixed Liabilities:
- Mortgages........................

Total..
Total Liabilities...............................
Net Worth(Deduct total liabilities from total assets and enter the difference here... _____
Total Liabilities and Net Worth..... _____

Assets and Liabilities at End of Year
Assets

Current Assets:
- Cash on Hand....................
- Cash in Bank.....................
- Notes Receivable................
- Accounts Receivable............
- Inventory Stock on Hand........
- **Total**..........................

Fixed Assets:
- Land................................
- Buildings..........................
- Equipment........................
- Furniture and Furnishings.......
- **Total**..........................

Other Assets:
- _____
- _____

Total..
Total Assets..

Liabilities

Current Liabilities:
- Notes Payable....................
- Accounts Payable................
- _____

Total..........................

Fixed Liabilities:
- Mortgages........................

Total..
Total Liabilities...............................
Net Worth(Deduct total liabilities from total assets and enter the difference here.... _____
Total Liabilities and Net Worth..... _____

Figure 2.24 Sample Balance Sheet

UNIT 3

COMMUNICATION IN BUSINESS

The Communication Process	C1-C3
The Communication Model	
Verbal and Nonverbal Communication	
Written Business Correspondence	C4-C26
Basic Business Letter-Writing Tips	
Business Letter Samples	
Address, Salutation and Complimentary Close Forms	
Correct Forms of Inside Addresses and Salutations	
The Complimentary Close	
Preparing Other Prevalent Written Communications	C27-C40
Interoffice Memoranda	
News Releases	
Reports and Manuscripts	
Parts of a Report	
Checklist for Writing Effective Communications	C41
Oral Communication in Business	C42-C48
Voice Qualities	
In-Person One-to-One Communication	
How to Do Machine Dictation	
Involvements With Speakers	
Giving a Speech or Oral Report	

Communication in Business

People are at the heart of the communication process. Interpersonal relationships are affected by both oral and written words, actions, and experiences of people as they interact with each other within and outside the organization.

In practical terms, effective communication is the glue that holds business together. Effective communication can result in timely, cost-effective decisions, improved employee morale, and satisfied customers. In contrast, ineffective business communication can result in the giving or receiving of incorrect or incomplete information, unnecessary stress and tension, unproductive decision making, and the possible loss of customers and profit.

This unit describes the communication process and suggests ways in which you can improve your written and oral communications skills in the office setting.

C1 The Communication Process

To communicate means to impart or to share. It is the transmission and reception of thoughts, feelings, and ideas between two or more parties. The need for effective business communication skills at a personal level becomes even more important in this time of dramatic change in the office environment. The human factor is the element that ignites information, and effective communication is the basis for effective interpersonal skills. Advancement on the job often depends on communication skills. Effective communicators are not born but develop through hard work and practice. To be an effective communicator, you must:

- Have the right attitude and be willing to work toward improvement.
- Have a reasonable command of the language.
- Have an adequate vocabulary.
- Have knowledge of the background and circumstances of the situation leading to the need for communication.
- Be able to look at a situation from the point of view of the other party.

C2 The Communication Model

One way to explain the communication process is through the use of the communication model (see Figure 3.1).

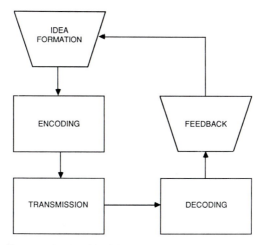

Figure 3.1 Communication Model

Idea Formation—The sender
- originates the need to communicate
- determines the message
- selects the communication medium depending on the speed of transmission necessary, the personalization necessary, the size of the audience, the length of the message, the cost of the transmission, and the accessibility of the communication media

Encoding—The sender puts the message into transmittable form by using verbal and nonverbal symbols and/or signals.

Transmission—The message is delivered or sent in person, on paper, by voice through telephone lines, through electronic technology to a CRT screen, or through other communication media.

Decoding—The receiver
- gets the verbal and nonverbal impact of the message
- interprets the message based on previous perceptions and experiences

Response/Feedback—The receiver
- acts on his or her understanding of the message as it has been interpreted. In essence, the receiver now becomes the sender of a new communication transaction.
- gives feedback by taking the action requested, verifying the interpretation of the message, asking questions about the message, or taking no action at all.

Communication in Business

The process described above continues until the desired result occurs. Communication is a complex process of thought that uses symbols, codes, words, or nonverbal messages to pass on information intended to influence the receiver. It is a continuous and interactive process between two or more people. As such, communication problems can result in inaccurate communication and ineffective interpersonal relationships.

C3 Verbal and Nonverbal Communication

Verbal Communication occurs in written or oral forms.

- Written communication occurs in letters, memos, reports, yellow pad notes, brochures, procedures manuals, contracts, forms, and other *hard copy* documentation formats. Audiovisual media such as slides, cassette tapes, and transparencies are considered *tangible* communication devices. Similarly, electronic media such as computer data base information, electronic voice storage and forwarding media, and miniaturized filmed versions of documents in the form of microfilm and microfiche also constitute tangible information.
- Oral communication, the spoken message, accomplishes work goals and provides the social contacts needed for good morale and job satisfaction. It includes activities such as telephone calls, dictation, interviews, conferences, training sessions, formal and informal speeches, department meetings, and planning sessions of all kinds.

Nonverbal Communication is sometimes characterized as silent messages and as something that goes beyond words. It includes all intentional and unintentional messages that are neither written nor spoken. It is as prevalent in the office as verbal communication, and sometimes its effect is even more powerful.

- Many nonverbal messages are *sent* and *received* as the written and oral communication processes take place.
- In written communication, nonverbal communication can be reflected in the quality of corrections, the type and/or color of the paper used, underlining for emphasis, and the length of a message.
- In oral communication, nonverbal communication can reflect the distance between people who are interacting; the amount of eye contact between participants; posture and seating arrangement; personal appearance; voice elements such as pitch, rate of

speaking, volume; and even characteristics of the physical environment in which the interaction is taking place, such as room temperature, lighting, acoustics, space allocation, and decor.
- Nonverbal cues can complement or contradict, can repeat or contrast, can regulate or confuse. Research indicates that if the nonverbal message conflicts with the verbal message, a receiver is more likely to find the nonverbal message believable. The more experience you have in understanding nonverbal messages, the better you can use nonverbal signals to complement and enhance the sending of messages, the giving of feedback, and the establishment of effective interpersonal communication.

C4 Written Business Correspondence

The purpose of this section is to describe the elements of effective business correspondence, provide samples of business letters, present forms of addresses, salutations, and closings in business letters, and specify memorandum, news release, and report preparation procedures.

C5 Basic Business Letter-Writing Tips

Write Promptly
- Do not procrastinate in providing a reply. A time lapse in replying to a message is a form of nonverbal communication that might be negatively interpreted by the receiver. The receiver might decide that you are disorganized or that you do not consider him or her important enough for a prompt reply.

Get Off to the Right Start
- Collect all the facts and related documents you need before you start writing.

Determine the Reason for Writing
- Assess and analyze the facts you have accumulated and decide upon a suitable course of action before you start writing.

Keep the Reader in Mind
- As you write, visualize the reader in terms of your knowledge of his or her prior attitudes, education, familiarity or involvement with the situation, or any other pertinent factors.

Communication in Business

- Assess the appropriateness of the medium selected for transmitting the message and how it will affect the reader. Here are several examples:

    Send an informal business letter to a client of many years; send a formal business letter to a prospective client.

    Make a telephone call to present a complaint to a vendor your firm has dealt with satisfactorily over a period of time rather than writing a letter of complaint.

    To inform employees of a policy change, use an interoffice memorandum; to inform employees of a forthcoming contest, use a flyer.

Follow the Five C's
- Produce a message that is coherent, clear, concise, courteous, and correct.

    Coherent—Make sure the message progresses logically after starting with a clear statement of purpose.

    Clear—Use simple, easy to follow, straightforward language.

    Concise—Make your message short and to the point.

    Courteous—Write in a tactful and friendly style that indicates concern for the reader.

    Correct—List places, dates, times, and other facts accurately and use correct spelling, punctuation, and grammar.

As you read the letter shown in Figure 3.2, notice how each of the 5 C's has been applied.

```
Dear Ms. Miller:

You are invited to a meeting of all our representatives
to be held in our main office at 55 Broad Street, Newark,
New Jersey, on Tuesday, December 15, 19--. The meeting
will start at 9 a.m., and you are invited to stay for
lunch as our guest.

We are planning an expansion of our business in your
territory over the next five years, and your reactions
to our plans would be helpful to us. Your suggestions
regarding advertising strategies and marketing potentials
would be welcomed either before or during the meeting.

Please let us know whether you expect to attend the
meeting and whether you will be able to stay for lunch.

                              Sincerely yours,
```

Figure 3.2 Use of the 5 C's

Recognize That the First Paragraph Is the Most Important Paragraph In the Letter
- Use the *you* approach in the first sentence whenever possible.
- Start in a pleasing way with the purpose of your communication.

Handle the Negatives Positively
- If you must say *no,* precede the negative statement with a positive statement to soften the blow.
- If you must say *no,* state what you *can* do.

```
We have enjoyed doing business with you for the past ten
years, but regret that because of slow payments this year
we are forced to cancel our credit arrangements with you.
We will, of course, be glad to accommodate you with cash
purchases.
```

Economize On Words
- Write as you talk.
- Choose words that are conversational rather than formal.
- Avoid redundant expressions.

Make the Tone of Your Letter Interesting
- De-emphasize the telling.
- Do not assume that everyone is familiar with the specialized vocabulary of your business; tailor your language for the reader.
- Use short sentences to avoid confusion in presenting details.
- Use active rather than passive verbs.

Mean What You Say
- Be honest in your writing.
- Don't promise what you can't deliver.
- Avoid words like "urgent" and "rush" unless you really mean them.
- Avoid being overly apologetic and gushy.
- Use *I* and *We* only when you are speaking for yourself or actually representing the sentiments of an entire group.

Know That the Second Most Important Paragraph Is the Last Paragraph
- End with something pleasant or specific.
- Make sure the reader knows the action to be taken.
- Say thank you only *after* the fact.

Communication in Business

Aim For Short Letters and Short Paragraphs Rather Than Long Ones
- Realize that a one-page letter is more apt to be read than a longer one.
- There should be at least three paragraphs per letter.
- The three paragraphs should reflect the introduction, the details, and the ending message.
- Try to convey one main idea per paragraph.

Remember That the Final Written Document Represents You
- Create a favorable impression by producing error-free correspondence.

C6 Business Letter Samples

The following sample letters are offered as guidelines. As you read the letters and then write your own, keep the business letter tips presented in the previous section in mind. For appropriate etiquette practices regarding inside addresses, salutations, and complimentary closings, see C24 through C26.

C7 Acknowledgment Letter (In Someone's Absence)

If your task is to handle someone's correspondence and certain decisions must wait until that person is able to deal with them, the polite thing to do is to write an acknowledgment letter.

```
Dear Mrs. Washington:

Thank you for inviting Mr. Reuben to give the keynote
speech at the Business and Professional Society
Conference on May 10, 19--.

Mr. Reuben is away on vacation at this time. He will
be returning next week and will contact you then.

                              Sincerely yours,
```

C8 Apology Letter

If something more formal than a telephone call is appropriate, write a note giving the reason for your regrets.

> Dear Mr. Caulder:
>
> Thank you very much for inviting me to speak at the Business and Professional Society Conference on May 10, 19--.
>
> I would have enjoyed meeting with your members and seeing some former colleagues, but unfortunately I am scheduled to take a business trip at that time.
>
> Please accept my apologies and offer my warm wishes to all of your members for a successful conference.
>
> Sincerely yours,

C9 Collection Letter

After several statement and reminder notices have been sent without results, the time comes to demand payment for an overdue account by means of a letter. Start with a lenient reminder letter as shown in Figure 3.3.

>   July 1, 19--
>
> Dear Mr. Rollins:
>
> Acknowledgement   We hope that you are satisfied with the computer that you bought from us on June 5.
>
> Statement of Facts   Under the conditions of the purchase, you made a down payment of $300 with a promise to pay the balance of $500 within ten days. However, almost a month has gone by and we have not yet received your payment.
>
> Action Requested   We would appreciate receiving a check for the outstanding balance of $500 in the return mail.
>
> Sincerely yours,

Figure 3.3 Collection Letter

If there is still no reply, send a more demanding note two weeks later:

>   July 15, 19--
>
> Dear Mr. Rollins:
>
> Have you overlooked something? According to our records, you owe us $500 as the balance due on a computer you purchased from us on June 5.
>
> The outstanding balance is more than a month overdue, and this is our second reminder that your payment has not been received. The outstanding balance represents your promise to pay $500 by June 15.
>
> Please act now and put your check for $500 in the mail today. Your attention to this matter will prevent us from having to take further action.
>
> Sincerely yours,

C10 Complaint Letter

If a verbal expression of dissatisfaction brings no results, turn to a formally worded but courteous letter. Wait until you are calm before writing because anger works against you. Figure 3.4 illustrates the parts of a complaint letter.

```
                    Dear Ms. Bender:

                    Our July shipment of frames arrived on
                    schedule, but unfortunately 100 of them
                    were damaged. Your shipping department
   Introduction     must confirm the packaging status of the
                    shipment before I can file a complaint
                    with the freight company.

                    I telephoned your shipping department
                    twice last week, and I was told that the
   Statement        matter would be investigated immediately.
   of Facts         Five days ago I spoke with Mr. Walter
                    Leahy in your shipping department, but
                    I have yet to hear the results of your
                    investigation.

                    Since I want to enter a claim for the
                    damage promptly and since we need to
   Action           order more frames to replace the broken
   Requested        ones, I would appreciate it if you would
                    give your immediate attention to our
                    problem.

                    Please telephone me by Friday at (201)
                    778-4243 with the information I need so
   Deadline Set     that I can proceed to file our claim with
                    the shipper and place a new order with
                    your firm.
                                          Sincerely yours,
```

Figure 3.4 Complaint Letter

Reply to the complaint letter. Figure 3.5 is a letter aimed at assuring the continuation of a business relationship after a problem has been solved.

```
                    Dear Mr. Litchfield:

                    As requested in your letter of July 15
   Introduction     regarding damaged frames, I contacted
                    Walter Leahy in our shipping department
                    to clarify your problem.

                    I apologize for the delay in contacting
                    you, but our shipping department--in spite
                    of numerous efforts--had difficulty obtain-
                    ing the necessary details from the carrier.
   Statement        Mr. Leahy now has the information you
   of Facts         need to enter your claim with the carrier,
                    and I have enclosed that information with
                    this letter. We have already placed an
                    order for 100 frames to replace the broken
                    ones.

                    Thank you for your patience. I hope that
   Establishment    our future transactions will continue to
   of Future        be as trouble-free and as mutually
   Goodwill         beneficial as they have been in the past.
                                          Sincerely yours,
```

Figure 3.5 Reply to the Complaint Letter

C11 Congratulatory Letter

Keep congratulatory letters short and sincere.

```
Dear Mario:

I was delighted to learn that you have been elected to
the office of president of Data Processing Professionals.
Those of us who know you realize that you are most
deserving of the position.

Your past record as an active and concerned member of the
organization well qualifies you for the vital leadership
the organization needs in this time of unprecedented
change. If I can lend assistance in any way, I will be
happy to do so.

Congratulations, Mario! Warm wishes for a successful
term as president.
                                    Sincerely,
```

The receiver of a congratulatory message may choose to reply:

```
Dear Philip:

How thoughtful of you to write a note congratulating me
on taking over as president of the Data Processing
Professionals.

Your good wishes and your willingness to support our
activities are certainly very much appreciated.
                                    Sincerely,
```

C12 Inquiry Letter

When a telephone inquiry is not possible, send a written request for information. Be specific about the information you seek.

```
Ladies and Gentlemen:

Our class is conducting a survey to find out which
types of letter and punctuation styles are currently
popular with business firms in our community and your
participation in our survey would be welcomed.

We are asking several companies to write us using the
letter and punctuation styles typical of their
correspondence. We would appreciate your taking part
in our survey.

Please reply to us on your company letterhead so that
we can collect a file of these, too. Your prompt reply
would be appreciated.
                                    Sincerely,
```

Communication in Business

Reply to inquiry, acknowledgment or receipt letter:

> Dear Ms. DiFiore:
>
> Thank you for inviting ABC Company to take part in your survey of letter and punctuation styles.
>
> We are always pleased to participate in activities generated by the schools in our geographic area, and we hope that you get a good response to your survey.
>
> Best wishes for the success of your project.
>
>   Sincerely,

C13 Form Letters

Preprinted and stored letters. When routine correspondence is mailed to a large number of people—to advertise a new product, to introduce a new salesperson, or to announce a change in location, for examples—there are two economical methods of handling it.

- One method is to preprint the body of a letter on the letterhead; the date, inside address, salutation, and other pertinent information can then be added at the time of mailing. A limitation of this method is that the spacing of the fill-in information will not be exact and the data entered on the typewriter probably will not match perfectly.
- Another method is to store the body of the letter in the memory of an electronic typewriter or on a floppy diskette that stores data for a word processor or personal computer; the pertinent variable information may be merged at the time of mailing. This method requires equipment capable of storing and merging text; however, the final letter copy will be professional looking and personalized.

> Dear (Variable 1):
>
> The enclosed check represents the proceeds of your loan, and the statement that appears with it shows the terms of your contract with us.
>
> Your monthly payments are $(Variable 2), payable on the (Variable 3) of each month, and the first payment will be due on (Variable 4). It is wise for you to meet your payments on time in order to maintain a good credit rating.
>
> Thank you for bringing your financial requirements to our company.
>
>   Sincerely,

C13 Form Letters

Boilerplate or stored paragraph letters. Sometimes there is a need to send a letter or variations of a letter frequently. In this case, a variety of paragraphs may be stored in an electronic typewriter's memory or on floppy disks accompanying a word processor or personal computer. These paragraphs can then be selectively recalled and merged to customize correspondence in particular situations.

Some possible stored paragraphs:

1. Thank you for your interest in establishing a charge account at the Clothes Rack.
2. Your application for a charge account has been approved and an account number has been established for you. Your credit card bearing your assigned number is enclosed.
3. We regret to inform you that your application for a charge account has been rejected at this time. You are encouraged to apply again at a future time, however, should your credit status change.
4. Your application for a charge account is pending action at this time due to some missing data. We need further information from you. The enclosed card and envelope are for your reply.
5. When your application file is complete, you will hear from us on the status of your application. In the meantime, we look forward to the possibility of adding your name to our roster of credit customers.
6. As always, we stand ready to satisfy your shopping needs for clothing with style. Won't you stop in soon to use your new credit card.
7. As always, we stand ready to satisfy your shopping needs for clothing with style.

If the above paragraphs were stored, several customized letters might be generated. For example:

- Newly approved charge account customers might receive a letter with paragraphs 1, 2, and 6.
- Rejected charge account applicants would receive letters with paragraphs 1, 3, and 7.
- Charge account applicants who need to supply further information pending a credit decision would receive a letter with paragraphs 1, 4, and 5.

For illustration purposes, the above example included only a minimal number of paragraphs. Usually a substantial variety of paragraphs are stored. Standard paragraphs are available in hard copy. An origi-

Communication in Business

nator of correspondence could select specific paragraphs from those available and order correspondence typed from the word processing center by telephone or on a word processing work order form.

C14 Gratitude or Thank You Letter

Avoid gushing phrases but show your genuine appreciation.

For a present:

```
Dear Armand:

It was so thoughtful of you to send me the Picasso print
for my birthday. Bill will have it framed for me this
weekend, and I will hang it in my office for all to see.

Thank you very much. Perhaps the next time you are in
town you will stop by for lunch and let me show you your
beautiful gift in its new setting.

                                          Sincerely,
```

For a favor:

```
Dear Lynn:

Thank you very much for giving me the data I needed for
my report. Since the report is crucial to future
departmental growth, you can imagine how important
your help was to me.

I know that you went out of your way to get the
information and your willingness to help is very much
appreciated.

                                          Sincerely,
```

To a speaker:

```
Dear Professor Mitchell:

Your recent presentation on "Demystifying the
Technologies" at our Professional Secretaries
International monthly luncheon meeting was a huge
success.

The members were most enthusiastic in their praise of
your dynamic and informative presentation.  Frequent
comments included: "I learned so much"; "The time went
by too quickly"; and "I feel more comfortable now about
the technologies."

On behalf of all the members present, I extend a sincere
thank you to you, Professor Mitchell, for your vital
role in the success of this month's program. We are
grateful to you for sharing your expertise with us.

                                          Sincerely,
```

C15 Introduction Letter

A letter introducing a person may either be mailed directly to the addressee or delivered to the addressee by the person being introduced. It should clearly state its purpose.

```
Dear Dr. Schaeffer:

I am pleased to introduce my friend, Professor Mark
Waters, whose work in mechanical engineering is
probably familiar to you. He is interested in visiting
your research laboratory and, at the same time, he
wishes to discuss a matter he believes will interest
you greatly.

I hope that your meeting will prove mutually beneficial.

                                        Sincerely,
```

or

```
Dear Professor Chen:

I am pleased to introduce to you Max Von Eben, my
colleague for the past five years.

Max and his family have decided to move to California
for business reasons, and it occurred to me that you
and he might derive some mutual benefit from meeting.
I would be grateful for any assistance or guidance
you could give Max.

                                        Sincerely,
```

C16 Order Letter

When a preprinted order form is not available, send a simple, detailed letter to make your request.

```
Ladies and Gentlemen:

Please send the following items to our branch office
at 166 Fifth Avenue, New York, NY 10017.

Qty.   Description              Unit Price     Total
1000   No. 204 Hinges, Copper   $1.00 each     $1,000.00
 500   No.  72 Corner Braces,
              Copper Plated     1.25 each         625.00

                                TOTAL          $1,625.00

We would appreciate your assistance in rushing this
shipment to us since a flurry of recent orders has
depleted our supplies.

                                    Sincerely yours,
```

C17 Payment Letter

If a letter is required to accompany a payment, give an explanation of the payment.

```
Ladies and Gentlemen:

Our check in payment of Invoice No. 473 is enclosed.

The amount of $784 on the check covers the invoice
total of $800, less your 2 percent discount for
payment made within 10 days.
                                    Sincerely yours,
```

C18 Recommendation Letter

On occasion, you may be asked to write a letter of reference for an employee or a co-worker. Keep the letter short, positive, and honest.

```
Dear Mr. Walter:

I am very pleased to recommend Geraldine Lepre to you
as a prospective office manager.

Geraldine has worked with our organization for four years
as a payroll clerk, bookkeeper, and office supervisor.
Because she has been a conscientious worker and has
eagerly accepted responsibilities, she has been able to
earn a supervisory position with our company despite a
rather short period of employment with us.

Because of her eagerness to improve and her ability to
get along well with others, she has been effective in
coordinating the steadily increasing office work in
our firm caused by the addition of several new product
lines.

I am sure that Geraldine would be an asset to your
company, and I wish her every success.
                                    ·Sincerely,
```

C19 Reservations Letter

Although most reservations for convention facilities or hotel accommodations are made by telephone, a letter is sometimes necessary to

C17-C21   Payment Letter

confirm the details of the reservations. Remember to give full details and to address the letter to the reservations manager at the hotel.

```
Dear Reservations Manager:

Please reserve a three-room suite for September 17, 18,
and 19 for our annual conference of sales managers.

The conference will open with a social gathering at
3 p.m. on September 17 and close with a brief business
meeting at 3 p.m. on September 19. One room should be
suitable for informal social meetings, one for product
displays, and one for formal meetings for 15 to 20
people.

A confirmation of this reservation within the next ten
days will be appreciated.

                                    Sincerely,
```

C20   Response to an Unsolicited Job Application

Try not to discourage the writer. At a future date, this application might be useful to you. Be straightforward and courteous.

```
Dear Ms. Staunton:

Thank you for submitting your application to join our
company as a programmer. Unfortunately, we have no
openings now in our data processing department.

We will place your application on file and should an
opening occur, we will contact you for an interview.
In the meantime, good luck with your job search.

                                    Sincerely,
```

C21   Response to Request for a Donation
Affirmative reply:

```
Dear Ms. Blackburn:

In response to your request for a donation toward prizes
at the "Games for the Handicapped," I am pleased to
enclose a check for $250 from Taylor Realty, Inc.

We support your effort annually because we recognize
its importance to those involved. On behalf of our
entire staff, best wishes to you and your organizers
for another successful and memorable event.

                                    Sincerely,
```

Communication in Business

Negative reply:

```
Dear Ms. Blackburn:

Thank you for inviting us to participate in your annual
"Games for the Handicapped" by means of a donation
toward prizes.

Unfortunately, we cannot assist you because it is our
policy to make one major donation yearly to the United
Way.

Please accept our regrets and our good wishes for a
very successful event.

                                      Sincerely,
```

C22 Sales Letter

Since the purpose of a sales letter is to sell a product or an idea, be positive and use the *you* approach. Let the reader know how he or she is involved in the action and arouse the reader's interest in reading the letter.

```
Dear Mr. MacDonald:

How would you like to increase the efficiency of your
office workers by 10 percent this summer? Tests in over
100 offices where Kool Air Conditioners were installed
proved that workers' efficiency improved 10 percent.

Greater efficiency means larger profits for your
organization; thus, the Kool Air Conditioner pays for
itself in just a short time. Spread the cost of the
air conditioner over one, two, or three years if you
wish. The money you spend to improve worker comfort
and morale, and thus improve productivity, will be a
wise investment.

Won't you call us today and let our engineers determine
your office air conditioning needs? Every day without
a Kool Air Conditioning unit is costing you money.

                                      Sincerely,
```

Cover letter with sales information:

```
Dear Mr. MacDonald:

We are pleased to enclose a catalog and price list of
Kool Air Conditioners as requested by our engineer,
Joe Hamilton, following his visit to your company.
It is Joe's opinion that the models marked with an
asterisk are those most suited to your office needs.

If you have any questions after you have had an
opportunity to look over the catalog, please call
us so that we can remove any doubts. We know that
you and your employees will be delighted with the
performance of the Kool Air Conditioner.

We are at your service, so call us for immediate
delivery.

                                      Sincerely,
```

C23 Sympathy or Condolence Letter

Be brief but compassionate.

```
Dear Peggy:

It was with much regret that I read today about your
brother's sudden death. Everyone who knew Joe will long
remember his cheerful ways and the many kindnesses he
provided for others.

May it comfort you to know that others share your loss.
Please accept my sincere sympathy at this time of deep
sorrow, and don't hesitate to call me if you need
anything.
                                    Sincerely,
```

Reply to a message of sympathy:

```
Dear Amy:

Your thoughtful note and donation to the Heart Fund
were very much appreciated by our family.

Joe was such a vital member of our family that we can
hardly believe what has happened. Your kind thoughts
will help sustain us through the trying weeks ahead
as we attempt to adjust to Joe's absence.
                                    Sincerely,
```

C24 Address, Salutation, and Complimentary Close Forms

When contacting individuals outside the organization, using appropriate protocol is important. This section discusses the correct method for a variety of situations.

Here are some general guidelines to follow:

- Always use a *courtesy title* (Mr., Mrs., Ms., Miss) if correspondence is addressed to an individual.
- If an individual has a professional title such as *Dr.* or *Esquire*, use the professional title instead of the courtesy title. When an abbreviation such as *M.D.*, or *Esq.* follows a name, do not use a courtesy title before it.

Communication in Business

- If you are uncertain about whether or not a woman is married, use *Ms.;* in most situations it is now the preferred title for a woman.
- Avoid using the salutations *Dear Sirs, Dear Madam,* or *Dear Mmes.* because they are obsolete.
- The complimentary closing *Sincerely* or *Sincerely yours,* is the most popular. Avoid using *Yours truly, Very truly yours,* or *Yours very truly,* because they are generally considered out of date.

C25 Correct Forms of Inside Addresses and Salutations

CATEGORY	ADDRESS	SALUTATION
For one or more individuals		
If addressee is male but his name is not known	Midtown Office Supply Co. Midtown Office Supply Company	Dear Sir **or** Dear Owner (preferred)
If addressee is female but her name is not known	The Towne Beauty Shoppe	Dear Owner
Man	Mr. Kenneth Simon	Dear Mr. Simon (Formal) **or** Dear Ken (Informal)
Two men (or women) with different surnames	Mr. Kenneth Simon and Mr. Frank Tice	Dear Mr. Simon and Mr. Tice (Formal) **or** Dear Ken and Frank (Informal)
Two men (or women) with the same surnames	Mr. Peter Lyons and Mr. Ralph Lyons Ms. Rita Harlow and Ms. Alice Harlow	Dear Mr. Peter Lyons and Mr. Ralph Lyons (Formal) Dear Peter and Ralph (Informal) Dear Ms. Harlow and Ms. Harlow (Formal) Dear Rita and Alice (Informal)
A married woman	Ms. Maria Coyle *unless* Mrs. has been expressed as her preference	Dear Ms. Coyle **or** Dear Mrs. Coyle (Formal) Dear Maria (Informal)
A woman, marital status unknown	Ms. Phyllis King	Dear Ms. King (Formal) Dear Phyllis (Informal)
A widow	Ms. Frederick Holly **or** Ms. Jane Holly *unless* Mrs. has been expressed as her preference	Dear Ms. Holly (Formal) **or** Dear Jane (Informal)

C25 Correct Forms of Inside Addresses and Salutations

A company, gender and names of owners unknown	The Fox Company	Ladies and Gentlemen
A company, owners female, names unknown	Good Deal Catering	Dear Owners or Dear Ladies
A company, owners male, names unknown	Sell Rite Athletic Shop	Dear Owners

Titles of selected government officials

President of the United States	President George Washington	Dear Mr. President
Federal or State Chief Justice of the Supreme Court	The Honorable Lena Chung	Dear Ms. Chief Justice
Federal or State Senator	The Honorable Frank Willing	Dear Senator Willing
Federal or State Representative	The Honorable Mary Simon	Dear Representative Simon
State Governor	The Honorable William Styne Governor of the State of New Jersey	Dear Governor Styne
Mayor	The Honorable Daniel Kelly	Dear Mayor Kelly

Other selected titles

Ambassador	The Honorable Charles Long The Ambassador of the United States	Dear Ambassador Long
Armed Forces Personnel	Colonel Thomas Flint, USAF (Give full rank, full name, and abbreviation of service branch)	Dear Colonel Flint
Dean of a School or College	Dean Jay Desaid	Dear Dean Desaid
Jewish Clergy	Rabbi Joseph Freeman	Dear Rabbi Freeman
Judge	The Honorable John Powers	Dear Judge Powers
Lawyer	Brenda Miller, Esq. or Ms. Brenda Miller	Dear Ms. Miller
Physician	Georgia Reeves, M.D.	Dear Dr. Reeves
President of a College or University	Dr. Gerard Waters, President	Dear Dr. Waters or Dear President Waters

Communication in Business

Professor	Professor Adeline Eastwood or Dr. Adeline Eastwood	Dear Professor Eastwood or Dear Dr. Eastwood
Protestant Clergy	The Reverend Mark Welsch	Dear Reverend Welsch
Religious Order Priest	The Reverend Joseph Byrne (Add initials of order, if any—The Reverend Joseph Byrne, C.S.C.)	Reverend Byrne (Formal) or Dear Father Byrne

C26 The Complimentary Close

The complimentary close is a short courteous phrase at the end of a letter. Note that only the first letter of the first word is capitalized. The letter style and punctuation style chosen determine the placement of the complimentary close (see E78).

Following is a list of complimentary close phrases in order of decreasing formality:

Closing	Use
Yours respectfully Very respectfully yours Respectfully yours	These are expressions of respect and are used in letters to dignitaries and those in high government, military, or religious positions.
Sincerely yours Yours sincerely Sincerely	These expressions are the most common. They are used with formal salutations.
Cordially yours Yours cordially Cordially	These expressions are used with informal salutations.

Yours truly and *Very truly yours* are considered formal closings; however, they are generally considered out of date and should be avoided.

C27 Preparing Other Prevalent Written Communications

Interoffice memos, press releases, and reports are other common business writing applications. General writing principles will be presented in this section. For specific formatting details, see Unit 5.

C28 Interoffice Memoranda

For intra-company communication when written documentation of a message is necessary, the interoffice memorandum or *memo*, is used. Memos make up a large part of written business communication. They transmit information between workers in the same department, between different departments, and even between distant branches of the company.

The primary advantage of the memo format is that it offers a fast, efficient, and uniformly organized method of presenting data. Memos are usually brief; however, they must be accurate and carefully written. At times, the memo format is used to deliver policy statements, directives, or official information and authorization. Copies of memos are usually kept on file.

Memo format is unique in that the guide words *DATE, TO, FROM,* and *SUBJECT* appear in the heading. These heading styles are often available on pre-printed forms, but the arrangement of the guide words frequently differs and is based on company preferences. Here are two examples:

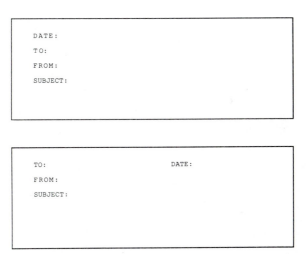

Memos can be prepared on half sheets (5 1/2" x 8 1/2") or on full sheets (8 1/2 " x 11"). The typical memo does not exceed one page (Figure 3.6). Memos are placed in special interoffice envelopes so they can be sorted separately from the outgoing mail.

Communication in Business

```
TO:    Suzanne Dennis, Registrar    DATE:    June 4, 19--
FROM:  Amy Lindner, Chairperson     SUBJECT: Room Change

       This is to confirm our conversation yesterday
regarding the scheduling of B0404-2806 Contemporary
Business.  I request a room change because there are
not enough seats to accommodate the number of students
enrolled in this section.

al:rm
```

Figure 3.6 Memo

Here are some guidelines for writing memos:

- Use the memo format adopted by your company.
- Be sure to fill in the information for each heading.
- Write clearly and be certain to verify all dates, numbers, times, and other critical information.
- Use short paragraphs, tables, and enumerations to simplify and clarify the presentation of data.
- An informal writing style is acceptable for routine messages; however, when writing a directive or policy statement memo, the writing should be formal.
- Place your initials next to your typed name on the *FROM* line if the message is routine; sign your name if a memo contains important information (i.e., procedural changes, directives), or if your initials might be confused with those of another employee.
- Use plain paper of the same weight and color of the first page if a second sheet is needed.
- For formatting instruction, see Unit 5.

C29 News Releases

When a new product is introduced, a senior managerial appointment is announced, or another notable event occurs, the occasion is frequently publicized by means of a news release (see Figure 3.7). This is a bulletin sent out to newspapers, trade magazines, and other pertinent segments of the press either ahead of the event or at the time of the event in an effort to obtain free publicity.

News releases are excellent communication devices. They can often be even more effective than paid advertisements and they build goodwill for the company.

C29 News Releases

```
                         NEWS RELEASE

Dr. Barbara Jacobsen, President      FOR RELEASE ON MARCH 14, 19--
The Office Technologies Institute
2000 Avenue of the Americas          Mailed:  March 11, 19--
New York, NY 10017
(212) 873-2000

                    OTI APPOINTS ACADEMIC DEAN

      New York, March 14 — The Office Technologies Institute has
announced the appointment of Dr. Lynn E. Mulder as the academic dean
of its New York City Branch.  Ms. Mulder succeeds Marshall Turner
who retired recently.  The announcement was made by President
Barbara Jacobsen at a press conference held at the school on
March 14.
      Dr. Mulder was formerly the Chairperson of the Office
Technologies Department at the Northside Business Institute in
Yonkers.  She earned her doctoral degree at New York University
and has served as a curriculum consultant for a number of
federally-funded vocational programs.  Dr. Mulder is the current
president of the New York City Business Educators Association
and has authored a text, The Office Specialist, published by
Chadwick House Publishers.  Dr. Mulder resides in Scarsdale.

                              ###
```

Figure 3.7 News Release

In large companies, a public relations department handles all news releases and other publicity. In such cases, official preprinted news release forms are used and no publicity should be given to the press directly by a department or an individual. When a public relations department does not exist, the news release is an effective way to solicit publicity.

Here are some guidelines for preparing news releases:

- Keep the contents to one page if possible.
- Write factually; avoid subjective comments.
- Apply the five *W's* of journalism and answer the following questions: *Who? What? When? Where?* and *Why?*
- Present the details by giving the most important ones first and the least important ones last.

Note the following details in the sample illustration:

- Standard typing paper and wide margins are used.
- The typing is double-spaced to permit editing.
- The sender's name and title, company name, address and telephone number are typed in a block at the top left.
- FOR IMMEDIATE RELEASE or FOR RELEASE ON (Date) are typed at the top right, and *Mailed (date)* is typed underneath.
- The story headline is typed in all caps and centered.
- The city and date are typed at the start of the first paragraph.
- The symbols ### end the copy.

C30 Reports and Manuscripts

Reports, surveys, and studies are prepared to present information to an individual or group of individuals so that better decisions can be made.

Reports come in two broad categories: the *information report*, which provides data; and the *research report*, which outlines a problem, presents facts and findings after research has been carried out, evaluates the data collected, and recommends a solution. The information report is informal and usually brief. The research report is complex and requires a more structured format. (See Unit 5, E94-E136, for formatting instructions.)

C31 Stages of Report Preparation

The amount of time spent preparing a report varies according to the complexity of the project, the availability of information, and sometimes even the time constraint under which information must be obtained; nevertheless, certain stages or steps in preparing a report are common. They include planning, investigating, outlining, drafting, and finalizing. A discussion of each step follows.

C32 Planning

At the outset, the report writer must clearly establish several factors. They are:

- **The purpose of the report.** This involves such considerations as knowing who the readers will be and what purpose the final report is to serve—information only; information and balanced assessment; information, assessment, and recommendation.
- **The problem to be solved.** A clear and specific statement of the problem to be investigated must be determined. It is usually

effective to attempt to present the problem in one broad statement. For example:

"To explore the possibility of adopting flextime scheduling at the Detroit branch of ABC Company."

- **The factors to be investigated.** Consideration should be given as to how the data should be gathered, who should be involved in the response, what information is needed to make the gathered information useful, and how worthwhile the results of the investigation might be.

  In the above example, the determination might be to construct a questionnaire that would be sent to all department managers to determine which positions in their departments could be staffed effectively using flextime scheduling.

- **The limiting factors.** Attention needs to be given to the constraints affecting the investigation process.

  In the above example, such concerns might include budgetary allocations, personnel available to conduct the investigation, time needed to tabulate the results, number of individuals to be surveyed, and time frames imposed for completing the investigation.

- **An overall presentation plan for the final report.**

Business Reports. The business report writer has three basic approaches by which to make the final presentation: the *direct approach;* the *indirect approach;* and the *modified approach,* a combination of the first two approaches. It is helpful at the outset for the investigator to make an outline of the main sections anticipated in the final report. These sections might be identified as follows:

Direct approach. The main ideas such as the summary, conclusions, and recommendations are presented first; the details follow.

Indirect approach. The details such as the introduction and findings are presented. They are followed by the main ideas such as the summary, conclusions, and recommendations.

Modified approach. A summary of the report appears first; the detailed information, such as the introduction and findings, follows; and finally, the conclusions and recommendations are given.

Formal research. In dissertations and other formal research projects, the following presentation sequence is usually observed and each section becomes a chapter of the manuscript.

Statement of the problem. The need and purpose of the study, the hypotheses (broad implications) of the study, and the limitations of the study (factors that affect the scope of the study) are given.

Review of the literature. Prior research in the field is summarized.

Design of the study. Information is given about selection, the preparation of the instruments used, and the method of statistical analysis.

Analysis of the results. The research discusses the hypotheses as they were reported with no interpretation; or interprets their meanings under a specific heading entitled *Discussion*.

Summary or conclusion. A synopsis of the problem, the literature, and the research design are first presented; conclusions and recommendations for future research are then given.

C33 Investigating

Information may be gathered from primary or secondary sources.

Primary research involves getting information first hand. Two often-used primary research methods for business report writing are the questionnaire and the interview. Experimentation and observation are commonly used primary methods in formal research. Questions must be carefully worded in a questionnaire so that it will yield true results. Interview procedures must be conducted uniformly; otherwise results will not be representative of the sample.

Secondary Research involves getting information from previously recorded or documented sources. Such materials are often found in libraries, through government services, through hard copy business reports (Moody's Manuals, Standard and Poor's, Datapro Reports), through computerized data bases (CompuServe, Dialog) as well as on microforms, records, videocassettes, and films.

An effective way to organize material in the research stages is to use an index card system (Figure 3.8). Using one index card for each fact makes it easier to organize the data in logical sequence in the writing stage. It also helps to keep the sources of information organized.

C34 Outlining

Once you have collected all the relevant data, make an outline of your report. The working plan you developed during the planning stage should be used as a guide. Include subheadings for topics to be included. Arrange the index cards you prepared in the investigation stage in sequence so that they lend support to the ideas you are presenting. Finally, think through the major ideas you plan to recommend.

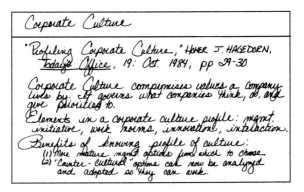

Figure 3.8 Research Notes on an Index Card

I. Summary (to be written last)
II. Introduction
III. Reasons for Considering Flextime
   A. Give reasons why the company is considering flextime.
      1. Cite comparative payroll expenditures.
         a. Use bar graph showing the payroll for the last five years.
         b. Use bar graph showing absenteeism figures by sex and marital status.
      2. Cite the results of a recent survey which show that both managers and employees favor a change to flextime.
      3. Cite reports from literature that support the change to flextime.
         Card No. 18
         Card No. 4
         Card No. 2, etc.
   B. Purpose of the Study
      1. To explore the possibility of adopting flextime.
      2. To identify specific jobs that lend themselves to flextime scheduling.
   C. Procedures
      1. Explain the procedures to be used in the survey.
      2. Explain how the questionnaire was developed.
      3. Explain how the sample was determined.
   D. Findings
      1. Give the details revealed by tabulating the questionnaires. (List the findings on a question by question basis as they appeared in the questionnaire.)
      2. Design charts or graphs to support the findings.

Communication in Business

    E. Conclusions
        1. Discuss those jobs that might qualify for flextime.
        2. Explain that the survey revealed that not all departments had jobs that would qualify for flextime.
    F. Recommendations
        1. Two departments seem to have the most jobs that lend themselves to flextime.
        2. A pilot program might be implemented in one department to determine the effectiveness of a change to flextime in some jobs.

C35 Drafting

After the outline is prepared, the writer begins to make a rough draft of the report. Ideally, this might be prepared at a text editor, such as a microcomputer, or dictated by the author into dictation equipment. In the absence of these alternatives, the traditional method would be to handwrite the report, or draft it at a typewriter. The *cut and paste* technique would be used for changes (see R16).

In the drafting stage, the report writer

- builds on the outline and adds detail and substance as the report is written paragraph by paragraph, one section at a time.
- decides what style of writing to use.
  Note: As you draft your report, you must keep your reader in mind and use an *impersonal* style, writing in the third person using, for example, *the writer. . ., the researcher*, etc.; or a *personal* style using *I's, we's,* and *you's*. Your decision should be based on the circumstances of the particular report. A formal report requires the impersonal style; on the other hand, your writing style can often be more forceful, interesting, and persuasive with the personal style. Your reader's preference as well as the reader's relationship to you should be considered in making your final decision. For example, when writing a report for your immediate supervisor, the personal style would be effective; however, a report to be considered by the operating officers of your company might be best if written in the impersonal style.
- rearranges the outline and embellishes the details, using the data collected on cards for reference and supportive information.
- strives for a logical arrangement of information, although sometimes it is necessary to prepare sections of the report out of sequence.

- uses a vocabulary level appropriate for the reader. Make sure technical expressions are not used if the reader is not familiar with them.
- revises, rewrites, analyzes data, and checks for accuracy over and over again.

C36 Finalizing

When the writer is finally satisfied that the rough draft is suitable in wording, detail, sequence, and adequacy of supporting data, the final copy of the report is printed. Before distribution, the final copy must be proofread carefully to ensure that it is accurate in all respects. If appropriate, the writer should consider placing the report in an appropriate binder to ease handling and to enhance its overall first impression on the reader.

C37 Parts of a Report

There are many sections that a writer might consider in presenting a report. It is important to recognize that all reports will not have every one of the sections. Those sections selected for use are determined by the writer. For specific illustrations, see Unit 5.

C38 Front Matter

Cover. The cover may be a special binder or a sheet of paper of similar quality to the inside pages. The title of the report should be on the cover.

Title Page. The title page includes the name of the report, the name and department or company of the originator, the name of the recipient, and the date—all attractively arranged.

Table of Contents. Each heading and its page number are shown to let the reader know what topics are to be covered and where to find them. Illustrations or tables might also be listed.

Letter of Transmittal. The letter of transmittal is presented at the writer's discretion. It might give an overview of the report, summarize its content, and possibly even offer to discuss the contents with the reader.

Abstract, Executive Summary, or **Summary**. In long reports, this section is included to summarize the main ideas of the report for the reader who does not have enough time to read the report in its entirety.

Foreword. The foreword is often found in published materials and its purpose is to strengthen the credibility of the work. It is written by someone other than the author, usually a well-known individual.

Preface. The preface, if included, enables the writer to present personal comments about the report.

Acknowledgements. The writer uses this section to give credit to individuals who helped with the report. Acknowledgements may be included as part of the preface.

C39 Body

Format. The report itself is organized into many sections and has many subheadings. This data may be presented in a variety of formats (see E99-E118).

Footnotes. When reference sources appear at the bottom of a page they are called *footnotes*. Each footnote must refer to a source cited in the bibliography (see E118-E132).

C40 Back Matter

End Notes. When reference sources are listed at the end of every section or chapter of the report, they are called *end notes* (see E118-E132).

Bibliography. A composite listing of the details of the reference sources used in compiling the report is called a *bibliography*. It may include books, periodicals, recordings, or other sources. It is usually alphabetically arranged by the author or editor (see E134).

Annotated Bibliography. A bibliography that includes a brief narrative statement about each reference used in compiling the report is known as an *annotated* bibliography.

Appendix. An *appendix* contains supplementary information, lengthy tables, and related forms that the reader might find helpful for reference purposes.

Glossary. A *glossary* is an alphabetical listing of terms and definitions to assist the reader in understanding difficult or technical terms.

Index. An *index* is an alphabetical listing of critical areas, words, or terms included in a report, with specific page number references.

C41 Checklist for Writing Effective Communications

Every piece of written communication, whether intended for business or personal use, is more effective and more likely to achieve its goals if it is written with the following elements in mind.

1. **Purpose**
    a. State one specific purpose.
    b. State the purpose clearly.
2. **Psychological considerations**
    a. Consider the feelings and philosophy of the reader.
    b. Make it interesting to the reader.
    c. Show sincerity.
3. **Completeness**
    a. Include all necessary facts.
    b. Answer the *Who?*, *What?*, *Why?*, *When?*, *Where?*, and *How?* questions.
4. **Clarity and conciseness**
    a. Use simple words that convey the specific idea.
    b. Use language understood by the reader; avoid slang, shortened words, contractions, English idioms, overused and outdated expressions.
    c. Place words and phrases correctly.
    d. Limit each paragraph to one idea.
    e. Include only the necessary information.
    f. Trim the sentences down to essential words and phrases.
    g. Use short—not choppy—sentences and paragraphs.
5. **Concreteness**
    a. Use words with specific meaning rather than general or abstract words.
    b. Use active writing rather than passive writing.
    c. Emphasize people rather than things.

Communication in Business

6. **Correctness**
   a. Use only true and unbiased facts.
   b. Employ appropriate and accurate letter mechanics.
   c. Always use accurate English—grammar, spelling, and punctuation.

7. **Coherence**
   a. Word each sentence so that it makes sense to the reader.
   b. Use logical sentence sequence.
   c. Use logical paragraph divisions.
   d. Use logical paragraph sequence.

8. **Courtesy**
   a. Select polite words.
   b. Instill a polite tone—tactful.

9. **Positivism**
   a. Choose cheerful and positive words.
   b. Organize the document so that it achieves it purpose.

10. **Effective beginning**
    a. Establish a *reader-centered* approach.
    b. Determine the best approach—inductive or deductive.

11. **Effective ending**
    a. Summarize with positive and complete sentences.
    b. Conclude with an active or convincing thought.

C42 Oral Communication in Business

Most office workers spend more time speaking than writing. Whether talking on the telephone, giving machine dictation, participating in a small or large group meeting or taking part in a one-to-one conversation, skillful oral communication will enable you to achieve desired results.

C43 Voice Qualities

How you speak will often affect the listener's perception of what you say. Some of the voice qualities that can affect a message are:

- *Tone*: indication of attitude and feelings; the overall style of delivery used.

- *Pitch*: degree of highness or lowness of the voice. Variations in pitch add interest and indicate meanings.
- *Volume*: quality that enables you to be heard. Volume should be influenced by the size of the room, whether or not a microphone is used, and the acoustics of the room.
- *Rate*: the speed of delivery. Delivery rates that are too slow or too fast will cause the listener to lose interest.
- *Enunciation*: the precision with which you express each word. Let your audience hear your words; be sure that word endings are audible— say "What did you say?" not "Wajasay?"
- *Pronunciation*: the correct expression of each word. Correct expression is the mark of an educated person—say "film" not "filum"; say "maintenance," not "maintainence."

C44 In-Person One-To-One Communication

- Learn the person's name and use it.
- Establish effective eye contact.
- Don't infringe on a person's personal work area. (For instance, don't put your handbag or briefcase on a person's desk.)
- Be businesslike.
- Be cheerful and appear interested in the conversation.
- Request feedback to clarify or confirm instructions.
- Be tactful.
- Be empathetic; try to put yourself in the other person's place.
- Be assertive, but not aggressive (see Unit 18, W19).
- Write down technical information while the conversation is taking place.
- Meet deadlines or provide an explanation beforehand if a deadline can't be met.
- Report on time for meetings and appointments; if you will be unavoidably late, call ahead with an explanation.
- After a long conversation, summarize what the understanding is at the end of the conversation.
- Be a good listener (see W18).

C45 How To Do Machine Dictation

As offices become more and more automated, machine dictation is becoming a necessary skill for originators, regardless of whether they are managerial or support personnel. Dictation is a skill and can be developed and improved through practice and perseverance.

Some dictation procedures and guidelines follow:

Prepare to Dictate
- Be certain you are familiar with the operation of the equipment or system you will use for the dictation.
- Assemble all the information you need before you start to dictate—files, addresses, dates, etc.
- Organize your thoughts in advance by making notes on the points you want to include. When replying to incoming correspondence, you might wish to jot down notes in the margins.

Begin the Dictation
- Identify yourself by name, title, and location.
- Identify the type of document to be dictated (letter, memo, telex, report).
- Give the date to be used.
- Identify the priority need, if any.
- Specify the number of copies needed.
- Give any special instructions about linespacing, formatting requirements, use of special paper, the length of the document—especially if it is extremely long or short—or any other necessary reminders.
- Let the transcriptionist know whether or not you will be dictating punctuation marks and paragraphs. Dictating punctuation and paragraphs handicaps the dictator because it disturbs the flow of thought. Therefore, dictating only unusual punctuation and formatting is usually best. Competent transcriptionists should be able to format dictation without depending on the dictator to supply routine punctuation and paragraph information.
- Use equipment-based systems to help the transcriptionist determine the length of the dictation and the corrections if you are using a desktop dictation unit.
Note: Some equipment enables dictators to record the beginning and ending of a document as well as out-of-sequence corrections on a special paper form called an *index strip;* other equipment provides for this by recording electronic or magnetic impulses.

Dictation Guidelines
- Hold the microphone or receiver about six inches from your mouth.
- Use a natural, conversational voice level and speed.
- Use appropriate inflections and pauses to help the transcriptionist determine punctuation and paragraphs, especially if they are not dictated.

C46 A Sample of a Dictated Letter to a Word Processing Center

- Spell out the name and address of the addressee.
- Spell out proper names and troublesome words.
- Provide subject line information for all memoranda.
- State any unusual punctuation desired, such as underlining, all caps, and exclamation points.
- Keep the quality of the dictation audible for the transcriptionist. Avoid fumbling with the unit, shuffling papers, and mumbling or chewing.
- Provide the transcriptionist with a handwritten copy of foreign names and addresses.
- Specify the number of columns for tables and statistical reports.

Closing Procedures
- Give your name, title, and preference for a complimentary close.
- Indicate whether there is to be an enclosure or attachment, and for whom carbon copies should be made, if any.
- Let the transcriptionist know if you have any special instructions for storing the dictated material permanently.

C46 A Sample of a Dictated Letter to a Word Processing Center

Good Morning. This is Roger Whittencamp, Administrative Assistant in the Personnel Department. I need to have a short letter typed on company letterhead with two copies. Please use today's date. I will not be dictating punctuation marks or paragraphs—instead, I will leave that up to you. The letter goes to Mr. Waldo (W-A-L-D-O) F. (as in Frank) Sanderson (S-A-N-D-E-R- S-O-N) (pause) Twelve Brian (B-R-I-A-N) Court (C-O-U-R-T), Phoenix (P-H-O-E-N-I-X) Arizona, Six-two-four-four-one (Pause) Dear Waldo (Pause) Your quarterly review is scheduled for the first of next month, and I would like to be certain that your file is up to date. (Pause) A record of the completion of continuing education courses would be helpful in your personnel assessment; therefore, if you have taken any courses from institutions granting C.E.U. (Capital C period Capital E period Capital U period) credit, please send me a copy of either a report card or a transcript that will serve to document the completion of the course work. (Pause) If I receive this information within the next two weeks, it will be placed in your file in time for consideration as part of your performance review. (Pause) If I do not hear from you in this period of time, I will assume that no course work has been taken. This would also be an appropriate time in which to send me any other material you would like to have included in your personnel file. (Pause) Sincerely, Roger (R-O- G-E-

Communication in Business

R) Whittencamp (W-H-I-T-T-E-N-C-A-M-P), (Pause) Administrative Assistant (Pause) Personnel Department (Pause). Please include a carbon copy notation to Bruce (B-R-U-C-E) Bender (B-E-N-D-E-R), Marketing Manager. Please call me at extention one-one-zero-four when this material is ready. Thank you, operator. This is the end of my dictation.

C47 Involvements with Speakers

Introducing a Speaker. Request information from the person you are to introduce in advance of the scheduled talk so that you can organize and plan your introductory remarks. Make every effort to keep the introduction short and simple.

- Make a warm, welcoming opening statement.
- Give a brief summary of the speaker's background and special interests, and highlight the credentials that support the presentation to be given.
- State the speaker's topic.
- Finally, introduce the speaker by name. Do this last so that the speaker clearly knows when it is time to take over.

Thanking a Speaker. Keep your remarks brief, but deliver them sincerely. Comment on the importance of the speech and then simply thank the speaker, expressing appreciation on behalf of everyone present.

C48 Giving a Speech or Oral Report

Prepare in Advance

- Establish the purpose of your talk. Is it to inform, persuade, entertain, or a combination of these?
- Research your audience. Who will be there, why will they be there, and how large is the group? What is the audience's interest in attending?
- Determine your topic and decide on the key ideas to be presented. Collect and organize reference materials. Prepare an outline or *frame* for your talk. It should include a stimulating opening to arouse your listeners and get them interested in the topic; a middle, which includes the details, examples, and facts that support your theme; and, finally, a conclusion, which reaffirms the opening statement and leaves the audience with an action-oriented, provocative thought.

C47-C48   Involvements with Speakers

- Produce your notes (Figure 3.9). Expand upon your outline until you have produced a speech that is an appropriate length for the presentation time allotted for your talk. Produce a set of notes from your outline on small index cards that summarize your major points.

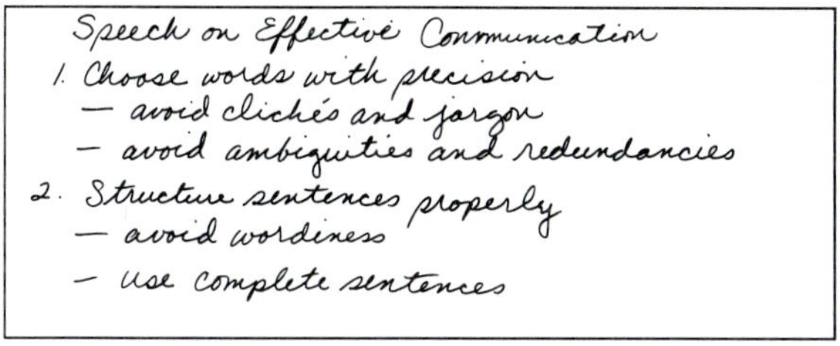

> Speech on Effective Communication
> 1. Choose words with precision
>   — avoid clichés and jargon
>   — avoid ambiguities and redundancies
> 2. Structure sentences properly
>   — avoid wordiness
>   — use complete sentences

Figure 3.9   Speech Notes

- Plan to use visuals if they will serve to clarify or emphasize your ideas. Transparencies, flip charts, slides, and handouts are just a few visual aids that might be considered. Keep in mind, however, that the visual aids should be used to supplement your talk, not substitute for it. Make sure that visuals are large enough for viewing by people in all parts of the room.
- Practice your talk. The inexperienced speaker may find it helpful to practice the presentation aloud to a friend, before a mirror, or into a tape recorder for a self-evaluation playback. Practice your talk with the visuals.

Making the Delivery
- Speak slowly, clearly, and loudly enough to be heard by everyone.
- Be enthusiastic; this is one of the most important qualities of a dynamic speaker.
- Be well prepared because preparedness breeds self-confidence.
- Don't read your talk; speaking from an outline or cue cards works best.
- Speak extemporaneously, never memorize.
- Use a conversational tone; think of this presentation as a broadened conversation.
- Take your time before you begin. Arrange your notes, look at the audience, and compose yourself. Don't be in a rush to begin.
- Keep your head up and look at people's faces in your audience. Try to sense your audience's reaction and respond to it.

Communication in Business

- Use your visuals effectively by referring to them in appropriate places and by making certain that the audience can see them.
- Avoid disturbing mannerisms such as rattling papers; saying "uhm," "you know," or other such expressions; using too many hand movements; or moving about too much.
- Use vocal variety in your delivery. Put highs and lows in your voice and use pauses to emphasize key points.
- Make certain that your body language complements your words. Try not to be stiff but stand straight, use movement at the podium carefully, dress appropriately, and take advantage of facial expressions and gestures to accentuate points.
- Avoid trite expressions, slang, and foul language.
- Involve yourself in your talk so that your presentation seems spontaneous.
- Always leave your group with a provocative thought, challenge, or question.

UNIT 4

DELIVERY AND SHIPPING SERVICES

Alternatives to Postal Delivery Services	D1-D8
Air Express	
Bus Delivery Service	
Courier Services	
United Parcel Service	
Other Alternatives	
Shipping Goods Within the United States	D9-D11
Documentation	
Obtaining Transportation Services	
Exporting Goods	D12-D23
Documentation Used	
Obtaining Export Services	
Importing Goods	D24-D32
Customs	
Clearing the Goods	
Clearance Documents	
Obtaining Import Services	
Transportation Terms	D33
Delivery and Shipping Log	D34

Delivery and Shipping Services

This unit discusses alternatives to the United States Postal Service for delivering office documents or packages both within and outside of the United States. Basic information about these alternatives is provided, and the list of related vocabulary at the end of the chapter should help you clarify terminology that is unique to delivery and transportation services.

D1 Alternatives to Postal Delivery Services

D2 Air Express

Some airlines offer *same day delivery* of important documents or packages in the United States as well as abroad. Refer to the Yellow Pages of your telephone directory to learn which airlines in your area offer air express service. Often a toll-free telephone call will tell you the special air express services available, the exact delivery schedule that will be followed, and the exact charges for sending your material from one location to another. Usually there are additional fees for pickup and delivery, for insurance over $100, and for packages exceeding 50 lbs.

D3 Bus Delivery Service

Bus companies often transport letters or packages for a fee based on the weight and size of the package and the destination. Depending on the areas to be served, arrangements can be made for pickup and/or delivery—again for an additional fee. Additional insurance can be purchased at minimal cost. C.O.D. deliveries are available only to businesses and organizations, not to individuals. As an example, one carrier limits packages to 100 lbs., 60" in length, and 141" in girth (distance around the thickest part); however, the limits vary with the bus company, so check the Yellow Pages under *Delivery Services* for the details regarding the specific carriers in your area.

D4 Courier Services

Couriers provide companies and individuals faster mailing service for packages, letters and all types of documents than can be obtained by regular mail. There are many courier companies from which to choose, and all of the major companies are now using computerized systems that give the sender up-to-the-minute information on the whereabouts of a

108

D1-D4 Alternatives to Postal Delivery Services

package or letter. This system is based on a special bar code that is placed on the airbill (written form completed by the sender; see Fig. 4.1). By means of a scanner, the material shipped is monitored from check in to delivery.

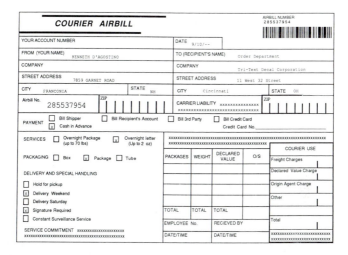

Figure 4.1 An Airbill

Courier services, rates, and reputations for meeting delivery schedules vary. Here are some features you might wish to consider when selecting a courier service.

Electronic Document Delivery. Some couriers in major cities can deliver laser-printer paper copies of computer correspondence within four hours.

Insurance. Besides the basic insurance protection offered by the courier, the customer has the option to purchase additional insurance.

Out-of-Delivery-Area Charges. Some couriers only deliver to selected cities or major population areas, and additional fees are imposed for deliveries beyond these delivery areas.

Payment. Businesses and organizations may set up accounts and be billed periodically for delivery costs. Individuals must pay ahead of time when using courier services.

Priority National Service. Some couriers offer an overnight service that provides the delivery of packages and letters by noon the next day in certain areas throughout the United States.

Delivery and Shipping Services

Quick Drop Boxes. Special boxes, similar to postal mail boxes, are located in centralized areas in large office buildings, industrial parks, or other busy locations. The courier service makes regular pickups daily at these locations; therefore, customers can avoid pickup charges, yet have the advantage of prompt pickup.

Rates. Rates need to be considered carefully because they vary from courier to courier and are based on the size, origin, destination, and type of service by which the material is being sent.

Redelivery. Most couriers redeliver a package the next day if delivery cannot be made on the first attempt.

Refunds. Some companies provide a refund on the delivery charge if materials are not delivered as promised. The customer must file a late claim form in order to obtain reimbursement.

Shipping Packs. Special envelopes are often supplied for materials to be shipped. Use of these envelopes facilitates delivery because the airbill is positioned in a uniform place on all documents. Additionally, when the package arrives it is apparent to the recipient that a special type of courier service was used, thereby emphasizing the importance of the package.

Toll-Free or Local Telephone Numbers. Most couriers have either toll-free numbers or local telephone numbers that can be used to obtain information, to schedule a package pickup, or to trace a package's delivery status.

Trace. Through computerization and optical scanning technologies, packages can be monitored from their check in with the courier to their delivery to the recipient.

D5 Steps in Choosing a Courier Service

The following steps should be helpful in planning the use of a courier service:

1. Use the local telephone number or toll-free telephone number to obtain information about the delivery areas served, the exact costs, the special services offered, and the transit time of several courier services.

2. Compare the information obtained, and weigh the various factors, alternatives, and reputations of the vendors.
3. Decide on the specific courier and the specific services you wish to use, and obtain a special pre-numbered airbill and mailing pack from the courier you have selected.
4. Complete the airbill carefully since this ensures that your materials will be delivered on time and to the right place. It will also control the billing and tracing for the package.

D6 Steps in Preparing an Airbill

1. Type all the information requested.
2. Enter the account number if the charge is to be billed to a business or an organization.
3. Type your name and your complete address in the spaces provided.
4. Enter the date the shipment is made.
5. Type the recipient's name and address and verify it for accuracy.
6. Specify the type of service desired and any special delivery or special handling services required, if any.

D7 United Parcel Service (UPS)

A frequently used alternative to the United States Postal Service is UPS or *United Parcel Service*. UPS can be relied upon for dependable, economical delivery of small packages (those weighing not over 50 lbs. and measuring not more than 108" in combined length and girth). Rates and delivery zones are similar to those for parcel post delivery, and charges vary with weight and distance; however, UPS delivery can be less expensive than United States Postal Service delivery for some packages. UPS can provide next day delivery, pickup service, and delivery of each package directly to the recipient's door.

D8 Other Alternatives

Railway delivery, truck delivery, and steamship delivery services afford other alternative methods for shipping goods. Your local Yellow Pages will provide you with the names of carriers who serve your area and whom you can call for specific information on rates, services, and procedures.

Delivery and Shipping Services

D9 Shipping Goods Within the United States

D10 Documentation

The *bill of lading* shown in Figure 4.2 (sometimes known as the *straight bill of lading*) is the standard contractual document used for all but express shipments between the shipper and carrier. (For express shipments, this document is referred to as the *express shipping contract*.) The bill of lading serves as a receipt for goods and as documentary evidence of ownership of goods, and is not negotiable.

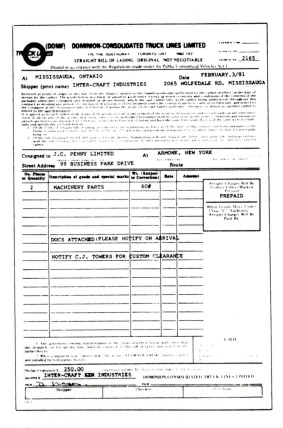

Figure 4.2 Bill of Lading

D11 Obtaining Transportation Services

When an organization is not large enough to have its own shipping department, it frequently uses freight forwarders or international freight forwarders. These are agencies that specialize in gathering small shipments (usually within a city or geographic area) and combining them into boxcarloads, containers, etc. They make up documents for shipments, take care of legal fees, arrange charges for freight, organize pickup and delivery, arrange for agents at the consignee's (recipient of the goods shipped) end, distribute documents, and provide any other required transportation services. Forwarders charge fees according to the value of the goods handled on each shipment. Freight forwarders often act as customs brokers as well.

D12 Exporting Goods

Shipping goods to foreign nations is more complex than shipping goods within the United States because of customs regulations, documentation, and foreign exchange problems.

D13 Documentation Used

A considerable number of documents are required to satisfy the demands of United States Customs and customs authorities in the importing country. The shipper may be required to provide all or most of the following documents.

D14 Confirmation of Sales

- An acknowledgement that the order has been received and will be shipped.

D15 Invoices

- Commercial Invoice: the standard invoice issued for all regular sales.
- Special Customs Invoice: needed by authorities in the importing country under certain circumstances.

Delivery and Shipping Services

D16 Special Certificates

- Certificate of Origin or Combined Certificate of Value and Origin: a declaration of the country of origin of the goods.
- Certificate of Mass (Weight List): needed when duties are calculated according to mass.
- Certificate of Health (Sanitary Certificate): required when animals or plants are being shipped.

D17 Export Permits

- May be required depending upon the commodity being exported and our relations with the other country.

D18 Import Permits

- Required by some countries.

D19 Bill of Lading

- The basic document required in any shipment (see D10).

D20 Export Entry Form

- Used by the customs department for statistical information.
- Required before goods valuing more than $500 may leave the United States.

D21 Shipping Notice

- Informs the importer that the shipment has been made.

D22 Packing List

- An itemized list of the contents of each package in the shipment.

D23 Obtaining Export Services

Because of the complexity of exporting, most large organizations employ their own experts, and smaller firms use a customs house broker (international freight forwarder) to prepare the documents and arrange for the transportation of the goods.

D24 Importing Goods

The responsibility for imported goods is usually included in the duties of the traffic manager or shipping department.

D25 Customs

Every article entering the United States must pass through United States Customs at official ports of entry. United States Customs controls both the entry of goods into the country and the collection of the required duties (tariffs) and taxes. There are customs offices in all major cities.

D26 Duty Rates

The rate of duty payable on goods entering the United States is determined by the classification of the goods and the tariff to be applied. Duty rates are calculated in three ways: *ad valorem* (a percentage of value), *specific* (according to mass, number, or size), or a combination of the two.

D27 Clearing the Goods

Goods are held in bond at a port of entry until they have been cleared; that is, until the importer has presented the required clearance documents and has paid the necessary customs duties and taxes.

D28 Clearance Documents

D29 Customs Entry Form

- Shows the items shipped, the method of transportation, duty and taxes payable, country of export, country of origin, names of the exporter and importer, and quantity of goods shipped.

D30 Customs Invoice

- Required for all shipments regardless of value. This invoice shows the transaction between the seller and the buyer.

Delivery and Shipping Services

D31 Packing List, Bill of Lading, Shipping Notice, and Import Permit

- See this unit, D18, D19, D21, and D22.

D32 Obtaining Import Services

Some organizations use a customs house broker (international freight forwarder) to clear shipments on their behalf. Customs house brokers clear shipments through customs, providing whatever assistance may be needed in the process (obtaining permits, finding out duty rates, preparing documents, etc.). The payment they receive is based on the value of the goods cleared.

D33 Transportation Terms

Ad valorem duty (Ad val., A/V) Customs tax levied on the value of imported goods.

Airbill Written form completed by the sender when using a courier service.

Bill of lading (b.l., B/L) Document issued by a carrier to a shipper acknowledging receipt of goods and promising to make delivery under the conditions stated.

Carload Shipment large enough to fill a rail boxcar.

C.O.D. (Cash on Delivery) Collection of the invoice value of the goods is made from the buyer when the goods are delivered.

Carrier Transporter of goods between the consignor and consignee.

Collect Recipient will be billed.

Consignee Recipient of the goods shipped.

Consignor Sender of the shipment.

Container service Shipments made in a metal container that may be carried by either road, rail, or sea (or all three) without the need for unloading and reloading.

Courier Commercial carrier providing for the rapid delivery of documents and packages.

D31-D34 Packing List, Bill of Lading, Shipping Notice, and Import Permit

Demurrage Charge for storage payable to a carrier for goods not collected within the time limit permitted.

F.O.B. (Free on board) Delivery of goods free of charge to the destination named (for example, F.O.B. Trenton).

Fishyback Trailer placed on a ship or barge.

LCL (less than carload) Quantity that is less than a full rail boxcar.

Manifest List of cargo that shows the masses, dimensions, values, destinations, and consignees.

Piggyback One method of transportation carried on the back of another (for example, a trailer on a flat railroad car).

Prepaid Sender will be billed.

Tariff Fee schedule of transporting companies or a government tax schedule on imports.

Third party bill Party other than the sender or the recipient will be billed.

Waybill (W.B.) Dispatcher's written description of goods shipped.

D34 Delivery and Shipping Log

Some companies keep a record of all packages shipped and received for better organization and for tracing purposes if a package becomes lost. This record is often in the form of a log as illustrated in Figure 4.3.

Delivery and Shipping Log
for the month of _____, 19___

Date	To/From	Incoming	Outgoing	Item	Contents	Shipping #	Rec'd/Sent by

Figure 4.3 Delivery and Shipping Log

UNIT 5

E DITING, FORMATTING, AND WORD PROCESSING

E

| Typewriting Operations | E1-E19 |

    Placement Information
    Finding the Starting Line (Vertical Placement)
    Finding the Center Point of the Paper
    Calculating Margins
    Basic Typing Techniques

| Categories of Keyboarding Equipment | E20-E25 |

    Electric Typewriters
    Self-Correcting Typewriters
    Electronic Typewriters
    Word Processors
    Personal Computers With Word Processing Software

| Corrections, Revisions, and Text Editing | E26-E37 |

    Making Corrections on a Typewriter
    Making Corrections and Revisions on a Text Editor
    Proofreading

| Style Practices | E38 |

| Typing Metric Expressions | E39-E41 |

    Symbols
    Numbers

Spacing Rules   E42

Typed Communications   E43-E93
- Charts and Graphs
- Envelopes
- Folding Correspondence
- Financial Statements
- Forms
- Legal Documents
- Letters
- Memoranda
- Post Cards

Reports, Essays, and Manuscripts   E94-E136
- Title Page
- Preface
- Table of Contents (Contents)
- Placement (Margins and Starting Lines)
- Spacing
- Headings
- Numbering Systems
- Ending the Pages
- Numbering the Pages
- Displayed Information
- Illustrations
- Quoted Material
- Footnotes and Endnotes
- Formatting Footnotes and Endnotes in Special Situations
- Textnotes
- Bibliography
- Index
- Typing Guide Sheet for Reports and Manuscripts

Word Processing Configurations   E137-E141
- Centralized Word Processing
- Decentralized Word Processing

The Word Processing Cycle   E142

Dictation Equipment   E143-E145
- Dictation Equipment Choices

Word Processing Terms   E146

Editing, Formatting, and Word Processing

Users of typewriters, text-editing equipment and word processors share common needs. They need to know how to operate their equipment effectively and how to produce typewritten work that meets the most exacting business and professional standards. Your keyboarding and formatting needs are addressed in this unit, regardless of the specific type of equipment you are using.

This unit provides a review of basic typewriter operations and acquaints you with some special features of typewriters, word processors, and personal computers used for text processing. Suggestions for proofreading are also given. The entire unit should be helpful to you as a reference for style and formatting practices. It should also provide some insight into the components and procedures of a word processing environment.

E1 Typewriting Operations

E2 Placement Information

Most typewriters are available with either *elite* type (12-pitch), which prints 12 characters to the inch; or *pica* type (10-pitch), which prints 10 characters to the inch. Some typewriters have dual-pitch capability that allows for typing in either 10- or 12-pitch. Still other typewriters are equipped with proportional spacing which means that the space allowed for each letter is proportional to the space required by each letter (Figure 5.1). All typewriters, however, permit six vertical lines to the inch.

```
ELITE TYPE
PICA TYPE
```
Variable Pitch (Proportional Spacing)

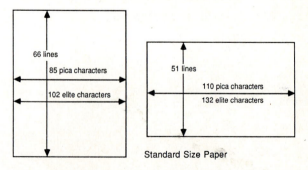

Figure 5.1 Spacing

E1-E6 Typewriting Operations

Read the manufacturer's manual that accompanies your typewriter so that you fully understand the scales, service keys, pressure settings, and special features of your particular machine.

E3 Finding the Starting Line (Vertical Placement)

E4 Determining the Line Count

```
Single Spacing      now is the time)      line count is 3
   (SS)             now is the time)
                    now is the time)

Double Spacing      now is the time)      line count is 5
                                    )
   (DS)             now is the time)
                                    )
                    now is the time)

Triple Spacing      now is the time)      line count is 7
                                    )
                                    )
   (TS)             now is the time)
                                    )
                                    )
                    now is the time)
```

Determining line count with single, double, and triple spacing

E5 Making the Vertical Placement Calculation

1. Count the total number of lines to be typed plus any necessary spacing.
2. Subtract the total number of typing lines and spaces from the lines on the typing paper.
3. Divide the result by 2 and add 1 to obtain your starting line. (Ignore any fractions.)

E6 Finding the Center Point of the Paper

Most typewriters indicate the center point for standard (let⸺ paper by means of an arrowhead or round mark on the ⸺ scale of the machine. Other typewriters provide ri⸺ markers against which to place the paper so tha⸺ lines up with the center point indicated on the ⸺

When there is no paper-guide scale on your machine:

1. Fold a piece of regular typing paper in half lengthwise.
2. Open the sheet. Insert it into your typewriter so that the left edge is against the paper guide, and note the point on the scale at which the fold appears.
3. If the number is a round one, such as 50 or 60, simply remember that number for future use.
4. If the number is not a convenient round number, pull forward the paper release, slide the paper over until the fold is on a round number, and adjust the paper guide so that it is tucked up tightly against the left edge of the paper. Leave the paper guide in that position permanently and remember the center point number.

Note: This technique is designed to assist in establishing the center point only when you first work with an unfamiliar typewriter.

E7 Calculating Margins

Divide the required line length by 2 and position your margin stops the resulting number of strokes on each side of the center point. For example, a 70-stroke line would be set with 35 strokes to the left of the center point and 35 strokes to the right of the center point.

E8 Basic Typing Techniques

Producing attractively typed material involves more than knowledge of the keyboard. Correct centering and tabulation techniques, display devices, and useful heading styles all contribute to a first-class finished product. These fundamental elements are outlined on the following pages. When using electronic typewriters, word processors, or software programs on a personal computer, some of these operations may be automatic; therefore, it is important to know the capability of the machine you are using so that you will use all of its features efficiently.

E9 Centering

Regular Centering
From the center point of the paper, backspace once for every two characters and spaces in the line to be typed. Then type the line.

HORIZONTAL CENTERING PROCEDURES

(Backspace once for each underscored character; do not backspace for any odd letter—for example, the last *s*.)

E7-E11 Calculating Margins

> **WP Note:** Automatic Centering is a standard feature on most text editors.

Spread (Extended Centering)
From the center, backspace once for each character and space *except the last*. Type the line, leaving *one* space between characters and *three* spaces between words.

```
S P R E A D   C E N T E R I N G
- - - - - -   - - - - - - - - -
```

(Backspace once for each underscored character and space—except the last one.)

E10 Decorative Devices

Use these sparingly in business applications because of the amount of typing time involved.

```
- - - - - - - -
  BORDERS              BORDERS
- - - - - - - -        _____
```

E11 Enumerations

When information is to be typed in sections or subsections, use a consistent pattern of numbers and letters, and/or indentions so that the reader can easily identify the relative importance of the material.

```
I.  -------
    A.  ------
        ------                (Remember to leave 2 spaces after each period)
        1.  -----
            -----             (Do not start a new subsection unless there
        2.  -----             are at least two subsections. There must be
            -----             an a and a b before adding section a; and a 1
    B.  ------                and 2 before adding a 1, etc.)
        ------
    C.  ------                (Line up letters and numerals):
        1.  -----             I.      1.      a.      A.
            -----             II.     2.      b.      B.
        2.  -----             III.    3. etc. c. etc. C. etc.
II. -------                   IV. (See Appendix, p. A7.)
```

> **WP Note:** Electronic typewriters and word processors can usually perform enumerations automatically; it is often called *automatic block indenting*.

E

123

E12 Heading Styles

Each of the following examples of heading styles may be centered, typed from the left margin, or pivoted (backspaced) from the right margin.

```
HEADING              Heading
HEADING              Heading
H E A D I N G        H e a d i n g
H E A D I N G        H e a d i n g
```

WP Note: Text editors can often produce **boldface** print that can be used effectively to **highlight** headings or key words in a document.

E13 Justifying the Right Margin

In typing, a justified margin means that all lines end evenly at the right margin. To accomplish this, follow these steps:

1. Set your margins for the required line length.
2. Draw a vertical line at the right margin setting.
3. Type a rough draft, but do not type any characters beyond the line at the right margin setting.
4. For each line, count the number of spaces between the last letter and the line drawn at the right margin.
5. Spread the number of extra spaces for each line evenly between the words in the line so that there are no large gaps.
6. Type the final copy, inserting the extra spaces as you proceed. Each line will now end evenly with the right margin.

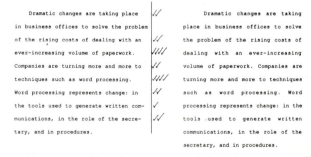

WP Note: Text editors and word processors can usually justify final copy by means of a command code.

E14 Leaders

Leaders are intended to take the reader's eye from one piece of information to another.

```
Open . . . . . . . . . . . . . . . . . . . open
Closed . . . . . . . . . . . . . . . . . . . . . . . . . closed
Patterned .. .. .. .. .. .. .. .. .. patterned
```

Remember these points when you use leaders:

- Leave a space at each end of the line of leaders.
- With open and patterned leaders, be sure to align the dots vertically—that is, notice if the first dot starts on an *odd* or *even* number, and then start all dots accordingly.
- If the right side is a figure column, end leaders two spaces before the column and align them vertically.

```
Books . . . . . . . . . . . . . . . . . . . . . . . $40.00
Pencils . . . . . . . . . . . . . . . . . . . . . .   5.00
Erasers . . . . . . . . . . . . . . . . . . . . . .   3.50
```

E15 Pivoting

Use this technique when a typed line must end at a particular point, or when succeeding lines must end at the same point.

1. Set the margins as usual, but set the right margin (or a tab stop) one space after the point at which you want the typing to end. For example, set the right margin stop at 91 for typing to end at 90.
2. Type the required words at the left margin and move the carriage to the right margin or tab.
3. Backspace from the right margin or tab stop once for every letter and space in the words to be pivoted.
4. Type the words. These will end exactly at the right margin or tab.
5. Continue until each line is completed.

```
Bloomsbury . . . . . . . . . . . . . . . . . . . . . . . . . . . Leon Edel
Blue Pages . . . . . . . . . . . . . . . . . . . . . . . . . . Ann Combose
Competitive Tennis . . . . . . . . . . . . . . . . . . . . Milton Dank
```

E16 Special Characters

Typewriters are not necessarily equipped with all the punctuation marks, symbols, or special characters you may need. Consult Table 5.1 to allow you to create your own.

Table 5.1 Special Characters

Special Character	Example	Method
Simple fraction	2/5	2 diagonal 5
Compound fraction	2 2/5	2 space 2 diagonal 5
Multiplication sign	2x5	lower case x

Editing, Formatting, and Word Processing

Table 5.1 Continued.

Division sign	$2 \div 11$	colon, backspace, hyphen
Minus	$12-3$	hyphen
Addition	$12 \neq 3$	diagonal over hyphen
Equal	$y=3$	two hyphens, one slightly above the other
Divide into (short)	$2)\underline{12}$	right parenthesis and underscore below number
(long)	$13)\overline{630}$	right parenthesis and underscore above number
Square root	$\sqrt{}$	v meeting diagonal and underscore
Cents	¢	c over diagonal
Dollars	$	S over diagonal
Pounds sterling	£	f over L
Degrees	$32°C$	o raised half line
Exponents	15^6	exponent raised half line
Chemical symbols	H_2SO_4	numbers lowered half line
Dash	--	two hyphens
Ditto	"	quotation marks
Does not equal	$\neq$	equal, backspace, diagonal
Exclamation mark	!	apostrophe over period
Square brackets	$\underline{/sic/}$	diagonals and underscores
Feet and inches	5'4"	apostrophe and quotation marks
Minutes and seconds	15'52"	apostrophe and quotation marks
Subscript	H_2O	type the number a half space below the letter in a chemical formula

Table 5.1 Continued.

Superscript	manuscript.³ 2⁴(exponent)	type the number a half space above the letter or number to which it refers
Section	§	Type S over S

E17 Tabulation Setup Procedures

To tabulate means to set up information in columns in an easy-to-read and attractive format.

```
✓Union City¹⁰        Morris Kiu         ✓$ 72,468⁸
 Trenton             Raj Kumar¹²           100,650
 Newark             ✓Daniel Keith           87,943
```

There are three methods of tabulation. The first stage in tabulation is to find the longest item in each column.

Method 1 (Arithmetic)
Planning the Job

1. Locate the longest item in each column (key item). Sometimes the key item is the column heading.
2. Decide on the number of spaces to leave between columns. Six is standard for most work but anywhere from two to twelve is acceptable. Three is standard for financial work, but two is acceptable.
3. Draw a plan showing columns and spaces, and note on it the character count of each key item and the amount of space to be left between columns.

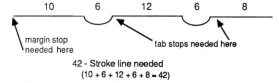

Setting the Machine

1. Clear any preset tab stops.
2. Clear any existing margin stops.
3. Set margins for the typing line needed for the table; that is, add all the figures on your plan and set the margin for that line width. Only the left-hand margin stop is necessary.
4. Set tab stops for the start of the second and all succeeding columns by spacing forward from the left margin for the number of characters in the key item in the column, plus the spaces in between, and then depressing the tab set key.

Editing, Formatting, and Word Processing

Column Headings

Blocked: simply start typing the headings at the left margin and at all tab stops.

```
SALES
$1025.12
```

Centered: center these headings over the columns.

A. Short Heads

```
    Sales
 $102,375.12
```

1. Follow instructions 1 to 4 for setting the machine.
2. Type the main table heading (title) and turn up a triple space.
3. Count the number of characters in the column heading. Subtract this number from the character count of the key item in the first column and divide the result by 2. (Drop any fractions.) Space forward the resulting number from the left margin stop and type the column heading.
4. Depress the tab key. Repeat the procedure given in step 3 for the other column headings.
5. Turn up a double space and type the remainder of the tabulation.

B. Long Heads

Long column heads will be the key item (longest line) for your column count. Your stop will, in fact, be set for the column head.

```
SALES BUDGET
  $17,000
```

1. Type the main table heading and turn up a triple space.
2. Type the column headings at the tab set points.
3. Center the column under the head as follows:
    a. Find the longest item in the column and count the characters.
    b. Subtract this character count from the heading count.
    c. Divide the result by 2. (Ignore any fractions.)
    d. Clear the margin.
    e. Tap the space bar by the number found and reset the margin.
    f. Depress the tab key. Repeat steps a, b, and c.

E17 Tabulation Setup Procedures

g. Clear the preset tab.
h. Tap the space bar by the number found and reset the tab.
i. Continue until all columns have been centered.
j. Type the rest of the table.

Method 2 (Backspace)
To establish margins with this method, start at the center point of the paper and backspace once for every two characters and spaces across the entire tabulation. Set left margin where backspacing ends. To set tabs, space forward once for each key item character and column character and depress tab set key. Repeat for all necessary tab stops. Deal with column heads as previously instructed.

Ruled Tabulations

- Set up your tabulation as already described.
- Type the horizontal rules as you proceed.
- Begin and end the horizontal rules at the left and right margins respectively.
- Note carefully the carriage returns needed to obtain the effect of a line of space above and below column headings, the body, and totals.

```
                        JANUARY TOTALS

                                                              DS
    _____
                                                              DS

           Chicago           New York           Los Angeles
                                                              SS
    _____
                                                              DS
           72,468            100,650            67,943
            9,005             20,725             6,319
           37,291              5,432            18,250
                                                              SS
    _____
                                                              DS
          118,764            126,807            92,512
                                                              SS
    _____
```

Boxed Tabulations

- Type the horizontal rules as you proceed and leave the vertical rules until you have finished the tabulation.
- Follow the points noted above for ruled tabulations.

Editing, Formatting, and Word Processing

- To insert the vertical rules, either use the notch or hole on your cardholder and a sharp pencil, or turn the paper sideways and use the underscore. The outside edges may be ruled but are better left open. Be sure to:

Keep the rules straight.

Place the rules in the center of the available space.

Begin and end the vertical rules at (not beyond) the bottom and top horizontal rules.

JANUARY TOTALS

Chicago	New York	Los Angeles
72,468	100,650	67,943
9,005	20,725	6,319
37,291	5,432	18,250
118,764	126,807	92,512

WP Note: The *Column Layout* feature of some electronic typewriters enables you to set up tables without calculations.

Method 3 (Judgment Placement)

In a busy business setting, it is often too time consuming to use either of the above methods to place tabulated material on a page. The judgment placement method enables the typist to *judge* where to set the margins and tabs for the table. A typist's skill improves with practice using this method.

- Study the table and estimate what margins could be set while still allowing sufficient space for all the columnar and intercolumn material.
- Set left and right margins so the margin areas will be even.
- Set tabs for each of the columns so the arrangement will be well-balanced and pleasing on the page.

E18 Tabulation Typing

In addition to the typing hints provided above, note the following suggestions:

Spacing

- Single or double spacing is acceptable. Use whichever will produce a tabulation that is attractive and easy to read.
- Triple-space under the main head and double-space under the column heads.

```
         Sales Report for Week Ending February 28, 19--
                                TS
         Monday      Tuesday         Friday      Total
                                DS
          317         298             312         927
```

Headings
Two-Line Headings
Align single-line headings with the *lower* line of two-line heads.

```
                  Sales
                Department             Total
                 $17,162              $44,865
```

Braced Headings
Braced headings are centered over a number of column headings as shown in Figure 5.2. Set margins and tab stops for column headings and type the main heading. To type the braced heading:

1. Find the width over which the braced heading is to be centered; that is, add the character count in the key items of the columns involved, plus the spaces between.
2. Count the characters and spaces in the braced heading.
3. Subtract the two results from each other and divide the result by 2.
4. From the tab stop set for the first of the columns over which the braced heading is to be centered, space forward the number found in step 3 and type the braced heading. Repeat this procedure for each braced heading.
5. Type the rest of the tabulation.

Editing, Formatting, and Word Processing

	Insurance Sold in the Week Ending February 23, 19--					
AUTOMOBILE		HOME OWNERS		TOTALS	
NEW	RENEWAL	NEW	RENEWAL	NEW	RENEWAL
$2,250	$4,500	$6,000	$8,000	$8,250	$12,500
1,000	3,500	2,400	6,500	3,400	10,000

Figure 5.2 Braced Headings

Space-Saver Headings

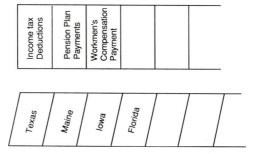

Figure 5.3 Space-Saver Headings

Note: Draw the lines *before* you type the words.

Numbers

- Whole numbers are aligned from the right (units, tens, hundreds, etc.).

```
 127
  32
 159
```

Separate digits into groups of 3 by means of spaces or commas.

```
12 141    12,141
```

132

E18 Tabulation Typing

- Decimals are aligned through the decimal point using a consistent style.

  ```
  9.00          9.          0.93           .93
  15.51   not   15.51       2.91    not    2.91
  ```

- Dollar signs are positioned to accommodate the longest line, but are typed only at the beginnings and ends of columns.

  ```
  $    37
     1,021
  $1,058
  ```

- Percent signs are placed after the figure. Type this symbol after each entry unless the word *percent* is included in the column heading.

  ```
   46%
   28
   26
  100%
  ```

Totals

Follow the spacing shown below unless space is limited.

```
127
 32    ← (Space)
159
```

Tabulations with Long Edge of Paper Inserted First

Set up your tabulation as shown in this unit, E17, but note this information: vertical line count is 51; number of possible strokes is 110 pica or 132 elite (Figure 5.4).

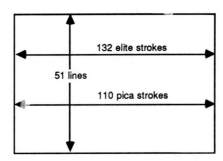

Figure 5.4 Tabulation Line and Stroke Counts

E19 Production Tips for Tabulations

- Try to get your table to fit on one page.
- Develop your judgment so that you can estimate the margin and tab-stop positions and avoid the need for meticulous, time-consuming calculations.
- Block all headings.
- Make a note of the settings for tabulations that you do frequently, such as regular reports.
- Avoid vertical and horizontal rules when possible.

E20 Categories of Keyboarding Equipment

A wide variety of equipment is available on which to prepare typewritten work. Your selection should be matched to your intended use.

E21 Electric Typewriters

When selecting a standard electric typewriter, consider carriage length, pitch size, and typeface capability. When complex financial statements are frequently required, a longer-length carriage of 15 inches or more may be advantageous. Dual-pitch typewriters make it possible to produce typewritten material in either pica or elite type at the flip of a switch (see E2). Typewriters that can accept interchangeable type elements or print wheels afford opportunities to personalize typewritten copy as well as to enhance the formatting and eye appeal of the finished page.

E22 Self-Correcting Typewriters

Usually sold at a slightly higher price, typewriters are available that are capable of correcting errors involving single characters or up to several lines of type. The increased cost involved is usually outweighed by the increased productivity provided by these machines.

E23 Electronic Typewriters

The electronic typewriter bridges the gap between standard electric machines and more sophisticated text-editing equipment. The features

E19-E24 Production Tips for Tabulations

vary with the make and model and may include some or all of the following:

- variable pitch
- automatic figure alignment
- automatic centering
- automatic justifying
- boldface capability
- text-editing (changing) capability
- memory capacity
- partial display
- communication capability
- mini-diskette storage capability

WP Note: Some electronic typewriters can also be linked to personal computers and used as printers.

E24 Word Processors

The capabilities of a word processor vary with the make and model but in general, they can be expected to perform as follows:

- Information that is keystroked (input/typed) is displayed on a video display screen so that the operator can see what has been recorded before the text (material) is printed in hard copy, final form.
- Text editing (changes) may be achieved without the need for retyping the entire document, and may range from altering a single character to inserting an entire page or moving previously typed material.
- Once the material has been keystroked and edited, the printing (playback) is automatic and the machine can produce error-free documents at high speeds.
- Storage capacity is provided. The equipment offers both internal and auxiliary electronic storage. The machine has a memory of its own and, in addition, permits what is in the internal memory to be transferred to an external storage device such as a magnetic card, floppy disk/diskette, hard disk, or host computer data base. The material in the auxiliary storage can be re-entered into the word processor at any time for reuse and for any necessary changes without the need for a total retyping.

Editing, Formatting, and Word Processing

- Repetitive typing is eliminated and documents can be personalized. Material being keystroked can be coded to stop at particular points during playback so that variable information such as names, addresses, and numbers may be inserted.
- Formatting (setting up) is automatic because the machine will automatically center, change margins, indent, justify, tabulate, and adjust spacing.
- Material suitable for printing purposes can be produced. Text keystroked into a word processor can be processed through a photocomposition unit to produce fully justified typesetting for much less cost than is possible with commercial typesetting (see R29).
- Merging of stored material is possible from among many stored form paragraphs. Just a few paragraphs may be selected and merged automatically to produce a complete document; or mailing lists on one storage device may be merged with form letters on another device to automatically produce error-free, individualized letters. (See Unit 3, C13.)
- Variety in appearance of the output is provided through pitch variations, the ability of the machines to accept interchangeable elements, and the capabilities of the printer used to produce the finished copy.
- Other equipment capability may include:

    sorting (the ability to arrange and present stored information in a desired sequence)

    searching (the ability to locate information such as a particular word, number, or group of words)

    searching and replacing (the ability to locate information such as a particular word, number, or group of words, and replace it with another word, number, or group of words)

    moving (lines, paragraphs, or columns)

    presenting (information in graphic form)

    accepting (typed documents through an optical character reader, thus eliminating re-keystroking)

    communicating (information to another word processor, personal computer, host computer, telex unit, facsimile device, or intelligent copier)

    data base (inquiry, retrieval, and input)

    computation and *records management* capabilities

E25 Personal Computers with Word Processing Software

A variety of software programs are available that permit personal computers to perform all of the functions of the electronic typewriter, and quite often many of the functions of word processing equipment as well. Different software packages require different microcomputer operating systems, have different operational commands, and are capable of performing a limited number or a wide variety of functions depending on the specific software program selected. Doing word processing on a microcomputer is effective; however, software programs must be selected with care because they differ widely.

E26 Corrections, Revisions, and Text Editing

E27 Making Corrections on a Typewriter

This section is directed to the typists who must resort to making corrections and revisions on a typewriter. Such corrections can be made by means of a typing eraser, correction fluid, or correction tape. Choose the right correction product for the job. If you select a covering aid, try to erase the error first to avoid show-through problems.

E28 Realigning

If you must make a typewritten change on a document *after* it is out of the typewriter, follow the procedures below. Be sure, however, that you are comfortable with the aligning scale mechanism on the typewriter. Practice with another sheet of paper first if necessary.

1. Reinsert the paper.
2. Check a line of typing against the writing scale on the clear plastic cardholder for correct horizontal placement.
3. Pull forward the paper release.
4. Gently adjust the paper so that the horizontal alignment is correct and the printing point or the vertical alignment scale rests at the center of a letter (Figure 5.5).
5. Push back the paper release.
6. If it is necessary to move the paper up or down, use the variable line spacer.

Editing, Formatting, and Word Processing

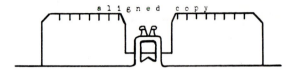

Figure 5.5 Realigning Copy

7. Check the alignment by putting the ribbon in the stencil position and typing a period. (Clean the key first.) You may have to adjust the alignment again.
8. Now type the correction.

E29 Spreading

When a long word must be replaced by a shorter one, follow these steps:

1. Erase the incorrect word.
2. If the new word is one letter shorter, simply use the half spacer, or hold the carriage with one hand and type with the other to allow 1 1/2 spaces at the beginning and end of the word.
3. On machines with typing elements, make this adjustment by reaching under the cover with the fingers of the right hand and pressing against the ribbon cartridge while typing with the left hand.

If several letters are involved in the change, spread the correct letters evenly so that they occupy the space of the erased word.

```
That books is . . .    The incorrect story . . .
That book  is  . . .   The  correct  story . . .
```

E30 Squeezing (Crowding)

When a short word must be replaced by a longer one, squeeze it in as follows:

- Erase the error.
- If there is only a one-character difference between the words to be changed, use the half spacer, or hold the carriage with one hand and type with the other to allow a half space at the beginning and end of the inserted word.
- On machines with typing elements, hold the ribbon cartridge as described in *Spreading* while you type the correction.

```
The  salution is...      Now is the time
The  salutation is...    Now is that time
```

If you need to make a correction close to the bottom of the page, roll the cylinder backward rather than forward to prevent the paper(s) from falling out and to eliminate the need for realignment. This is a particularly useful tip when carbon copies are involved.

E31 Making Corrections and Revisions on a Text Editor
E32 Common Text-Editing Features

Electronic typewriters, word processors, and personal computers with word processing software are equipped to handle changes in text and format. This section describes the most common text-editing features found on such equipment.

- *Automatic centering*: keyboard commands enable centering to take place automatically.
- *Automatic decimal alignment*: a feature that provides for the automatic alignment of decimal points or commas in vertical columns.
- *Footers*: setting up type to automatically appear at the bottom of each page, such as consecutive page numbering.
- *Headers*: setting up a line of type to appear at the top of each page, such as a running side heading and page number on a report.
- *Automatic headers and footers*: helpful in long documents; equipment can automatically place running headers or footers on pages in documents.
- *Automatic margins, tabs, line length, and pitch settings*: many terms are used for this feature; commonly called *standard format* and usually represented in pre-programmed settings that represent the most frequently used format arrangements.
- *Automatic underlining*: keyboard commands control the starting and stopping of the underline.
- *Automatic word wrap (wraparound)*: the right margin is automatically determined for the typist by the equipment or software program.

Editing, Formatting, and Word Processing

- *Blocking*: a specific area—word, line, paragraph, sentence, or page— is designated or set off in order to be changed or used for some specific purpose such as MOVE, COPY, PRINT, ADJUST (Change margins); LINESPACING (Change linespacing); or DELETE.

Example: A paragraph that is *blocked* can be MOVED or COPIED. Study Figures 5.6 and 5.7.

MOVE: Through keyboard commands, a segment of previously typed material is set off (blocked and sometimes visually highlighted or set off with codes); it is then repositioned (Figure 5.8).

COPY: Through keyboard commands a segment of previously keyboarded material is set off (blocked and sometimes visually highlighted or set off with codes); it is then recopied and appears a second time at another desired point in the document (Figures 5.9, 5.10 and 5.11).

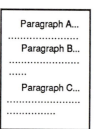

Figure 5.6 Original Document

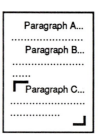

Figure 5.7 Blocked Paragraph Indicated

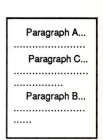

Figure 5.8 After the MOVE Command

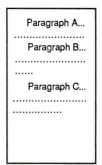

Figure 5.9 Original Document

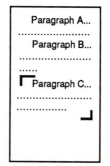

Figure 5.10 Blocked Paragraph Indicated

Figure 5.11 After the COPY Command

E32 Common Text-Editing Features

- *Communication capability*: software can automatically translate recorded documents into specific codes for telecommunication purposes through a *modem* (a device that converts signals from one form to a form compatible with another kind of equipment) and telephone lines (see Unit 9, I62).
- *Global search and replace*: specific words can be located throughout the document and changed as directed by the operator via keystroke commands. For example, "IBM" can be changed throughout the document to "International Business Machines" or vice versa.
- *Hyphenation options*: a software program can handle hyphenation decisions or can verify the accuracy of hyphenation decisions.
- *Index generator*: some software can provide for the automatic indexing of document filenames in a directory.
- *Margin justification*: this feature enables the equipment to print the final copy with flush (even) left and right margins.
- *Repagination*: the equipment will determine where pages will end. If insertions or deletions are made, the equipment will automatically rearrange the pages in the document. For example, if a ten-page document has been keyboarded and then the operator deletes two long paragraphs on page 3, all of the pages in the document will be readjusted to compensate for the paragraphs that were removed. The pages will be renumbered if the document has been coded for headers or footers.
- *Revisions and corrections*: three types of corrections can be made easily, usually by cursor movement:

    Overtype—for equal value corrections; simply type correct strokes right over incorrect strokes.

    Delete—to erase or remove characters from the screen; after letters are removed, the text automatically closes up the missing spaces.

    Insert—to add or make room for additional characters in already existing text.

- *Spelling verification*: software can provide for the checking of the words in a document against a dictionary of pre-programmed words, as well as words that can be added to the dictionary by the user. A spelling program, however, does not check the accuracy of homonyms, context, or sentence structure.
- *Widow/orphan adjust*: software can be programmed not to separate lone lines or partial lines from the rest of the paragraph at the end of a page.

Editing, Formatting, and Word Processing

E33 Common Operational Features

Some operational procedures in working with text-editing equipment are:

- *Booting up*: starting the system by turning on the power, inserting the diskette, and getting into the desired program mode. Each machine has a specific sequence of steps; be sure these are followed correctly.
- *Cursor movement*: directional arrows with labels often move the cursor (or screen printing point):

    UP↑   DOWN↓   LEFT←   RIGHT →

- *Copy/Backup*: make another exact copy of a document or a whole diskette for protection purposes.
- *Escape/Cancel*: get out of the present mode of operation and enter another mode of operation.
- *Load*: enter a particular program into the system.
- *Recall/Retrieve*: access information that was previously recorded.
- *Save/Store*: retain keyboarded information in the internal memory or on a magnetic medium, such as a floppy disk, a hard disk, or a minicomputer data base.
- *Scroll*: move the text up, down, or sideways on the screen so that a specific area of text may be viewed.
- *Understand action prompts*: sometimes messages appear on the screen that require the operator to respond by means of keystrokes or attention to other matters before further processing can continue. Examples include:

    Delete? Y/N? (Operator must type *Y* for *Yes* or *N* for *No*.)

    Password? (Operator must type the appropriate password before processing continues.)

    Printer not ready. (Operator must check the printer to be certain it is plugged in, turned on, has enough paper, has no problem with the print device, etc.)

- *Understand status prompts*: messages are often sent by the equipment to the operator to let the operator know what is happening (in the system) at a given time. Examples include: *loading diskette, diskette is full, invalid code name, disk drive A in use.*

- *Use help screens*: call up special screens that are made available by the program to help the operator clarify procedures on how to perform specific operations.
- *Use menus*: choose from a list of possible functions that are shown on the screen.

E34 Proofreading

E35 Steps in Proofreading

Always proofread

- *before* removing the paper from the typewriter by using the paper bail method. To do this, you go back to the top of the document and read the copy line for line moving the paper bail under each line as you read it.

  or

- *before* printing out the hard copy from a word processor or personal computer. On some equipment, it is wise to turn off any screen graphics so that the proofreading can be accomplished without interference.

After the copy has been removed from the typewriter or from the printer, proofread again as follows:

- Look at the format to be certain it is correct.

  Check for the date, paragraph indentions, attractive placement on the page, appropriate horizontal spacing, and other style concerns.

- Read the contents.

  As you read, look for typing, spelling, and punctuation errors; and editing errors such as dates that are wrong, numbers that are not the same, sentences and paragraphs that do not make sense, lines left out, words misused, or any other information that does not appear correct.

- Check on anything that you are unsure about or that seems unusual or unclear to you.

  Use a dictionary, do calculations, and verify uncertain items with an appropriate reference source or the originator of the document to be certain that the data is correct.

Editing, Formatting, and Word Processing

- Read again—slowly, carefully, and with the expectation of finding errors.
  You will find errors only if you proofread with the expectation of finding them.
- Sign your name or submit the document as mailable.
  Remember that your initials appear at the bottom of a letter and that any typewritten work that you submit is a reflection on you. Take pride in the accuracy and quality of the work you submit; it is your autograph of excellence.
- Be sure that all enclosure materials are attached.

E36 Proofreading Pointers

For *short* correspondence:

- Pay attention to dates—check the spelling of months; the correctness of the day and year; the correct projection of dates; and the accuracy of the day and the week on the calendar date associated with it.
- Verify some of the sections of typed work where errors are often unnoticed, such as: the spelling of names; the use of courtesy titles such as Mr., Mrs., and Ms.; the use of the correct two-letter state abbreviation; and the appropriate inclusion of an enclosure, subject, or copy notation line.
- Check to see that words are not repeated at the beginnings or ends of lines.
- Be certain that the format is consistent: use courtesy titles in letters but not in memos.
- If copying from previously typed material, lay your typed copy over the original and hold them up to the light. If lines are not the same length, investigate.
- If typing a repetitive letter, read and type each subsequent letter from the one just typed.

For long reports, manuals, or work consisting of several pages:

- Make a style sheet indicating spelling, punctuation, and placement notes to assure consistency throughout the copy. Keep the style sheet handy and use it as needed in adding new pages and in making revisions.
- Be sure that tables are placed in the right places in the body of the manuscript.

- Scan pages by number to be certain that none have been overlooked.
- Check to see that all inserts have been included. Count the number of paragraphs in the original notes and in your final copy.

For technical data and statistical tables:

- Two people, one reading aloud and one checking, may be needed to verify technical data.
- If two people cannot do the proofreading, proofread carefully yourself using the techniques presented. Do your own proofreading twice at two different times. A lapse between the proofreading efforts should help locate mistakes.
- If the draft is typewritten, lay a ruler under each line; this will help you keep your place in the copy as you proofread.
- If columns were typed down the pages, proofread across the page; proofread down the page if columns were typed across the pages.
- Fold the original copy and proofread the two copies side by side.
- Count the number of entries in each column and compare the number. Check the sequence of the data as it was presented.

E37 General Proofreading Guidelines

- Use the dictionary.
- Look for omissions of terminal letters and/or the adding of letters when they are not necessary.
- Mentally repeat syllables of long words containing many vowels; it is very easy to leave out a syllable.
- Verify the spelling of words with double letters.
- Be aware of errors caused by poor spelling, inadequate research, and inconsistent formatting.
- Use apostrophes, dashes, abbreviations, and homonymns correctly.
- Check the dictionary or other reference sources to verify word division.
- Be consistent in typing numbers and letters.
- Recognize and use proofreading symbols correctly.
- Look for omissions of entire lines of copy.
- Be certain the wording is logical and that the material makes sense.

(See inside back cover for list of proofreader's symbols.)

Editing, Formatting, and Word Processing

E38 Style Practices

Provided in this section is information on correct style practices as they relate to the typing of metric expressions and spacing after punctuation marks. For information on the current style practices used with the following, consult the sections indicated:

Abbreviations: See G54.

Capitalization: See G64.

Numbers: See G82.

Roman Numerals: See Appendix, page A7

Word Division: See G88.

E39 Typing Metric Expressions

Note: See Appendix, pages A5-A6 for a complete table of metric units, symbols, and conversions.

The style to be used in typing common metric terms, units of measure and their symbols is as follows:

E40 Symbols

- Use only the symbols associated with the SI metric system.
- Use symbols rather than full metric terms with numbers.

    30 m   **not**   30 meters

- Use lower case, except when the symbol is derived from the name of an individual.

    mm for millimeter

    N for Newton

    C for Celsius

- Leave a space between quantity and symbol.

    2.75 m

    The degree sign occupies the space in temperature expressions.

    32°C

- Do not start a sentence with a symbol.

    Distance is expressed in meters.   **not**   m is used to express distance.

- Do not pluralize metric symbols—both the singular and plural forms are the same.

    1 kg   75 kg

- Symbols are not abbreviations. Use a period only if the symbol occurs at the end of a sentence.

    He bought 0.75 kg of cherries.

    He bought 0.75 kg.

- Show square and cubic symbols by means of exponents (numerals typed a half line higher).

    16 m^2 32 cm^3

- Use the diagonal (/) to represent *per*.

    He drove at 60 km/h.

E41 Numbers

- Express fractions as decimals.

    2.75 kg   **not**   2 3/4 kg

- Use a zero in front of the decimal point when no whole number is shown.

    0.75 kg

- Use spaces or commas to group figures into blocks of three. This applies to groupings on both sides of the decimal point. The space may be omitted in four-digit numbers unless these numbers are listed in a column with other numbers of five digits or more.

    17 243.57 m   or   17,243.57 m

- When times are based on the 24-hour clock (military style), use four digits and separate hours and minutes with a colon.

    04:30   16:22

E42 Spacing Rules

Observe the spacing rules shown in Table 5.2 when you type punctuation marks and symbols.

Table 5.2 Spacing Rules for Punctuation Marks and Symbols.

Punctuation Mark	Spacing	Example
Apostrophe		
as possessive	no space	The boy's hat . . .
as omission sign	no space	Aren't you coming?
Colon		
as punctuation	two after	He bought: a rabbit, a hen . . .
as time	none before or after	10:30 p.m.
as ratio	none before or after	3:6 is as 1:2
Comma	one after	An apple, a pear, and an orange.
Dash	two hyphens without spaces	He can—he said.
Diagonal or Slash	no space	3 3/5; and/or; 31 km/h
Exclamation mark	two after	Good grief! What next?
Hyphen	no space	mother-in-law
Parentheses	one before the opening and one after the closing	Can you (as a friend) do this?
Period		
at sentence end	two spaces	Go home. It's time.
after abbreviations		
one abbreviation in caps	one space	Mr. J. Jones
two abbreviations or more in caps	no space	C.B.C.
any abbreviations in lower case	no space	b.c.c.
after initials	one space	Mr. E. B. Long
Question mark	two after	Can you? Will you?
Quotation marks	one before opening quote and one or two after completing quote (if a punctuation mark ends the closing quote, use the spacing required by that punctuation mark)	Mr. Winters asked, "Is the letter ready?"
Semicolon	one after	She went east; he went west.
Addition	one on each side	3 + 2 = 5

Table 5.2 Continued.

Ampersand (&)	one before and one after	Smith & Wesson
At (@) (each costing)	one on each side	2 @ $15 = $30
Cent sign	one after	He paid 15¢ for it.
Decimal	no space	1.05
Degree symbol	no space	30°
Division	one on each side	6 ÷ 2 = 3
Dollar sign	one before	He paid $15.
Equality	one on each side	6 × 2 = 12
Feet	no space before, one after	he was 6′ tall
Inches	no space before, one after	he was 6′ 2″ tall
Minutes and seconds	no space before, one after	he ran in 5′ 6″
Multiplication	one on each side	6 x 2 x 12
Number (#)	one before, none after	She lives at #3, Tenth Avenue.
Percentage (%)	none before, one after	5% plus 10%
Subtraction	one on each side	6 − 2 = 4

See this unit, E39, for spacing in metric expressions.

E43 Typed Communications

This section contains information on how to produce typed documents quickly and easily.

For typed examples of the following communications, consult the sections indicated:

Agendas: See O4.

Itineraries: See A25.

Meeting Announcements: See 03.

Minutes: See O12.

News Releases: See C29.

Memos: See C28.

E44 Charts and Graphs

Charts and graphs are an invaluable tool to the report writer as well as to a speaker making an oral presentation. Computer programs can be used to prepare graphic aids (see I 11). If charts and graphs need to be

Editing, Formatting, and Word Processing

produced without the aid of a computer, these suggestions should be helpful.

- Draw in pencil a very light outline of the chart to be completed. Draw this to scale if necessary.
- Use your typewriter for the outside horizontal and vertical lines and as much other data as you can. (A compass or any small, round object can be used for a pie chart.)
- Neatly insert any other necessary lines by hand, but use a ruler for straight lines.
- Erase whatever may remain of your light pencil outline.

E45 Line Graph

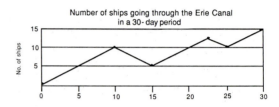

E46 Vertical Bar Graph

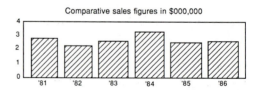

E47 Horizontal Bar Graph

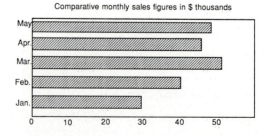

E45-E51   Line Graph

E48   Pictogram (Picture Graphs)

Information in Figure 5.12 is shown using symbols or illustrations.

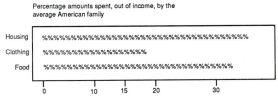

Figure 5.12   Pictogram

E49   Pie Chart

Information in Figure 5.13 is shown as sections of a circle.

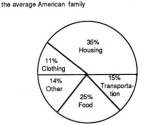

Figure 5.13   Pie Chart

E50   Envelopes

E51   Standard Envelopes

Shown in Figure 5.14 are the two most frequently used sizes of business envelopes: the Number 10 (large) envelope and the No. 6 3/4 (small) envelope.

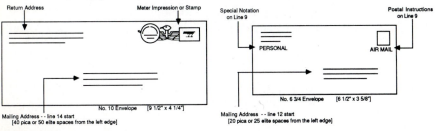

Figure 5.14   Business Envelopes

Editing, Formatting, and Word Processing

E52 Guidelines for Addressing Standard Envelopes

- Always use a courtesy title in the envelope address.
- Follow the style and punctuation pattern used in the letter.
- Type carefully and spell accurately.
- Single-space.
- Try to balance line lengths.
- Indent any continuation lines by three spaces.

```
Dr. Mary Ann Mathews, Chairperson
Department of Business Education and
   Office System Administration
Mountain View College
Avon, CT 06001-0000
```

- Use a two-letter state abbreviation (see inside front cover).
- Use one or two blank spaces between the two-letter state abbreviation and the ZIP (Zone Improvement Plan) Code.
- Type delivery and any other instructions (such as *Confidential*, *Personal*, and *Hold for Arrival*) on the left-hand side underneath the return address on line 9.
- Always use the postal ZIP Code. Locate it on letterheads, return addresses or in the ZIP Code directory. The ZIP Code must be the last item typed. The Postal Service is now encouraging the use of ZIP + 4 in addresses to provide additional delivery directions. The four extra digits are separated from the ZIP Code by a hyphen.
- If an attention line is used in the letter, it should appear either as the second line of the inside address, or a double space below the inside address.
- If envelopes with pre-printed return addresses are used, type the sender's name or department name or number above the inside address to expedite handling if it is returned.
- All words in an address should be written out. If an abbreviation must be used, be certain that it is correct. Use the abbreviations requested by the post office to set up computerized mailing lists, or to take advantage of OCR (Optical Character Reader) scanning.

Apartment	APT	Street	ST
Road	RD	Boulevard	BLVD
Building	BLDG	Heights	HTS
Drive	DR	Avenue	AVE

E52 Guidelines for Addressing Standard Envelopes

See Appendix, page A2 for other permissible abbreviations. Figure 5.15 is a completed standard envelope format.

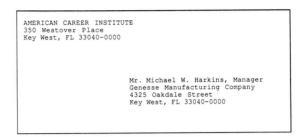

Figure 5.15 Standard Envelope Format

- If you are to benefit from the advantages offered by the optical character scanning equipment used in the post office follow these procedures (see also L40):

Type within the proper address area of the envelope.

Type in all capital letters.

Use no punctuation marks.

Use single line spacing.

Use standard typefaces—no script or italics.

Use abbreviations requested by the post office (see Appendix, page A2). Figure 5.16 shows a completed OCR-style envelope address.

Use standard envelope sizes suggested by the post office.

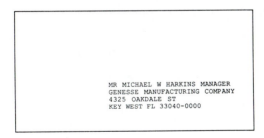

Figure 5.16 OCR-Style Address

E53 Large Manila Envelopes

- Be certain that the return address appears in the upper left-hand corner.
- Center the recipient's address on the envelope, or use a label for the address and attach it to the center of the envelope.

E54 Addresses Typed on Continuous Form Labels

- Insert the first label in the typewriter (use the paper bail rollers to hold it firmly) with the remaining quantity still attached and stacked behind the typewriter.
- Type the required information. Move up to the next label, type the next address, and so on.
- Separate labels when all the typing has been completed.

Note: Be sure addresses are typed in the appropriate style (see E52).

E55 Chain Feeding Envelopes

When many envelopes (or post cards) must be typed at one time, chain feeding is a useful technique. It permits a continuous supply of envelopes to be fed into your typewriter.

- Place a stack of envelopes on the desk, flap side up and with the open flap pointing away from you.
- Insert the first envelope into the typewriter.
- Type the first envelope address.
- Insert the next envelope immediately behind the first one.
- One roll of the cylinder will remove the first envelope and position the second.

E56 Interoffice Envelopes

Interoffice envelopes are used to send documents within the branches and departments of a specific company. They are most frequently the size of the number 10 standard envelope or 8 1/2" x 11" in size. Interoffice envelopes are designed to be reused as Figure 5.17 shows.

E53-E57 Large Manila Envelopes

Figure 5.17 Interoffice Envelope

E57 Folding Correspondence

Small Envelope (No. 6 3/4)

Enclosures should fit envelopes as closely as possible. Follow folding instructions in Figure 5.18 for folding letters to fit a small envelope.

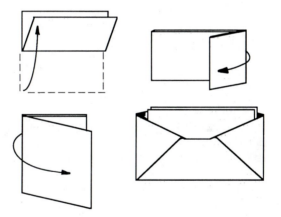

Figure 5.18 Small Envelope

1. Place letter face up on desk. Fold in half.
2. Fold right third to left, making the fold slightly less than one-third of the way over.
3. Fold left third so that it is 1/4 inch short of the other.
4. Insert last folded edge first.

Editing, Formatting, and Word Processing

Large envelope (No. 10)
Follow the instructions shown in Figure 5.19 for folding letters into large envelopes.

1. Place letter face up on desk. Fold slightly less than one-third up towards top.
2. Fold down top of letter.
3. Insert so that second fold goes in first.

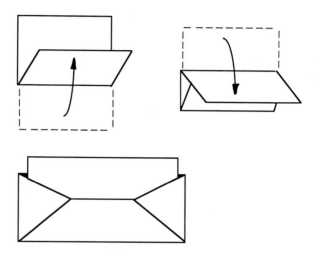

Figure 5.19   Large Envelope

Window Envelopes
When you use window envelopes, be sure the enclosure fits the envelope snugly so that the address (including the postal code) cannot shift out of the window area.

Window envelopes—letter (Figure 5.20)

1. With sheet face down, top toward you, fold upper third down.
2. Fold lower third up so address is showing.
3. Insert sheet into envelope with last crease at bottom.

Window envelopes—invoices and other forms (Figure 5.21)

1. Place sheet face down, top toward you.
2. Fold back top so address shows.
3. Insert into envelope with crease at bottom.

E58 Speedy Envelope Sealing and Stamping by Hand

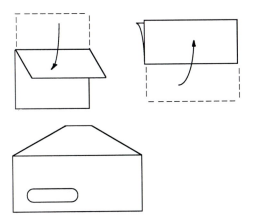

Figure 5.20 Window Envelopes (Letter)

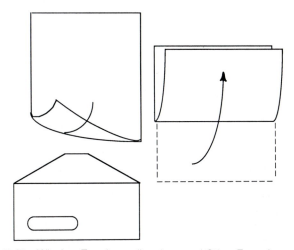

Figure 5.21 Window Envelopes (Invoices and Other Forms)

E58 Speedy Envelope Sealing and Stamping by Hand

Sealing

- Use a damp sponge or other moistener.
- Assemble ten envelopes one behind the other with flaps open and glued side up (Figure 5.22).
- Run the sponge over the first two or three envelopes. Seal them.
- Continue until all envelopes are sealed.

Editing, Formatting, and Word Processing

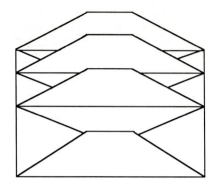

Figure 5.22 Sealing

Stamping

- Assemble ten envelopes so that the stamp area is visible (Figure 5.23).
- Moisten a horizontal row of ten stamps.
- Quickly attach a stamp to each envelope.

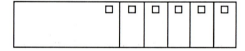

Figure 5.23 Stamping

 ## E59 Financial Statements

- Financial statements (Figure 5.24) are reports prepared regularly for management that show the worth of the company and the operating results.
- Financial statements usually contain a descriptive column and money columns. Leave six to eight spaces after the first column. Leave two or three spaces between the money columns.
- Follow the techniques of tabulation (see this unit, E18).
- Plan the job so that the final statement is both attractive and easy to read. (Use larger than normal paper or insert the long edge of the paper first, if necessary.)
- Use leaders if they will make the report easier to read.

```
                    MARTIN KOLCHESKI
                    INCOME STATEMENT
              FOR THE YEAR ENDED MARCH 31, 19--

  Income
    Gross Sales .........................    $92,206.45
      Less Returns and Allowances......        969.59
    Net Sales............................                  $91,236.86


  Cost of Goods Sold
    Merchandise Inventory, April 1, 19--..    $ 9,462.20
    Purchases.........................54,943.15
      Less Returns and Allowances.......   496.96
                                             54,446.19
    Cost of Goods for Sale................   63,908.39
      Less Mdse.Inv.,March 31, 19-- ....   11,220.25
    Cost of Goods Sold....................                  52,688.14
    Gross Profit..........................                 $38,548.72


  Expenses
    Salaries Expense......................   $13,731.24
    Delivery Expense......................     1,560.60
    General Expense.......................       510.80
    Insurance Expense.....................        62.00
    Supplies Expense......................       440.80
    Depreciation Expense..................       534.16
       Total Operating Expenses...........                  16,839.60
    Net Income............................                 $21,709.12
```

Figure 5.24 Financial Statement

E60 Forms

See Unit 8, *Handling Forms*; also *Legal Documents*, this unit, E61.

- When you type on lines, note that the descenders on longer characters should just touch the printed line.

    grey

- Set tab stops for frequently recurring positions.
- Stay within the boundaries set by the preprinted form.

E61 Legal Documents

There is nothing particularly difficult about typing legal documents. Simply apply normal rules of style (see G53) and, with minor modifications explained below, the rules of manuscript typing (see this unit, E94-E136).

- If you are employed by a legal firm, follow the style guide of your particular office.
- Corrections are permitted in most offices, but you must use either a correcting typewriter or an eraser. Liquid paper, correcting tape, and erasing tape are not permitted.
- Text editors are often used to prepare legal documents.

Editing, Formatting, and Word Processing

E62 Typing Preprinted Legal Forms

- When the available space is longer than necessary, center the matter to be typed and fill any remaining space with ruled lines or hyphens.
- Fill in large spaces by ruling or typing a large Z (Figure 5.25).
- Keep your typed line within the margins set by the printing on the form.
- Use single spacing where space is limited.

Figure 5.25 Preprinted Legal Form

E63 Typing Entire Legal Documents

Figure 5.26 illustrates the following steps.

- Start approximately 10 lines down on the first page.
- Leave 12 pica spaces or 15 elite spaces for left margins and 10 pica spaces or 12 elite spaces for right margins if you use plain paper (1 inch on both sides).
- Stay inside the ruled lines if you use ruled legal paper (8 1/2" x 11" paper is commonly used now).
- If ruled legal paper is used, type the copy to within 1 inch of the ruling on each side.
- Leave a 1-inch bottom margin.
- Number continuation pages on line 7. Continue typing on line 10.
- Double-space. Indent paragraphs by 10 spaces.
- Note that the attestation section is single-spaced.

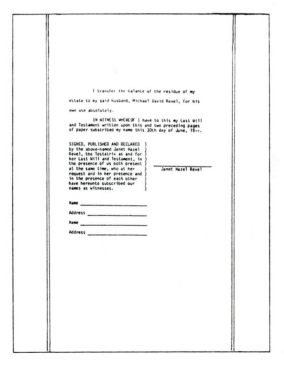

Figure 5.26 Legal Document

Editing, Formatting, and Word Processing

E64 Letters

E65 Basic Letter Parts

Figure 5.27 illustrates the basic letter parts.
Figure 5.28 shows additional letter parts.

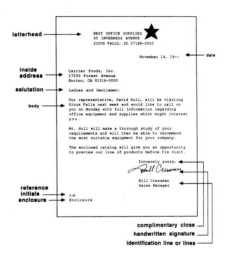

Figure 5.27 Basic Letter Parts

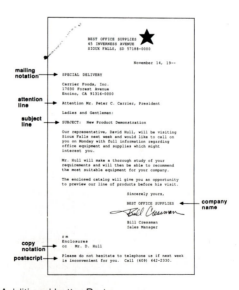

Figure 5.28 Additional Letter Parts

E66   Basic Letter Styles

Most business letters are typed in one of the four basic styles and in one of the two punctuation patterns illustrated.

Full Block Style

- All lines start at the left margin.

Modified Block Style—Standard Format

- Date and complimentary closing start at the center.
- All other lines start flush with the left margin.

Modified Block Style With Indented Paragraphs

- Date and complimentary closing start at the center.
- Paragraphs are indented.

Editing, Formatting, and Word Processing

Simplified Style

- Uses the full block style and open punctuation formats.
- A subject line typed in all capital letters replaces the salutation. The word "subject" is omitted.
- A one-line writer's identification replaces the complimentary closing. This line is typed in all capital letters.

Basic Punctuation Styles
Open Punctuation

- Punctuation is not used after the date, inside address, salutation, complimentary closing or identification unless these end with an abbreviation.

Mixed Punctuation

- A colon follows the salutation.
- A comma follows the closing.
- Punctuation is not used after the date, inside address, company name, or identification unless these end with an abbreviation.

Note:

Any one of the two punctuation styles illustrated may be used with any letter style.
Attention lines, subject lines, mailing notations, enclosures, reference initials, and copy notations have ending punctuation only if they end with an abbreviation.
The postal code is never punctuated.

E67 Letter Placement

- Letters should be typed on the page so that they are attractively framed by a balanced amount of white space.

E67-E68 Letter Placement

- For speed and efficiency, use one margin setting for all your letters. Use either a 50-space pica or a 60-space elite stroke line or set margin stops at the starting and ending points indicated by letterhead design.
- Type the date a double or triple space below the printed letterhead. For a short letter, leave eight to ten lines between the date and inside address; for a long letter, leave only four lines. Allow four to five lines for the signature.

Where more precise placement than suggested above is needed, use the guide in Figure 5.29.

```
PLACEMENT GUIDE
The date should be typed a double space or so below the printed letterhead.
```

Word Count	Stroke Line	Pica Margin* Settings	Elite Margin* Settings	From Date to Inside Address
up to 100 words (short letter)	40 pica/50 elite	22-62	25-75	8 to 10 lines
100 to 100 w0rds (medium letter)	50 pica/60 elite	17-67	20-80	6 to 8 lines
200 or more words (long letter and two page letter)	60 pica/70 elite	12-72	15-85	4 to 6 lines

*These figures represent exact margins if the left edge of the page is at [i]0[r] on the aligning scale.

Figure 5.29 Placement Guide

E68 Mailing Notations

- Type mailing notations at the left margin midway between the date and inside address in all capitals.
- Use only when a special mail service such as *express* or *registered* mail service is used.
- Leave one blank line before or after the mailing notation line.

REGISTERED

ABC Industries
106 Anderson Avenue
Berkeley, CA 94704-0000

E69 Date

- Never abbreviate when typing the date.
- The style below is most frequently used:

    November 17, 19—

- The military services use an inverted style for typing the date:

    17 November 19—

E70 Inside Address

- Use at least three typed lines.
- Attempt to keep line lengths approximately equal.
- Avoid abbreviations as much as possible.
- Indent any continuation lines by three spaces.
- Always include a courtesy title—Mr., Mrs., Ms.—or a professional title—Dr., Reverend, The Honorable—if the letter is directed to an individual.
- *Ms.* is now the generally accepted preferred title for a woman; however use *Mrs.* or *Miss* when it has been designated as a personal preference.
- Professional titles and special titles such as Professor, Reverend, and Senator are not usually abbreviated, but Doctor (Dr.) may be.
- Do not show title *and* degrees—use one or the other, but not both (B. Turcotte, Ph.D. or Dr. B. Turcotte).
- Check the proper form of address if you are writing to a prominent person in public life, politics, the clergy or the military (see C24 and C25).
- Position in the company may be shown in these ways. Note the use of the comma.

```
Mr. F. Sharman, President
Seaview Golf Club

Mr. F. Campagnilia
President, BM Industries

Ms. Jayne Tobias-Smith
Director of Human Resources
Collingwood Specialties, Inc.
```

- When street names are composed of numbers, use *words* for one to ten and use *figures* for numbers over ten.

  160 Seventh Street

  One Park Place

  32 South 14th Street

  1440 - 65th Street

  P.O. Box 225

- Separate the town from the state with a comma.
- Use the two-letter abbreviation for the state (see inside front cover).
- Type the ZIP Code on the last line of the inside address; it should be separated from the two-letter state abbreviation by one or two spaces.

E71 Attention Line

- The attention line is used to route a business matter through a specific person or department.
- Type the attention line two lines below the inside address, centered or starting from the left margin.
- The current trend is to direct correspondence to a particular person in the first line of the inside address rather than use the attention line.

            Attention Mr. J. Dunn, Chairperson

            Attention: Ms. Nancy Scott

            Attention: Traffic Department

            Attention: Registrar

E72 Salutation

- Type the salutation two lines below the inside address (or attention line if there is one).
- Capitalize the first word and all nouns.
- Use an individual's name if it is known and if it appears in the first line of the inside address.

  Dear Ms. Warren

Editing, Formatting, and Word Processing

- Use an appropriate salutation for a letter to an unnamed individual or group.

  ```
  Dear Reservations Manager
  Dear Department Managers
  ```

- A letter with an attention line always has a salutation of *Gentlemen* or *Ladies and Gentlemen.*
- See C25 for help in selecting the appropriate salutation.

E73 Subject Line

- Type the subject line two lines below the salutation, centered, or starting from the left margin—depending on the letter style and desired emphasis.
- The words "Subject," "Re" or "In re" may precede the subject title, account number, or other notation that may be designated as the topic of the document.
- The term "Subject" is never used to introduce the subject line in the simplified letter style.

Style Choices:

```
SUBJECT:  ANNUAL SALES CONVENTION
Subject:  Annual Sales Convention
Annual Sales Convention
RE:  Annual Sales Convention
```

E74 Body

- Begin typing the body two lines below the salutation or subject line.
- Single-space; double-space between paragraphs.
- A business letter usually has at least three paragraphs.

E75 Displayed Information

Numbered Lists
Short lists may be keyboarded within sentences.
    A list is an effective way to (a) summarize facts; (b) present a sequence of steps; or (c) help the reader retain key information.

Numbered Sentences

- Leave a line of space above and below each numbered item.
- Single-space each numbered item and double-space between them.

E73-E75 Subject Line

- Either line up the numbers (or letters) with the existing left-hand margin (as Figure 5.30 shows), or indent five spaces from the left and right margins and set new margins for the listing if emphasis is desired (as shown in Figure 5.31 for quoted material).
- Set a tab four places from the left margin and depress the tab for the second and succeeding lines.

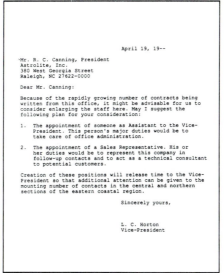

Figure 5.30 Numbered Sentences

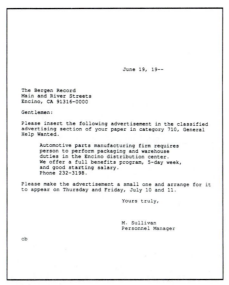

Figure 5.31 Inset Information

E76 Quoted or Inset Information

- Leave a line of space above and below any information that has been quoted or that must be set off from the rest of the body.
- Indent five spaces from the left and right margins.
- Single-space.
- Type shorter quotes (two lines or less) within the body of the material, using quotation marks.

E77 Tabulated Information

Figure 5.32 shows placement of tabulated material.

- Follow the rules of tabulation. (See this unit, E17.)
- Leave a line of space above and below the table.
- If the tabulation has a *short* line length (i.e., narrower than the margins you usually set for your letters), set up the tabulation normally.
- If the tabulation is a *long* one (i.e., longer than the line length you would usually set for your letters), first calculate the tabulation and *then* set your margins for the rest of the letter. Set your margin stops five spaces to the right and to the left of the tabulation line length. This will guarantee that your tabulation stays within the line length of the letter.

```
Dear Mr. McMaster:

Please send us a quotation on each of the following
items:

      5 in. steel casing         SC4   5 sections
      1.5 in. Logan pump          LP1   4 sections
      3 in. twist steel cable    TS7   400 ft.

Please show f.o.b. point to Philadelphia, Pennsylvania.
```

Figure 5.32 Tabulated Material

E78 Complimentary Closing

- Type the complimentary closing a double space below the body.
- Capitalize the first word only:

    Cordially yours

    Sincerely yours

- Sometimes a writer may choose to use a more personal closing such as *Best wishes, Regards,* or *With regards* in place of a formal closing.
- See C26 for help in selecting the appropriate complimentary closing.

E79 Company Name in Closing

- Avoid using the company name in the closing unless company preference demands it.
- Type the company name in capitals a double space below the complimentary closing.

```
Sincerely yours,
GRANATO GRAIN COMPANY
```

E80 Handwritten Signature

- Allow three or four blank lines for the writer's signature. You may allow as many as six lines if there is a large bottom margin.
- The writer may wish to use a special title in the typed signature but handwrite an informal signature.

```
       Sincerely yours,
       
       Bob
       
       Dr. Robert L. Gross, Chairperson
       Social Science Department
```

- Courtesy titles such as Ms., Mrs., or Miss may be written in parentheses before the signature; however, Mr. is *never* written as part of the handwritten signature.

```
   Cordially,                        Sincerely,
   (Ms.) Deanne Brynton              Deanne Brynton
   Deanne Brynton, Editor            Ms. Deanne Brynton, Editor
```

- If you are authorized to sign a letter in the dictator's absence, you may use one of the following forms; however, it is best not to let the recipient know that the signature is not an official one as this might be interpreted as an insult. It is best to let the reader believe that the writer signed the letter.

```
   Barbara Davidson              Linda Evers
     by Linda Evers                for Barbara Davidson
```

Editing, Formatting, and Word Processing

E81 Writer's Identification Lines

- Type the identification line or lines below the closing or company name.
- Use them as balancing lines. That is, if you have only a small amount of space left at the lower edge of the sheet, leave four lines prior to the identification lines. Stretch this to seven lines if there is a surplus of space to be used.
- Show the name of the dictator/originator and the position that person holds.
- A male does not usually indicate *Mr.* in the closing.

```
Grant Parker, President

M. Chantrell (Miss)  or  (Miss) M. Chantrell  or  Mary Chantrell

Louis J. Langley, Ed.D.  or  Dr. Louis J. Langley
```

- One or two lines may be used depending on the amount of information to be included.
- Never let an identification line extend beyond the longest line of the letter.

```
                    Alicia Fedorsen, Comptroller
                    United Retail Store Association

                    Suresh Habai Desai, Ph.D.
                    Dean, School of Business

                    Stephen M. Yotcowski, Chairperson
                    Department of Administrative
                       Office Services
```

E82 Reference Initials

- Type reference initials at the left margin two lines below the identification lines.
- Company preferences often dictate the specific style to use.
- If the dictator/originator's name is typed in the identification, it is not necessary to show the initials; however, the typist's initials should always be shown.
- If the dictator's initials are to be shown, they should be presented first and the typists' initials presented second.
- If two sets of initials are to be shown, a colon or diagonal may be used to separate them.

  Style Choices:

      `lf` (only typist's initials shown)

    `PHE:lf` (both dictator's and typist's initials)

  `PHEllis:lf` (dictator's initials and last name shown if not in identification)

E83 Enclosure Notation

- Use this notation when something is to be included with the letter or document.
- Type the notation one or two spaces below the reference initials.
- It is preferable to write out the term "Enclosure" or "Enclosures."

Style Choices:
```
Enclosure

Enclosure Check $453.95

Enclosures

Enclosures:
    1.  Check No. 204 for $250
    2.  Invoice B424
    3.  Credit Memo 42
```

E84 Copy Notation

- Use this notation when one or more people are to receive copies of the letter.
- Type the notation one or two spaces below the enclosure notation at the left margin.
- The *cc* initials (representing carbon copy) are still used most frequently even though the copies may be photocopies rather than carbon copies. Some writers prefer to use the single *c* to represent the fact that a copy has been sent without any special concern as to how it was reproduced.

Style Choices:
```
c M.R. Franklin, Data Processing
```
   or
```
cc M.R. Franklin, Data Processing
cc: Walter K. Dennehy
```
   or
```
c: Walter K. Dennehy
```

- The *c* or *cc* notation may be followed by a colon. If it is, two spaces follow the colon.
- When the copies are to be sent to a number of people, the list of names may be typed. As copies are earmarked to their respective

Editing, Formatting, and Word Processing

envelopes, a checkmark may be placed next to each person's name. (A highlighter pen may also be used to signal the recipient.)

```
cc:    Ms. Allice Foster
       Mr. Donald Orafice
       Ms. Lena Tillman
       Mr. Frank Untereiner
```

The following example shows that this copy has been designated for Ms. Tillman:

```
cc:    Ms. Allice Foster
       Mr. Donald Orafice
     √ Ms. Lena Tillman
       Mr. Frank Untereiner
```

E85 Postscript

- Use a postscript to add emphasis or to include something omitted in the body.
- The letters *PS* may be used; however, the position of a postscript at the end of a letter identifies it as an afterthought. The current trend is to omit the introductory initials.
- Type it a double space below the last item.
- Type the notation with single spacing and in the same style as the paragraphs in the letter.

Style Choices:

```
Remember, John, get in touch with me as soon as you can.
(No introductory initials used.)

P.S. Let me hear from you soon.
```

- A second postscript (post postscript) may be used as well. It is represented by the letters *PPS*. The post postscript is typed in the same format as described above.

E86 Headings on Multiple Page Letters

- When letters take up more than one page, on successive pages type a heading showing the addressee, the page number, and the date.

```
line 7      Cooper Lumber Co.       2           June 18, 19--
(TS)
            check will be received from you within the next few days.
            If this check is not received, the matter will be . . .
```

```
line 7        Seattle Lumber Supply Company
              Page 2
              June 18, 19--


(TS)
              the check will be received from you within the . . .
```

- Use the same quality stationery as used for page 1, but use a plain sheet (unless your firm has printed continuation-page stationery).
- Type the heading on line 7. Continue the body of the letter a triple space under the heading.
- The addressee's name is the first line of the inside address on page 1.
- Do not carry a divided word from one page to the next.
- Do not have fewer than two lines of a paragraph at the foot of one page or at the top of the continuation page.
- Never use the continuation page to type only the closing lines of a letter.

E87 Other Special Notations

Addressee Notation

- To include special instructions regarding the delivery of mail at its destination, special notations such as *Confidential, Please Hold for Arrival, Personal,* and *Please Forward* may be used. These notations are keyboarded in *all capital letters* both in the letter and on the envelope.
- Type the addressee notation at the left-hand margin a double or triple space above the inside address of the letter in the same way that the mailing notation is typed (see E65, Figure 5.28).
- Type the addressee notation two lines below the return address in the upper left-hand corner of the envelope (see E51, Figure 5.14).

Blind Carbon Copy

- When the distribution of the carbon is not to be shown on the original, a *blind carbon copy* notation should be used on the carbon copies only.

```
bcc Mr. D. Wilson or bc Mr. D. Wilson
```

Editing, Formatting, and Word Processing

- Either take out the carbon pack, remove the top sheet and first carbon and reinsert the remainder of the pack, or place a piece of scrap paper over the original and type.
- The *bcc* notation is placed a double space below the last reference line at the left margin.

E88 Additional Business Letter Styles

In addition to the basic letter styles described in this unit, the following styles are also used occasionally in some business situations. The body of each letter in Figures 5.33 and 5.34 provides examples of the occasions on which these letter styles might be useful.

```
                                              1414 Duquesne Parkway
                                              Austin, TX 78701-0000
                                              May 4, 19--

Ms. Ruth Tait, Manager
Allied Retail Stores, Inc.
7 East 7th Avenue
Atlanta, GA 30308-0000

Dear Ms. Tait:

You will be introduced to a personal business letter by means of this sample.
Notice that this letter is typed on plain white paper and that the sender's
address is typed above the date line.

This letter has been typed in modified block style--standard format; however,
it might have been typed with indented paragraphs or in full block style as
well.

If you want to order merchandise, request information, lodge a complaint, or
contact an individual or organization regarding business matters, this is the
type of letter to use.

Finally, notice that there are no reference initials because the author of
the letter is also the typist.

                                              Sincerely,

                                              Lynne Marie Lyons

                                              Lynne Marie Lyons
```

Figure 5.33 Personal Business Letter

E88-E89 Additional Business Letter Styles

```
                         E. R. BENJAMIN
                       EXECUTIVE OFFICES
                    EVANSTON CONSULTING SERVICES
                       EVANSTON, IL 60201-0000


                                April 6, 19--


    Dear Mr. Denniston:

            This letter style is favored by many government departments and agencies,
    civil services offices, and even by some senior executives for their personal
    correspondence. It is known as the official style.

            This letter style is really very much like a basic business letter. Its
    most distinguishing feature, however, is that the inside address appears as
    the last item. The letter may have blocked or indented paragraphs and may be
    typed in either the open or mixed punctuation style.

            If the letter includes a postscript, enclosure, or copy notation, these
    are typed in their usual position following the typed name and identificaton
    lines of the sender.

            Quite often this is fine quality paper with the sender's name embossed
    at the top. This could also be a letter typed on monarch or baronial size
    paper rather than standard letter size paper.

                                       Sincerely yours,

                                       E R Benjamin

                                       E. R. Benjamin
                                       Chairman of the Board

    ac

    Mr. S. Denniston
    247 Barrington Street
    Alpena, MI 49707-0000
```

Figure 5.34   Official Style

E89 Form Letters

- When you need to send the same basic letter to many people, but you want to make a few individual changes, use a form letter.
- Word processing equipment handles the preparation of form letters very efficiently.
- The ultimate goal is to prepare form letters that appear to be individually typed.
- For methods of organizing the preparation of form letters, see C13.

E90 Letters on Small Stationery

- The names given to stationery that is smaller than standard are *Monarch* (Figure 5.35) and *Baronial.* (Figure 5.36)
- They are used most frequently by senior business executives to add distinctiveness to their letters or when it is necessary to particularly catch a reader's attention.
- Set margins of 12 elite or 10 pica strokes from each side and follow all the other typing rules contained in this section. (See E88, *The Official Letter.*, Figure 5.34.)

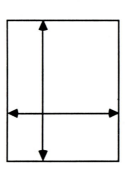 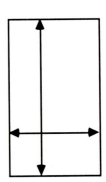

Figure 5.35 Monarch (7 1/4" x 10 1/2") **Figure 5.36** Baronial (5 1/2" x 8 1/2")

E91 Tips on Rapid Letter Production

- Remember that the full block style with open punctuation requires the least typing effort.
- Set one margin for *all* letter lengths and adjust the available space between date and inside address.
- Set tabs for all needed indentions in advance.
- *Block* attention and subject lines (i.e., start them at the left margin).
- Do not type the company name if this is shown in the letterhead.
- Organize all the materials you need ahead of time.
- Proofread your work *before* you take it from the typewriter.
- Use a ruler or a line-a-time device to hold your place in the copy when working with a complicated document or small type.
- Aim to compose directly at the keyboard of a typewriter, text editor, or personal computer.

E92 Memoranda

Interoffice memoranda, or *memos,* are used when written communication between company employees is necessary (Figure 5.37).

- Inside address, salutation, and complimentary closing are not used.
- Use block style and a consistent line length (60 pica, 70 elite).
- Titles are not needed in the *To* and *From* sections but may, as a matter of courtesy, be used in the *To* section only.
- The formatting for carbon copies, enclosures, postscripts, and multiple pages is exactly the same as for letters.
- The manner in which the originator's name is shown in the closing is a matter of preference. Some alternatives include: only the originator's initials are shown at the end of the memo; the originator's full name is typed about five lines down from the last paragraph so that his or her signature can be placed above the typed name; the orginator initials or signs the memorandum next to the typed name that appears on the *From* line and no closing signature or initials are typed.
- Memos are usually preprinted forms but they can also be typed on plain paper.
- Memos are usually sent in special reusable interoffice envelopes (see E56).

```
                    M E M O R A N D U M

                                          Date:  June 14, 19--

To:     Dean Thelma Washington, School of Business Administration
From:   Robert Fourman, Chairperson, Economics Department
Re:     Reappointment Request for All Adjuncts

        Dr. Frederick Sforza and Dr. Adele Fischer have served as
        adjuncts in the economics department for the past two
        years.  They have recently been evaluated by Personnel
        Advisory Committee members and by the students in their
        respective classes.  In each case, the evaluations have been
        very favorable; and, as a result, I would like to reappoint
        both Dr. Sforza and Dr. Fischer for the fall academic
        semester.

        If you need further information, I will be happy to supply
        it; otherwise, I look forward to hearing your position on
        this matter.

        lc

     c  Dr. Stephen Hecht, PAC Chairperson
```

Figure 5.37 Memorandum

Editing, Formatting, and Word Processing

E93 Post Cards

Post cards are useful for sending brief notices, announcements, or messages. Post cards can also be pre-addressed to help expedite replies if they are mailed with letters that require a brief and fast response (Figures 5.38 through 5.40).

```
The ABC Company
20 Tower Drive
New London, CT 06320-0000


                                    Ms. Hilda S. Turner
                                    57 Stonehedge Street
                                    Wilmington, DE 19803-0000
```

Figure 5.38   Post Card (Address)

```
                                              August 4, 19--

Dear Ms. Turner:

     This is to remind you that the next meeting of the
Wilmington Chapter of Professional Secretaries International
will be held on Wednesday evening, August 13, at 6:30 p.m. at
the Silver Fox Restaurant.

     Following dinner, our guest speaker will be Dr. Harriet
Hurley, a noted author and lecturer in office technologies.
Call (302) 764-8993 by Friday, August 8, for a reservation.

                              Betty L. Grayson, Secretary
```

Figure 5.39   Post Card (Message)

```
     _____  Yes. I will be present for the June Meeting of the
            Business Professionals Association.

     _____  Sorry, I will not be able to be present for the June
            Meeting of the Business Professionals Association.


     _____    _____
     Name of Respondent              Date
```

Figure 5.40   Pre-Addressed Post Card

E94 Reports, Essays, and Manuscripts

For guidance on *writing* reports, see Unit 2, C30-C40.

- Reports, essays, and manuscripts are so similar in their typed form that the instructions provided here apply specifically to reports used in business, to formal academic essays, and to material being prepared for publication.
- Use a good-quality, plain white, letter-size, unpunched bond paper; type on *one* side of the sheet only. Use onion skin for copies. Always keep a copy of any report, paper, or article submitted for publication.
- Reports, essays and manuscripts usually consist of a title page, contents page, body, and bibliography. Complex or very long documents may also contain a preface, appendices, and an index.

E95 Title Page (Cover Page)

The title page shows the document title (topic), name of the author, author's title, and submission date (Figure 5.41). It may also contain the name of the person or company to whom it is submitted (Figure 5.42).

- Balance the layout so that the page is attractive and easy to follow.
- For a business report, a conservative, simple style is best; decorative borders should be avoided.

Figure 5.41 Centered Title Page

Figure 5.42 Detailed Title Page

E96 Preface (also known as the Introduction, Abstract, Foreword, Synopsis, Summary, or Digest)

The preface outlines the purpose of the report, its scope and limitations, the methods of rearch employed, the major ideas in the report, the name of the person who authorized it, and any special observations or acknowledgements (Figure 5.43).

- Type the preface as a separate page and place it between the body and the title page.
- Use the same margins, placement, and spacing as for page 1 of the body but leave the page unnumbered.

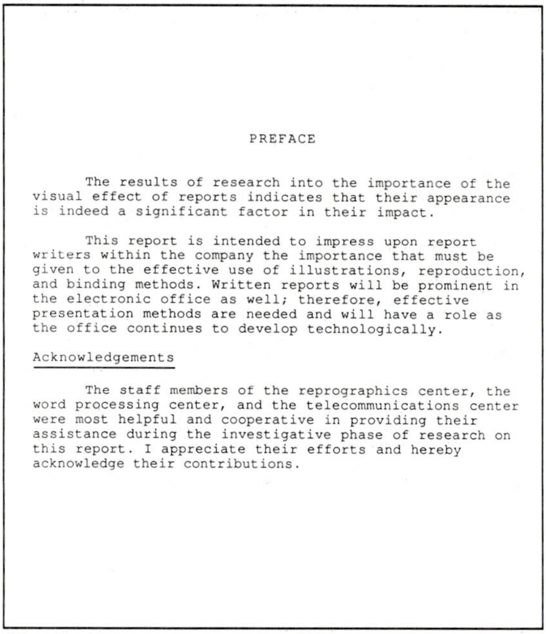

> **PREFACE**
>
> The results of research into the importance of the visual effect of reports indicates that their appearance is indeed a significant factor in their impact.
>
> This report is intended to impress upon report writers within the company the importance that must be given to the effective use of illustrations, reproduction, and binding methods. Written reports will be prominent in the electronic office as well; therefore, effective presentation methods are needed and will have a role as the office continues to develop technologically.
>
> Acknowledgements
>
> The staff members of the reprographics center, the word processing center, and the telecommunications center were most helpful and cooperative in providing their assistance during the investigative phase of research on this report. I appreciate their efforts and hereby acknowledge their contributions.

Figure 5.43 Preface

E97 Table of Contents (or Contents)

The contents page lists each major section (and sometimes subsections) of the document and appropriate page numbers. It is needed only in lengthy reports (ten or more pages) and should be prepared *after* the rest of the report has been typed so that accurate page numbers may be included (Figure 5.44).

- Use the same margin settings as in the body.
- If the contents list is a short one, center the material vertically on the page. No page number is needed.

- If the contents list is a long one and likely to occupy more than one page, type the heading on line 13 and finish typing 6 lines up from the bottom edge. Start the continuation page on line 7. Use Roman numerals to number these continuation pages.
- The contents page should follow the heading pattern and/or numbering system used in the report, essay, or manuscript itself.

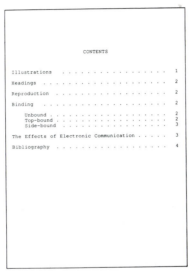

Figure 5.44 Table of Contents

E98 Placement (Margins and Starting Lines)

Table 5.3 Placement for Margins and Starting Lines.

	Unbound	Topbound	Sidebound
Starting line, page 1	13	15	13
Starting line, page 2, etc.	7 (page number line 4, center or right side)	10 (page number bottom right corner or center)	7 (page number line 4, center or right side)
Left margin (strokes from left edge)	10 pica, 12 elite (1 inch)	10 pica, 12 elite (1 inch)	15 pica, 18 elite (1 1/2 inches)
Right margin (strokes from right edge)	10 pica, 12 elite (1 inch)	10 pica, 12 elite (1 inch)	10 pica, 12 elite (1 inch)
Bottom margin	1 inch (6 lines)	1 inch (6 lines)	1 inch (6 lines)

Editing, Formatting, and Word Processing

E99 Spacing

Use double spacing and a five-space paragraph indention. (In business reports where there may be an important reason for saving space, single spacing is acceptable.) Use single spacing for displayed information (long quotations, numbered listings, footnotes, and bibliography).

E100 Headings

The effective use of headings and subheadings in a report serves an important function. These divisions help organize the material and emphasize the report's key topics to the reader (Figure 5.45).

```
                    MAIN HEADING (FIRST CATEGORY)
                              (DS)
    -----------------------------------------------------------------
    -----------------------------------------------------------------
                        (DS)
    SIDE HEADING (SECOND CATEGORY)
    -----------------------------------------------------------------
    -----------------------------------------------------------------
                        (DS)
    Side Heading (Third Category)
    -----------------------------------------------------------------
    -----------------------------------------------------------------
                        (SS)
        Indented/Consistent Style Heading (Fourth Category)
    -----------------------------------------------------------------
    -----------------------------------------------------------------
                        (SS)
        Paragraph Heading (Fifth Category). --------------------
    -----------------------------------------------------------------
```

Figure 5.45 Report Headings

- Use headings and subheadings to organize the material, to show relationships, and to indicate the relative importance of the separate sections of the report.
- Try to limit yourself to three or four categories of headings. Never use any more than five levels of headings.
- Suggested typing styles for various categories of headings are:

  First category . . . . Main Headings (Capitals, centered)

  Second category. . . . . . Side Headings (Capitals, flush left)

Third category . . . . Side Headings
(Initial capitals, flush left, underscored)

Fourth category . . . . Indented/Consistent Style
(Initial capitals, indented 5 spaces, underscored)

- To speed your typing if you are working from a draft, decide on heading categories *before* you start typing and then code each heading in the job (e.g., number them from 1 to 5).
- Note that an extra line of space must be left *below* main heads and *above* all other headings.

E101 Numbering Systems

Some formal reports may need a numbering system to make the location of material easier. Use either one of the following two systems:

E102 Decimal Style

1. A major topic.
    1.1 A section of the major topic.
        1.11 The next subdivision.
        1.12 A second point at this level.
    1.2 A second section of the major topic.
2. The next major topic.
    2.1 A section of the next major topic.
    2.2 The second point at this level.

E103 Number/Letter Style

1. A major topic.
    A. A section of the major topic.
        1. The next subdivision.
            a. Part of 1, above.
            b. Another part of 1, above.
    B. Another section of the major topic.
2. The next major topic.
    A. A section of this major topic.
    B. Another section of this major topic.

Editing, Formatting, and Word Processing

> ### THE BUSINESS REPORT: ITS FINISHED APPEARANCE
>
> Research, organization, and writing skills are needed in the preparation of an effective business report, but these ingredients alone will not guarantee that the report will achieve the desired effect. The final layout and appearance must be carefully considered since they can greatly influence the reader.
>
> ILLUSTRATIONS
>
> The writer must not only try to make the report easy to read but easy to understand as well. Writers must remember that words are not the only tools that are available.
>
> Pearlman and DuBose offer this advice:
>
>> Take advantage of the paper on which your letter or report is printed. Think of the blank space as part of the message. Use it to break up large blocks of material that offer little relief to the eye of the reader.[1]
>
> Laird makes a strong case for the use of illustrations.
>
>> Quite often, words are not as dramatic in presenting the data for a report as are graphic forms of communication. Graphics are effective ways of sharing key statistics, noteworthy trends or startling contrasts. Bar charts, pie charts, trend lines: all these help your reader get key ideas better than words can--provided the data has something significant to say.[2]
>
> HEADINGS
>
> The more important parts of the message or report--whether a word, a phrase, or an idea--should be emphasized. "Headings and subheadings pinpoint
>
> ---
> 1. Daniel D. Pearlman and Anita DuBose, *Letter Perfect*, Bobbs-Merrill Educational Publishing, Indianapolis, Indiana, 1985, p. 40.
> 2. Dugan Laird, Writing for Results: *Principles and Practice*, Addison-Wesley Publishing Company, Reading, Massachusetts, 1978, p. 201.

> and summarize ideas for easy absorption by the reader."[3] Page after page of closely printed material is boring to read. Break the text into short units topped with suitable headings or titles to enhance readability.
>
> REPRODUCTION
>
> The type of report and its functions will influence the kind of reproduction method used. Photocopies may be appropriate for reports to members within your own company, but reports to shareholders should be reproduced by offset or some other process that will produce printlike, quality copies. A number of questions need to be answered before a reproduction process is selected.
>
>> When determining the most appropriate method of reproducing information, consider the quality of copies desired, the quantity of copies desired, the amount of time and money to be spent on materials and labor, and the speed desired.
>
> BINDING
>
> A reader's first impression of a report is affected by its binding. Three types of binding are common:
>
> Unbound
>
> If the report is no more than ten pages long, staple it at the top left-hand corner. Use a binding on a longer report.
>
> ---
> 3. Dorothy Farmloe, *Creative Communications for Business Students*, Holt, Rinehart and Winston, Toronto, Canada, 1977, p. 186.
> 4. Jo Ann Lee, Louis C. Nanassy, and William Selden, *Reference Manual for Office Workers*, 2d ed., Glencoe Publishing Company, Encino, California, 1986, p. 288.

Figure 5.46 Format of Business Report

Figure 5.46 (continued) Format of Business Report

E104 Ending the Pages

Each page should have a bottom margin of about 1 inch (6 lines). As a reminder, use a pencil to mark a point 4 to 6 centimeters from the end of the page *before* you begin typing, watch the paper-ending indicator on your machine, or use a guide sheet (see this unit, E136). Be sure to follow these rules.

- Type at least two lines of a paragraph at the foot of one page and always type at least two lines at the top of the next page.
- Do *not* divide the last (or first) word on a page.
- Do *not* type a heading on one page and the body on the next so that the heading is isolated.

E105 Numbering the Pages

E106 Introduction (Table of Contents and Preface)

- Leave these pages unnumbered unless many pages are involved.
- Use Roman numerals or letters of the alphabet if several pages are involved within each section.

E107 Body

- Leave the first page unnumbered.
- Number second and succeeding pages either at the top (line 4) at the center or right side, or at the bottom (four lines up) at the right side.

E108 Ending (Appendixes, Bibliography, Index)

- Leave these pages unnumbered unless several pages are involved.
- Use Roman numerals, Arabic numerals in parentheses, or letters of the alphabet if several pages are involved within each section.

E109 Displayed Information

E110 Numbered Lists

- Indent five spaces on each side or align with the margins.
- Single-space, but double-space between each item.

```
            1.  ------------------------------------
                --------------------
            2.  ------------------------------------
                --------------------
```

- Set a tab four places from the left so that alignment is simplified.

E111 Tabulated Material

- Follow the rules given for tabulations. (See this unit, E17-E18.) Do *not* let your table extend beyond the margins of the body of the text.
- Single spacing is preferred.
- Leave a blank line above and below the table.
- Type footnotes related to a table below the table rather than at the foot of the page.

E112 Illustrations

- For information on typing tables, charts, and graphs see this unit, E44-E49.

E107-E117 Body

- If a list of illustrations is required, type this in numbered sentence format and insert it in the report after the body and before the bibliography.

E113 Quoted Material

E114 Short Quotations (Three or Fewer Typed Lines)

Type these within the body of the report and within quotation marks. End them with a raised numeral indicating a footnote reference.

E115 Quoting Complete Sentences

Use quotation marks, begin the quotation with a capital, and end it with a period.

> Typists should be aware that, "Quotations of just a few lines are double-spaced and typed within quotation marks."[2]

E116 Quoting Parts of Sentences

Use the ellipsis, 3 spaced periods (. . .), to indicate that not all of the sentence from which the quotation is taken has been used.

> Typists should be aware that quotations and paraphrases ". . . of just a few lines are double-spaced."[1]
>
> Typists should be aware that quotations ". . . of just a few lines . . ."[1] are double-spaced and may be introduced and ended by an ellipsis.

Note: Use *four* periods if the closing ellipsis comes at the end of the sentence.

> Typists should be alert to the fact that "an ellipsis at the end of a sentence requires the ellipsis plus an extra period . . . ."[2]

E117 Long Quotations (More Than Three Typed Lines)

- Leave a line of space above and below long quotations.
- Single-space the quoted material.
- Indent five spaces on each side of the margins.
- Do not use quotation marks.

Editing, Formatting, and Word Processing

- Indent the first line an additional five spaces if you are quoting from the beginning of a paragraph.

  Dorothy Farmiloe says on this subject:

  > An appendix is the place to put supplementary material not essential to the report but which may aid the reader's understanding of it in some way.[2]

- If the quote opens part way through a sentence, use an ellipsis (. . .) to begin the quotation (see E116).
- If the quote closes with an incomplete sentence, use the ellipsis plus a period at the end (see E116).

E118 Footnotes and Endnotes

Footnotes and endnotes are used for two purposes:

- To provide additional useful information on a particular topic to that noted in the body of the report

  7. For more detailed information on the population of major cities in the United States, consult the statistical data published annually in almanacs and yearbooks.

- To identify the source of information quoted exactly or paraphrased (a summary of someone else's ideas)

  8. James MacGregor Burns, <u>Leadership</u>, Harper & Row Publishers, New York, 1978, p. 223.

Footnotes usually appear on the page on which quoted material appears. However, it is acceptable to type these notes on a separate sheet headed *Notes* and attach it to the end of the body. These are called *endnotes* (see E124).

E119 Basic Style Patterns

Footnotes or endnotes may follow one of two basic style patterns. The format should be determined *before* you proceed with collecting notes so that you will organize your research notes in such a way as to make the drafting of the report easier.

E120 Business Style

    1. Tom Peters and Nancy Austin, A Passion for
Excellence, Random House, New York, 1985, p. 189.

E121 Academic Style

    ¹ Tom Peters and Nancy Austin, A Passion for
Excellence (New York: Random House, 1985), p. 189.

> **Note:** The illustrations in this text will follow the business style format; however, they can be easily changed by placing the city of publication, name of the publisher, and year of publication in parentheses as shown above. Note too, that the footnote reference number is typed as a superscript in the academic style illustration.

E122 Numbering Footnotes and Endnotes

- Use Arabic numerals and number each quotation or reference consecutively throughout the report. Asterisks may be used when only a very few references are needed.
- In the body, type the reference numbers a half line above the regular typing line at the *end* of the quotation or reference and outside any punctuation.

    . . . spacing is as you would expect."²

In the footnote or endnote itself, the numeral may or may not be raised.

E123 Typing Footnotes

When footnotes must be typed on the page on which the reference appears, be sure you leave enough space at the bottom of the page. As a rule, allow four lines for each footnote that you type. This allows for space between each footnote and a 1-inch bottom margin.

- When typing is complete on a page, turn up *one* line under the body and type a 1 1/2 to 2-inch underscore.
- Turn up a double space and begin typing the footnote reference.
- Single-space footnote references and double-space between them.

Editing, Formatting, and Word Processing

- The numbers assigned to each footnote may be typed on the line followed by a period and two spaces, or they may be raised above the line with the next character immediately following.
- Follow the style and spacing illustrated in Figure 5.47. This style will suit most applications, but some academic institutions may have particular requirements that must be followed.

Show author(s) in the sequence of given name and family name.

Underscore book titles and put quotation marks around the titles of articles.

Punctuate footnotes as shown by using commas to separate each item and by using a period at the end of each footnote.

Indent at the outset of each new footnote.

```
       There must be at least two lines of a paragraph at the end of one
page and the top of the next page for an appropriate page ending.
_____
       1.  Harold T. Smith, The Office Revolution: Strategies for Managing
Tomorrow's Workforce, Administration Management Society Foundation, Willow
Grove, Pennsylvania, 1983, p. 4.

       2.  Abraham Zaleznik, "An Introduction to Work in the 21st Century,"
Personnel Administrator, December 1983, p. 28.
```

Figure 5.47 Footnotes

E124 Typing Endnotes

When quotation references (footnotes) are typed as a separate sheet, follow the formatting rules presented below. (See Figure 5.52.)

- Start typing the page on line 13.
- Use the heading *Notes*.
- Single-space each reference and double-space between references.
- Place the sheet after the body of the document and in front of the bibliography.
- The numbers assigned to each footnote may be typed on the line followed by a period and two spaces, or they may be raised above the line with the next character immediately following. Follow one style consistently throughout.

```
            1.  This is acceptable ...
                  or
            ¹This is acceptable ...
```

E124-E127 Typing Endnotes

- If continuation pages are required, start on line 7 and continue to follow the page numbers already sequenced.

If the manuscript illustrated on pages 186 and 187 entitled, *The Business Report: Its Finished Appearance*, had been typed with endnotes instead of footnotes, the endnotes would appear as they do in Figure 5.48.

```
                              NOTES

    1. Daniel D. Perlman and Anita Dubose. Letter Perfect. Indianapolis, Indiana:
       Bobbs-Merrill Educational Publishing, 1985, p.40.

    2. Dugan Laird. Writing for Results: Principles and Practice. Reading,
       Massachusetts: Addison-Wesley Publishing Company, 1978, p.201.

    3. Dorothy Farmiloe. Creative Communication for Business Students. Toronto,
       Canada: Holt,Rinehart and Winston, 1977.

    4. Joann Lee, Louis C. Nanassy, and William Selden. Reference Manual for
       Office Workers, 2d ed. Encino, California: Glencoe Publishing Company,
       1986, p.288.

    5. Eleanor Hollis Tedesco and Robert B. Mitchell. Administrative Office
       Management: The Electronic Office. New York: John Wiley & Sons,
       1984, p.638.

    6. Tedesco and Mitchell, p.638.
```

Figure 5.48 Endnotes

E125 Formatting Footnotes and Endnotes in Special Situations

E126 References to Anthologies and Collections

Show the author and the work cited (in quotation marks) from the anthology or collection, the title (underscored) plus the name(s) of the editor(s), and the place of publication, publisher, and year of publication.

> 5. Abraham T. Collier, "Business Leadership and a Creative Society," Executive Success: Making It in Management, edited by Eliza G. C. Collins, New York: John Wiley & Sons, Inc., 1983, p. 22.

E127 References to Books

The standard footnote content includes footnote number, author, book title, publisher, place of publication, year of publication, and page number(s).

> 1. Alvin Toffler, The Third Wave, William Morrow and Company, New York, 1980, p. 64.

For two authors, list their names in the order shown on the title page of the book.

>   3.   Thomas J. Peters and Robert H. Waterman, Jr., <u>In Search of Excellence</u>, Harper & Row Publishers, New York, 1982, p. 308.

For more than three authors, you may show the first author and then the words "et al." The words "et al" are not underscored. Use this style consistently throughout if you choose to use it instead of listing all the names.

>   8.   Jo Ann Lee et al., <u>Reference Manual for Office Workers</u>, 2d ed., Glencoe Publishing Company, Encino, California, 1986, p. 40.

E128 An Edition of a Text

No special notation is made for the first edition of a text. For the second and subsequent editions, the footnote reference should show the edition as it would be stated in ordinary terms: 2d edition, 3d edition, 4th edition, etc.

>   9.   Rosemarie McCauley and Keith Slocum, <u>Business Spelling and Word Power</u>, 2d ed., Bobbs-Merrill Educational Publishing, 1983, p. 42.

E129 Unknown Author

If the author of a publication is unknown, begin the footnote with the name of the publication.

>   26.   <u>Twenty Facts on Women Workers</u>, United States Government Printing Office, U. S. Department of Labor, Washington, D.C., 1972, p. 3.

E130 References to Periodicals and Newspapers

Show the author's name, article title (in quotes), periodical or newspaper name (underscored), volume number (optional), month and year of publication, and page number(s).

>   15.   Marilyn Machlowitz, "Coping With Ambivalence: The Woman Manager's Balancing Act," <u>Working Woman</u>, February 1981, p. 42.
>
>   16.   Pamela Moreland, "Rebellion in the Typing Pool," <u>The Bergen Record</u>, March 2, 1981, p. 19.

E131 Nonprint Sources

For recordings, tapes, interviews, speeches, works of art, microforms, and performances, you need to use your judgment and attempt to provide sufficient information so that the reader can identify and locate the source if necessary.

```
     27.  La Cage aux Folles, Original Cast Recording, RCA Red Seal
Stereo Records, 1983.

     28.  Personal interview with Mr. Martin Farnsworth, Fidelity
National Bank, San Francisco, California, July 14, 19--, 4 hours.
```

E132 Shortened and Recurring References

After a book or periodical has been footnoted in full or is cited in the manuscript content once, shortened references may be used following any of the styles below:

Latin abbreviations may be used; none of these expressions should be underscored.

- **ibid** (short form of *ibidem,* meaning *in the same place*): refers the reader to the *immediately preceding* footnote. This term can be used at any time in endnotes, but in footnotes only if the entry to which it refers appears on the same page.

```
     8.  Terence E. Deal and Allan A. Kennedy, Corporate Cultures,
Addison-Wesley Publishing Company, 1982, pp.203-204.

     9.  Ibid.  (Exact work including page numbers)

     10.  Ibid, p. 301.  (Exact work but different page)
```

- **op. cit.** (*opere citati,* meaning *in the place cited*): this refers the reader to a previously cited work but a different page number.

```
     22.  Deal and Kennedy, op. cit., p. 211
```

- **loc. cit.** (*loco citato,* meaning *in the place cited*): this refers the reader to the previously cited work.

```
     23.  Deal and Kennedy, loc. cit.  (Refers to footnote 8 above—the
same work on the same page.)
```

E133 Textnotes

In short reports, in reports where the number of reference sources is limited, or in reports where there is no bibliography, it is acceptable to insert bibliographic data in parentheses within the body of the report as in Figure 5.49.

Editing, Formatting, and Word Processing

```
       In writing about the mythology of innovation, the story about
  how the "Post-It Note Pads have become a staple in the American office--
  and a $200 million winner for 3M" helps us understand the quirks and
  time lags that often affect innovation.    (Tom Peters and Nancy Austin,
  A Passion for Excellence, Random House, 1985, p.115.)
```

Figure 5.49   Textnotes

If a bibliography will be provided, the textnote might be abbreviated even further as in Figures 5.50 and 5.51.

```
       In writing about the mythology of innovation, the story about
  how the "Post-It Note Pads have become a staple in the American office--
  and a $200 million winner for 3M" helps us understand the quirks and
  time lags that often affect innovation.    (Tom Peters and Nancy Austin,
  1985, p.115.)
```

Figure 5.50   Abbreviated Textnotes

```
       When Peters and Austin write about how the "Post-It Note Pads
  have become a staple in the American office--and a $2 million
  winner for 3M," they help us understand the quirks and time lags
  that often affect innovation (1985, p.15.)
```

Figure 5.51   Abbreviated Textnotes

E134 Bibliography

The bibliography is an alphabetical list of *all* the resources consulted by the author in the preparation of the report. Usually shown in each entry are the author(s), title, place of publication, publisher, and date of publication.

E134 Bibliography

```
Kanter, Rosabeth Moss.  Men and Women of the Corporation.  New York:
     Basic Books, 1977.
Kruse, Bettijune and Benedict Kruse.  Dictionary of Word Processing.
     Encino, California:  Glencoe Publishing Co., Inc., 1983.
Walt, Harold R., "Toward 2000."  Management World, January, 1983,
     pp. 9-10.
```

Use these guidelines for preparing a bibliography.

- Type the bibliography on a separate page (or pages).
- Use the same margins as for the body of the report. Start the first page on line 13 and succeeding pages on line 7.
- Center and capitalize the main heading.
- Single-space each reference and leave a double space between them.
- Follow the punctuation shown in Figure 5.53.
- Note that authors are listed by surnames (family or last names) first.
- When the work either does not have an author, or the author's name is not known, position the work in alphabetical order by the first word in the title, ignoring *A*, *An* or *The*.
- Start the first line at the margin and indent the second and subsequent lines of the same entry five or ten spaces, but be consistent.
- If there are two works by the same author, replace the author's name the second time with six hyphens (------).
- In most cases, all sources would be listed in alphabetical sequence; however, if the bibliography is extensive, the listing may be divided into sections according to the types of references cited. For example:

    By the importance of the reference sources: *primary, secondary*

    By the kinds of publications: *books, periodicals, unpublished works*

The illustrations in the NOTES (Figure 5.52) and BIBLIOGRAPHY (Figure 5.53) show the following situations cited below by author names only:

> *one-author text* — Drucker, Peter F., People Performance . . .
>
> *two-author text* — Wilkes, Mary and C. Bruce Crosswait, Professional . . .
>
> *three-or-more author text* — Laird, Donald A. et al., Psychology . . .
>
> *article in a periodical* — Mayer, Richard, "Don't . . .

Editing, Formatting, and Word Processing

article in a newspaper — McGahey, Richard, "High . . .

no author name available — "Office Automation, Personnel . . .

personal interview — Personal interview with . . .

second work in the bibliography by the same author ------. Technology . . .

government publication — <u>Brief Highlights</u> . . .

editor as author — Collins, Eliza G., Editor . . .

```
                              NOTES

    1.  Peter F. Drucker, People and Performance: The Best of Peter
Drucker on Management, Harper & Row Publishers, New York, 1977, p. 42.

    2.  Ronald L. Applbaum and Karl W. E. Anatol, Effective Oral
Communication in Business and the Professions, Scientific Research
Associates, Inc., Chicago, Illinois, 1982, p. 6.

    3.  Mary Wilkes and C. Bruce Crosswait, Professional Development:
The Dynamics of Success, 3rd ed., Harcourt Brace Jovanovich, Inc.,
New York, 1987, pp. 171-176.

    4.  Kenneth R. Mayer, "Group Communication Skills for Future Office
Workers," Business Education Forum, February 1983, p. 13.

    5.  Mary Wilkes and C. Bruce Crosswait, pp. 86-90.

    6.  Donald A. Laird et al., Psychology: Human Relations and Work
Adjustment, McGraw-Hill Book Company, New York, 1983, p. 262.

    7.  Peter F. Drucker, Technology, Management, and Society,
Harper & Row Publishers, New York, 1970, pp. 109-115.

    8.  Richard Mayer, "Don't Be Hoodwinked by the Panacean Conspiracy,"
Management Review, June 1983, pp. 23-24.

    9.  "Office Automation, Personnel, and the New Technology," Personnel
Journal, October 1980, pp. 817-820.

   10.  Brief Highlights of Major Federal Laws on Sex Discrimination in
Employment, U. S. Government Printing Office, Washington, D.C., August,
1980, p. 4.

   11.  Peter F. Drucker, Technology, Management, and Society, p. 84.

   12.  Richard Mayer, p. 23.

   13.  Personal interview with Ms. Alice Forrestal, Brandwine Associates,
Silver Springs, Maryland, March 14, 19--, 2 hours.

   14.  Ronald L. Applbaum and Karl W. E. Anatol, p. 67.

   15.  Richard McGahey, "High Tech, Low Hopes," New York Times, May 15,
1983, p. E-21.

   16.  Eliza G. Collins, Editor, Executive Success: Making It In
Management, John Wiley & Sons, New York, 1983, p. 47.
```

Figure 5.52 Notes

```
                              BIBLIOGRAPHY

Applbaum, Ronald L. and Karl W. E. Anatol. Effective Oral Communication
     in Business and the Professions, Chicago, Illinois: Scientific
     Research Associates, Inc., 1982.

Brief Highlights of Major Federal Laws on Sex Discrimination in Employment.
     Washington, D.C.: U. S. Government Printing Office, August 1980.

Collins, Eliza G., Editor. Executive Success: Making It In Management.
     New York: John Wiley & Sons, 1983.

Drucker, Peter F. People and Performance: The Best of Peter Drucker on
     Management. New York: Harper & Row Publishers, 1977.

------. Technology, Management, and Society. New York: Harper & Row
     Publishers, 1970.

Laird, Donald A. et al. Psychology: Human Relations and Work Adjustment.
     New York: McGraw-Hill Book Company, 1983.

Mayer, Kenneth R. "Group Communication Skills for Future Office Workers."
     Business Education Forum, February 1983, pp. 11-13.

Mayer, Richard. "Don't Be Hoodwinked by the Panacean Conspiracy," Management
     Review, June 1983, pp. 23-25.

McGahey, Richard. "High Tech, Low Hopes." New York Times, May 15, 1983,
     p. E-21.

"Office Automation, Personnel, and the New Technology." Personnel Journal,
     October 1980, pp. 815-823.

Personal Interview with Ms. Alice Forrestal, Brandwine Associates, Silver
     Springs, Maryland, March 14, 19--, 2 hours.

Wilkes, Mary and C. Bruce Crosswait. Professional Development: The
     Dynamics of Success, 3rd ed. New York: Harcourt Brace
     Jovanovich, Inc., 1987.
```

Figure 5.53 Bibliography

Note: The page numbers in the NOTES section may be different from those appearing in the BIBLIOGRAPHY. The page numbers in the NOTES section represent those pages on which the specific citation actually appears. The page numbers in the BIBLIOGRAPHY represent *all* the page numbers in the article. Note, too, that *no* page numbers are given for texts in the BIBLIOGRAPHY.

E135 Index

An index is an alphabetical listing of all topics and their page numbers. It is often provided with very lengthy reports and academic papers.

Indexes will vary considerably with the nature of the material. However, use the same margins, and starting and finishing lines as the rest of the document, and plan your work so that the information is easy to follow.

Editing, Formatting, and Word Processing

E136 Typing Guide Sheet for Reports and Manuscripts

To simplify the layout task, rule a typing guide backing sheet with a broad felt-tip marking pen that shows top, bottom, and side margins. Type line numbers at the left side (see Figure 5.54).

- Place this backing sheet behind the top copy and in front of the first sheet of carbon paper.
- Allow the numbers at the right of the guide to extend beyond the top copy so they can serve as a guide to the lines remaining on a page.
- Type just within the frame indicated on your guide.

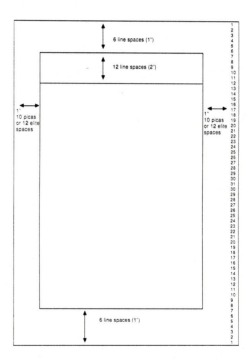

Figure 5.54 Typing Guide Sheet

E137 Word Processing Configurations

The organization of the word processing facility in an office will vary with the size and needs of the firm. It may range from a large, self-contained, fully-equipped (centralized) department to a single, independent unit used by one operator or shared by several secretaries (decentralized). In some organizations both environments co-exist (hybrid).

E138 Centralized Word Processing

If a word processing department is centralized, it is a separate department of the firm with its own budget and it reports directly to management. Several organizational structures are possible. For example, the department may be responsible for

- all the firm's typing and secretarial support services, with one manager responsible for correspondence (typing) services and one manager responsible for administrative (secretarial support) services;

or

- the firm's correspondence (typing) only may be centralized. The administrative (secretarial support) staff might be administered by the separate departments to which they belong. Fewer and fewer organizations have centralized word processing departments; the trend is toward decentralized centers.

Supervisors of a centralized word processing department are often required by management to keep a record of the work that is accomplished daily by their operators. Figure 5.55 is an example of a log that can be used for this purpose.

A typical word processing department may include a supervisor, a *lead* specialist, one or more specialists, one or more operators, and one or more proofreaders, depending upon the size of the firm and its particular volume of work.

			DAILY WORK OUTPUT			
OPERATOR NAME				DATE		
DOCUMENT NUMBER	TYPE OF WORK	ORIGINATORS NAME	NUMBER OF LINES/PAGES	TIME USED		
				HOURS	MINUTES	

Figure 5.55 Word Processing Activity Log

E139 Decentralized Word Processing

The two basic forms of decentralized word processing environments are the *satellite center* and the *single-unit station*.

E140 Satellite Centers

Satellite centers are small word processing centers set up to serve individual departments. There may be several "satellite" or "distributed word processing centers" within an organization, each independent of the others and each organized specifically to serve special departmental needs. This arrangement brings the authors and originators of documents (principals) closer to the word processing support staff, expedites the handling of confidential or rush jobs, and facilitates the handling of special projects. For these reasons, this structure is growing in use.

E141 Single-Unit Workstation

Increasing numbers of secretaries now have sophisticated electronic typewriters or personal computers instead of standard electric typewriters. In some instances, a personal computer or word processor may be available to a group of secretarial or administrative support personnel for special project jobs such as repetitive letters, long reports, data base research needs, and the like. In such cases, the use of the special equipment is shared on an "as needed" basis.

E142 The Word Processing Cycle

Basically, the flow of work in a word processing environment follows in the typical cycle shown in Figure 5.56.

E139-E145 Decentralized Word Processing

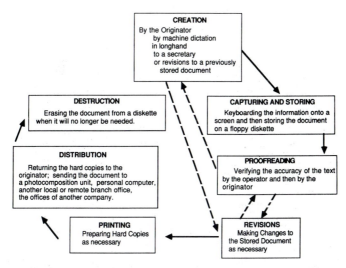

Figure 5.56 The Word Processing Cycle

E143 Dictation Equipment

Because of the high cost of word processing equipment, the machines must be kept working constantly if the greatest cost efficiency is to be achieved. Because in-person dictation is slow and deciphering handwriting is time consuming for the typist, machine dictation equipment is an essential component of a word processing system.

E144 Dictation Equipment Choices

Dictation machines are of two types:

- *independent portable or desktop units,* which are very similar to small tape recorders and consist of a recorder, a microphone, and a separate transcriber
- *centralized recording and transcribing units* with a telephone hookup to permit remote dictation

E145 Centralized Recording Devices

Automatic changer (also known as discrete media recorder): This type of equipment permits continuous central recording without the need to insert a new cassette, tape, etc., when one tape is full. The recording medium is changed automatically. Long periods of dictation are possi-

Editing, Formatting, and Word Processing

ble, and transcription can be under way while dictation continues.
Endless loop: The recording tape is sealed into a tank and is not removed or touched. Such a system offers automatic, unattended use 24 hours a day. A supervisory console (or monitoring panel) enables dictation to be directed automatically to the secretary who can deal with it most rapidly. With this system, transcription can be under way a very short time after the dictation.

Telephone Hookup
Telephone hookup to a central recording device may be made through a private and separate telephone system or through the regular telephone service. The telephone receiver is used for recording in both systems.
Private systems (purchased or rented) not supplied by the public telephone service. Three types are available:

- *nonselector* equipment: connected to one recorder only (if the recorder is in use, the dictator must wait)
- *manual selector:* dictator can select a vacant recorder
- *automatic selector:* dictator is automatically connected to first free recorder

Telephone company system: equipment provided by your local telephone service is connected with the centralized recording equipment. Access to the recording device is gained by dialing particular numbers, and dictation is possible from any extension telephone or from any outside telephone.

Note: Advice on efficient dictation techniques is provided in Unit 3, C45.

E146 Word Processing Terms

Boilerplate A term used to describe what appear to be individually typed communications but are in fact form letters or form paragraphs combined with variables.

Codes Special instructions such as stop codes, underscore codes, backspace codes, and tab codes, keystroked into the recording media. During playback the use of these codes results in the special instruction being carried out.

Communicating word processors Text can be automatically transmitted from one unit to another compatible unit via an internal network or over telephone lines.

Continuous loop See *endless loop recorders*.

C.P.U. The central processing unit of the computer.

CRT (Cathode Ray Tube) A video screen that displays the operator's input in electronic word processing systems prior to playback.

Cursor A symbol on a CRT that indicates where the next character will be displayed.

Data base An extensive and continuously updated file of information on a particular subject or subjects.

Disk drive The device that makes possible the recording of text onto magnetic media.

Downtime Time when equipment is not operating correctly because of some malfunction.

Dumb terminal A text-editing terminal of a computer-based system that relies on the computer for its instruction.

Endless loop recorders A continuous-flow dictation system in which magnetic tape is sealed in a tank and loops around constantly.

Electronic mail The use of electronic means (telephone lines, private networks, or satellite networks) to transmit printed information.

Floppy disk/diskette A flexible magnetic storage medium.

Footer Page identification used at the foot of a page.

Formatting Setting margins, indents, etc., for various typing set-ups, such as letters and reports.

Global search and replace The capability of the word processor to locate a particular word or expression in stored information and replace it automatically with another word or expression.

Hard copy A typed or printed document on paper.

Editing, Formatting, and Word Processing

Header Page identification used at the top of a page.

Input The first stage in the processing of a typing job, such as the word originator's (author's) dictation.

Keyboarding or keystroking Inputting material into the system via an electronic keyboard.

Mag cards Magnetic cards that record text as it is being typed.

Menu List of operator choices supplied by the system.

Modem (modulator-demodulators) Device that enables computers and terminals to communicate over telephone circuits.

MT/ST (magnetic tape Selectric typewriter) The first of the word processing machines—introduced by IBM in 1963.

Optical Character Recognition (OCR) Units that can scan and enter typed material directly into the word processing system without the need for retyping (see I30).

Output The completed job.

Peripherals Items of equipment that may be attached to the system such as printers, photocomposers, telecommunications devices, or OCR units.

Playback or playout Printing out of recorded material.

Prerecorded Material that has been put onto disk or tape for reuse, such as paragraphs for form letters, legal documents, collection letters, etc.

Principal Person who initiates work and requires secretarial services.

Search Locating specific places in recorded material.

Scrolling The movement of text on a visual display.

Shared logic systems Several operators at several keyboard terminals use the memory and processing powers of one computer or C.P.U. simultaneously.

Shared resource system A system with a central disk drive and controller, and work stations that have their own intelligence.

Smart terminal Text editing terminal that has its own computer power but shares the printing and/or storage facilities of the computer.

Standalone Machine that operates independently from any other machine. (Has the ability to store, recall and revise).

Text Printed or written matter.

Text editing Revising recorded information on electronic typing systems for automatic playback.

Throughput The time involved in actually processing the job from initiation to completion.

Time sharing Several terminals from different organizations may be connected to a large computer system with the cost of the computer being shared.

Transcribing unit Playback component of a dictation machine.

Turnaround time The time taken between the beginning and the completion of a job once it has been given to the word processing operator.

Video display See *CRT*.

Wraparound The automatic process of carrying an incomplete word from one line to the next.

UNIT 6

F ILING SYSTEMS AND RECORDS CONTROL

Data Versus Information	F1
The Records Cycle	F2
Creation	F3
Maintenance and Use	F4-F16
Elements of a Good Filing System	
Parts of a Typical Correspondence File	
Filing Fundamentals	
Steps in Filing	
Alphabetic Indexing	F17-F41
Alphabetic Sequencing	
Names of Individuals	
Names of Companies	
Special Concerns in Sequencing	
Titles	
Geographic/Compass Terms	
Other Special Situations	
Numbers	
Filing Systems	F42-F50
Alphabetic Filing	
Geographic Filing	
Subject Filing	
Numeric Filing	

Retention	F51
Transfer	F52
Destruction	F53
Records Storage Equipment	F54-F61

    Vertical File Cabinet
    Lateral File Cabinet
    Visible Files
    Open Shelf Files
    High Density Movable Files
    Mechanical Files
    Electronic Power Files

Systems Control	F62-F68

    Charge-Out Procedures for Borrowing Filed Materials
    Color Coding
    Follow-Up or Reminder (Tickler) Systems
    Procedures Manual
    Reading File
    Ratios

Elements of a Comprehensive Records Management Program	F69
A Summary of Factors to be Considered When Evaluating a Records System	F70
Micrographic Storage	F71-F73

    Microforms
    The Advantages of Microfilm

Electronic Filing	F74-F79

    Diskette Filing
    Indexing
    Disk Utilization
    Storing Electronic Information
    Retrieving Electronic Information

Insurance Record Maintenance	F80
Related Vocabulary	F81

Filing Systems and Records Control

Records in today's office take a variety of formats—paper (hard copy), cassette tapes, computer printouts, cards, microforms, charts, maps, photographs, drawings, floppy disks, and magnetic tapes are some examples. Essentially a *record* is some form of information that has been generated or received by a company. This information appears or is stored (saved) in a format that serves as evidence of a transaction so that it can be retrieved for future reference.

This unit describes the basic principles of record handling and control that can be applied regardless of the format used to store and retrieve information. Since all records are sequenced through a five-phase cycle from their creation to their destruction, the unit will explain the records cycle, describe filing systems and record storage and control procedures, and provide basic information on micrographic and diskette records. A listing of terms related to records management will complete your orientation to this important area of administrative support.

F1 Data Versus Information

There is a difference between data and information. Data are represented by numbers, words, symbols, or combinations of these. Therefore, 101286, S, read, #, and 7B are examples of *data*, or raw facts.

Data interpreted by individuals become *information*. When people organize data or add their perceptions to data, the end result is information. For example, an individual may perceive *101286* as the date October 12, 1986, an account number, an employee number, or a passbook number depending on circumstances, context, or other related experiences. Similarly, the letter *S* might be interpreted as *Small*, the # symbol as a proofreading symbol for *leave a space*, and *7B* as a shoe size meaning *size 7, medium width*.

Keep in mind that since information depends on interpretation and analysis by people, the perceptions may be correct—but they may also be incorrect! Finally, data captured on paper, electronically, magnetically, on film, or in other retrievable form constitute *records*.

F2 The Records Cycle

Filing is merely one element—although an important one—in a properly managed records system. Like people, records have a life cycle. There are five stages in the life cycle of a record (Figure 6.1).

F1-F2 Data Versus Information

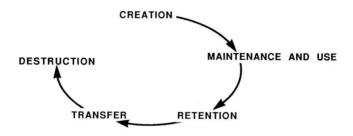

Figure 6.1 The Records Cycle

Creation is the stage in which a record is conceived, prepared, or received by an organization. Records may be created by keyboarding; by preparing a form; by having a computer generate a printout, report, or bill; by having a word processor produce a piece of correspondence or a report; by writing a check or voucher; by signing an agreement; by dictating into a cassette; by writing a document in longhand, etc. Basically, a record is created when data are captured on paper, in magnetic encoding, in electronic impulses, on film, or in any other form that provides evidence of documentation.

Maintenance and Use is the *filing* phase of the cycle. In this stage, it is presumed that the records are stored efficiently and accurately so that they can be retrieved (found) quickly.

The **retention** phase of the records cycle acknowledges that all records will not be needed forever. In this stage, records are assessed to determine their life span. Most records are *active* (heavy use) for a period of time, and they become *inactive* (diminished use) for another period of time before they are no longer necessary to an organization. **Retention** is the process of determining the guidelines for the active and inactive storage needs of an organization's records as they are classified by type.

Transfer is the process of carrying out the guidelines imposed by retention decisions. The *record retention schedule* provides written documentation of the active and inactive storage periods for each type of record. When the records become inactive, they are removed from the active file location and placed in an inactive file location. The movement of documents from one location to another is known as **transfer**.

Destruction provides for the final removal of records from the system. This may involve destroying the records in a variety of ways—shredding, burning, recycling. Destruction could also take place by erasing data on a cassette, disk, or other magnetic medium, as well as by deleting data from an electronic data base or file.

Filing Systems and Records Control

F3 Creation

Before information is captured to be included in a records system, some key questions should be answered:

Is this record needed?

Is this an original record or a duplicate record?

How many copies are actually needed?

Does this record provide all the information required?

Does all of the data on this record need to be part of the system?

Does the paper record need to be a part of the system or can key information be extracted, maintained, and manipulated just as effectively by electronic means?

Is this information available from another source within the organization?

Does the value of having this information justify the cost of creating and maintaining a system for this record?

A major problem in records management is placing too many records into the system in the first place.

F4 Maintenance and Use

Filing is a systematic process for the maintenance and use of records. Basic filing procedures should be followed whether the organization is large or small; whether the filing is centralized or decentralized; or whether the medium filed is paper, magnetic tapes, floppy disks, microforms, films, or pamphlets.

F5 Elements of a Good Filing System

- The information retrieved is *accurate*.
- The retrieval procedures are *logical*.
- The data retrieved are *up-to-date*.
- The system is *cost effective*.
- The system is *expandable*.

F6 Parts of a Typical Correspondence File

F7 Guides

Main (primary) and *auxiliary* (secondary) guides (folder-size cardboard with metal tabs) are used to separate file folders into divisions and subdivisions to facilitate filing and retrieval. *Special guides* are used when particular subjects or correspondents are frequently referred to and must be quickly located. These guides are shown in Figure 6.2.

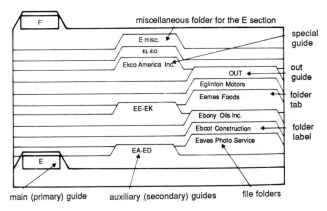

Figure 6.2 Parts of a Typical Correspondence File

F8 Folders (Legal or Letter-Size)

- **Individual.** An *individual* folder is placed alphabetically in the file behind the proper subdivision for each person, organization, or subject.
- **Miscellaneous.** Correspondence concerning a new person or subject is placed in a *miscellaneous* folder in the proper subdivision until at least five papers have accumulated. An individual folder is then prepared and moved to the appropriate position.

Folder Tabs

Folders are available in a variety of *cuts* that leave a tab visible in the file drawer or on the file shelf (Figure 6.3).

The same cut may be used for all folders in a system, or cuts may be varied to stagger folders so that one folder tab is not obscured behind another. For shelf filing, folders, guide cards, and outguides are available with tabs at the side for easy visibility.

Filing Systems and Records Control

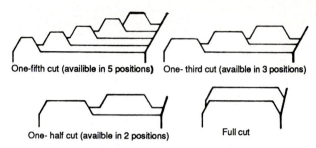

Figure 6.3 Folder Tabs

Folder Labels

Folder captions are usually typed on labels available in roll or sheet form and in various colors. Captions should be typed neatly in a consistent style, and the labels should be positioned carefully so that the captions can easily be seen. Color may be used to indicate particular years, departments, and other information needing special emphasis.

F9 Filing Fundamentals

- Label the outside of each file drawer (Figure 6.4).

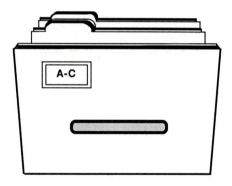

Figure 6.4 File Drawer

- Use the straight-line technique for file folders and guides (Figure 6.5).
- Use one guide for each 2 to 4 inches or every 10 to 20 folders. There should be approximately 30 guides (average) per standard file drawer.
- Use folders of the same size and weight to make retrieval easier.

F9 Filing Fundamentals

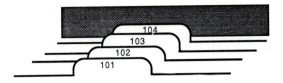

Figure 6.5 File Folders

- Captions on labels should be consistent—same type style and same location on each folder (Figure 6.6).

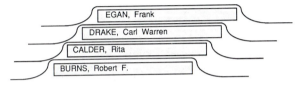

Figure 6.6 File Folder Labels

- Create a file folder for every 5 or more sheets for the same subject or customer.
- File folders should be no more than 1 inch thick. Use the scores (lines needing to be creased) at the bottom of the folder to provide for expansion to 1 inch.

When the 1-inch capacity is reached, start another folder. Example: If the *Directives* file has reached its capacity, rearrange the file with two folders as shown in Figure 6.7.

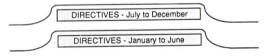

Figure 6.7 Creating New File Folders

- Maintain 4 inches of workspace in a file drawer to allow room for expansion.
- Attach small pieces of paper and clippings to 8 1/2" by 11" paper before putting them in the file so they don't get lost.
- When possible, file at a regular time interval daily.

215

Filing Systems and Records Control

F10 Steps in Filing

The five steps in filing are:

1. Inspecting
2. Indexing
3. Coding
4. Sorting
5. Storing

F11 Inspecting

Inspecting means that all documents must be routinely checked to ensure proper release for filing. No document should be filed until somebody has released it (indicated that all necessary action has been taken). Initials, a rubber stamp, or a carbon copy of a reply attached to the original document as shown in Figure 6.8 are generally considered as filing releases.

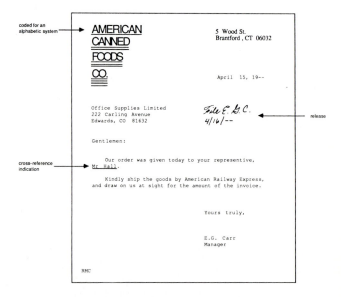

Figure 6.8 Document Released for Filing

F12 Indexing

Indexing is the most critical step in the filing process. It is the *mental process* of determining the caption (title, topic) under which the item will be filed. Being able to index properly presumes a knowledge of the overall filing system and the ability to make decisions about the role of specific documents in relation to the overall system. The indexing decision is made permanent when the next step—*coding*—has been completed.

F13 Coding

Coding means identifying on the record where it is to be filed.

- The word(s) under which the document is to be filed is(are) underscored or circled, or the appropriate caption is inserted.
- The filing units may be indicated by the use of one or more underscores, if required.

Unit 1	Unit 2	Unit 3
Liontos	James	Antiques
American	Canned	Foods

- In the case of a numeric system, the appropriate number or code is written on the document.

Note: Coding makes refiling easier if papers taken from the system must be replaced.

F14 Cross-Referencing

Cross-referencing means indicating in one or more places where a record may be located. Records are filed under the most important classification and cross-referenced under the other(s).

Cross-references are advisable when a document refers to more than one subject, or when a file might be looked for under more than one heading. For example:

- for names containing several important words

    Brown, Pearce, and Rowe, Architects

    New Orleans Home Mortgage Authority

Filing Systems and Records Control

- for names with similar sounds but different spellings

    Noel—Nowell

- for companies referred to by initials and the meaning of the initials is known

    NYSE   New York Stock Exchange

Three cross-referencing devices are:

Cross-referencing sheets. Specially designed letter-size sheets that may be filed inside the cross-referenced folder as though they were correspondence (Figure 6.9). They direct the searcher to the correct folder.

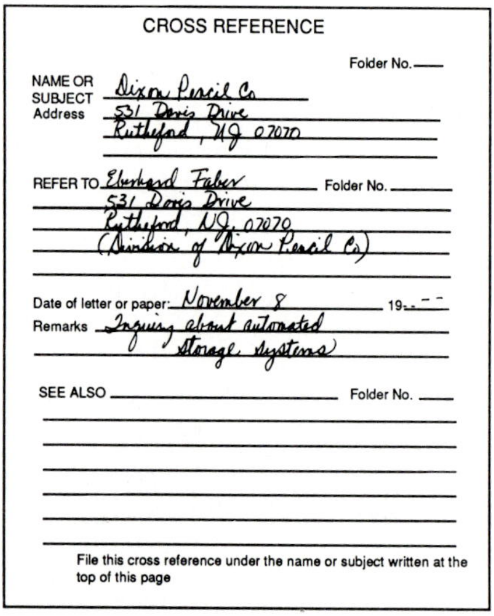

Figure 6.9   Cross-Reference Sheet

Cross-referencing folders. Tabbed half-folders placed in the file drawer or shelf in the cross-referenced position as though they were actual folders. They are labeled to indicate the position of the actual correspondence folder (Figure 6.10).

Cross-referencing index cards. Small cards kept in a separate file drawer. They are used in a large system where many cross-references occur (Figure 6.11).

F15 Sorting

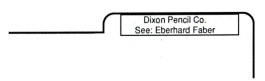

Figure 6.10 Cross-Reference on a Half-Tab

```
DIXON PENCIL CO.
531 Davis Drive
Rutherford, NJ 07070

See:    Eberhard Faber
        531 Davis Drive
        Rutherford, NJ 07070

Note:   Eberhard Faber is a division of
        Dixon Pencil Co.
```

Figure 6.11 Cross-Reference Card

F15 Sorting

Sorting involves prearranging items to be filed. If there are a number of items to be filed, it is best to do a rough sort first (putting like items together), and then a fine sort (placing items in the same order as the file). Example:

File Type	Rough Sort	Fine Sort
100 letters for an alphabetic file	Sort into piles of A-D, E-H, I-N, O-T, U-Z first.	Take the A to D pile and arrange the A's, B's, C's, and D's in exact file sequence. Do the same with the other piles.
100 invoices for a numeric file with a number range of 100 to 500	Sort into piles with 100's together, 200's together, 300's together 400's together, and 500's together.	Take the 100-199 pile and put it in numerical order from 100 to 199. Do the same with the other piles.

Sorting racks like the ones in Figure 6.12 are helpful in prearranging documents for filing.

Filing Systems and Records Control

Figure 6.12 Typical Desktop Sorters

F16 Storing

- Place documents in chronological order in a file with the most recent date on top.
- Place all documents in the file in the same order with the letterhead to the left when the folder is in the file.
- Keep a *miscellaneous* folder at the back of each alphabetic or numeric division to hold correspondence that is not designated for a specific file. Open an *individual* folder once five or more papers have been accumulated for one particular topic or customer name.
- Remove paper clips from items to be filed; staple papers in the upper right-hand corner.
- Do not overcrowd file drawers or shelves. Allow 4 inches of unused space.
- A folder should hold a maximum of 100 sheets or 1 inch of paper. Do not exceed the space provided by the scores or creases.
- Suspension folders in cabinets keep materials neater and make files easier to handle.
- Mend torn papers with tape before placing them in the file.

F17 Alphabetic Indexing

Before names or other captions (places or subjects) can be placed in alphabetic order, they must be *indexed*. Indexing means determining the most important part of a name or caption and then bringing that word or words to the front, if necessary. The indexed version of the name or caption should be typed on the file folder, index card, or record container.

Normal Order
Laura I. Fleming
Jack Reiss Plumbing Company
The Complete Essays of
Mark Twain

Indexing Order
F̲leming, Laura I.
R̲eiss, Jack, Plumbing Company
T̲wain, Mark (The) Complete Essays (of)

- Commas are used to indicate that the parts of a name or caption have been rearranged.
- Small, unimportant words are ignored for indexing purposes.

F18 Alphabetic Sequencing

Since the alphabet is the basis of many filing systems, one uniform set of rules for placing names in alphabetic order must be followed by everyone who works with or uses the files. The following rules are those recommended by the Association of Records Managers and Administrators, known as ARMA. ARMA is a nationwide, well-respected, and recognized organization of professionals who are involved with and spokespersons for standards in records handling.

F19 Identification of Units

Each part of the name or caption is considered a separate filing *unit*, working from left to right until a comparison point is reached.

Unit 1	Unit 2	Unit 3
Brown,	J.	
Brown,	Joseph	
Browne̲,	J.	John

For correct filing order, always follow the rule, "Nothing comes before something." This rule and the illustration above make it clear that incomplete names are filed before complete names.

Filing Systems and Records Control

F20 Names of Individuals

- Surnames (last names) are considered first; given names (first names) or initials second; middle names or initials third.
- A surname standing alone precedes a surname with initials.
- A surname with initials precedes a surname with a full given name.

Johnson

Johnson, N.

Johnson, Nadia

> **Note:** Names of married women should be alphabetically sequenced by their own names, not by their husband's names.
>
> Jones, Sara (Mrs. Robert)
>
> Jones, Sarah (Mrs. Allan)

When alphabetizing foreign names, if you can make the distinction, place the surname first. If you are unsure which is the first name and which is the surname, consider each part of the name in the order in which it is written but cross-reference the name as well.

James Lee Chung   File as: *Chung, James Lee*

Abdur Nandir   File as: *Abdur Nandir* and cross-reference as *Nandir, Abdur*

F21 Prefixes in a Surname

Prefixes in a surname (d', O', de, Von, Mc, Mac, Du, Del) are considered part of the surname.

DeAngelis, John

DeDominicus, Francis

DeLucia, Paul

Dumont, Frank

F22 Names of Companies

Company names are filed as written unless the company is named after a person.

E Z Car Care Center (4 units)

East Hill Cleaner

F20-F24   Names of Individuals

If the company is named after a person, it is indexed so that the family name is considered first.

Normal Order	Indexing Order
Michael Waltham Electronics	Waltham, Michael Electronics
Wayne Waters Travel Agency	Waters, Wayne Travel Agency

If the *whole* name is the one under which the company is commonly known, it should be filed following the normal order and not indexed. Providing a cross-reference in this case is recommended.

Normal Order	Indexing Order
Helen Elliott Candy Company	Helen Elliott Candy Company
Sara Lee Kitchens	Sara Lee Kitchens

Foreign language equivalents of *the* (le, la, il, el), and Old English forms (Ye) are considered prefixes; that is, part of the name.

El Matador (one unit)

La Scala Dining Room (three units)

Le Chien Elegant (two units)

Ye Olde Cheese Factory (three units)

F23   Special Concerns in Sequencing

F24   Abbreviations

Spell out abbreviations if you are sure of the actual name. Show the abbreviated form on the file folder tab or index card. Always spell out *Saint*.

Caption Order	Indexing Order
St. John's Bookstore	Saint John's Bookstore
Samosa Bros., Inc.	Samosa Brothers Incorporated
Sanitary Inspectors, Inc.	Sanitary Inspectors, Incorporated

Filing Systems and Records Control

F25 Apostrophes

Ignore apostrophes in alphabetic sequencing—no matter where they occur. Notice, for example, how the name *Lela's* fits into the list. Remember to use *all* letters in any possessive word or contraction.

LeLarge, Inc.

Lela's Hair Stylist

Lelas, T.

L'Elegant Beauty Salon

L'Elegante, Inc.

> **Note:** Some offices ignore the *s* if it comes after the apostrophe, but current practice is to ignore the apostrophe and include the *s*.

F26 Hyphenated Names

Ignore the hyphens in a hyphenated name, and consider the hyphenated words as *one* word. This rule applies to the names of individuals and organizations.

	Unit 1	Unit 2	Unit 3
Canadian-American Pen Co.	Canadian-American	Pen	Company
James William Curtis	Curtis	James	William
Ellen Curtis-Brown	Curtis-Brown	Ellen	
Winston Curtis-Jones	Curtis-Jones	Winston	

F27 Initials (Single Letters)

Names consisting of initials only are placed before all other names starting with the same letter. Each initial is considered a separate unit.

	Unit 1	Unit 2	Unit 3	Unit 4
CAC Realty	C	A	C	Realty
CIAG Insurance	C	I	A	G
Cabaret Dance Studio	Cabaret	Dance	Studio	

When the meaning of the initials is known, such as in the names of organizations, treat the single letters as separate units for filing purposes. In such cases, however, it is advisable to cross-reference under the name as it would be spelled out. For example:

PBS   File as three units: P, B, S, but cross-reference as *Public Broadcasting Service, SEE: PBS*

F28 Small Words (an, and, of, by, on, &, the)

Ignore small words for sequencing purposes, but type them in the caption on the file label. They may be placed in parentheses if desired. If *the* begins a name, it is moved to the end; if it occurs elsewhere, it may be typed in parentheses.

Fernando The Butcher	Fernando (The) Butcher
The Valley School of Dance	Valley School (of) Dance (The)

F29 Titles

F30 Titles and Degrees

Disregard titles and degrees for alphabetic sequencing purposes, but type them after the name on folders and labels.

Normal Order	Caption Order
Mrs. Jane Alexander, B.A.	Alexander, Jane (B.A.) (Mrs.)
Dr. Ronald H. Draper	Draper, Ronald H. (Dr.)

Note: If a title is part of a person's given name or a business name, it is filed as written.

Lord Simcoe Hotel	Lord Simcoe Hotel
Sir Nicholas Restaurant	Sir Nicholas Restaurant
Sister Gabriella	Sister Gabriella

Filing Systems and Records Control

F31 Seniority and Other Designations

Seniority terms such as *Jr.* and *Sr., II* and *III* are always considered for filing purposes. *Jr.* and *Sr.* are alphabetized in their abbreviated form, and *II* and *III* are indexed in numeric order.

	Indexing Order
Frank Williams Sr.	Frank Williams
Frank Williams, Jr.	Frank Williams, Jr.
Frank Williams, III	Frank Williams, Sr.
Frank Williams, II	Frank Williams, II
Frank Williams	Frank Williams, III

F32 Titles in an Organization's Name

Abbreviated titles in firm names are treated as if they were spelled out—except for Mr., Mrs., and Ms.

	Indexing Order			
Mrs. Wagner's Pies	Captain	Jim's	Seafood	Restaurant
Capt. Jim's Seafood Restaurant	Lady	Jane's	Bridal	Gowns
Lady Jane's Bridal Gowns	Mr.	Speedy	Cab	Company
Mr. Speedy Cab Company	Mrs.	Wagner's	Pies	
Sir Walter's Car Wash	Sir	Walter's	Car	Wash

F33 Geographic/Compass Terms

F34 Geographic Names

Consider each part of a geographic name as separate, but remember that hyphenated geographic terms are considered as one unit.

	Unit 1	Unit 2	Unit 3	Unit 4
New Haven Pharmacy	New	Haven	Pharmacy	
San Francisco Car Rental	San	Francisco	Car	Rental
Wilkes-Barre Restaurant	Wilkes-Barre	Restaurant		
Winston-Salem Novelties	Winston-Salem	Novelties		

F31-F37 Seniority and Other Designations

F35 Compound Words or Compass Points

Whether the original form is solid, spaced, or hyphenated, each word in a compound word should be considered a separate item.

Indexing Order

United Airlines	Mountain	View	Condos
Mountain View Estates	Mountain	View	Estates
Mountainview Condos	Tippy-Tu	Charcoal	Haven
Tippy-Tu Charcoal Haven	United	Air	Lines

Note: In Tippy-Tu Charcoal Haven, *Tu* is not recognized as a word; therefore, it is not considered a separate unit.

Each element in a compound compass point is treated as a separate unit regardless of whether the term is spaced or hyphenated.

Indexing Order

Northeast Shippers, Inc.	North	East	Printers
Northern Lights Boutique	North	East	Realtors
North-East Printers	North	East	Shippers Inc.
North Eastern Publishers	North	Eastern	Publishers
North East Realtors	Northern	Lights	Boutique

F36 Other Special Situations

F37 Associations, Societies, Organizations, Banks, Churches, Colleges, Schools and Universities

If the identifying word in the name (*Bank, College, University*) is the first word in the name, place that word last.

Caption Order	**Indexing Order**
Fidelity Union Bank	Fidelity Union Bank
Bank of Fresno	Fresno, Bank (of)
Holy Name Society	Holy Name Society
University of Maryland	Maryland, University (of)
College of St. Elizabeth	Saint Elizabeth, College (of)

Note: Cross-reference, if necessary, to avoid confusion (see F14).

Filing Systems and Records Control

F38 Boards, Committees, Estates, Trustees

Boards, etc., are rearranged to bring the most important word to the front.

Normal Order	Indexing Order
Estate of D. Chung	Chung, D., Estate (of)
Board of Governors	Governors, Board (of)

Note: Cross-reference, if necessary, to avoid confusion (see F14).

F39 Governments and Their Divisions

Government agencies and departments are filed under the name of the particular government (federal, state, municipal) with further subdivisions where necessary.

Normal Order	Indexing Order
Internal Revenue Service	United States Government Treasury Department Internal Revenue Service (8 units)

Note: All government agencies are filed under United States Government, then the name of the department, and finally the name of the body or commission.

F40 Identical Names

Identical names are filed alphabetically by location as follows:

a. Alphabetize first by city or town.
b. If cities or towns are identical, alphabetize by state. Thus: Springfield, Illinois comes before Springfield, Massachusetts.
c. If the name, city or town, and state are identical, alphabetize by street name. If the street name is a number, spell out the number.
d. If street names are identical and a direction is part of the address (North, South, Southeast), consider the direction as the next unit.
e. If all of the above units are identical, consider the house or building number and arrange them in numeric sequence.

General Manufacturing Co., 440 Main Street, Burlington, Vermont

General Manufacturing Co., 4 Vine Street, Rochester, Nevada

General Manufacturing Co., Main Street, Rochester, New York

General Manufacturing Co., 73 F̲ifth Avenue, Schnectady, New York

General Manufacturing Co., 49 T̲hird Avenue, Schnectady, New York

General Manufacturing Co., 440 W̲ashington Street South, Schnectady, New York

General Manufacturing Co., 109 Williams Street, Schnectady, New York

General Manufacturing Co., 1̲100 Williams Street, Schnectady, New York

F41 Numbers

At the beginning of a name. Numbers expressed in figures are sequenced in numeric order as a group before the complete alphabetic file. Names that start with numbers expressed as words are filed alphabetically.

Indexing Order

Two Brothers Cafe	1(st)	Avenue	Grocery
13th Street Bakery	1̲3(th)	Street	Bakery
1986 Researchers	1̲986	Researchers	
Alexander Anderson, III	A̲nderson	Alexander	III
First Place Realtors	F̲irst	Place	Realtors
1st Avenue Grocery	T̲wo	Brothers	Cafe

Within a name. Numbers expressed as figures anywhere in a name, except as the first word, should be filed immediately before the first similar name without a figure. If numbers are spelled out, regardless of where they appear in a name, they should be considered separate units—except that hyphenated words such as *twenty-first*, and *sixty-three* are considered one unit.

Indexing Order

Betty's Eighth Street Cafe	Betty's	8th	Avenue	Diner
Betty's 8th Avenue Diner	Betty's	E̲ighth	Street	Cafe
The Route 46 Car Wash	C̲olumbia	200	Tower	Club
Route Four Graphics	Columbia	Tw̲enty-two	Club	
Route 72 Plaza Shopping	Columbia	T̲ypewriter	Service	
Emerson's Six-Foot Club	E̲mersons	Six	Foot	Club
Safe-Clean Maintenance	R̲oute	4̲6	Car	Wash

Filing Systems and Records Control

Safer One-Hour Cleaners	Route	72	Plaza	Shopping
Safer, Peter	Route	Four	Graphics	
Scenic Route Travel	Safe	Clean	Maintenance	
The Columbia 200 Tower Club	Safer	One	Hour	Cleaners
Columbia Typewriter Service	Safer	Peter		
Columbia Twenty-Two Club	Scenic	Route	Travel	

F42 Filing Systems

Records may be arranged alphabetically, by geographic location, by subject, by number, or by a combination of letters and numbers.

F43 Alphabetic Filing

- Names and subjects are filed in simple alphabetic order (Figure 6.13).
- Main guides indicate each letter of the alphabet.

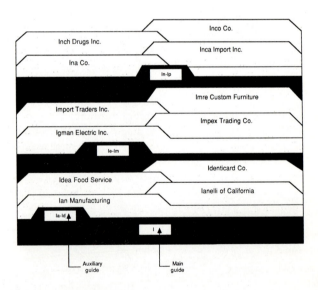

Figure 6.13 Simple Alphabetic File

- Auxiliary guides break down each letter of the alphabet into sections. Folders are arranged alphabetically by name behind these guides. The user merely looks for the first two or three letters on the auxiliary guide and then looks behind the guide for the folder being sought.
- This system is simple, easy to operate, but difficult to expand.
- This system is used in small organizations where specialized breakdown by subject or location is not needed.

F44 Geographic Filing

- Files are grouped by geographic location (Figure 6.14) from the largest geographic division to the smallest (e.g., from state to town).

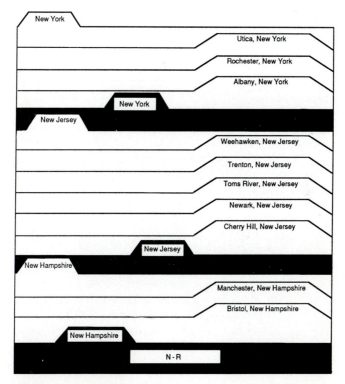

Figure 6.14 Typical Geographic File

Filing Systems and Records Control

- The largest divisions (states) appear on the main guides, and the cities or towns on the auxiliary guides. File folders for correspondents in each city or town are placed alphabetically behind these guides.
- In an international filing system, the largest divisions would be country names followed by cities, towns, etc.
- This system is useful to firms or departments whose main interest is territorial data (e.g., sales records); however, it should be noted that successful operation of a geographic system demands sound geographic knowledge.

F45 Subject Filing

- Subject filing means organizing records by topic (i.e., the content of the material), and then arranging the files alphabetically by those topics (Figures 6.15 and 6.16).

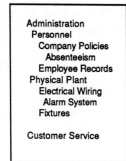

Figure 6.15 Subject File Master List

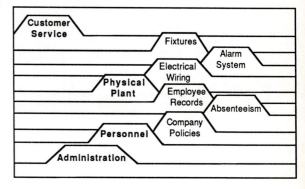

Figure 6.16 Simple Subject File

- There are two main sections to a subject file: the file itself, and an accompanying index, which can be a typed list of the file folder captions or a card file with one card representing each caption.
- The main guide indicates the main topic breakdown in the filing system. Auxiliary guides indicate any necessary subdivisions of the topic. Folders are placed alphabetically by topic behind the appropriate guide.

- An alphabetic master list or card index should show all the main subject divisions, auxiliary (secondary) divisions, and individual folder categories to facilitate retrieval.
- Establishing subject classifications demands care and considerable knowledge of the organization's activities.
- With this system, never open (label) file folders with a caption such as *Miscellaneous* or *General.*
- With this system, never file folders with names of individuals; *Comptroller Directives* is a better caption than *Arnold Franco's Directives.*
- Many cross-references are likely to be required.
- This system is used when subject matter is more important than correspondents' names.

F46 Letters and Numbers Used in Subject Filing

Subject filing may also be set up by means of letters and numbers used in combination, or by numbers used alone. Such systems are particularly useful in large, centralized filing systems because they can overcome the difficulties generally associated with simple alphabetic subject systems. These variations offer flexibility, diminish misfiling possibilities, eliminate uneven workload problems, and ease expansion difficulties.

Alpha-Numeric
A combination of letters and numbers is used. Main topics are given letters and related subtopics are assigned numbers.

A	Administration
A1	Personnel
A1-1	Company Policies
A1-1-1	Absenteeism
A1-2	Employee Records
A2	Physical Plant
A2-1	Electrical Wiring
A2-1-1	Alarm System
A2-2	Fixtures
B	Customer Service

Decimal

All material is grouped into ten or fewer main categories. Each of the ten major subjects may be subdivided into ten more parts and so on indefinitely.

100	Administration
110	Personnel
111	Company Policies
111.1	Absenteeism
112	Employee Records
120	Physical Plant
121	Electrical Wiring
121.1	Alarm System
122	Fixtures
200	Customer Service

Duplex-Numeric

A combination of numbers is used. Each primary topic is given a consecutive number, and secondary and tertiary (third subdivision) topics are subdivided downward from that number.

1	Administration
1-1	Personnel
1-1-1	Company Policies
1-1-1-1	Absenteeism
1-1-2	Employee Records
1-2	Physical Plant
1-2-1	Electrical Wiring
1-2-1-1	Alarm System
1-2-2	Fixtures
2	Customer Service

Subject-Numeric

Subject groups are assigned alphabetic codes (usually of three letters), and secondary and other categories are represented by numerals.

ADM.01	Personnel
ADM.01-0	Company Policies
ADM.01-0-1	Absenteeism
ADM.01-1	Employee Records
ADM.02	Physical Plant
ADM.02-0	Electrical Wiring
ADM.02-0-1	Alarm System
ADM.02-1	Fixtures

F47 Numeric Filing
F48 Sequential Numeric System

- There are four parts to a numeric filing system: an accession register, a card file, a numeric file, and a miscellaneous file (A to Z).
- As new files are opened, the number to be used for the new file is determined by consulting the *Accession Register* (Figure 6.17), a record of file numbers already allocated. The next unused number is allocated to the new file.

ACCESSION REGISTER	PAGE 5
Number	File Name
108	S. K. Sports Shoes
109	Tesco Distributors
110	Evergreen Nurseries
111	
112	
113	
114	

Figure 6.17 Accession Register

- Main guides are used to indicate round numbers and auxiliary guides are used to break down the round numbers into smaller categories (Figure 6.18).

Note: Some companies use both name and number on the file folder; but where confidentiality is required, number only is used.

- The system must have a complementary card system (Figure 6.19) arranged alphabetically that shows the client's name, address, assigned number, and any other pertinent information. If the file number is unknown, the alphabetic card index is consulted and the file number is easily located.
- A miscellaneous file usually follows the main numeric file. This *A to Z* file is used to store documents for which there is no indi-

Filing Systems and Records Control

Figure 6.18 Typical Numeric File

Figure 6.19 Card System for Numeric Filing

vidual file folder assigned. Unless there are at least five or more documents in a particular category, a numeric folder is not assigned; therefore, if a paper is to be placed in a numeric file for which there is no specific file set up, a card is made out for the card file with an M notation. In Figure 6.20 the paper is placed in the G miscellaneous folder in alphabetical order in relation to papers that are already in the folder.

- When more than five documents for *Garson Industries* are accumulated in the G miscellaneous folder, the next number is assigned from the accession book, the card in the card file is

F48 Numeric Filing

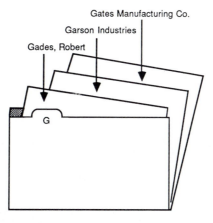

Figure 6.20 Miscellaneous File

modified as shown in Figure 6.21, and a new folder with the assigned number is added to the main file. All the papers related to the *Garson Industries* account are now removed from the *G* miscellaneous folder and placed in the numbered folder.
- Numeric filing offers accuracy, confidentiality, and unrestricted possibilities for expansion.
- This system is used by lawyers, doctors, jobbers, or in any situation where records are classified by numbers, and where records are continually added.

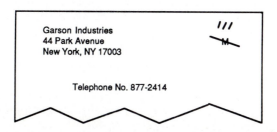

Figure 6.21 Modified Miscellaneous File

Filing Systems and Records Control

F49 Skip Numbering

Skip numbering is a *nonconsecutive* numbering system in which names are arranged in alphabetic sequence and assigned numbers with intervals or skips. As new names are added to the file, they are placed in between the original names and are assigned numbers that are available. Example: If a file has numbers 100 to 199 available, Adams might be assigned 106; Green, 135; Miller, 150; Winters, 193; and Zimmer, 198. If Walters is added later, it might be given number 180, Black might be given 114, etc. If all 100 numbers are taken, the system can be expanded by changing 100 to 1000 and 199 to 1990 as necessary.

F50 Terminal Digit Filing

- In this type of numeric filing system, numbers are read from right to left in equal groups of numbers (i.e., the first two numbers at the right hand are *primary*; the next two are *secondary*; and the rest are *tertiary*, or third, in importance).

    File Number 271832 is read as 32 18 27

- To file or retrieve, users first look under section 32 of the file, then under section 18, and finally under section 27.
- Users of this system include insurance companies and hospitals, where the primary and secondary digits could identify the type of claim or service and the tertiary numbers identify the individual's name.

F51 Retention

Retention policies must be developed if an effective records system is to be maintained. These policies should be established through a team approach rather than by one individual. The larger the volume of records, the more complex the job of determining a retention schedule. Some of the major steps involved in implementing records retention follow.

Take an inventory of existing records
Identify and qualify the records created and processed by the firm. This can be done through a physical inventory (actually counting all the records), or through a survey; that is, using a questionnaire to determine the number and types of records.

Classify the records

The records determined in the inventory are classified by *record series*. A record series is a group of identical or related records that is normally used and filed as a unit and that permits evaluation as a unit for retention scheduling purposes. Examples of record series include: purchase orders, customer service correspondence, employment applications, deeds, and vouchers.

Once the records are classified by record series, they are classified further by at least three additional categories:

Record or Nonrecord. *Record* copies are official copies— possibly original copies. *Nonrecords* are convenience copies or duplicates. Provision must be made to retain the designated *record* copy.

Active or Inactive. *Active* records are generally categorized as those records that are used at least once per month per file. Those used less than once per month are categorized as *inactive* records. Some judgment must be made on the future need to retrieve records from each record series.

Value of the Record. Record appraisal must include an evaluation of each record series based on its value to the organization from a variety of perspectives—legal, fiscal, historical, operational, administrative and research. Certain records should be designated as *vital records*, representing documents that are critical to the operation of the organization and which could not be replaced or would be difficult to replace (i.e., financial statements, tax records, historical documents, contracts, deeds, etc.). Such vital records should be given preferential handling and storage.

Analyze the records

The records that have been identified and classified should be analyzed by a team representing employees trained by consultants, consultants themselves, or a records manager.

Authorize a retention schedule

Recommended retention policies for each record series should be authorized in writing by representatives from major operational areas of the firm such as the legal department, the accounting department, the finance department, and others.

Prepare the records retention schedule

The approved retention procedures should be published as a master list (Figure 6.22).

Filing Systems and Records Control

Record Series	Dept.	Retention of Original		
		Total Period	In Dept.	In Storage
Advertising Releases	Sales	2 yrs.	2 yrs.	--
Agreements--Patents	R & D	20		20 Vaulted
Applications--Service				
Approved	Cust. Serv.	Indefinitely	1 yr.	Indefinitely
Not Approved	Cust. Serv.	2	1 yr.	1 yr.
Bank Reconciliations	Acctg.	4 yrs.	1 yr.	3 yrs.

THE LEXINGTON COMPANY
MASTER RECORDS RETENTION SCHEDULE
19--

Figure 6.22   Sample Master Records Retention Schedule

Evaluation of the retention schedule
The retention schedule should be evaluated at least once each year. Department heads should be required to verify existing schedules and identify areas needing change. The records team or committee would then reappraise the specific records identified.

F52 Transfer

The retention schedule determines the fate of each record series. *Transfer* is an orderly process that involves moving the inactive records to designated locations. Inactive storage locations could be within the same department, in a centralized records center, or in remote record storage areas.

The type of business determines the type of transfer method used. Two methods are typical.

Perpetual Transfer
In certain environments, a file is transferred to inactive storage when a particular case is closed or a job is completed; therefore, the transfer can occur at any time. Real estate, medical, legal, and construction companies are examples of businesses whose records are best suited to perpetual transfer.

Periodic Transfer
Transferring files to inactive storage at a designated time, such as the end of a year, quarter, or other designated period, is periodic transfer. Two such plans are common.

- *Two-Period Method.* Duplicate files with identical guides are maintained—one for active files and one for inactive files, usually from the previous period. In this method, the documents in the inactive drawers are either destroyed or put in boxes and moved to the records center. The active file drawer documents are then moved into the inactive drawers. Current transactions are then placed in the active file drawers. (See Figure 6.23.)
- *Maximum/Minimum Method.* At a given time, all records older than six months are moved to an inactive storage area. This leaves the current records representing the last six months in the active file.

Figure 6.23 Active/Inactive File Arrangement

F53 Destruction

Not all records should be destroyed by placing them in the wastebasket. Certain records—particularly confidential information—*by law* require special handling. Certain state and federal laws also prescribe specific methods of destruction. Some of these methods are:

Selling disposable records to a salvage company, a method which applies only to documents not requiring special handling.

Shredding documents using equipment that can vary from electric wastebasket models to high speed, high volume shredding and baling equipment.

Macerating and pulverizing records by the use of chemicals that disintegrate the paper into dust or pulp.

Burning the records in incinerators, a method required for some government documents or bearer-type instruments.

To provide for the systematic disposal of records, a *destruction tickler file* can be established from the dates indicated on the retention schedule. A *destruction register*, which records the records that are destroyed and the respective date of destruction, is often kept to permanently document destroyed records.

F54 Records Storage Equipment

F55 Vertical File Cabinet

- Manufactured in two- to five-drawer models.
- Five-drawer model provides 25 percent more filing space than the four-drawer model (Figure 6.24).
- A compressor built into each file drawer holds the paper upright.
- Manufacturer standards differ; therefore, consider structural reinforcement of frame, fire resistance, and size when purchasing.
- Drawers may be fitted with a frame over which hanging folders may be hooked to serve as file folders or to house other folders.
- Used for personal use or in a small office setting.

F56 Lateral File Cabinet

- Also known as *side opening file* (Figure 6.25).
- Projects fewer inches into the working aisle than the 28 inches needed for the vertical file; therefore, is space saving.
- Same comments as vertical file apply.

F57 Visible Files

- Documents are arranged in an overlapping sequence on a tray (Figure 6.26).
- Provide fast reference to many documents at a glance by means of a visible caption strip.

F54-F57 Records Storage Equipment

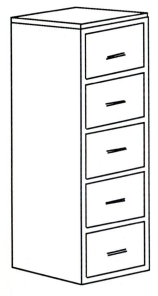

Figure 6.24 Vertical File Cabinet

Figure 6.25 Lateral File Cabinet

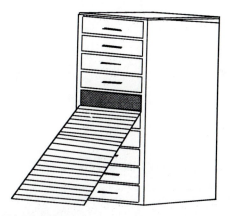

Figure 6.26 Visible File

- No guides are necessary.
- Color-coding may be used for retrieval.
- An effective way to house card-type documents.
- Cabinets are available in a variety of styles and sizes.
- Useful for records that need to be posted or updated frequently, such as inventory cards or time cards.

Filing Systems and Records Control

F58 Open Shelf Files

- The open shelf files shown in Figure 6.27 occupy less aisle space (about 50 percent less) than vertical cabinets.
- Offer great adaptability because shelves can be rearranged to house computer printouts, tape reels, and other non-standard documents, as well as file folders.
- Records are exposed and not protected from humidity, dirt, and other potentially harmful elements.
- Color-coded labels can enhance retrieval.
- Useful for offices with large record holdings where space is at a premium.

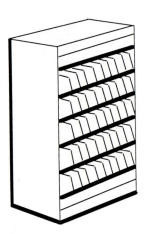

Figure 6.27 Open Shelf File

F59 High Density Movable Files

- Space-saving due to movable rows that are easily moved electronically or manually (Figure 6.28).
- Same advantages as open shelf files.
- Built-in safety features so that personnel cannot be caught between moving shelves, and so that the unit can be closed and locked to permit unauthorized use of records.
- Effective when there is a large volume of records, and when space is at such a premium that open shelves cannot meet required filing needs; or when security and confidentiality of record retrieval is a concern.

F58-F60   Open Shelf Files

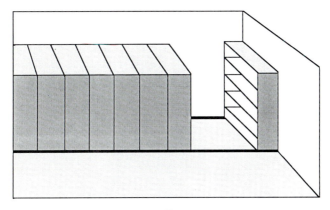

Figure 6.28   High Density Movable Files

F60 Mechanical Files

- Deliver files to workers by means of a foot control or push button hand controls.
- Can be carousel, rotary (rotate horizontally), or wheel (rotate vertically) types.
- Available with flat shelves, tubs, hanging folders, trays, and file boxes.
- Can be arranged as a rotating file in the center of several desks to permit multiple retrieval.
- For high volume filing and retrieval needs when many documents of the same type and size require storing and frequent retrieval (Figure 6.29).

Figure 6.29   Mechanical File

Filing Systems and Records Control

F61 Electronic Power Files

- Storage is automated. The location and replacement of a particular item (record, tape, bin, folder) is requested by push button command from the console (Figure 6.30).
- System is controlled by an operator who uses a simple keyboard console.
- After operator keys in the record identification command, the mechanism moves the appropriate location, bin, or container to the operator.
- Shelves are adaptable, and some units can house different document shapes simultaneously, if necessary.
- System can be interfaced with a computer by using magnetically encoded labels on stored items.
- Filed materials remain protected within the unit or chamber itself.
- Permit random filing of documents.

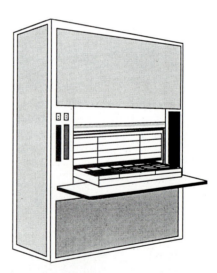

Figure 6.30 Electronic Power File

F62 Systems Control

F63 Charge-Out Procedures for Borrowing Filed Materials

- Every filing system should have an efficient charge-out system for establishing the whereabouts of a record or file when it is on loan.
- When materials are borrowed, a dated *Charge-Out Requisition* describing the record or file should be completed in duplicate (Figure 6.31).

```
              CHARGE-OUT REQUISITION
Material requested _____
Date requested _____ Date to be returned _____
Requested by _____
Signature of the recipient _____
Department _____ Telephone Extension _____
```

Figure 6.31 Charge-Out Requisition

- The copy of the Charge-Out Requisition should be kept in a tickler file according to the date the document is to be returned (see F65).
- The data on the Charge-Out Requisition should be written on an *outguide* (Figure 6.32) or an *outfolder* (Figure 6.33). While the record is out on loan, an outguide or outfolder should be used to replace the document in the file. Outguides are satisfactory for single documents; outfolders are best for replacing complete folders because new records can be safely stored in them while the folder itself is out on loan.
- Strict follow-up of overdue material is advisable to ensure that borrowed material is returned.

Filing Systems and Records Control

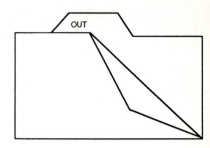

Figure 6.32 Outguide   **Figure 6.33** Outfolder

- Should documents that are borrowed by one person be given to another person (rerouted), the borrower should inform the file department, and the outguide and follow-up record should be changed to show the new borrower's name.

F64 Color Coding

Color can be added to folders, labels, guides, or other storage media to identify records and to make filing and retrieval easier and faster.

Color can counteract the monotony of filing and it can also help improve security. By color-coding special records and folders that should not leave the file area, a visible check of security is provided. In open shelf files, color coding can help locate misfiles.

Some ways in which color can be added to files are:

- Bars of color can be used on labels in uniform locations for identification.
- Twelve colors can be used to identify each month of the year in a distinctive manner.
- One color may be used for all the transactions in a given year.
- Groups of alphabetic characters may be assigned specific colors to aid in sorting and filing.
- Major divisions of a file can be assigned different colors.
- Colored labels may be used to indicate days of the week.
- Different colored *outguides* for different weekdays, months, or quarters will help distinguish those documents or folders that are out of the file for an excessive amount of time.

F65 Follow-Up or Reminder (Tickler) Systems

A good follow-up system ensures that documents requiring future attention or needing to be returned to the file are brought forward at the proper time. Any document that requires handling at a future date should have the request recorded in a follow-up or *tickler file* before the document is placed in the file. In the case of records to be returned by a designated date, there should be appropriate tracking so that the borrowed materials are returned or so that the return date is extended as necessary. If materials are returned ahead of time, the charge-out request form is removed from the tickler file.

There are two basic follow-up systems.

Desk Calendar
On the appropriate day, a note is made of the reminder request and the location of the material (see W30).

Chronological File or Tickler File
Sometimes referred to as the follow-up file or *pending* file (Figure 6.34).

- Thirty-one folders (one for each day of the month) and 12 folders (one for each month) are labeled.
- The folders are placed in a file drawer.

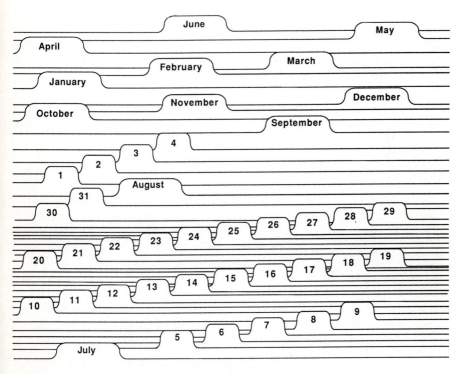

Figure 6.34 Chronological or Tickler File on July 5.

Filing Systems and Records Control

- A follow-up request for the current month is filed in the appropriate *day* folder. If the follow-up is for a future month, it is placed in the appropriate *month* folder.
- Material in each day's folder is dealt with on the appropriate day, and the empty folder is then moved to the back of the *day* folders.
- At the beginning of each month the previous month's empty folder is moved to the back, and papers from the current month's folders are transferred into the daily folders.
- Dates of weekends or holidays are not used for bringing forward correspondence.
- For a very large system, daily folders for a year might be set up.

Note: The material in the folder may be the original, a copy, or simply a note to serve as the follow-up.

A tickler file is identical to the follow-up file, except that it is in card form and is housed in a small card index container. Reminder notes are made on separate cards and these are inserted behind the appropriate day or month guides.

F66 Procedures Manual

A procedures manual that describes the key elements of the records program should be an integral part of the system control design. This manual can be used for reference, to train employees, and to identify procedures and responsibilities. The manual will help systematize and standardize procedures. It must be kept up to date for effectiveness (see W2).

F67 Reading File

In some organizations, a copy of every piece of outgoing correspondence is kept on file in chronological order. This file is kept separately from the regular filing system. One month's correspondence is kept in one folder and, at the end of the month, the whole file is transferred to a binder with the latest material placed on top. The binder can hold three months of data. Each time a new month of data is added to the binder, the last month's data is removed and discarded. This reading file provides a chronological record of all correspondence placed in the file. Longer retention periods may be assigned if three months of correspondence for review is not enough.

 Ratios

At times, it becomes necessary to document the productivity of the files. Two such measures might be helpful.

Accuracy Ratio
To determine how accurate the filing system is, keep an actual count for a period of time—one month, for example—of all the items retrieved from the file. Keep a record of all the items requested from the file. Then perform the following computation:

```
     1448              Items Found
     1500              Items Requested
1448 ÷ 1500 = 97%     (Accuracy Ratio)
```

> **Interpretation of Accuracy Ratio.** An accuracy ratio lower than 99.5 indicates that there is a problem in retrieving the records. Attention needs to be given to the physical arrangement of the files, the accuracy with which the operators work with the files, the effectiveness of the charge-out system, and the procedures used in indexing and coding the documents.

Activity Ratio
Keep a tally of all the records removed from the file for a particular length of time. Determine how many records are in the entire file. Perform the following calculation:

```
     450              Records Retrieved from the file in a month
    1500              Records in the Entire File
450 ÷ 1500 = 30%     (Activity Ratio)
```

> **Interpretation of Activity Ratio.** An activity ratio below 5 percent is considered low. This indicates that records are being kept and not used. Consider reassessing whether or not certain types of documents should be kept at all, find out if duplicate records are being kept elsewhere, or consider shortening the active storage period and moving the records to the inactive storage area sooner.

Filing Systems and Records Control

F69 Elements of a Comprehensive Records Management Program

According to ARMA, the following elements and functions are necessary for a complete records management program:

- A records management administrator and staff
- Forms management and control
- Reports management and control
- Correspondence management and control
- Records management procedures manual
- Active files management and control
- Inactive files management and control (records center)
- Vital records management and control
- Records inventory and appraisal
- Records retention and disposition schedule
- Micrographics management and control
- Copy reproduction and control
- Directives management and control
- Mail management and control
- Archives management and control

F70 A Summary of Factors to be Considered When Evaluating a Records System

The following questions should be asked when setting up or evaluating a records system:

- Should the documents be filed at all?
- Does the system provide for quick retrieval according to the way the document will be sought—by name, geographic location, number, or date?
- Is a logical pattern followed for grouping data in file folders and under main headings and subheadings?
- Have vital records been given appropriate special handling and housing?
- Have security or confidentiality requirements been considered in devising and operating the system?

F69-F71 Elements of a Comprehensive Records Management Program

- Is the equipment appropriate for the volume of data in the file now?
- Will the equipment be able to provide for future expansion of the records?
- Does the system lend itself to use and retrieval by more than one person at a time if this is necessary?
- Is there a procedures manual available?
- Are color-coding and an appropriate guide and folder system being used to facilitate retrieval?
- Are people being properly trained to use the record system?
- Is there a provision for charge-out and follow-up?
- Is there a provision for the periodic transfer of inactive files?
- Is there an up-to-date retention schedule?
- Are the retention schedule decisions based on sound input from legal, accounting, regulatory, operational, and administrative departments?
- Is the filing system being evaluated periodically to verify its effectiveness?
- Are guides plentiful and folder labels neatly arranged and typed?
- Are activity ratios and accuracy ratios determined periodically?
- Is floor space being used effectively?

F71 Micrographic Storage

Microrecords (small records) involve the microminiature recording of documents on film. Such records are being used more and more to ease the increasing need for records storage. Storing information in microrecord form provides better protection for the record, fast access to information, simplicity of copying, improved ease and cost of transmittal, and—most importantly—a savings of storage space. It is estimated that microrecords can save up to 98 percent of the storage space needed for original documents.

Micrographics is the term that describes the full range of services for creating and using microrecords. Basic equipment needed in a micrograhics environment includes:

- a *camera* to film (record) documents.
- a *processor* for duplicating the exposed film. Processing may take place on the company's premises or the film might be sent to a service bureau for processing.
- a *microfilm reader* to magnify the microfilm to readable size.
- a *storage unit* to house the microfilm media.

Other equipment that might also be found includes:

- a *printer* to produce hard copy printouts of the microfilmed documents in the same size as the original document.
- a *duplicator* to make inexpensive duplicate copies of previously developed film.

Note: The reader and printer may be combined into one unit rather than two separate units.

F72 Microforms

Microform is a generic term representing the array of formats that microrecords may take. The choice of microform depends on the nature and the amount of the material to be stored. Microforms may be:

- **Reels**. Reels (Figure 6.35) are rolls of uncut film used when all the microfilmed documents are related to each other. This media is most useful for documents that are serial (successive) in nature, such as newspapers and other publications. Reels offer the lowest processing cost. The length of a reel determines how many frames (images) can be held. Reels take a long time to search, update, and load into readers.

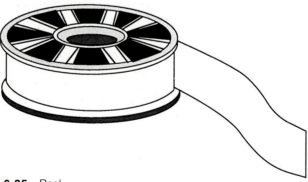

Figure 6.35 Reel

- **Cartridges or Cassettes**. Reel microfilm can be encased in a plastic container called a cartridge (Figure 6.36). Cassettes involve the encasing of microfilm in a two-cartridge plastic container. Cartridges and cassettes are easy to store, handle and load to readers; they cost more to process, however.

F72 Microforms

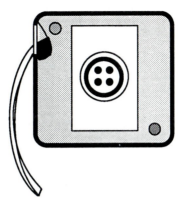

Figure 6.36 Cartridge

- **Film Jacket**. A film jacket (Figure 6.37) is two thin pieces of clear, film-like material that are sealed on two sides while two sides are open. Jackets are further subdivided into channels so that strips of microfilm can be inserted from an open end. Individual frames of film can be inserted at any time. Each jacket is like a file folder housing information on one particular topic. Master files are usually housed in this format, which is often the 4" x 6" size. Film jackets are best suited to active systems where frequent updates and retrievals are involved.

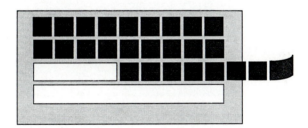

Figure 6.37 Film Jackets

- **Aperture Card**. This microform combines the advantage of electronic data processing with the advantage of microfilm because the 80-column standard input card (Figure 6.38) can be coded with related data as the basis for retrieval. Only one document is housed on an aperture card. The punched card version is now obsolete, having given way to computerized storage and retrieval techniques. Oversized records and documents used in engineering, architecture, and construction are often stored on this microform.

255

Figure 6.38 Aperture Card

- **Microfiche.** A piece of microfilm containing many images arranged in a grid pattern is referred to as microfiche—pronounced *micro-feesh* (Figure 6.39). The number of frames on each piece of fiche is determined by the reduction ratio used in filming. A microfiche is usually 4" x 6" and is suited to housing filmed versions of entire reports or computer printouts. It can be likened to a file folder because it has a label along the top to identify its contents which, as in a file folder, is typically related to one specific topic. A microfiche is easily duplicated. A special camera called a *step and repeat* camera can film microfiche directly.

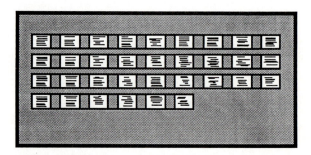

Figure 6.39 Microfiche

- **Ultrafiche.** Ultrafiche is like microfiche, but it is produced at much higher magnification or reduction ratios, permitting the storage of hundreds and even thousands of documents in a very small area of film. The images appear about the size of pinheads. An ultrafiche is used for large catalogs, books and other areas of micropublishing.
- **Ultrastrip.** This microform is a short length of microfilm containing highly reduced images. It is popular for high-speed storage and retrieval units and in small business office operations.

Newest developments in microforms include updatable microfiche and microfiche with color images.

(For microfiche storage and retrieval systems, see Unit 9, I31, I47, I48.)

F73 The Advantages of Microfilm

- Fast and easy retrieval of many documents
- File integrity, because the master copy never leaves the file
- Reproducibility, because fiche copies are inexpensive to make
- Space savings of about 98 percent
- Permanence, provided archival film is used
- Security, because vaulting is possible
- Legal protection, provided proper filming standards are maintained
- Ease and economy of distribution
- Can be used in a COM or CAR automated environment (see I47 and I48)

F74 Electronic Filing

Newer electronic equipment is being used more and more frequently to store and control information. Using electronic equipment to maintain records involves careful indexing and filming procedures, too. This time, however, the information is most likely to be stored on a diskette, hard disk, or in the computer's memory (see I32).

There are certain elements necessary for successful electronic filing.

F75 Diskette Filing

Files consist of related information stored on a diskette or on fixed disks. A diskette file is like a separate folder in a file drawer. Just as a file folder contains related information on a specific subject, so should diskettes be used to store related documents.

Any combination of files can be stored on a diskette, but each file or document stored must have its own unique *filename*. Filenames are usually from one to eight characters long. You will need to abbreviate, but don't do so to the extent that documents lose their identity. A good filename is one that will enable you to remember the document stored—for example, *MAILST* is a good name for a mailing list, and *DATSH* is a good name for a data sheet. Whenever you create, revise, or delete a document, you must use a document name.

Filing Systems and Records Control

F76 Indexing

A good index is the key to finding data in electronic storage, but creating a good index is no easy matter. Sometimes a powerful sorting program is available, and a master index can be created that can then be searched by department, originator's name, document name, or document number. If such a sorting program is not available, a two-level index can be maintained. An index of the disks would be kept, identifying the general content of each disk, such as accounting records, quarterly reports, market form letters, etc. Another index would be kept identifying the specific documents on each diskette. When documents are added or deleted, the index should be changed accordingly. In the absence of software-managed indexing, a manual index must be kept by the opertor of a personal computer or text editor.

F77 Disk Utilization

Indexing data on disks is important. But the length of time that data is to be stored on the disks must be considered also. Generally, information may be stored on disks for permanent, extended, or temporary time periods. It is important for the originator of the document to specify its retention period.

Permanent Storage. Mailing lists, form letters, and other records that will be used over and over again are kept on file permanently, even though they might be updated or changed later. Lengthy records, such as 50-page reports, may be kept on one diskette. Long documents are typically indexed by the type of record. If there are many shorter permanent records from one department or from one originator, the diskettes are indexed by the name of the department or originator with a separate index for each disk by document name.

Extended Storage. Those documents that need to go through several revisions or that are written, developed, and revised over a period of time are given extended storage. After the document is completed, it is usually erased or maintained for permanent storage. Extended storage documents are often stored under the originator's name. One diskette might be allocated for the storage of a long document.

Temporary Storage. Correspondence and other material with a revision cycle of less than one month is kept for temporary storage only. Diskettes can be color-coded by the operator to keep track of material that is stored on a temporary basis. Operators have their own coding systems. One such system involves assigning a different color code to each operator. A second color code—which is the same for all operators—represents the weeks in a month. Thus, red (operator code) and blue (first week of the month code) enable the operator to re-use a diskette one month later, allowing for the *temporary storage* for one month of the data on the disk. The second week of the month's diskette would be color coded red (operator code) and green (second week of the month code), etc. A similar scheme may be used for shorter temporary storage by using a color for the operator code and another color for each day of the week.

F78 Storing Electronic Information

Once data are keyboarded and stored, consideration must be given to the importance of the data. Often a *backup* copy of a diskette (Figure 6.40) is made when the information stored involves heavy keyboarding or is particularly important. Diskettes require special handling. Here are some guidelines:

- Do not touch the exposed area of the diskettes.
- Do not bend or scratch the diskettes.
- Store diskettes away from magnetic fields, in their jackets when they are not being used, and away from the sun.
- Store diskettes upright.
- Always write the label of the diskette *before* placing it on the disk.
- Store diskettes under normal humidity and temperature conditions (from 50° to 125° Fahrenheit).
- Avoid contact with static electricity from carpeting.

Figure 6.40 Floppy Disk

Filing Systems and Records Control

F79 Retrieving Electronic Information

Documents are retrieved from diskettes by referring to filenames. In sophisticated systems, a dictionary-type listing of all the document names in the file may be provided. Sometimes keywords or descriptors can be used to enhance the retrieval process when there is a heavy volume of information in storage. In enhanced computer-assisted retrieval environments, items can be sought by providing a series of key words (see Q24).

F80 Insurance Record Maintenance

Even though insurance companies are expected to maintain accurate and up-to-date records, it is sometimes a good idea to keep separate records of insurance policies, premium due dates, policy expiration dates, and other pertinent information, in the office of the policy holder(s). The following list suggests methods of maintaining insurance records:

1. Prepare a *tickler file* (see F65) for each new policy to serve as a reminder of the premium due date and the policy expiration date.
2. Place the tickler file so that it automatically receives attention a week to ten days before the premium due date and approximately one month before the policy expiration date. These time allowances will provide for any policy modifications or advance arrangements necessary for premium payment.
3. Include on the tickler file card sufficient information to identify the policy: type, number, issuing company, name of insured, amount of premium, and where to send payment.
4. Maintain an insurance file record for each policy. Include all of the information included in the tickler file as well as a summary of the details of coverage and the exclusions. Attach these records to the policy itself when and if it is canceled, lapsed, expired, or placed in storage.
5. Keep policy records separate by the name of the insured.
6. If it is helpful to view the total insurance program at a glance, maintain a list of policies according to type, amount, issuing company, policy number, and yearly premium. This record may be organized by type of coverage, with sufficient space left between types to allow for the addition of new policies.
7. Maintain a yearly schedule of premiums due. The format may be a monthly listing or a calendar chart.

F79-F81   Retrieving Electronic Information

F81   Related Vocabulary

In addition to those terms already defined in this unit, the following terms may also be useful:

Access Register Used in numeric filing to record the file numbers already allocated and the next number to be assigned.

Archival Records The permanent records of an organization.

Back-Up Copy Extra copy of a vital or important record that is prepared and kept as a precaution.

Blip Coding A mechanism found in many microfilm cameras providing a square mark below the frame on a microrecord to be used in electronic retrieval.

Block Numeric A numeric filing system in which blocks of numbers are assigned to particular subject groupings. For example: 0-99 Teachers; 101-199 Administrators; 201-299 School Board Members, etc.

Caption The heading (or description) used on a file folder label.

Case File A file containing only material relating to a specific action, event, person, place, or thing.

Centralized Records Gathering and storing all the records of an organization in one location within the organization.

Chronological Filing Filing by date (see F65).

Decentralized Records Storing records in respective departments within the company.

Direct Access System A filing system in which a person can locate a past record by going directly to the file and looking under a specific name. Alphabetic filing systems are direct access systems.

Dispersal Sending copies of vital records to locations other than the place where the original is housed.

Filing Placing records in their appropriate file drawers or cabinets.

Given Name An individual's first name.

Guides Dividers in file drawers or shelves to separate groups of records.

Index A list of the topics, titles, or documents in a file.

Indexing The selection of the caption under which a document is filed.

Indirect Access System Filing system in which an index must be used to determine the specific code assigned to the record. Numeric filing systems are indirect access systems.

Odometer An indexing method of retrieving images that associates microrecord frames with linear distance in a file.

Outfolder A substitute folder used when a whole file folder is removed from a file cabinet or shelf.

Outguide A special guide used to substitute for a folder or a record that has been removed from the file.

Reading File A chronological file of extra copies of correspondence.

Reduction Ratio The ratio between the size of the original document and its photographically reduced image on microfilm.

Relative Index An index listing in alphabetic order giving all topic names in a subject filing system; also a cross-reference index or an index used with a numeric filing system.

Rerouting The process of lending a record out on loan to another borrower without first returning the record to the file room.

Secondary Guide A special guide used in cabinets or shelves to highlight frequently referenced sections of the file.

Soundex A filing system based on the phonetic spelling of a name.

Superseded Outdated.

Surname An individual's last name.

System A series of interrelated tasks or procedures followed to achieve a major goal.

Updatable Microfilm A process based on the ability of a piece of microfiche to be rearranged.

Variadex An alphabetic filing system in which the second letter of the surname name or first filing unit is color-coded.

UNIT 7

GRAMMAR, USAGE, AND STYLE

Grammatical Terms — G1

Correct Sentence Structure — G2-G4
  Sentence Construction Hints
  Sentence Flaws to Avoid

Punctuation — G5-G42
  Apostrophe
  Colon
  Comma
  Dash
  Exclamation Mark
  Hyphen
  Parentheses
  Period
  Question Mark
  Quotation Marks
  Semi-Colon
  Underscore

Selecting the Right Words — G43-G48
  Avoiding Trite Expressions
  Frequently Confused Words
  Misused Words
  One Word or Two?
  Words with Accompanying Prepositions

Grammar, Usage, and Style

Spelling   G49-G52
  Guides for Improving Spelling Ability
  Some Helpful Spelling Rules
  Frequently Misspelled Words

Style Mechanics   G53-G90
  Abbreviations
  Capitalization
  Numbers
  Plurals
  Word Division

Additional Reference Sources   G91

Improper use of language skills—punctuation, spelling, parts of speech, word division—hinders effective communication. This unit highlights key information needed to make effective English usage decisions. It is intended to serve as a good resource for future reference especially in areas where grammatical errors are commonly made. The information in this unit is not intended to replace a dictionary, a thesaurus, or a complete handbook of language usage, all of which are thorough and reliable reference sources.

Six major areas are covered in this unit: grammatical terms, correct sentence structure, punctuation, selecting the right words, spelling, and style preference in written communication.

G1 Grammatical Terms

The grammatical terms listed below represent some of the basic labels or parts of speech into which traditional English grammar words are classified. You may wish to refer to this list as you proceed with this unit.

Adjective A word that modifies (describes) a noun or pronoun.

> *long* dress; *fast* typist

> *Compound Adjective:* Two or more words that combine to describe a noun.

> a *good-looking* man, a *ten-speed* bicycle

Adverb A word that modifies a verb, adjective, or another adverb.

> She types *quickly*. That *rather* old typewriter . . .

Antecedent The noun or pronoun to which a pronoun refers.

> When *Sue* went shopping *she* forgot to buy cheese.

> Every *person* is entitled to express *his or her* opinion.

Appositive (In apposition) Expression that provides additional but nonessential information about a previously mentioned noun or pronoun.

> Our tour guide, *who wears a black beret,* is very experienced.

Grammar, Usage, and Style

Case The English language has three cases:

Nominative (subjective) (initiates action): I, he, she, we, they, who

He can type.

Objective (receives action): me, him, her, us, them, whom

Give *them* the book.

Possessive (ownership): my (mine), your (yours), etc.

We use *his* typewriter.

Clause A group of words in a compound or complex sentence containing both subject and predicate.

While the sun is shining . . .

Restrictive Clause: A group of words that is essential to the meaning of the sentence.

The man *who had a broken leg* limped home.

Non-Restrictive Clause: A group of words that does not affect the meaning of the sentence.

The man, *whose leg was broken last week,* is our chief accountant.

Conjunction A word or words used to connect sentence parts.

and, but, as well as, not only . . . but also

Gerund A form of the verb (ending in *ing*) that is used as a noun. Note that a noun or pronoun modifying a gerund is in the possessive case.

He appreciated *their* offering to help.

We approve of *their* coming with us.

He refused to go despite the crowd's urging.

Mood The mood of a verb shows the type of action of the verb and can be either:

Indicative: a statement of fact

She *can* drive a car.

Imperative: a command (frequently used with an exclamation mark)

G1 Grammatical Terms

>Close the door.
>
>Stop it!
>
>*Subjunctive:* a wish or conjecture
>
>If I *were* you . . .

Noun The name of a person, place, thing, animal, action, or concept.

>*Proper noun*: person—Richard Rogers
>
>>place—United States
>
>*Common noun:* thing—apple
>
>>animal—dog
>
>>action—labor
>
>*Abstract noun* (concept): love
>
>*Collective noun* (groups of things): committee, team

Number Singular or plural of nouns, pronouns, or verbs.

>apple/apples; him/them; she runs/they run

Object The part of a sentence that receives the action.

>The sun is shining on *us*.

Paragraph A series of sentences developing *one central purpose or idea.* The *topic* sentence opens the paragraph and the *transitional* one ends it, forming a link with the paragraph that follows.

>Golf is a game that many people play. Most of my friends are golf fanatics, and they particularly enjoy competition. (transitional)
>
>The club in town runs four major tournaments each season to test every golfer's skill . . . (topic)

Parenthetical Expression A word, phrase, or clause that does not change the meaning of a sentence but adds some expression to it.

>Every sales representative—63 to be exact—attended the conference.

Grammar, Usage, and Style

Participle A form of the verb in either present or past tense (freezing, frozen) that is used as an adjective.

Freezing January temperatures are uncomfortable.

Phrase A group of related words without a subject and predicate that functions as a single part of speech.

on the other hand,

Predicate The verb and its modifiers.

The sun *is shining brightly today*.

G2 Correct Sentence Structure

Sentences may be long or short, simple or complex. However, regardless of length, they must always be grammatically sound.

G3 Sentence Construction Hints

- Select your words with care. Use words only in their exact, precise meanings and contexts. Avoid wordiness.

  WORDY: The customer was mad because when he returned the merchandise the clerk was rude and she refused to give him the refund he was entitled to.

  BETTER: When the customer returned the merchandise, he was annoyed at the clerk's rudeness and refusal to refund the money.

- Be grammatically consistent. Avoid disagreements in number, tense, or mood.

  INCONSISTENCY IN NUMBER: Every one of the branch offices had their own sales quotas.

  CORRECTION: Every one of the branch offices had *its* own sales quotas.

Note: Certain indefinite pronouns, such as *anyone, each, everyone, everything, someone, either, neither, nobody,* and *another,* are always singular; therefore, a singular pronoun should be used.

G2-G3 Correct Sentence Structure

INCONSISTENCY IN TENSE: The vice-president of finance *approved* the higher dividend, and then the board of directors *rejects* it.

CORRECTION: The vice-president of finance approved the higher dividend, and then the board of directors rejected it.

INCONSISTENCY IN MOOD: We would appreciate it if you *can* come early.

CORRECTION: We would appreciate it if you *could* come early.

- Use parallel (balanced) structure to make your writing flow smoothly.

    NOT PARALLEL: Do you think *writing* or a *messenger* would be faster? (Here, *writing* is a participle; *messenger* is a noun.)

    CORRECTION: Do you think *the mail* or a *messenger* would be faster? (Here, *mail* and *messenger* are both nouns.)

- Avoid masculine bias whenever possible.

    Some nouns may be applied both to males and females: client, customer, student, employer, employee, professor. Try to word sentences with these nouns so that you avoid the use of *he* as a generic term applying to both males and females.

    WEAK: An *employer* should recognize that *he* is a role model for *his* workers.

    WEAK: An *employer* should recognize that *he or she* is a role model for *his or her* workers.

    BETTER: *Employers* should recognize that *they* are role models for *their* workers.

Note: Changing the wording from singular to plural or rewording the sentence to avoid the generic nouns will often help eliminate masculine biases in writing.

- Position modifiers properly. Closely related parts of a sentence should be placed close together to avoid ambiguity.

    IMPROPERLY PLACED MODIFIER: Having been previously trained on the equipment, the office manager asked Mary to demonstrate it.

    CORRECTION: The office manager asked Mary, who was previously trained on the equipment, to conduct the demonstration.

G

Grammar, Usage, and Style

- Use the active voice as much as possible. When the active voice is used the subject performs the action, making the writing style more interesting for the reader.

    WEAK: His name *will be seen* in lights. (Passive voice)

    BETTER: He *will see* his name in lights. (Active voice)

- Avoid excessive coordination. Too many *ands* or *buts* make reading cumbersome and boring.

    TOO MANY ANDS: I attended a meeting, and she stood up and took her time and started a long monologue on her new idea.

    CORRECTION: I attended a meeting during which she stood up and began a long monologue on her new idea.

- Place the part to be stressed at the beginning of the sentence.

    STRESS IMPROPERLY PLACED: They do more work than a human being in the same time, and they threaten many jobs, but computers calculate rapidly and we must use them.

    CORRECTION: We must use computers, in spite of their threat to many jobs, because they can calculate so rapidly.

G4 Sentence Flaws to Avoid

- Sentence fragment (incomplete thought)

    Although the singer is good.

    CORRECTION: The singer is good.

- Shifted constructions

    Because of an oil shortage and we are losing money, the plant will have to shut down.

    CORRECTION: Because of an oil shortage and a loss of money, the plant will have to shut down.

    or

    Because we are suffering from an oil shortage and are losing money, we will have to shut down.

G4 Sentence Flaws to Avoid

- Subject-verb disagreement

   His contribution to the school's funds were extremely high.

   CORRECTION: His contribution to the school's funds was extremely high.

   The president, as well as her staff, have arrived.

   CORRECTION: The president, as well as her staff, has arrived.

- Incorrect case

   We do not approve of them arriving late.

   CORRECTION: We do not approve of their arriving late.

Note: A noun or pronoun preceding a gerund (e.g. arriving), is written in the possessive case.

   Me and my brother are going shopping.

   CORRECTION: My brother and I are going shopping.

- Adjective and adverb confusion (see G46).

   He did a real good job.

   CORRECTION: He did a really good job.

   Note: In most cases, if *very* would be appropriate in the sentence, *really* is the correct choice between *really* and *real*.

   Kathy played good yesterday.

   CORRECTION: Kathy played a good game yesterday.

   or

   Kathy played well yesterday.

Note: *Well* answers the question, *How? Good* is an adjective and modifies a noun (game). *Well* is an adverb and modifies a verb (played).

- Comma fault (Do not use commas carelessly.)

   The woman with the broken leg, could not walk.

   CORRECTION: The woman with the broken leg could not walk (see this unit, G13).

Grammar, Usage, and Style

G5 Punctuation

Punctuation marks are designed to give a sentence meaning and expression by showing the relationships among its various parts.

Note: If you have difficulty choosing the appropriate punctuation for a sentence, it may be that your sentence has been improperly structured. Revise the sentence into a form that you know is correct.

G6 Apostrophe (')

G7 Contractions

When a letter or number is omitted, use an apostrophe: don't, doesn't, 'tis, I'll, Hallowe'en, '45, you're

You're sure Hallowe'en falls on October 31?

The class of '85 was a large one.

G8 Plurals

Although plurals of many isolated letters or words are formed by adding *s* only (see this unit, G83), an apostrophe is used before the *s* in cases where confusion might result with the addition of *s* only.

Please dot all the i's.

One can never earn too many A's.

G9 Possessives

To form the singular possessive, add an apostrophe plus *s* ('s).

Singular	Possessive
boy	boy's
woman	woman's
witness	witness's
secretary	secretary's
Joan Haslam	Joan Haslam's
Charles	Charles's

The boy's coat and the woman's shoes were dirty.

Joan Haslam's responsibility is to pay the secretary's salary.

You are invited to Charles's party tonight.

Note: Where the addition of apostrophe plus *s* would add a new syllable that would make pronunciation difficult, add the apostrophe only.

| Jesus | Jesus' |
| goodness | goodness' |

To form the plural possessive, add an apostrophe if the plural noun ends in *s* (s'); add an apostrophe plus *s* ('s) if it does not.

Singular	**Possessive**
boys	*boys'
women	women's
witnesses	*witnesses'
children	children's
gentlemen	gentlemen's

Boys' coats and women's shoes are on special this week.

The two witnesses' testimony continued all day.

The children's bulletin board was blank.

*The *s* after the apostrophe is omitted in most plural words ending in *s* to make pronunciation easier. The words noted above are examples.

Individual Ownership
Phil's and Maya's marks were good last term.
Apostrophes in both names make it clear that Phil had a high mark and Maya had a high mark, but they did not get the same mark.

Joint Ownership
John and Sarah's apartment is spacious.
The apostrophe in the latter name tells you that the apartment is shared by John and Sarah.

Expressions relating to time or measure employ the possessive

Could I have a dollar's worth of peanuts, please?

Justin will be home in two months' time.

She was released with one week's pay.

Grammar, Usage, and Style

G10 Colon (:)

G11 Direct Quotations

Introduce a quotation of more than three lines with a colon.

When you are feeling downhearted, remember these lines from the poem "Smile":

We know the distance to the sun.
   The size and weight of earth.
But no one's ever told us yet
   How much a smile is worth.

G12 Introductory Statement Followed by Lists or Series

Use a colon to introduce a list.

The agenda is as follows: . . .

They brought the following: . . .

We still need these dishes for the staff party: stroganoff, rice, salad, and broccoli.

G13 Comma (,)

The comma is the most common punctuation mark and is often misused and overworked. Apply common sense to your writing by asking yourself if there is need for a pause where you have placed the comma. Remember, "When in doubt, leave it out!"

G14 Adjectives

When two or more adjectives precede a noun, or when several adjectives follow the noun they are describing, use a comma.

He is a punctual, efficient employee.

That employee, punctual and efficient, deserves a raise.

Note: Do not use a comma between the adjectives if they are connected by *and*, *or*, or *nor*.

He is a punctual and efficient employee.

When the first adjective qualifies the second, omit the comma.

a large, red hat

a bright red hat

G15 Compound Sentences

When two independent clauses (clauses that express a complete thought and could stand alone as sentences) are joined by a conjunction and have *different* subjects, use a comma. (An exception is permitted if the sentence is very short and the conjunction is *and*.)

Our former office manager demanded a very high standard of work, but the new one is more interested in quantity than quality.

Exception: Our former office manager demanded high standards and the new one does not.

When two verbs share one subject, no comma is necessary.

Our former office manager demanded high standards and also insisted upon a high production rate.

G16 Correspondence

Dates
Separate the day from the year by a comma unless using the international date method.

September 1, 19--

1 September 19--

Place Names
Place commas after the street address and the town or city.

140 Franklin Drive, Reno, Nevada

Chicago, Illinois, is known as the "Windy City."

Names and Titles
Separate the name from the title with a comma.

Mr. J. Barry, Jr.

R. Newsome, Sales Manager

Grammar, Usage, and Style

G17 Non-Restrictive (Non-Essential) Clauses and Words or Phrases in Apposition

Non-restrictrive clauses and phrases are expressions that are not essential to the meaning of the word they modify but add information. They need a comma at the beginning and end to separate them from the remainder of the sentence.

The rain, which falls constantly in April, makes grass grow.

but

Only the rain that falls in April makes our grass grow.

Words or phrases in apposition explain something about the subject. They, too, require a comma at beginning and end.

The woman, hat in hand, came in from the rain.

Fred, an Irishman, was an excellent football player.

Use a comma on either side of the phrases beginning: *as well as, together with, in spite of, or, like,* and *such as*.

The man, as well as his wife, is coming to dinner.

Actors in New York, like those in Los Angeles, work hard.

Note: Restrictive clauses and phrases do not require commas because they are essential to the meaning of the sentence.

The man who held the smoking gun was the obvious killer.

The acid rain that fell around Omaha damaged the crops.

Note: Do not be trapped into using a comma between the subject and the verb unless these are separated by a non-restrictive clause

Incorrect: The small boy with curly hair, played the tuba.

Correct: The small boy with curly hair played the tuba.

or

The small boy, who had curly hair, played the tuba.

G17-G21 Non-Restrictive Clauses and Words or Phrases in Apposition

G18 Omission of Words

Insert a comma to indicate that one or more words have been omitted.

He traveled the scenic route; she, the most direct one.

Here, *traveled* is implied after *she.*

G19 Parenthetical Expressions

Parenthetical expressions are words that are not necessary to the meaning of a sentence but give added emphasis to it. These may occur at the beginning or in the middle of a sentence.

G20 At the Beginning of a Sentence (Introductory)

Place a comma after an introductory word, phrase, or clause.

Yes, Edgar is expected tonight.
Under the circumstances, it was the best decision.
When the rain stopped, we all went out for dinner.

G21 Within a Sentence

Place the parenthetical word(s) within commas.

Everyone knew, *of course,* that Edna would be captain.
The oldest person was, *however,* very dissatisfied.
England is, *without doubt,* a beautiful country.

The following words and phrases are common introductory and parenthetical expressions that should be set off with commas.

accordingly	consequently	fortunately
also	finally	further, furthermore
as a matter of fact	first, first of all	however
besides	for example	in fact

Grammar, Usage, and Style

in my opinion	nevertheless	thus
in other words	obviously	well
in the meantime	of course	without a doubt
meanwhile	otherwise	yet
moreover	personally	
needless to say	therefore	

G22 Series

In a series consisting of three or more elements in which the last item is preceded by *and*, *or*, or *nor*, place a comma before the conjunction and between the other items.

Her favorite colors are green, purple, and orange.

The visitors were expected to behave politely, to ask questions, and to return to the hotel by noon.

Note: Some authorities consider the final comma before a conjunction optional. However, modern business usage suggests inclusion of the comma.

G23 Dash (—)

A dash is a separating device. Use it to enlarge upon a point or to give emphasis to a statement.

He went west—Los Angeles, San Francisco, and Las Vegas—for the holidays.

Roger lost a tough battle—and I don't blame him for being disappointed.

The teacher—I'm pleased to say—gave them extra help.

Kate plays excellent tennis—she has lost only one match out of twenty this month.

G24 Exclamation Mark (!)

Use an exclamation mark to indicate surprise, enthusiasm, strong emotion, or a command.

Happy Birthday, Dad!

Stop, thief!

Use the exclamation mark after the interjections *Ah* and *Oh*.

Ah! What low prices.
Oh! How beautiful.

When a single exclamatory word is used as a sentence, use the exclamation mark.

Help!
Wait!

G25 Hyphen (-)

Use a hyphen to join words or syllables.

G26 Compound Adjectives and Words

When two or more words are used in combination immediately preceding the noun they modify, join them with a hyphen to form a compound adjective.

They went away for a four-day holiday.
My car has an eight-cylinder engine.
Her brother is a good-looking man.

When each adjective separately describes the subject, use a comma.

Her brother is a big, strong man.

G27 Fractions

Use hyphens for fractions used as *adjectives* and *adverbs* but not those used as nouns. When used as nouns, fractions are often followed by *of*.

Two thirds of the residents are employed downtown.
A two-thirds vote is necessary for the bill to pass.

G28 Numbers

Use a hyphen when the spelled-out number consists of two or more words.

The band consisted of twenty-nine musicians.

G29 Prefixes

Many prefixes require the use of a hyphen after them.

A post-mortem is required when a person dies from unknown causes.

The ex-Senator attended the ceremony.

G30 Parentheses ( ) and Brackets [ ]

G31 Parentheses

Use parentheses with explanatory material incidental to the context. The expression is made by the author of the sentence.

Grammar (essential to every student) is high on the priority list.

Also use parentheses to give reference.

Letter styles (Chapter 3) was the next topic covered.

G32 Brackets

Use brackets to set off inserted matter that is incidental to the context. The insertion is made by someone other than the author, such as an editor's comments or explanations.

In 1984 she [Ferraro] was the first woman to receive a major party's nomination for vice-president.

G33 Period (.)

Use a period after a sentence, an abbreviation, and with figures in various contexts. A period at the end of a sentence is followed by two spaces. All other periods are followed by one space.

The sun came up very early that day.
Mr. S. Eby
U.S.S.R.
I.R.S.

a.m.
Ph.D.
1.82 percent
2:55 p.m.
6.667

> **Note:** If an abbreviation closes a sentence, only one period is needed at the end of that sentence.
>
> The goods should have been shipped C.O.D.
>
> Use a period instead of a question mark when you are making more of a demand than a request.
>
> Would you kindly forward your check at once.
>
> (Compare with: Did you receive the check we sent?)

G34 Question Mark (?)

Use a question mark:

after a direct question

    How much does it cost?

to express doubt (place the question mark in parentheses and use after the doubtful term)

    He was born in 1947(?).

Do *not* use a question mark:

after an indirect question

    I asked him how much it cost.

after a request

    Will you please find out the cost.

G35 Quotation Marks (" ")

Quotation marks are used in two ways:

G36 Direct Quotes

The man cried, "Stop, thief!" and then fired.

He said, "Stop, or I'll shoot."

Did he say, "Stop, or I'll shoot"? No, he did not.

"If you don't stop," he said, "I'll shoot."

G37 Titles

Titles of articles, essays, sermons, speeches, poems, and parts of magazines and books are indicated by quotation marks.

The poem, "Ode on a Grecian Urn," by Keats, is famous.

When you read Chapter 5, "Punctuation," study the section entitled "Comma."

> **Note:** Use single quotation marks for the second quote when a quote within a quote must be indicated.
>
> She said, "I heard him say 'Be on time.'"

Punctuation

Commas and periods are always placed *inside* quotation marks.

The manager said, "Your report is due tomorrow."

Colons and semicolons are always placed *outside* quotation marks.

Chapter 12 is entitled, "Punctuation"; please read it before our next class.

Exclamation marks and question marks are placed *inside* quotation marks when they belong with the quoted words only, and *outside* when they belong with the entire sentence.

When the alarm sounded, he shouted, "Fire!"

Have you read the article, "Effective Business Communication"?

G38 Semicolon (;)

The semicolon has three main uses.

G39 Compound Sentences

If a comma is used in either of the two independent clauses, use a semicolon before the conjunction.

It was a hot, humid day; and we were concerned about the temperature in the data processing center.

Separate independent but related clauses, which are not connected by a conjunction, with a semicolon.

The wind was high; the sea was rough.

The letters were dictated; they were then keyboarded on the text editor.

G40 With Conjunctive Adverbs

The words *then, however, thus, hence, indeed, accordingly, besides,* and *therefore* are considered adverbs rather than conjunctions and should be preceded by a semicolon when used between the clauses of a compound sentence.

He scheduled a meeting for tomorrow morning; however, no definite time has been set.

G41 Series

Use a semicolon for clarity when the items being separated contain commas.

Most of the executives were present: Hugh Fine, President, New York; Elizabeth Byrnes, Treasurer, Iowa; Todd Honeker, Secretary, Maine; and Amy Scott, Historian, California.

G42 Underscore (__)

Use the underscore (underline) in handwritten or typewritten material to indicate titles of books, plays, works of art, magazines, newspapers, words that need emphasis, and foreign expressions.

Hard Times is a fine novel by Charles Dickens.

The last issue of Forbes contained an interesting article.

Have you seen Michelangelo's sculpture, the Pieta?

Please tell Bill that this order is rush.

G43 Selecting the Right Words

To eliminate communication barriers, the writer or speaker must select the right words so that the message is received and understood. To be effective, business correspondence and oral expression should be straightforward and natural. The complexity of the English language

Grammar, Usage, and Style

sometimes causes confusion and, as a result, words are misused. This section will help you overcome some common communication barriers; however, since no one source could possibly supply you with answers to all of the problem situations you might encounter, be prepared to do further research in the dictionary and/or one or more English usage books.

G44 Avoiding Trite Expressions

Let one word do the work of three or four whenever possible; do not use cliches or old-fashioned expressions in the hope of making a good impression on the reader. Outdated words and expressions cause communication barriers. Table 7.1 lists words to avoid and those to use.

Table 7.1 Avoiding Trite Expressions

Avoid	Use	Example
(We) acknowledge receipt of	Thank you	Thank you for your letter . . .
(We) are in receipt of your	We have received	We have received our shipment of . . .
At all times	Always	We always enjoy our business association with you.
At an early date	Soon, immediately	We hope to have an answer soon.
At this point in time	Now, at present	Your representative is here now.
cognizant	aware	I am certain you are aware that . . .
Due to the fact that	Because, since, as	Because the workers are on strike . . .
Enclosed please find	Enclosed is (are)	Enclosed is my check for . . .
Encounter difficulty	Have trouble, need help	If you need help, please call us.
Free of charge	free, at no charge	We will make the repair free if . . .
In a position to	can	As soon as I can . . .
In due course	As soon as, when	My client will pay as soon as she is able.
In re	regarding, about	Your suggestion regarding the annual bonus . . .
In the amount of	for	Your check for $10 arrived today.

G44-G45 Avoiding Trite Expressions

Table 7.1 Continued.

In the event that	in case, if	If it rains, the game will be called.
In the near future	Soon, shortly	You can expect to hear from us soon.
In view of the fact that	Because, since	They had to go because he said so.
I remain	Do not use.	
May we anticipate an early reply?	May we hear from	May we hear from you soon?
Of the opinion that	think	I think this is a good time to . . .
Per	a	The cost was $16 a dozen.
Reiterate	restate, state again	I wish to restate the facts.
Tell Jim or myself	tell Jim or me	Why not tell Jim or me the details?

G45 Frequently Confused Words

Words that sound alike but have different meanings are called *homonyms*. Homonyms often pose a challenge for writers and transcriptionists. Never guess when it comes to selecting which like-sounding words to use. This list represents some of the most frequently confused words. If you need to look up other words, add them to Table 7.2 so that they will be readily available to you.

Table 7.2 Frequently Confused Words

Word	Meaning	Example
accept	to receive	Please accept this present from us.
except	not including	Everyone except Julio was invited.
access	a way or means of approaching, getting or using	The password enabled him to access the information in the computer's data base.
excess	over abundance; too much	She went on a diet to get rid of her excess weight.
adverse	hostile	Arguing with a customer has an adverse effect on business.
averse	opposed	Politicians are averse to being blunt.

285

Grammar, Usage, and Style

Table 7.2 Continued.

advice (n.)	counsel	Their advice was freely given.
advise (v.)	to recommend	Please advise me of the best action to take.
		The lawyer was eager to advise the client.
affect (v.)	to move or to touch (mind)	Love will affect a child positively.
effect (n.)	consequence, result	The price increase had a negative effect on sales.
effect (v.)	to accomplish	We will do all we can to effect prompt delivery.
alternate	one of two choices	She took the scenic route; we took the alternate one.
alternative	choice of several	When four roads meet, the driver has three alternatives: turn right, turn left, or go straight.
assistance	help, aid	The temporary secretary provided the assistance we needed.
assistants	helpers	The managers and their assistants were present.
billed	sent a bill, charged	He was not billed for the broken lamp.
build	to construct	The ordinance would not let the contractor build on the site.
capital	city where the government of a country or state is located	Austin is the capital of Texas.
	money or property a company uses in carrying on business	The new computer was a capital expense.
	an upper case letter	The first word of a sentence always begins with a capital letter.
capitol	building in which a legislative body meets	Many state capitol buildings are fine examples of outstanding architecture.
choose	to select	Please choose the one you want.
chose	past tense of choose	He chose the blue one.

Table 7.2 Continued.

cite	to quote	The witness was asked to cite an example.
sight	view	What a wonderful sight the ocean was!
site	location	The new site for our home has been chosen.
coarse	rough, common	The unfinished table has a coarse surface.
course	path, way	Every ship's captain must plot a safe course.
	division of a meal	We ate the seven-course meal slowly.
	outline of a subject to be learned	The teacher prepared the course of study for Grade 11 English.
complement	to fill up or complete	Use alyssum to complement the flower arrangement.
compliment	polite expression of praise	It is kind to pay a compliment.
council (n.)	administrative body	The San Antonio Council meets this week.
counsel (n. or v.)	guidance	Ask for counsel from someone with experience.
	to advise	Parents should counsel their children wisely.
decent	respectable	Returning a lost article is the decent action to take.
descent	decline, downward motion	The elevator's descent from the tenth to the ground floor was fast.
dissent (n. or v.)	disagree(ment)	The dissent between players caused their team to lose.
defer to	to respect the opinion of	It is customary for young people to defer to older people.
	to postpone	Shall we defer the meeting until next week?
differ	to be unlike	Their opinions differed, so they reached a compromise.
defective	faulty	The defective computer was returned to the store.

Table 7.2 Continued.

deficient	incomplete	This office is deficient—it has no typewriter.
desert (n. or v.)	to abandon	The ruler was deserted by his followers.
	barren land	Sand is everywhere in the desert.
dessert	sweet course	The dessert after dinner will be Baked Alaska.
eligible	fit to be chosen	Your training makes you eligible for this job.
illegible	unreadable	That doctor's writing is illegible.
emigrant	person leaving country	Sanjay is an emigrant from Kenya.
immigrant	person entering country	Joe Chan is an immigrant to Canada.
eminent	distinguished	The Queen of England is an eminent lady.
imminent	about to happen	They were told a hurricane was imminent.
formally	according to form, rule	Please dress formally for the Prime Minister's dinner.
formerly	previously	His mother's family was formerly from Poland.
foreword	preface	A book often contains a foreword.
forward	in front	Please go forward ten paces.
hear	to listen	A bird's song is pleasant to hear.
here	in this place	Bring the files here, please.
incite	to stir up	The union leader incited the workers to riot.
insight	penetration with understanding	A year in India will give you an insight into some Asian cultures.
its	possessive form of *it*	The lion protects its young.
it's	contraction for *it is*	It's the end of the year on December 31.
last	final	The last train left at 2:30 p.m.

G45 Frequently Confused Words

Table 7.2 Continued.

latest	most recent	What is the latest news on world food supplies?
later	farther on in time	The later we dine, the hungrier we will be.
latter	second of two	Sue and Carol came together; the latter drove.
loose (adj.)	free	Because his shoe was loose, it fell off.
lose (v.)	to be deprived of	They may lose their place if they are not here soon.
moral	concerned with distinction between right and wrong	Children's moral behavior is patterned after adults' behavior.
morale	mental condition or attitude	The morale in our office is very high under the new manager.
overdo	to go too far	If you overdo the exercise, you may be injured.
overdue	late, past the due time	The March payment is long overdue.
passed	past tense of *to* pass	Every student passed the exam.
past	beyond in time or place	It is now past midnight.
personal	one's own	Each member is entitled to a personal opinion.
personnel	body of workers	All our personnel are trained.
peruse	to examine carefully	Please peruse the report and give me your opinion.
pursue	to follow with intent to catch	The tiger pursued the deer.
precede	to go before	A precedes B in the alphabet.
proceed	to go on	Let us proceed with the meeting.
principal	chief, major; capital, sum	The principal cause of car accidents is careless driving.
principle	fundamental truth	Accounting principles require considerable study.
	personal code of conduct	Albert Schweitzer's high principles brought him world renown.

Table 7.2 Continued.

stationary	unmoving	A statue is stationary.
stationery	writing materials	Most firms have printed stationery.
their	possessive form of *they*	Their house is very large.
there	in that place	Take this cake over there, please, Jill.
they're	contraction for *they are*	They're late for the meeting.
weather	atmospheric conditions	The weather forecast called for rain.
whether	which of two alternatives	I do not know whether or not they are coming.
whose	possessive form of *who*	Whose hat is this?
who's	contraction for *who is*	The one who's first gets the prize.
your	possessive form of *you*	Make sure you take your own pen.
you're	contraction for *you are*	When you're in Spain, speak Spanish.

G46 Misused Words

Certain words and phrases are frequently misused. The following is a list of the most commonly misused expressions and their acceptable forms.

among and **between**

Use *between* when two items are referred to; *among* for more than two items.

The argument is only between you and me.

Please solve the problem among all of you.

and etc. and **etc.**

etc. means "and the rest" or "and so forth;" therefore *and etc.* is redundant.

One to the second power, two to the second power, etc., can be calculated easily using an electronic calculator.

G46 Misused Words

and/or
Avoid using *and/or*. It is better to write a sentence as follows:

Either the administrative assistant or the secretary may provide the support work for an executive.

anyplace and **anywhere**
Use *anywhere* only. Avoid using anyplace.

Is there a restaurant anywhere near here?

anyways and **anyway**
There is no such word as *anyways*.

He had to be present anyway.

bring and **take**
Use *bring* to this place (here); and *take* to that place (there).

Will you bring the report when you come?

Take these books home with you when you go.

can and **may**
Can implies capability; *may* signifies a request or probability.

An athlete can usually run fast.

May my friends join me for the conference?

The meeting may take place in Dallas, Texas.

come and **go**
Use *come* when implying "here;" *go* when meaning "there."

The hostess is expecting twenty guests to come for lunch.

I am going to Florida for Easter vacation.

every which way and **in all directions**
Every which way is slang and should be avoided. *In all directions* is preferred.

The traffic seemed to be moving in all directions at the same time.

Grammar, Usage, and Style

enclosed herewith and **enclosed**
Avoid using enclosed herewith; it is a trite expression.

Enclosed is my data sheet for your review.

good and **well**
The adjective *good* must modify a noun; *well* is used as an adverb or adjective.

She did a good job. (*good* as an adjective)

He did well. (*well* as an adverb)

I am well. (*well* as an adjective)

in regards to and **in regard to**
In regard to is correct.

Call me in regard to your recent order.

lay and **lie**
Lay means "to place" and requires a direct object; *lie* means "to recline" and can stand alone.

Edith was asked to lay the documents on the desk.

Robert had to lie down every afternoon while he was recuperating from his illness.

real and **really** (see G4)
Real is an adjective that describes a noun; *really* is an adverb.

She ran a really effective meeting.

She is wearing a real diamond bracelet.

seeing as how and **since**
Seeing as how is slang and should be avoided. *Since* is preferred.

Since you read the report carefully, you can summarize it for us.

shall and **will**
In formal English, to indicate:
future: use *shall* in the first person (I shall, we shall); *will* in the second and third person (you will, he will, they will).

We shall submit the report tomorrow.

She will make the decision this week.

G46 Misused Words

determination: use *will* in the first person (I will, we will); *shall* in the second and third persons (you shall, he shall, they shall)

We will strike if agreement is not reached.

You shall return by 10 p.m.

Note: In modern usage, *will* is increasingly used in all persons to express both future and determination.

I expect I will have a good trip. (future)

I will complete this report by tomorrow no matter what happens. (determination)

some place and **somewhere**
Some place is incorrect.

I left my glasses somewhere.

than and **then**
Use *than* for making comparisons; use *then* when referring to time.

The tall boy is much stronger than the short one.

First came the caviar; then came the pheasant.

there is and **there are**
Is refers to a singular noun; *are* refers to a plural one.

There is only one Queen of England.

There are many books to be sold.

who and **which**
Who refers to a person; *which,* to a thing.

The man who delivered the computer was very polite.

The telephone, which is near the door, is within easy reach.

you're and **your**
You're is the contraction for you are; *your* is the possessive of you.

You're one of our very best workers.

Your workers are going to receive a pay increase.

G47 One Word or Two?

If you are in doubt, refer to the list below.

all ready (all prepared): They are all ready to go.

already (adv.) (past the time): It is already too late for lunch.

all right (acceptable, satisfactory): Everyone agreed that the office layout was all right. (Alright: incorrect spelling of *all right*.)

all together (in unison): The choir should sing all together.

altogether (adv.) (entirely): Your holiday was altogether too expensive.

any time (adj. and n.) (used with a specific time in mind): If you have any time next week, please call.

anytime (adv.) (used when no specific time is intended): You are welcome here anytime.

any way: Is there any way in which we can help?

anyway (adv.) (in any case): Anyway, the game had already been won. (There is no such word as *anyways*.)

every day (each day): It is good to practice every day.

may be: The children may be going out this afternoon.

maybe (adv.) (perhaps): Maybe the children will go out soon.

no body: There was no body found in that murder case.

nobody (pronoun) (no one): Nobody came to the party.

some time (adj. and n.) (used with a specific time in mind): Snow usually falls some time in January.

sometime (adv.) (used when no specific time is intended): He promised to call her sometime.

sometimes (adv.) (on occasion): Sometimes it is difficult to sit up straight.

G47-G50   One Word or Two?

G48 Words With Accompanying Prepositions

Certain words in English must be accompanied by a particular preposition. For example:

accompanied *by*	She was accompanied by her mother.
according *to*	According to the news, the damage was great.
capable *of*	Jim is capable of doing that job well.
comply *with*	If you agree, please comply with my request promptly.
concur *in* (something)	Everyone did not concur in that decision.
concur *with* (people)	The president concurred with the manager.
conform *to*	The building does not conform to specifications.
different *from* (not *to* or *than*	Bill is quite different from Ned.
plan *to* (not on)	Let us plan to stay slim while on vacation.
superior *to* (not than)	One twin is superior in intelligence to the other.
surrounded *by*	That farmhouse is surrounded by fields.
try *to*	Please try to see it my way.

G49 Spelling

Anyone who can spell accurately possesses a valuable skill and is viewed as an attentive and careful person. Like any skill, spelling can be improved in direct proportion to the attempts made to improve. Spelling is closely related to reading ability, vocabulary development, and proofreading skill. Having *word sense* is a critical skill that office workers need to strive to develop.

G50 Guides for Improving Spelling Ability

- Recognize that spelling can be improved and make a commitment to do so.
- Aim for precision in the pronunciation of words.

Grammar, Usage, and Style

- Develop and use memory aids:

    There's a rat in *sepa<u>rat</u>e*.

    p<u>ie</u>ce of *pie*

- Be conscious of misspelled words and keep your own list of troublesome words for study and reference.
- Think in syllables as this is helpful in word division and proofreading.
- Classify words into groups and apply spelling rules whenever possible:

    Example: *i* before *e* except after *c*

    Or when sounded like *a*

    As in neighbor and weigh

- Develop skill in using the dictionary.

G51 Some Helpful Spelling Rules

Dropping the Final E

Drop the final *e* from the root word when adding a suffix beginning with a vowel: <u>i</u>ble, <u>a</u>ble, <u>i</u>ng, <u>e</u>r, <u>e</u>d and <u>o</u>r are examples.

give becomes giving; write becomes writer

Exceptions: Do not drop the final *e* from words ending in *ce* and *ge* when adding the suffix *able*:

trace becomes traceable

change becomes changeable

or when adding a suffix beginning with a consonant: *

complete becomes completely

hope becomes hopefully

require becomes requirement

*There are exceptions to this rule however, so check your dictionary for specific cases.

Adding Word Endings

When adding a suffix (word ending) that begins with a vowel, double the final consonant if all three conditions below are met:

- if the word ends in a single consonant (except *x*)
- if the consonant is preceded by a single vowel
- if the word is pronounced with the accent on the last syllable.

Example:

> control—ends in a single consonant; the single consonant *l* is preceded by the vowel *o;* the accent is on the last syllable when pronouncing *control;* therefore: controller, controlling, controlled

Words that end in *y* preceded by a consonant usually require that the *y* be changed to *i* before adding the suffix except those beginning with *i*; words ending in *y* preceded by a vowel do not change the *y* to *i* before adding the suffix.

Examples:

study becomes studies, studied, studying

destroy becomes destroys, destroying, destroyed

Plurals

(See this unit, G8, G9, and G83.)

G52 Frequently Misspelled Words

The words listed in Table 7.3 frequently pose spelling problems. Take time to study these words often. If you have trouble with spelling, check your dictionary.

Table 7.3 Frequently Misspelled Words

absence	advisable	ascertain	bulletin
accidentally	all right	assessment	business
accommodate	amortize	attitude	calendar
achievement	analysis	bachelor	campaign
acquaintance	analyze	bankruptcy	carriage
acquiesce	apparently	beginning	catalog
acquisition	argument	believe	category
advantageous	arrears	beneficiary	champagne

Grammar, Usage, and Style

Table 7.3 Continued

changeable	forty	neighbor	restaurant
chauffeur	fourteen	neither	rhythm
column	friend	nickel	schedule
commitment	fulfill	ninety	seize
committee	gauge	ninth	separate
concede	government	noticeable	similar
congratulate	grammar	occasionally	simultaneous
conscience	grateful	occurred	sincerely
conscientious	grievance	occurrence	skillful
conscious	guarantee	omission	sponsor
convenience	handkerchief	omitted	subpoena
correspondence	harass	oversight	substantial
courteous	height	pamphlet	subtle
courtesy	hors d'oeuvres	parallel	subtly
criticism	hundredth	permissible	succeed
debt	hypocrisy	perseverance	suing
deceive	inasmuch as	personnel	surprise
defendant	incidentally	persuade	susceptible
definitely	indictment	phase	synonym
dependent	indispensable	possession	tariff
desirable	intercede	precede	technique
development	irrelevant	preferable	temperament
dilemma	itinerary	prejudice	thoroughly
disappoint	jewelry	prerogative	unanimous
discreet	leisure	privilege	useable
dissatisfied	library	procedure	vacuum
dividend	liaison	proceed	vice versa
efficiency	license	professor	warehouse
eighth	lien	promissory	Wednesday
embarrass	lieutenant	pronunciation	weird
en route	lightning	psychiatric	whether
etiquette	loose	psychology	wholly
exaggerate	lose	peruse	wield
exceed	lying	questionnaire	withhold
exercise	maintenance	queue	woolen
exhaustible	meantime	receipt	writing
extension	mileage	receive	yield
facsimile	miscellaneous	recognize	
fascinating	mischievous	recommend	
February	mortgage	reference	
foreign	necessary	resistance	

G53 Style Mechanics

Both the writer and the transcriptionist must be concerned with detail. Rules on abbreviation styles, capitalization principles, numeral usage, and guidelines for word division are presented below.

G54 Abbreviations

Generally, abbreviations should be avoided because it is possible for them to be misinterpreted or misunderstood. However, they are acceptable in statistical or tabulated matter. Let the following slogan guide you in a decision as to whether or not to abbreviate: WHEN IN DOUBT, SPELL IT OUT! Follow these rules when using abbreviations:

- Use only commonly accepted abbreviations that cannot be misunderstood.
- Use capitals only if the word being abbreviated is a word that should be capitalized.

    Nov.   etc.   Mon.   et. al.

    Note: Most abbreviations consisting only of initial letters are capitalized—for example, I.O.U., U.S.

- For companies, agencies, unions, and societies, use only the abbreviations shown in the legally registered title—for example, the abbreviations in the organization's letterhead.
- Use the ampersand (&) *only if used in official company names,* but never in text matter.

    Braithewaite & Singer   Zimmer & Co., Inc.

- Abbreviate months or days of the week in tabular material only where space is very limited.

G55 Addresses

- For special abbreviations on envelopes, see Appendix, page A2.

Grammar, Usage, and Style

G56 Business Terms

Table 7.4 contains standard abbreviations that are frequently used in such business communications as forms and tables.

Table 7.4 Business Terms

Abbreviation	Meaning
acct., a/c	account
A.D.	Anno Domini (in the year of our Lord)
ASAP	as soon as possible
amt.	amount
assoc., assn.	association
asst.	assistant
B/L	bill of lading
B/S	bill of sale
Blvd.	boulevard
bros.	brothers
bul.	bulletin
C	hundred or Centigrade
c.i.f.	cost, insurance, freight
carbon copy	c.c., cc
c/o	care of
Co.	Company
c.o.d.	cash on delivery
Corp.	corporation
C.P.S.	Certified Professional Secretary
cm	centimeter
cr.	credit
d/b/a, dba	doing business as
dept.	department
D.D.	Doctor of Divinity
D.D.S.	Doctor of Dental Surgery
doz.	dozen
dr.	debit
Dr.	Doctor

Table 7.4 Continued

ea.	each
e.g.	for example
enc.	enclosure
e.o.m., EOM	end of month
Esq.	Esquire
et al.	and others
exp.	expense
ext.	extension
FBI	Federal Bureau of Investigation
FCC	Federal Communications Commission
FDIC	Federal Deposit Insurance Corporation
FIFO	first-in, first-out
f.o.b.	free on board
FRB	Federal Reserve Board
ft.	feet, foot
FTC	Federal Trade Commission
fwd.	forward
FY	fiscal year
FYI	for your information
gal.	gallon
gds.	goods
GHQ	General Headquarters
gm	gram
GNP	Gross National Product
govt.	government
Hon.	Honorable
hp.	horsepower
ht.	height
Hwy.	highway
ibid.	in the same place
ICC	Interstate Commerce Commission
ill., illus.	illustration, illustrated
in.	inches

Table 7.4 Continued.

Inc.	Incorporated
incl.	inclusive
inv.	invoice
IOU	I owe you
I.Q.	intelligence quotient
ital.	italics
J.D.	Doctor of Jurisprudence
J.P.	Justice of the Peace
Jr.	Junior
jt.	joint
L	fifty
lab.	laboratory
lat.	latitude
L/C	Letter of Credit
LIFO	last in, first out
L.S.	in place of the seal
Ltd.	Limited
lv.	leave
M	thousand
M.A.	Master of Arts
M.B.A.	Master of Business Administration
M.C.	Master of Ceremonies
M.D.	Doctor of Medicine
mdse.	merchandise
mfg.	manufacturing
Mgr.	Manager
misc.	miscellaneous
mkt.	market
Mr.	Mister
ms.	manuscript
Ms.	Miss or Mrs.
n	net
n/c, NC	no charge
n.g.	no good

Table 7.4 Continued

no.	number
N.S.F.	not sufficient funds
n/10	net ten days
O/P	out of print
opt.	optional
O/S	out of stock
P/A	power of attorney
PBX	private branch exchange
pd.	paid
pfd.	preferred
Ph.D.	Doctor of Philosophy
pg.	page
pkg.	package
P.O.	Post Office
pop.	population
pr.	pair
Prof.	Professor
P.S.	postscript
pt.	pint, part
qt.	quart
qtr.	quarter
qty.	quantity
rec.	receivable
recd.	received
ref.	reference
reg., regd.	registered
rev.	revised
Rev.	Reverend
R.F.D.	Rural Free Delivery
R.R.	roural route
R.S.V.P.	reply, if you please
rt.	right
rte.	route
sav.	savings

Grammar, Usage, and Style

Table 7.4 Continued

sec., Secy.	Secretary
SEC	Securities Exchange Commission
Sen.	Senate, Senator
shpt.	shipment
sic	so, thus
sq.	square
Sr.	senior
St.	Street, Saint
std.	standard
Supt.	Superintendent
Treas.	Treasurer
twp.	township
U.N.	United Nations
Univ.	University
UPI	United Press International
V	five (Roman Numeral)
VIP	very important person
vol.	volume
vs., v.	versus
wk.	week
wt.	weight
yd.	yard
yr.	year

G57 Dates and Times

- If the abbreviations B.C. or A.D. are to be shown, use them only when dates are numerals.
- Use a.m. and p.m. (upper or lower case—lower case preferred) when hours are shown as numerals (not to be used when 24 hour clock is used).

1948 A.D., 11:45 p.m., 13:30

G58 Measurements

Metric (See Appendix, pp. A4 thru A6.)

G59 Places

States (See inside front cover.)

G60 Compass Points (in technical material only)

Abbreviate using capital letters.

N   NE   W   SW   NNW   SSE   etc.

G61 Publication Terms

Some common abbreviations used in publishing follow.

ch., chap.	chapter	p., pp.	page(s)
div.	division	sec.	section
fig., figs.	figure(s)	v., vs.	verse(s)
ill., illus.	illustration, illustrated	vol., vols.	volume(s)
l., ll.	line(s)		

G62 Titles After Names

Some common abbreviations following a person's name are:

Jr., Sr., M.A., B.A., M.D., Esq.

R. A. Kahn, Ph.D

Dr. R. Farmer, Jr.

Use a comma before and after the abbreviation when it appears in the middle of a sentence.

Dr. R. Farmer, Jr., will speak at our annual meeting.

G63 Titles Before Names

(See C24 and C25.)

G64 Capitalization

Proper capitalization gives importance and emphasis to words. It is used to identify sentence beginnings and proper nouns. There is some disagreement among authorities on specific capitalization rules, but the trend today is toward a decreased use of unnecessary capitalization in business writing.

In general, capitalize proper nouns and words that begin a sentence. Each of the following sections identifies specific instances where capitalization is necessary.

G65 Academic Field

Capitalize as follows:

Specific Courses: Linguistics I, Spanish 307, Biology 203

Degrees: B.A., Ph.D., M.Sc., LL.B., Ed.D., M.B.A.

Titles: Professor William Chiu, Dr. Yvonne Borden

Note: Language names are always capitalized.

Carl enjoyed French and Japanese, but he did not like accounting or science.

G66 Advertising Trademarks

Capitalize trademarks.

Dove, Shake and Bake, Tide, Xerox

G67 Astronomical Bodies

Capitalize astronomical bodies.

The Great Bear, The Milky Way, Venus, Mars

Note: When *sun*, *moon*, or *earth* are used with other astronomical bodies, they should be capitalized also.

G68 Calendar Dates and Holidays

Capitalize festivals and holidays as well as the months and days of the year.

Easter Sunday	Rosh Hashana	Martin Luther King Day
Valentine's Day	the Fourth of July	Cinco de Mayo
Halloween	Hanukkah	

> **Note:** Do not capitalize the seasons unless the season is being personified (that is, referred to as though it were a living being).
>
> Does your heating system protect you from Old Man Winter's chill?
>
> **but**
>
> Our spring line of dresses will arrive shortly.

G69 Family Relationships

Capitalize words that show family relationships when the word precedes the person's name or is used in place of the person's name.

Uncle Bob is here.   Mom is a good cook.

Is Dad home?

but

Do not capitalize words showing family relationships when such a word is preceded by a possessive pronoun.

My sister's boyfriend is nice.   I like my aunt's new car.

I met my uncle at the airport.

G70 Geographic Terms

Compass points should be capitalized only when a specific place is intended.

The Jones family went out West for their vacation.

He drove west from his last stop in Chicago.

The golf courses in South Carolina are lovely.

How far south do you plan to drive?

G71 Government and Political References

Capitalize as follows:

Acts, Treaties

   the Statute of Limitations

   the Universal Code

   the Wagner Act

   the Vocational Education Amendment

Grammar, Usage, and Style

Bodies

The Federal Bureau of Investigation

The Chamber of Commerce

The Iowa Division of Motor Vehicles

The Supreme Court of the State of New Jersey

Parties

the Republican Party and the Democratic Party

but

Both parties had to agree to the format of the presidential debates.

Titles

> **Note:** Usually only the titles *President, Vice-President, Senator,* and *Supreme Court Justice* are capitalized. Others are lower case unless they precede the name of the person.
>
> the lieutenant governor of New York
>
> the United States ambassador to Italy
>
> Senator Robert E. Dugan

G72 Institutions

Capitalize names of institutions.

Harvard University

The University of Maryland

The Mount Carmel Institute for the Blind

Beth Tzedec Synagogue

G73 Letter Openings and Closings

Capitalize the first word in the salutation of a letter, plus all nouns and titles in the salutation.

Dear Friend	Ladies and Gentlemen
Dear Mr. and Mrs. Barker	Dear Ms. Smith

Capitalize only the first word in the complimentary close of a letter.

Sincerely yours	Very truly yours

G74 Monuments and Parks

Capitalize names of monuments and parks.

The Statue of Liberty
Central Park
the Liberty Bell
the Boston Commons
the Washington Monument
Washington Square Park

G75 Nationalities, Languages, Races

Capitalize nationalities, languages and races of people.

Asian
Hispanic
Chinese
Black
Italian
Caucasian

G76 Organizations

Capitalize names of organizations. **Note:** Minor words—of, the, and—are not capitalized.

the Benevolent and Protective Order of Elks

Association of Records Managers and Administrators

Professional Secretaries International

the Girl Scouts of America

G77 Places

Names of specific places, such as continents, countries, nationalities, bodies of water, provinces, cities, valleys, mountains, regions, and localities, should be capitalized.

The Hudson River
Essex County
the St. Lawrence River
the Appalachian Mountains
the Lincoln Tunnel
the Golden Gate Bridge

Grammar, Usage, and Style

> **Note:** Do not capitalize these nouns when they are used in the plural. Only the actual names are capitalized.
>
> the Atlantic and Pacific oceans
>
> the Jordan and Nile rivers
>
> the Holland and Baltimore-Washington tunnels
>
> Morris and Bergen counties

G78 Publications

Capitalize all the important words in titles of plays, books, articles, newspapers, magazines, operas, pictures, and long poems.

In Search of Excellence	The Barber of Seville
Office Automation and Administration	Beethoven's Fifth Symphony
the New York Times	Gone With the Wind

> **Note:** Titles of books, plays, works of art, magazines, newspapers, words that need emphasis, and foreign expressions should be underlined as well as capitalized.

G79 Punctuation Marks

Capitalize the first letter after the following:

Colon when it introduces a complete sentence or a series of complete sentences.

> The Pocono Mountains are beautiful: The mountains, lakes, and streams provide year-round recreation.
>
> She made three suggestions: Get everyone to take part, invite only the officers to take part, have a representation of five officers and five members take part.

but

> She made three suggestions: all participate, officers only participate, representatives participate.

Period, Question Mark, Exclamation Mark

> Please come. If you insist.
>
> Are you coming? No, thanks.
>
> Do come! It is not possible.

Quotation marks when a complete sentence is quoted.

> The visiting dignitary said, "It is my pleasure to be here."

but

> The visitor's "pleasure to be here" was hampered by the bad weather.

G80 Religious References

Capitalize words with religious significance.

The Koran	God
Buddhism	Good Friday
Judaism	Talmud

G81 Time

When representing clock time, *a.m.* and *p.m.* are preferred.

> The luncheon will begin at 1 p.m.
>
> **Note:** When *o'clock* is used, the number is written out.
>
> The luncheon will begin at one o'clock.

G82 Numbers

Figures or words? As a rule in business writing, *general* numbers are expressed in words and *specific* numbers are expressed in figures.

Nearly three hundred people attended the workshop.

There were 295 people present.

Some specific guidelines are given below regarding when to use figures and when to use words. When in doubt, consult these guidelines.

Use Figures For

numbers above 10	Send 15 radios.
a series of numbers	Send 15 radios, 2 television sets, and 4 cassette recorders.
with abbreviations or symbols	3 lbs., 2 in., 6 p.m., #84

Grammar, Usage, and Style

money	
a series of round amounts	$25, $100, $44
a series of amounts including cents	$25.11, $143.45, $9.50
a series of amounts in cents only	17¢, 28¢, 10¢
house or building numbers (except the number one)	15 King Street, Apartment 804, **but** One King Street
street names above ten	402 30th Street
dates	February 17, 19--
percentages	We saved 20 percent
mixed numbers	His salary increased 1 1/4 times.
clock time (except with o'clock)	The appointment was at 2:30 p.m. The class started at 13:30 (military time for 1:30 p.m.).
large numbers	They counted 10,432,086 people in the census.
exact unit of time	The trip took 2 years, 7 months, and 10 days.
decimals	0.47, 7.3 million
exact age	She will be 4 years, 3 months old on Tuesday.
ratios	5:2 or 5 to 2
business forms, documents, serial or size numbers	Invoice 468, Order 2071, Policy No. 14-56-7722, Lot No. 9, size 8 shoe
temperature	The temperature rose to 95°F today.
measures and measurements	49° (49 degrees), 30 miles, 22 feet, 4' 5"

Use Words For

numbers under ten	They sent us five sets.
street names under ten	240 Fifth Avenue
numbers beginning a sentence	Eighteen employees were honored for their attendance.
date (formal usage)	November eighth, nineteen hundred eighty-six

unit of time	He stayed for six months.
round numbers	Two thousand years, thirteen hundred soldiers
fractions standing alone	Three quarters of the group attended the demonstration.
legal documents and formal correspondence	Two thousand dollars, nineteen hundred
age and anniversary	Elsie is eighteen today. It's their fifteenth anniversary.
approximate numbers	Approximately three hundred people were present.

Note: When two numbers are used consecutively, spell out the lower number.

Buy twelve 22-cent stamps, please.

G83 Plurals

G84 Abbreviations, Letters, Numbers, Words

Form the plural by adding 's.

and's and but's	the 1900's or 1900s
in two's and three's	the pro's and con's
the 5 C's or 5 Cs	YMCA's or YMCAs (If letters are uppercase, or if numbers are involved, the apostrophe may be omitted.)

G85 Hyphenated Words

As a rule, pluralize the principal word.

editors-in-chief	sisters-in-law
men-of-war	

If no noun is contained in the compound word, add s to the end of it.

get-together, get-togethers
write-up, write-ups

Grammar, Usage, and Style

G86 Nouns

Generally, form the plural by adding *s*.

desk, desks; employer, employers; fuse, fuses

Exceptions to the above rule are as follows:

- To words ending in *s, ch, sh, x* or *z*, add *es*.
- For nouns ending in *y* preceded by a consonant, change the *y* to *i* and add *es*.

  city, cities; community, communities

- To nouns ending in *y* preceded by a vowel, add *s* to the singular to form the plural.

  attorney, attorneys; monkey, monkeys; tray, trays

- Some nouns have irregular plural forms.

  man, men; foot, feet; mouse, mice

- Some nouns remain the same in the plural.

  sheep, sheep; fish, fish; series, series

- Some nouns are always used in the singular form even though they seem to have a plural feeling or meaning.

  arthritis, economics, ethics, news, politics

- Some nouns are rarely or never used in the singular; they are almost invariably plural.

  acoustics, clothes, goods, premises, statistics, tactics

G87 Foreign Words

Foreign words often have irregular plural endings.

Singular	Plural
analysis	analyses
curriculum	curricula
datum	data
phenomenon	phenomena
memorandum	memoranda
medium	media

Note: Consult the dictionary for the correct way to form plurals of specific words. Don't guess. The first spelling listed is usually **preferred**.

G88 Word Division

Before you contemplate word division, remember that it is better to avoid it. If you absolutely must divide a word, follow these guidelines.

- Consult the dictionary if you are in doubt about the correct division.
- Make the reader's task easy by giving a strong indication of the entire word before the division point.
- Have no more than two successive lines ending with a division.

Never Divide

- words of one syllable or words pronounced as one syllable

    brought   stopped   healed

- proper names

    Jonathan   Portugal   Micheline

- short words (fewer than six letters)

    after   alone

- contractions or abbreviations

    haven't   Ph.D.

- the last word in a paragraph or on a page
- words in which only one or two characters would be separated

    mounted   largely   oblique   ready

- numbers (unless they are very long)

    $2147.75

G89 Dividing Words

Always divide words between syllables. Specifically:

- as close to the center as possible

    communi-cation

- after prefixes

    contra-dict

Grammar, Usage, and Style

- before suffixes

    lov-able

- between double consonants when the root word does not contain double consonants

    run-ning   occur-rence

    but

    stall-ing   bluff-ing

- after the vowel when there is a one-letter syllable followed by a consonant

    regulate: regu-late   separate: sepa-rate

- between the vowels when there are two one-letter syllables

    radiator: radi-ator   anxiety: anxi-ety

- at the hyphen when the term is already hyphenated

    self-control

G90 Dividing Related Expressions

Avoid dividing parts of a related expression, but if division is essential, choose a logical breaking point and one that will not confuse the reader.

Addresses:	37 Bayview Avenue	Division: 37 Bayview Avenue
Dates:	May 24, 1987	Division: May 24, 1987
Geographic Locations:	Weehawken, New Jersey	Division: Weehawken, New Jersey
Money (very large amounts only):	82 million	Division: 82 million
Names:	Professor B. Castens	Division: Professor B. Castens

G91 Additional Reference Sources

For additional reference sources on dictionaries, English usage books, and other helpful information, see Unit 15, *Queries: Locating Information.*

UNIT 8

HANDLING FORMS

System Flowcharts	H1
Forms	H2
Forms Used in Basic Business Activities	H3-H27

    Purchasing (Buying)
    Receiving
    Stockkeeping (Inventory Control)
    Producing
    Selling
    Shipping
    Billing
    Collecting
    Disbursing
    Preprinted Forms
    Basic Business Forms
    Specialized Forms

Rubber Stamps and Die Plate Stamps	H28
Principles of Forms Design	H29

Handling Forms

In all firms, regardless of size, nature of business, or type of ownership, certain departments have similar organization because they deal with the same fundamental activities. These activities are purchasing, receiving and inventory control, producing, selling, shipping, billing and keeping records of money received and paid. These separate activities are linked by means of forms, each designed for a particular purpose and each prepared in sufficient quantities to satisfy the firm's needs.

This unit describes the flow of activity around *purchasing* and *sales*, the two systems that are the lifeblood of any business organization. As you study the illustrations in the unit, you will see the interdependence of the various departments involved. You will also be able to identify the forms used at various stages of activity. Information about how forms and related supplies can be used as time savers and suggestions for designing a form are also presented in this unit.

H1 System Flowcharts

Flowcharts are graphical representations in which symbols are used to represent operations, data flow logic, and equipment. The *system flowcharts* in Figures 8.1 and 8.2 illustrate the components and flows of data for a typical purchasing system and a typical sales system.

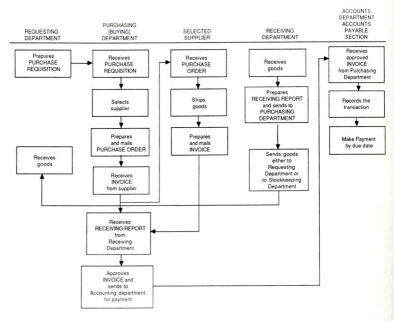

Figure 8.1 Flow of Activities in a Typical Purchasing System

H1-H3 System Flowcharts

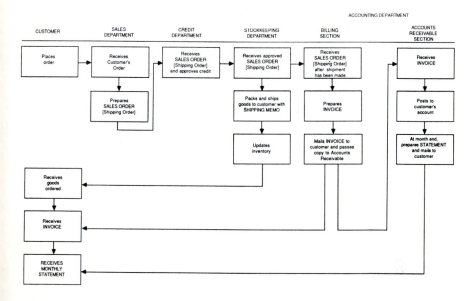

Figure 8.2 Flow of Activities in a Typical Sales System

H2 Forms

A *form* is a document that has specially designed spaces for the printing, writing, or keyboarding of information.

Business transactions are supported by forms that create, cancel, confirm, clarify, and complete a transaction. Forms can also be used to gather, report, and summarize information.

Forms can take on a variety of shapes and sizes as depicted in Figures 8.3, 8.4, and 8.5. They can also be depicted in a variety of mediums.

H3 Forms Used in Basic Business Activities

Forms differ in appearance from company to company. Some forms are prepared in longhand or on a typewriter as the illustrations in this unit demonstrate. When a computer is used, the forms will look a little different from those illustrated, but their effect will be the same. In each of the illustrations below, note that *only the minimum* number of copies of each form is indicated.

Handling Forms

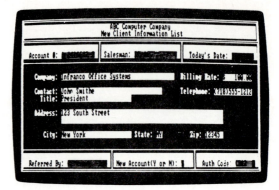

Figure 8.3 Sample Business Form on CRT

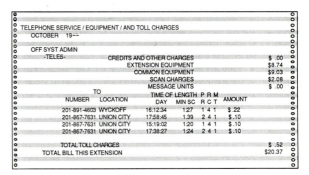

Figure 8.4 Sample Business Form—Computer Printout

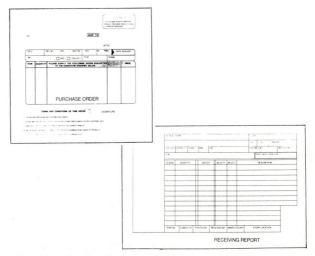

Figure 8.5 Other Sample Business Forms

H4 Purchasing (Buying)

Purchasing involves obtaining everything an organization needs in its operation—from paper clips to delivery trucks. In a small company, buying may be done quite informally (a telephone call or a letter, for example), but a large company needs forms to control and record purchasing functions. In most organizations, buying is handled by a purchasing department that acts only on receipt of an approved *purchase requisition* (Figure 8.6).

Figure 8.6 Purchase Requisition

H5 Purchase Requisition

- An approved purchase request from within the organization.
- Two copies: one to the purchasing department
  one for issuing department file

H6 Purchase Order

- Figure 8.7 is a purchase order prepared from the purchase requisition and sent to the vendor (supplier) who offers the best price and delivery terms.
- Three copies: one to supplier
  one to receiving department
  one for purchasing department file

Handling Forms

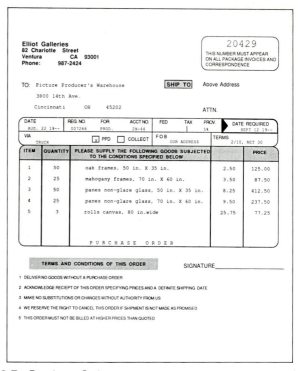

Figure 8.7 Purchase Order

 Receiving

Goods received must be matched against the original purchase order for accuracy in quantity and condition. It is the responsibility of the receiving department to make the check and complete a *receiving report* on the incoming goods.

H8 Receiving Report

- Figure 8.8 is a receiving report prepared after incoming goods have been checked against the purchase order.
- Four copies: one to accounts payable department
   one to purchasing department
   one to inventory control or stockkeeping department
   one for receiving department file
- The items ordered are delivered to the appropriate department, and payment is handled by the accounts payable department.

322

H7-H11   Receiving

Figure 8.8   Receiving Report

H9   Stockkeeping (Inventory Control)

The stockkeeping department is responsible for the storage, care, and distribution of finished goods and raw materials.

H10   Inventory (Stock) Record

Kept for each product; shows quantity received and issued, and the balance presently on hand.

- Only one copy is essential.

Note: In many situations today, this record is computerized. Additions and deletions to the inventory are made by keystrokes on a computer terminal and periodic computer printouts provide the inventory record (Figure 8.9).

H11   Stock Requisition

- Sent to the purchasing department by the inventory control clerk or stockkeeper when it is necessary to replenish supplies that have reached minimum quantity levels.
- Dealt with by the purchasing department as though it were a requisition.

323

Handling Forms

```
ELLIOTT GALLERIES
82 Charlotte St.
Ventura    CA    93001

Phone:  987-2424
```

			PERPETUAL INVENTORY CARD				
ITEM: Oak frames, 50 on. X 35 in						Maximum: 200	
CODE: S342			STOCK NO: PR89			Minimum: 20	
Date	Mdse. on order		STOCK				
			Recieved		Issued		
19--	P.R.#	Amt.	P.O. #	In	S.R. #	Out	Balance
June 6							130
July 7					347	10	120
July 13					703	35	85
July 27					912	50	35
Sept. 11	7266	50	20 429	50			85

Figure 8.9 Inventory Record

- Two copies: one to purchasing department
  one for inventory control or stockkeeping department file

Note: In computerized operations, the computer can be programmed to automatically reorder supplies or raw materials when a stated minimum quantity has been reached.

H12 Producing

In manufacturing firms or in service businesses, an authorization form is required before the actual production of goods or servicing of equipment can begin. Obtaining maintenance service may also require the preparation of a *work order*.

H13 Work Order (Production Order)

- The work order (Figure 8.10) is given to the person, division, or unit doing the job.
- Two copies: one for the worker, division or unit doing the job
  one for the production department or requesting unit's file

H12–H15 Producing

Figure 8.10 Work Order

H14 Selling

A customer who wishes to buy merchandise or services places an order with a firm.

H15 Sales Order (Also known as Shipping Order in some organizations)

- Usually prepared by a sales representative or sales department clerk after taking an order in person, by telephone, or through the mail.
- Six copies: one to credit department
  one to customer
  one to inventory control or stockkeeping department
  one to shipping department
  one to accounts payable department
  one for sales department file

Note: In more automated environments, orders may be received via telex equipment, by facsimile equipment, or by other forms of electronic mail or telecommunication services. Orders may also be confirmed using these devices (see T36).

In retail sales situations, a *sales slip* (Figure 8.11) is issued at the time of sale and given to the customer with the goods purchased.

- Three copies: one to customer
  one to accounts receivable department—when sale is a credit one
  one for sales department file

Handling Forms

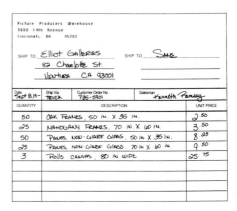

Figure 8.11 Sales Slip

 Shipping

When goods are shipped, acknowledgement of their receipt is frequently necessary. The form used to obtain the acknowledgement may be a copy of the invoice or it may be a shipping memo.

H17 Shipping Memo (Delivery Receipt)

- Signed by the customer and given back to the carrier on receipt of the merchandise (Figure 8.12).
- Two copies: one (signed) to customer
                 one (signed) for shipper

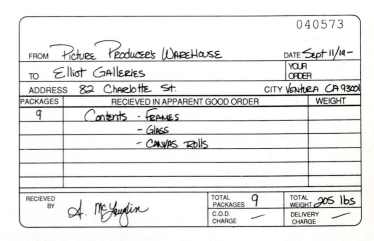

Figure 8.12 Delivery Receipt

H16-H20   Shipping

H18   Bill of Lading

- The standard shipping document that serves as a contract between the cosignor (the supplier) and the carrier of the goods.
- Used for rail, water, air, or road transportation of goods.
- Signed by the customer or carrier (See D10.)

H19   Billing

After the supplier has shipped the order or after delivery of the merchandise, the customer is billed (sent an *invoice* similar to the one in Figure 8.13).

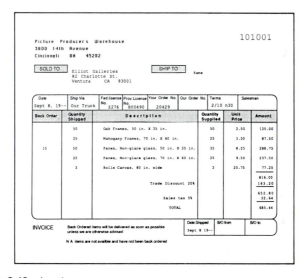

Figure 8.13   Invoice

H20   Invoice

- Sent by the billing section of the accounting department to the customer.
- Shows details of the merchandise ordered, cost, shipping charges, terms of payment, discounts applicable, taxes due, and total amount due.
- Three copies: one to customer
                  one to accounts receivable department
                  one for billing section file

Handling Forms

- Additional copies of the invoice may also be used by:

    credit department

    accounting department

    sales department (to acknowledge order or to indicate that shipment was made)

    inventory control or stockkeeping department

    shipping department (as a packing slip)

If the total order cannot be shipped, the invoice shows that fact. For example, if only 30 of the 50 oak frames ordered were available for shipment, 20 would be entered in the *back order* column and 30 in the *quantity* column. The outstanding 20 would be shipped and invoiced at a later date.

H21 Credit Invoice

- Issued by the billing section of the accounting department to a customer in case of returned or damaged merchandise or an overcharge.
- Tells the customer that his or her account is reduced (credited) by the amount shown.
- Three copies: one to customer
    one to accounts receivable department
    one for billing section file

H22 Collecting

If a customer does not pay for each order as it is invoiced, the customer is sent a monthly statement as shown in Figure 8.14.

H23 Statement

- Sent by the accounts receivable section of the accounting department to the customer.
- Itemizes purchases, returns, and payments made during the month and shows the total balance due.
- Three copies: one to customer
    one for collection follow up
    one for accounts receivable file

H21-H26   Credit Invoice

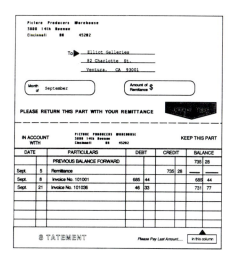

Figure 8.14   Monthly Statement

H24   Disbursing

Disbursing—the paying out of funds by a company—is carried out either by the accounts payable section or by the payroll section of the accounting department. The *accounts payable* section makes all the company's payments other than payroll. The *payroll* section handles salaries and wages for employees (see B56).

H25   Preprinted Forms
H26   Basic Business Forms

When the size of the business does not justify custom-printed forms, preprinted forms may be purchased at a stationery or office supply store. These forms may then be rubber stamped with the company name, address, and form number, if desired. Preprinted forms that may be purchased include, but are not limited to, the following:

Billing forms (duplicate and triplicate)

Carbon set memos

Delivery receipts

Handling Forms

Invoices

Ledger sheets and accounting pages

Purchase orders

Receipts for cash

Requisition forms

Sales order books

Statements

Time and payroll forms

H27 Specialized Forms

Preprinted business forms are also available for specialized business uses. For example, tax forms, banking forms, and insurance forms are available from the respective agencies. Preprinted forms can be purchased for specific types of businesses as well. Some of these include medical charts, real estate listing cards, shipping labels, wills and other legal documents, and restaurant dinner checks.

H28 Rubber Stamps and Die Plate Stamps

In some situations, rubber stamps can be used in place of forms to provide necessary information. Information can be stamped on documents to indicate date of receipt, date of shipment, priority in handling, departmental routing of documents, and filing information. Rubber stamps can be specially imprinted with an individual's or a company's name, address, the date and other information. An individual's signature can also be simulated on a rubber stamp. Inks, stamp pads, racks, and kits to make your own stamp sets are available.

Self-inking die plate stamps are the ultimate in ready-to-use stamps. These stamps can affix six items at a time—day, month, year, action taken, by whom, for department or company—or they can provide any or some of these items. Self-inking numbering machines are also a handy office tool.

H29 Principles of Forms Design

Cumbersome forms, redundant and unclear questions on forms, and poorly designed forms are time wasters. Business forms should be designed with the goal of speeding up the flow of information. The following elements are essential to good forms design:

- Keep the *user* in mind when designing forms.

  — Use standard terminology.
  — Use clear captions.
  — Allow ample space for filling in information.

- Preprint as much information as possible so that the user has very little to write.
- Use *box design* (check boxes) for variable data, and place boxes to the left whenever possible

Incorrect	**Correct**
Marital Status:_____	Marital Status: ☐ Married ☐ Single

- Give each form a title. The title should be short, specific, and appear at the top of the form.
- Arrange items on forms with similar information grouped together. Items should be placed on the form in the same sequence in which they will be used later.
- Place clear, simple instructions for filling out a form near the section to which they apply.
- Take advantage of time-saving features by

  — placing responses at similar tab stops
  — placing addresses so they can be used in window envelopes
  — placing routing instructions on each copy of a form
  — color coding copies to make routing faster and easier

- Keep the form layout and design simple.

  — Have adequate margins for appearance, binding, or filing needs.
  — Use standard typefaces.

Handling Forms

- Consider handling needs and the length of time the material is to be filed when selecting the paper weight.
- Make the use of ruling, shading and white space attractive.
- Keep vertical spacing the same as the typewriter spacing used in your company.
- Provide adequate space for certification, approvals, signatures, etc.
- Set horizontal spacing for typewriters used in your company (either 10 or 12 pitch) if form will be filled in by typewriter.

■ Be economical in forms design.

- Avoid using more than one color ink unless absolutely necessary.
- Use standard paper sizes: 8 1/2" x 11"; 4" x 5 1/4"; 4" x 5 1/2".
- Consider two-sided printing only if appropriate.
- Consider reducing print size to get the information on one side only.

■ Consider processing requirements in your forms planning.

- As the form is being designed, give thought to the use of carbon sets, no-carbon-required paper, colored copies, continuous form paper, side-punched holes, or other special needs.
- Special form-design paper can be purchased to block out the spaces on your form. It is available with different typewriter spacing.

Other good forms management practices indicate that you should provide for the following:

■ Date forms and assign specific numbers to each form. Keep a record of each form and its changes and developments.
■ Keep a functional record file of every form in the company to prevent the duplication of information on forms.
■ Keep a specification file of all company forms. That is, keep one copy of each form arranged by its size, type of paper used, and special printing requirements. This file can help you save money on printing by batching orders for additional forms and by limiting form sizes.

For additional forms management procedures, see Unit 6, *Filing Systems and Records Control.*

UNIT 9

INFORMATION PROCESSING

The Automated Office	I1-I3
Criteria for an Effective Information Processing System	
The Historical Development of Information Processing	
The Computer's Role in Information Processing	I4-I11
Steps Involved in the Information Processing Cycle	
Computer Components	
Information Processing Devices	I12
Input Devices	I13-I31
Magnetic Ink Character Recognition (MICR)	
Magnetic Tape or Disk	
Optical Mark Reading (OMR)	
Paper Tape	
Punched Cards	
Magnetic Media Data Entry Devices	
Computer Terminals	
Transaction Terminals	
Electronic Mouse	
Joystick	
Light Pen	
Touch-Sensitive Screen	
Digitizers	
Voice Input	
Facsimile Equipment	
Telex Equipment	
Optical Character Recognition (OCR)	
Computer Input Microfilm (CIM)	

Information Processing

Storage Devices — I32-I38
- Magnetic Disk Hardware
- Floppy Disks
- Magnetic Tape Hardware
- Magnetic Bubble
- Semiconductor Secondary Storage
- Optical Disks

Processing Devices — I39

Output Devices — I40-I52
- Visual Display
- Impact Printers
- Intelligent Copiers
- Non-Impact Printers
- Plotters
- Magnetic Tape and Magnetic Disk
- Computer Output Microfilm (COM)
- Computer Assisted Retrieval (CAR)
- Photocomposition Units
- Facsimile Units and Telex Units
- Voice Output
- Voice Messaging (VMX)

Distribution Devices — I53-I60
- Standard Telephone Lines
- Coaxial Cables
- Microwave Transmission
- Communication Satellites
- Fiber Optics
- Cellular Radio
- Local Area Networks (LAN)

Technological Subsystems in the Integrated Office — I61

Computer-Related Terms — I62

I

The primary purpose of the office in an organization is to communicate timely and up-to-date information so that effective decision making can take place; therefore, the office is the *nerve center* of an organization's information processing system.

Information processing involves getting the *right information* in the *right medium* at the *right time* to the *right person* or *persons* in the *right place* or *places* in order to provide for effective decision making.

Regardless of how large or small your office may be, this unit serves as an invaluable reference by which to discover how automation affects the performance of traditional office work and how it can improve office productivity.

I1 The Automated Office

Office work generally falls into two categories: *administrative work*, which is more often the non-structured tasks, such as message handling, scheduling, researching, and analyzing; and *clerical work*, which involves more structured tasks, such as calculating, filing, posting, and sorting. Improvements in office automation today are directly affecting both the administrative and clerical aspects of office work.

To be able to make sound business decisions, it is necessary to have accurate and timely information. The office serves an organization by providing information that may take one or more of the following forms:

- data (numbers, symbols)
- text (words)
- graphics (drawings, charts, graphs)
- image (microfilm, videotape)
- voice (speech)

Information processing is a system—that is, the coordination of people, procedures, and equipment designed to provide the user with the most accurate and timely information. The diagram in Figure 9.1 illustrates this system.

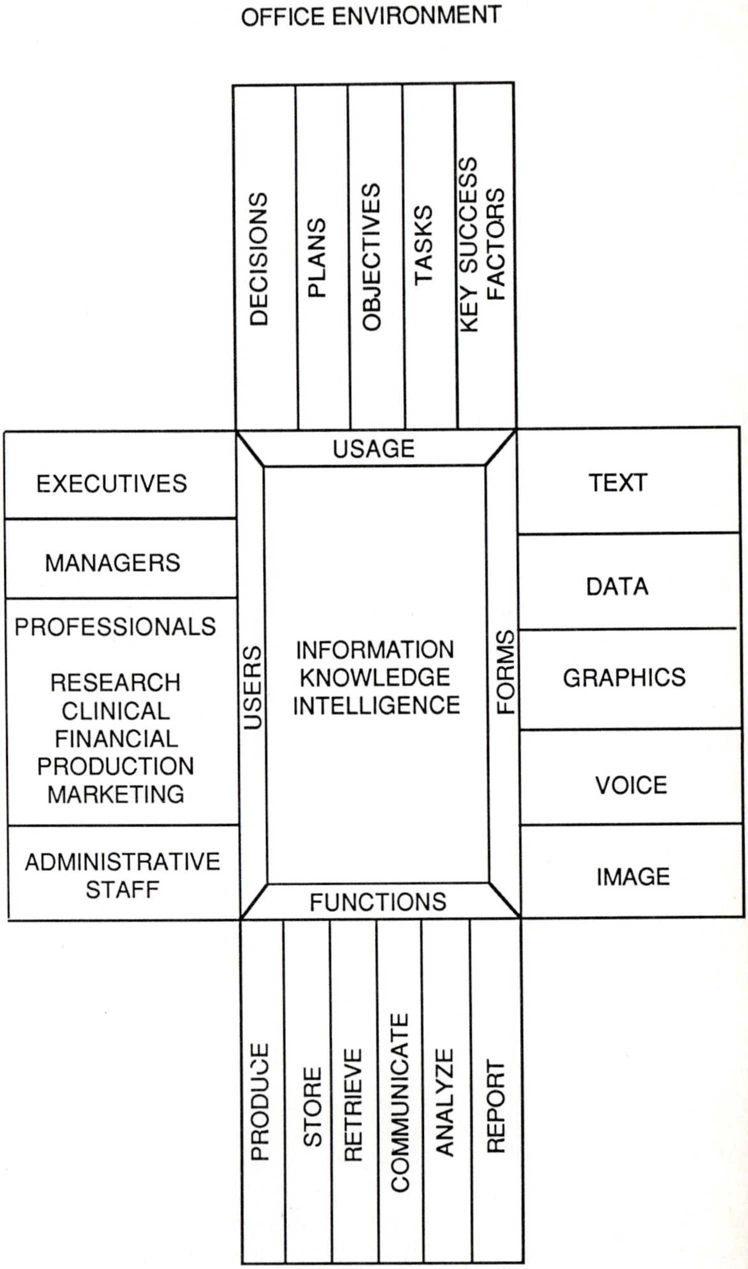

Information Processing

OFFICE ENVIRONMENT

- DECISIONS
- PLANS
- OBJECTIVES
- TASKS
- KEY SUCCESS FACTORS

USAGE

EXECUTIVES
MANAGERS
PROFESSIONALS
RESEARCH
CLINICAL
FINANCIAL
PRODUCTION
MARKETING
ADMINISTRATIVE STAFF

USERS

INFORMATION
KNOWLEDGE
INTELLIGENCE

FORMS

TEXT
DATA
GRAPHICS
VOICE
IMAGE

FUNCTIONS

- PRODUCE
- STORE
- RETRIEVE
- COMMUNICATE
- ANALYZE
- REPORT

Figure 9.1 Information Processing System

I2 Criteria for an Effective Information Processing System

To achieve an effective information processing system, the following criteria must be evaluated:

- **The productivity of the system**

    An appropriate blending of people, procedures, and equipment must be used at every step of the information processing cycle from input to storage, processing, output, and distribution (see I5).

- **The capability of the equipment**

    Equipment purchases must be controlled so that there is compatability of operational functions of the equipment used.

- **The effectiveness of the distribution/communication facilities**

    Since information can be stored or distributed in analog mode (wave length communication) or digital mode (pulse or code communication), there is often a need to convert from one mode to another in order to communicate information from one piece of equipment to another, especially when communicating over distances.

- **The acceptance of the system by personnel**

    To ensure the acceptance of the automated environment, people need to be provided with the motivation for change. They must be involved in the change process from the very beginning, and must be provided with adequate training and support as they adjust to the new procedures and equipment.

I3 The Historical Development of Information Processing

Historically, information processing subsystems have developed *concurrently* yet *independently* as shown in the following diagram. The future dictates that these subsystems *consolidate* and *merge*. The ultimate goal of office automation is the achievement of an integrated office environment (Figure 9.2) in which the work of all employees is automated and coordinated. In this integrated environment, the computer would be at the center of all office activities and would provide for the interrelationship and shared use of all the data in the system. The following diagram shows the evolution of the integrated office environment.

Information Processing

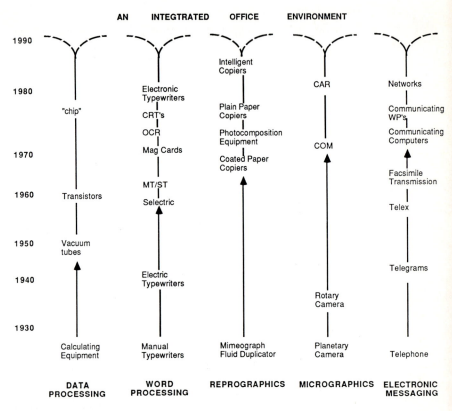

Figure 9.2 An Integrated Office Environment

I4 The Computer's Role in Information Processing

Today's business firms are faced with the need to handle an ever-increasing volume of data. As a result, both large and small firms are turning to the computer as the single most important information processing component.

I5 Steps Involved in the Information Processing Cycle

There are five phases in the information processing cycle.

- **Input**. The device, process, or channel involved in placing the data into the system.

14-17 The Computer's Role in Information Processing

- **Storage**. The data is saved or filed on internal or external storage devices.
- **Processing**. The data is manipulated, calculated, sorted, or rearranged in order to make it more meaningful to the user.
- **Output**. The end result of the processing that has been designed to meet the user's special needs.
- **Distribution/Communication**. Getting the output to the user in a timely and appropriate format.

Let's trace the above steps as they are applied in the presentation of a week's pay to an employee.

Input: From a source document (employee time card), raw data (hours worked) are entered into a computer via one of the input media discussed later.

Storing: The facts, consisting of the information to be processed (hours worked and rate of pay) and the instructions for processing (calculate the rate), are fed into the computer's memory locations.

Processing: All required calculating, processing, and other related instructions are carried out [(regular hours x hourly rate) + (overtime hours x overtime rate)—deductions = net pay.]

Output: The amount of the paycheck is determined and printed out in a payroll register format.

Distribution/Communication: The net pay for each employee is deposited into each employee's account at a local bank, or a paycheck is prepared and distributed to the employee.

16 Computer Components

17 Types of Computers

Computers differ in size, storage capacity, processing speeds, and cost. Three major categories are:

- **Mainframe Computers**

    Mainframes are the largest computers in size. They provide the greatest speed and storage capacities and they are also the most expensive. They have the ability to support a number of microcomputers and handle the information processing needs of very large organizations and/or divisions of state and federal governments.

Information Processing

- **Minicomputers**

    Minicomputers are powerful computers in and of themselves. They may be linked with mainframe computers for enhanced storage and processing potential. Microcomputers and computer terminals may also be linked to minicomputers.

- **Microcomputers**

    Microcomputers are personal desktop computers that vary greatly in their capabilities. They may be *dumb terminals* linked to a minicomputer or mainframe. Such terminals have limited input, processing, storage, and retrieval capabilities on their own. They may be *intelligent workstations* that have substantial memory, storage, and processing capabilities on their own. Intelligent workstations may also be linked to mainframes or minicomputers, or to other intelligent work stations at local or remote locations.

Computer hardware refers to all the electronic and mechanical parts of the device, such as readers, printers, and tape and disk drives. *Computer software* refers to all of the instructions that tell the computer to perform certain operations.

I8 The Central Processing Unit (CPU)

The CPU receives instructions and information from the input device, stores the information until needed, recalls the information and instructions, performs the needed calculations or comparisons, and takes whatever other action may be required. The CPU has three parts:

- **Primary Storage (Memory) Unit**

    All data and instructions must be received here before the computer can start its work. This unit provides for the *temporary* storage of data. The storage area contains a number of *addresses* (storage locations). The size of the computer determines the number of possible storage locations.

- **Arithmetic/Logic Unit**

    Responsible for processing the data, this unit can do calculations and take logical action (compare possible courses of action and decide between alternatives).

- **Control Unit**

    This unit controls the entire system (input and output devices and central processing unit) and sees that everything is working in accordance with the instructions (program) it has received.

19 Programming

The computer can make rapid calculations but it cannot *think*. It is told how to solve a problem by means of a *program*. The program instructs the machine to perform a fixed operation or group of fixed operations on given data.

The programmer (the person who writes the program) must attempt to foresee every possibility and every alternative that could arise in the solution of a problem. Therefore, the programmer must work in a systematic fashion and take each problem carefully and meticulously through the following stages before feeding the program into the computer:

1. Define the problem.
2. Plan the solution—develop a visual, step-by-step procedure.
3. Code the solution into a computer language.
4. Test the solution.
5. Make revisions as necessary to achieve desired results.

From the *statement* of the problem, the programmer develops either a *flowchart*, a *structure diagram*, or some other type of coded diagram to illustrate the steps involved in solving the problem. In flowcharting, *symbols* are used; in structure diagrams, *lines and comments* are used.

The following problem and accompanying diagram (Figure 9.3) illustrate the flowcharting of a solution.

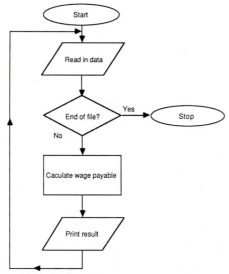

Figure 9.3   Flowcharting a Solution

Information Processing

PROBLEM: Wage payable = (hours worked x hourly rate) + (overtime hours x overtime hourly rate)—deductions

- From the input device, the computer receives the information needed (wage rate, hours worked, deductions).
- Each time information is input, the question *Is this the last piece of information?* is asked. If the answer is *yes*, then the process is complete and the machine stops. If the answer is *no*, the computer moves on to the next stage to receive the next item.
- The computer is instructed to complete all the necessary calculations to establish the amount payable to the employee.
- At the last stage, the computer is instructed to print out the result of the calculation in the form of a paycheck, a report, a transfer of funds to a bank account or a combination of these actions.

I10 Computer Languages

Computers operate on instructions presented in words and digits. There are several computer languages, but four are most frequently used.

- **Cobol** (COmmon Business Oriented Language): particularly suited to perform business-related tasks.
- **Fortran** (FORmula TRANslation): designed primarily to perform mathematical and scientific calculations.
- **Basic** (Beginners All-purpose Symbolic Instruction Code): most widely used on small business microcomputer systems and for personal computing.
- **Pascal:** a logical and easy-to-learn general purpose language that is growing in acceptance.

I11 Microcomputer Software Packages

Although users can write their own programs for a microcomputer, most users purchase commercially available software packages.

Microcomputer software consists of two types: *system software*, which controls and supports the operations of the computer system as it performs its tasks; and *application software*, which consists of programs that direct the computer to do specific, special-purpose tasks.

Some popular single-function application software packages provide programs as follows:

- *word processing:* provides for the automation of the creation, editing, and printing of documents.

- *data base management:* provides for the creation, maintenance, and use of data records and files that can be easily accessed to obtain data displayed on the screen, printed in hard copy, or communicated to another location.
- *spread sheet:* serves as a replacement for the traditional worksheet in that the program generates a user-defined worksheet in rows and columns on the screen. The user can change one item and all related items will reflect changes as appropriate.
- *accounts receivable:* keeps records of amounts owed to customers, prepares monthly statements, and produces credit management reports.
- *accounts payable:* produces checks, keeps track of purchases made and amounts owed to suppliers. May also produce cash management reports.
- *inventory control:* records all changes to inventory, notifies management of items needing reordering, and provides management with comparative inventory status reports.
- *sales analysis program:* analyzes sales data to produce management reports, analyzes sales by salespersons, customers, products, and regions.
- *payroll program:* maintains employee work records, produces paychecks, earnings statements and other documents, as well as various payroll and tax reports for management and governmental agencies.
- *graphics program:* enables the user to quickly and easily produce charts or graphs from reports or data base information.
- *communication program:* enables two microcomputers to send and receive messages and provides the ability to send messages from a microcomputer to a host computer.
- *tutorial program:* interactive training program that teaches the user how to operate a piece of equipment; use a software package; or learn and reinforce a new skill, such as how to keyboard using correct fingering.

Integrated software packages are relatively new and are becoming popular with certain business firms. Integrated packages combine the ability to do several general purpose applications in one software program—typically data base management, word processing, spread sheets, and graphics. Most integrated packages require significant memory capacity and, in some cases, compromise on the power, speed, and flexibility of single-function packages. An advantage of some integrated packages is the ability to do *windowing*—that is, the ability to view displays from several documents on the screen at one time.

I12 Information Processing Devices

Systems can be designed that incorporate a wide variety of equipment and technologies—each interacting with the other. Table 9.1 suggests some of the most common devices. Each of the devices listed will be described briefly in the sections that follow.

Table 9.1 Information Processing Devices

INPUT DEVICES	STORAGE DEVICES	PROCESSING DEVICES	OUTPUT DEVICES	DISTRIBUTION DEVICES
Magnetic Ink Character Recognition (MICR)	Magnetic Disk Hardware	Mainframe Computers	Visual Display	Telephone Lines
Magnetic Tape or Disk	Floppy Disks	Minicomputers	Impact Printers	Coaxial Cables
Optical Mark Reading (OMR)	Magnetic Tape Hardware	Microcomputers	Non-Impact Printers	Microwave
Paper Tape	Magnetic Bubble Memory	Other specialized equipment with built-in microprocessors	Plotters	Communication Satellites
Punched Cards	Semiconductor Secondary Storage		Magnetic Tape and Magnetic Disk	Fiber Optics
Magnetic Media Data Entry Devices	Optical Disks		Computer Output Microfilm (COM)	Cellular Radio
Computer Terminals			Computer Assisted Retrieval (CAR)	Local Area Networks (LAN)
Transaction Terminals			Photocomposition Units	
Electronic Mouse			Facsimile Units and Telex Units	
Joystick			Voice Output	
Light Pen			Voice Messaging	
Touch Sensitive Screen			Intelligent Copiers	
Digitizers				
Voice Input				
Facsimile Equipment				
Telex Equipment				
Optical Character Recognition (OCR)				
Computer Input Microfilm (CIM)				

I13 Input Devices

Before data can be fed into the computer, it must be *recorded* in an acceptable format. The part of a record that contains a specific piece of information (such as an employee number or an account number) is referred to as a *field*. A set of related records is known as a *file* (all office employees or a set of accounts receivable records).

I12-I18   Information Processing Devices

Information may be recorded from *source documents*, such as invoices, sales slips, and orders; or it can be accepted directly into the computer from either optically read documents or input terminal keyboards. All computers accept one of the following input devices and most can accept a number of them.

I14   Magnetic Ink Character Recognition (MICR)

A special ink containing a trace of iron is used to imprint the MICR code on documents. The iron is magnetized, and sorting machines sense it and interpret the data. This device is used by banks for processing checks.

I15   Magnetic Tape or Disk

A random access storage device onto which data can be keyed directly without the need for cards. Data are stored on the surface of each disk as small, magnetized spots arranged in circular tracks. The encoding is done by means of a typewriter-like keyboard.

I16   Optical Mark Reading (OMR)

In this system, pencil marks on cards or sheets are scanned and interpreted by the computer. Market research surveys would be a typical example of the use of OMR.

I17   Paper Tape

Paper tape is a strip of paper on which data can be recorded in the form of punched holes. Such tapes may be made by different business machines including cash registers. Paper tape is inexpensive but fragile, slow to read, and impossible to reuse. This medium is rarely used today.

I18   Punched Cards

The card has numbered columns and rows that are punched by a keypunch machine. Each batch of punched cards is verified (checked), sorted, and put onto a reader where the holes in the cards are read and converted into electronic impulses by the computer. Punched cards are almost obsolete in favor of other faster and more accurate input methods.

Information Processing

I19 Magnetic Media Data Entry Devices

Key-to-Disk devices provide for the recording of data from a keyboard directly to a magnetic disk. *Key-to-Tape devices* provide for the entry of data directly from a keyboard onto magnetic tape. The aim of these systems is to bypass the paper tape and punched card processes and be able to record directly on the magnetic medium.

I20 Computer Terminals

A computer terminal consists of a keyboard and a cathode ray tube (CRT) screen. The terminal can be in the same room as the computer or a considerable distance away. The operator enters the data, views the information on the screen, makes any necessary changes, and then enters the data directly into storage. New records can be added and existing ones can be changed immediately. This is the most widely-used form of input/output hardware.

I21 Transaction Terminals

These terminals are used to capture data at the point-of-origin. They are used widely in banks, retail stores, shipping and receiving departments, and other worksites for source data information. Automated teller machines used in banks provide a frequently-used example.

I22 Electronic Mouse

The Mouse is an electronic visual input device used to move the cursor on the screen, to issue commands, and to make responses and menu selections. A hand-held device is used to move the cursor to screen locations and/or icons (drawings) that, in turn, prompt the computer to a specified action.

I23 Joystick

The joystick is a visual input device that is popular for microcomputer video games. It looks like a gear shift level set in a box and is used to move the cursor on the display screen.

I24 Light Pen

The light pen uses photoelectric circuitry and enables the user to write on the CRT display screen. This pen-shaped device enables the computer to calculate the coordinates of the points that the pen touches on the screen, even though these points of light are finite.

I25 Touch-Sensitive Screen

With the touch of a finger or pointer on the display screen, data may be entered into the system. Menu selection is its most frequent use.

I26 Digitizers

Graphics tablets and *graphic pens* are examples of digitizers. They are visual input devices that enable the user to convert drawings and other graphic images on paper or other materials into digital data which is then entered into a computer system.

I27 Voice Input

Voice input systems are now in the frontier stages of development; however, there are some voice data entry terminals that are now being used that permit the direct entry of data into a computer system by verbal communication of a human operator. These units rely on *voice recognition* microprocessors that analyze and classify speech patterns for computer entry.

I28 Facsimile Equipment

Transmitting units can send handwritten, alphanumeric (consisting of both letters and numbers), graphic, and photographic data via telephone lines. Transceiver units can both send and receive information.

I29 Telex Equipment

Alphanumeric data can be sent from one telex unit to another, spanning domestic as well as international areas (see T40).

Information Processing

I30 Optical Character Recognition (OCR)

Optical character recognition provides a method of direct input of data from a source document into a computer system. Recently developed OCR readers can read a greater variety of typefaces from work prepared on typewriters, word processors, and computer printers. The technology is based on the principle that certain shapes can be sensed by sophisticated optical reading devices (scanners). OCR readers can be connected to electronic mail equipment and can, as a result, send telex messages and store-and-forward messages. They can also produce output in the form of floppy disks which can later be used on word processors, personal computers, or photocomposition equipment. As an input device, it is based on the use of paper in the office. More advanced OCR readers will be faster, more accurate, and more versatile because they will be able to read a broader range of type faces, type sizes, paper colors, and paper thicknesses.

I31 Computer Input Microfilm (CIM)

Computer input microfilm is not yet a fully-developed technology. The ultimate goal of this technology is to be able to scan microrecords so that they can be used as input media.

I32 Storage Devices

Data fed into a computer must be temporarily stored in the primary storage unit to await processing, and data that has been processed may also have to be stored temporarily or permanently. However, since there is a limit to how much data may be stored in primary storage, secondary (auxiliary) storage is required when processed data is to be retained for future use. Secondary storage can be achieved in a number of formats. Some of the most common are described below.

I33 Magnetic Disk Hardware

Magnetic disks are now the most common form of secondary storage. They provide high storage capacity at a reasonable cost, in additon to direct access capability. The formats include: removable, easy-to-handle *disk packs* that are thin metal or plastic disks resembling phonograph records mounted together; nonremovable *fixed disk* assemblies that provide for higher speeds and greater recording densities; and *Winchester disk modules* that place magnetic disks in a sealed module or cartridge and are significantly faster and more reliable than open disk packs.

I34 Floppy Disks

A floppy disk is a small, single, and flexible magnetic disk mounted to rotate freely inside a protective plastic jacket. The 5 1/4" floppy disk is the most popular secondary storage device for microcomputers. The 8" floppy and the 3 1/2" microfloppy are also used (see F78).

I35 Magnetic Tape Hardware

Magnetic tape provides for the recording of data in the form of magnetized spots on the iron oxide coating of plastic tape, much like that used by home tape recorders. Magnetic tape formats include *reels, cartridges,* and *cassettes*—all of which provide a high-density, high-speed, and popular storage medium.

I36 Magnetic Bubble

The use of magnetic bubble storage is increasing. Its important advantage is its ability to retain stored data even when the power is off, but it is currently slower than other forms of semiconductor memory.

I37 Semiconductor Secondary Storage

Plug-in circuit boards that can be added to certain microcomputers to enhance their storage capability.

I38 Optical Disks

The optical disk uses laser or electronics technology to embed data into the recording medium. It allows large files of records to be stored and retrieved rapidly. One of the major limitations of the current *laser optical system* is that information cannot be erased once it has been written on a disk.

Information Processing

I39 Processing Devices

Mainframe, minicomputers, and microcomputers handle the processing functions which include sorting, calculating, comparing, priority setting, and summarizing. The components of a computer's central processing unit represent the area that controls the processing functions according to instructions received from the program (see I6).

Other specialized equipment—such as word processors, PABX units, copiers, OCR units, facsimile and telex units, and many others—have their own built-in microprocessors that direct specific functions and operations.

I40 Output Devices

The function of output devices is to convert processed data from electronic impulses into a form that is intelligible to human beings, or into machine-readable form. There are two basic types of output devices: those that provide permanent (hard copy) records such as statements, reports, and checks which are known as *print-outs*; and those that provide temporary, visual displays (soft copy) which are known as *readouts*. The type of output is related to the eventual use of the information, whether for storage and use in future processing or for immediate use in a visible form.

I41 Visual Display (CRT)

Information is displayed on a screen that may be located nearby or at a great distance from the computer. Printers can be linked with CRTs if a permanent record of the readout is required.

I42 Impact Printers

Impact printers form characters and other images on paper by means of the impact of mechanical type fonts and an inked ribbon against paper. *Ball-shaped elements, daisy wheel printers,* and *thimble printers* are letter-quality impact printers. Another form of impact printer is the *dot matrix printer*. These printers form characters by printing a series of dots, and provide a less expensive way to print text because neither a daisy wheel nor a ball-head is needed. The dot matrix patterns range from widely-spaced patterns to near letter-quality (NLQ). However, dot matrix printers are considered draft-quality rather than letter-quality because the dot pattern is not as easy to read as as fully formed character. Dot matrix printers are capable of producing graphics as well as characters.

I43 Intelligent Copiers

Intelligent copiers are capable of receiving electronic messages and printing out high-speed, quality printed results in hard copy form from stored input (see R32).

I44 Non-Impact Printers

Non-impact printers are normally quieter than impact printers. There are several types of non-impact printers: *ink jet printers,* which spray tiny ink particles against the paper from fast-moving nozzles and provide higher quality output than dot matrix printers; *thermal printers,* which use heated wire to print dox matrix type characters on special heat-sensitive paper; *laser printers,* which combine laser technology and microcomputer technology to produce output so fast that they are referred to as page printers rather than character or line printers. The cost of laser printers is generally much higher than that of other printers, but they also provide higher quality output.

I45 Plotters

Plotters produce graphic output using a variety of pen and ink processes. The graphic output can be in color.

I46 Magnetic Tape and Magnetic Disk

Output data may be placed on magnetic tape or magnetic disk media. In these formats, the information may be duplicated, retained indefinitely, used as input for new processing, or reformatted (off-line) at a later time in another medium such as Computer Output Microfilm (COM).

I47 Computer Output Microfilm (COM)

Microfilming and computers have been linked in a system known as Computer Output Microfilm (COM). In this system, computer output is transferred directly into film instead of into a printout. The need for paper is virtually eliminated for every document put on COM. This is a popular output alternative.

I48 Computer Assisted Retrieval (CAR)

In Computer Assisted Retrieval (CAR), the computer is linked to the searching of microrecords. Microfilmed records can be located within seconds and the microform can be read on a separate viewer or on the screen of the terminal from which the request was initiated. If a paper copy is required, it can be printed on the retrieving device. CAR can also be interfaced with other automation components, such as phototypesetters, word processors, electronic message systems, and personal computers; in this way, it becomes an effective tool by which to manage the indexing and accessing of documents.

I49 Photocomposition Units

Text can be transferred from a personal computer, from OCR equipment, from a word processor, or from any other computerized unit to a photocomposition unit. The ultimate output from a photocomposition unit is professional-looking hard copy (see R29).

I50 Facsimile Units and Telex Units

Facsimile equipment scans a page and sends an electronic signal over telephone lines to a receiving station, where a dot-matrix or laser printer reconstructs the page. Facsimile equipment can transmit and reproduce any free-form, black-on-white image, and can provide twenty-four hour sending/receiving capability.

I51 Voice Output

The microcomputer revolution has helped create breakthroughs in the development of voice output devices. *Audio response units* and *speech synthesizers* allow the computer to verbally respond to inquiries or commands.

I52 Voice Messaging (VMX)

Voice store-and-forward or voice messaging systems (VMX for Voice Mail Box) enable the user to send oral messages by telephone and computer. This is a one-way conversation delivered to a computer. The computer in turn delivers the oral message when the recipient of the call

I48-I57 Computer Assisted Retrieval (CAR)

addresses a specific voice mailbox number. The computer can be programmed to deliver the same message to a number of people (broadcast mode) or to one individual (point-to-point mode). This technology is becoming popular in field sales environments because of the need to act quickly on telephone information. It is also known as computer-based message system (CBMS).

I53 Distribution Devices

One of the major components of a data communication system is the communication channel or link between the sending and receiving devices. Some of the most common ones are discussed below.

I54 Standard Telephone Lines

Ordinary telephone lines, which consist of copper wires twisted into pairs, are used extensively for communicating information in *analog* form.

I55 Coaxial Cables

Groups of copper and aluminum wires wrapped to insulate and protect them are known as *coaxial cables.* These are being used in office buildings for local area networks and permit high-speed data transmission.

I56 Microwave Transmission

Microwave antennas transmit high-speed radio signals between earthbound relay stations spaced approximately 30 miles apart.

I57 Communication Satellites

Earth microwave stations beam signals to communication satellites that have been placed in stationary orbits about 22,000 miles above the equator. The communication satellites beam the signals to other satellites that transmit the signals to other earth stations thousands of miles away. The use of satellites to send information has made global or wide-area networks possible.

Information Processing

158 Fiber Optics

Fiber optics technology uses cables consisting of hair-like strands of glass fibers that conduct the light generated by laser beams at transmission speeds resembling the speed of light. This technology is already seriously competing with other forms of communications media, and its use in the future is expected to become widespread.

159 Cellular Radio

An advanced form of mobile telephone service combining radio and computer technology to provide telephone service to moving vehicles. This is expected to become an important communication medium for mobile voice and data communication.

160 Local Area Networks (LAN)

Local area networks connect information processing devices within a limited physical area such as an office building or other worksite. They form the basis for integrating a multiple-vendor environment within an organization. LAN provides for the sharing of text processors, computer files and memory, different types of printers, communications among all devices of a system, communication to the outside world, and various other services, such as electronic mail and voice processing.

Note: The above communication channels make telecommunications technologies possible (see Unit 17).

161 Technological Subsystems in the Integrated Office

As the office is becoming increasingly automated, more and more businesses are seeking to merge a number of existing independent subsystems for the processing and communication of information in the form of data, text, images, graphics, or voice. Consult the index of this handbook for more information on the most recent developments in office automation in specific technological areas, such as electronic mail, facsimile transmission, computer assisted retrieval, computer output microfilm, intelligent copiers, teleconferencing, and data base management.

I62 Computer-Related Terms

Access The operation of seeking, reading, or writing data on a storage unit.

Address An identification for a storage location in the memory of a computer.

Analog An analog transmission system that sends data in a continuous wave form, whereas a digital system breaks data down into separate digital units for transmission.

Artificial Intelligence The development of software whereby a computer may be used to solve problems that appear to require reasoning and intuition.

ASCII (AMERICAN STANDARD CODE FOR INFORMATION INTERCHANGE) A standard eight-bit code used for information interchange between equipment of different manufacturers.

Analog Computer Computer designed to deal with problems of measurement (e.g. the flow of liquid, temperature changes).

Audio Response Unit An output device that provides the spoken word as the output. Also known as a voice synthesizer.

Backup Standby equipment or storage media for use if the primary equipment fails.

BASIC A simple high-level language that stands for *Beginners All-purpose Symbolic Instruction Code.*

Batch Processing Grouping related information and processing it at one time. Batch processing makes the most efficient use of computer hardware.

Baud Transmission speed of data in bits per second.

Binary Number System A numbering system that uses only two digits (0 and 1) as its base.

Bit The smallest unit of information recognized by a computer. It is an abbreviation for BInary digiT. The binary number 101 is composed of three bits.

Information Processing

Buffer A storage device used in the transmission of data that provides a temporary location for the transmitted data to occupy until the proper unit is ready to receive it.

Bug A program defect that causes the computer to operate incorrectly or not at all.

Byte A group of eight bits, usually treated as a unit. One byte can store one unit of information. Memory capacity of a computer is measured in bytes.

CAD (Computer Aided Design) An automated design and drafting system that speeds the design process by eliminating many tedious time-consuming tasks previously performed by hand.

CAI (Computer Aided Instruction) Using a computer as a teaching device as well as for reinforcement of learning through the use of special tutorial software programs.

CAT (Computer Aided Transcription) Taking down information using machine shorthand, and then using a special-purpose computer to transcribe the machine shorthand tapes into hard copy.

CP/M (Control Program for Microprocessors) A disk operating system for 8-bit personal computers.

Cassette A standard tape cassette. Provides an inexpensive way to store programs and data.

Channel A path along which signals can be sent.

Chip A tiny piece of semiconductor material containing microscopic electronic components; use of the chip has resulted in the creation of small, powerful computers.

COBOL (COmmon Business-Oriented Language) Programming language particularly suitable for business-related tasks.

CPU (Central Processing Unit) The brain of the computer that is responsible for arithmetical, logical, and control functions.

Crash A machine's hardware or software failure that prevents a system from functioning.

Data Bank A collection of data pertaining to a given subject or application.

162 Computer-Related Terms

Data Base A comprehensive and continuously updated collection of files of data on a particular subject in a single location. This electronic filing cabinet contains a series of files that can be sorted, analyzed, and stored.

Debugging A procedure to identify and correct any mistakes or malfunctions found during the testing of a computer or computer program.

Digital Computers Computers designed to perform arithmetic and logical operations.

Disk A device for storing data. A flexible disk is known as a *floppy disk*.

Disk Drive An electromechanical device that stores information on or recalls information from a disk.

Disk Operating System (DOS) A program that manages the interaction between a computer and its peripherals. The disk operating system and the operating system of the software must be compatible. Some examples are TRS DOS (Radio Shack), Apple DOS (Apple Computer), and IBM DOS (IBM Personal Computer).

Distributed Data Processing Decentralized data processing where, for example, branch offices have their own microcomputers that are linked to a main frame computer at another location. This speeds up the company's information processing functions because some of the processing can be handled away from the main frame computer and then fed into it.

Dump To transfer the contents of all or part of a storage device, usually from a central processing unit, into an external storage unit.

Encription To scramble or convert data prior to its transmission to prevent unauthorized use of the data.

Feasibility Study Part of the process of systems development in which the needs of the users are determined, the costs and benefits are determined, and a written proposal is made regarding the project that is proposed.

File A collection of related records.

FORTRAN (FORmula TRANslation) Programming language used primarily for mathematical and scientific procedures.

Information Processing

Hard Disk A rigid disk made of hard, plastic-like material, used to store and retrieve programs and data. A long-lasting storage medium with a great deal of storage capacity.

Hardware The equipment or devices that make up a computer system (e.g. the printer, the disk drives, the CRT screen).

Icon A small figure on a video display that looks like a familiar office device; for example, a wastebasket for *destroy*; a file folder for *store*.

Input The data entered into the computer or the act of entering information into the computer.

Interactive The user responds to screen prompts, and the computer responds to user answers to the prompts or to the user's performance or actions. For example, in typing tutorial software, the user types and, upon completion, the computer lets the user know how many words per minute were typed and how many errors were made.

Interface The boundary between two parts of a computer system, often consisting of a piece of electronic circuitry, that allows devices to communicate with each other.

Intelligent Copier A programmable copier capable of simple copying or of assembling stored information, copying, and distributing it to other compatible equipment (see R32).

Intelligent Terminal A terminal with its own built-in microprocessor.

Keyboard The device used to enter information into the computer, usually consisting of a standard set of typewriter keys and various special keys.

Keypunch A device that punches the holes in cards.

MS-DOS A disk operating system for 16-bit personal computers. (Also known as PC-DOS.)

Memory A device or series of devices capable of storing information in the computer temporarily or permanently in the form of patterns of binary zeros and ones.

Microcomputer A small computer for home use or for small business use.

Microprocessor A central processing unit contained on a single chip.

Minicomputer A small, yet powerful, computer that can be used on its own or connected to a main frame computer.

Modem Derived from the words MOdulate-DEModulate. A device attached to the computer to convert its digital signals into signals for transmission to other computers over a communication line.

Monitor A television receiver or cathode ray tube used to display computer output.

Off-Line Processing of transactions through a computer as they actually occur—as in banking where an account is updated as deposits are made.

Output Information or data transferred from the internal memory of the computer to some external device such as a screen, a printer, or some other piece of equipment.

Peripherals Equipment separate from the computer that can be connected in different ways to the central processing unit and memory, and that forms the system's input and output devices, such as printers, disk drives, and terminals.

Point of Sale Terminals Bar code sensors or wand readers that capture data from price tags or codes. These terminals automatically record product identification and price, and update inventory records.

Printer A device for producing paper or *hard* copies of data output by a computer.

Program A series of instructions carried out by the computer in sequence. The program must be written in a language the computer understands.

RAM (Random Access Memory) The memory into which information can be put (written) and from which it can be instantly copied (read). RAM is the *working memory* of the computer into which applications programs can be loaded and then run.

ROM (Read Only Memory) Memory circuit in which stored information is built into the chip at the time of manufacture and which cannot be subsequently changed.

Random Access Access to particular items in a file (or disk) without the need for searching the whole file.

Information Processing

Real-Time Processing Processing the data on transactions as they actually occur, such as in airline and hotel reservations.

Service Bureau Commercial businesses that will handle your information processing work for a fee.

Software The programs and instructions governing the operation of the computer that direct it to perform specific functions.

Source Document The original written record of an activity, such as a purchase order or sales invoice (see B76).

Standalone A device that is completely self-contained.

Structured Programming A programming method that uses a *top down* program design and a limited number of control structures in a program to create highly structured *modules* of program code.

Subsystem A system that is a component of a larger system.

Systems Analyst An employee who studies ways of improving office routines involving the computer.

Terminal A device for entering or receiving data from a computer.

Time Sharing A system that allows several different persons to share a computer (usually a mainframe) for different purposes at the same time.

Turnaround Time Time between the submission of a job to the computer center and the return of the results.

Turnkey System A system devised for the untrained purchaser in which all the necessary hardware, software, and systems development are provided.

Video Display A TV screen that displays information going into and coming out of the machine.

Video Display Screen The standard video display is 80 characters (or columns) wide, and 24 or 25 lines in length. Some screens can expand type size or scroll to 132 characters. The standard size screen for personal computers is 12 inches, measured diagonally.

Voice Mail A variation of electronic mail where digitized voice messages, rather than electronic text, are accepted, stored, and transmitted.

Voice Recognition Unit An input device that converts spoken words into binary digits.

Voice Response Unit A terminal that generates output in a voice-like response.

UNIT 10

JOB SEARCH AND APPLICATION

The Search	J1-J2
Sources of Job Leads	
The Application	J3-J11
The Letter of Application	
The Data Sheet	
The Application Form	J12
The Interview	J13-J15
Preparing for the Interview	
Presenting Yourself at the Interview	
Follow-Up	J16
Resume Log	J17
Final Thoughts	J18

J1-J2 The Search

Finding the right job requires careful thought and considerable effort. You need to know about yourself and your skills as well as about the job opportunities avilable in the community in which you are seeking employment. This unit contains some ideas on how to search for the job you want, how to present yourself to best advantage in a written application, how to promote yourself effectively in an interview, and how to effectively follow up after an interview.

J1 The Search

J2 Sources of Job Leads

Classified Newspaper Advertisements. The newspaper is an excellent source of employment opportunities in a given geographical area. Don't read only the headings or titles of the help wanted ads; they may be misleading. Read the entire advertisement. You might find that you qualify and that the job would interest you after all. Do not be discouraged if you do not have precisely the qualifications listed. Often, you do not have to meet every qualification stated in the advertisement—only most of them. Go ahead and apply if a particular advertisement appeals to you. Carefully follow the directions given in the advertisement for making an application.

Most classified ads are *signed ads* that give the name and address and/or telephone number of the hiring company. Some ads are *blind ads* in which no company name is mentioned, and a box number is given for a written reply. Blind ads are not often used and are generally for higher-level positions.

State Employment Agencies. Free job placement along with vocational counseling, testing, and statewide placement are provided through state employment agencies. Your nearest state employment office can be found by looking in the telephone directory under the caption for your state name. The listing is often found under *Labor, Department of* and *Employment Services* or a variation of these titles. Since this is a public service office, you'll have to be patient and persistent to get the help you need. **Note:** Don't overlook possible job opportunities that are available through town, county, state, and federal government offices and agencies.

School/College Placement Offices. Students can take advantage of their school's placement services by registering for assistance. Many employers prefer to work with school or college placement offices that strive to match employees with potential employers.

Job Search and Application

Private Employment Agencies. Private employment agencies act both for the job seeker and the prospective employer. They offer personalized service but they often charge a fee. When the job seeker accepts a *non-fee paid* position, he or she is obligated to pay the service charge, which is usually based on the starting salary. *Fee paid* is the term used if the employer is willing to pay the service charge fee. *Fee reimbursable* means that you, the job seeker, will pay the fee first and, after a satisfactory trial period, the hiring company will reimburse you. A *partial fee* paid calls for the job seeker and the hiring company to split the agency fee. Private agencies perform a valuable service for both employer and employee; however, they should be selected with care.

Friends, relatives, and associates. Don't overlook this source of help. Letting family, former instructors, neighbors, and other professional acquaintances know that you are looking for employment can sometimes give you an edge in learning about job vacancies in their own companies. This is sometimes referred to as *networking*.

Yellow Pages of the Telephone Book. If you are interested in a job in a specific field, locate companies in that field through the yellow pages of the telephone directory and then contact those companies directly. For employment outside your local area, consult the nearest telephone company office or public library for access to other cities' telephone directories.

Professional Associations and Professional Journals. Job leads can be obtained from contacts with members of professional organizations such as *Professional Secretaries International, Association of Records Managers and Administrators* and the *Administrative Management Society*. Additionally, a classified section usually appears in publications put out by these organizations.

Direct Contact. Once you have identified where you want to work—even if you do not know whether or not there is an opening—make a phone call to obtain the name of the contact person in the personnel office. Send a letter of application and data sheet (or resume) to that person. You may find that there is an opening or—at the very least—your application will be kept on file for future consideration.

J3 The Application

An application letter and data sheet essentially *sell* you and are often fundamental steps in applying for a position. It is important to prepare an informative and attractive letter and resume for a prospective employer. These documents are the employer's first impression of you, and may be the deciding factor in whether or not you are invited for an interview.

J4 The Letter of Application

Your letter of application should be well-organized and carefully worded. The following outline of a letter of application (Figure 10.1) indicates how such a letter might be organized.

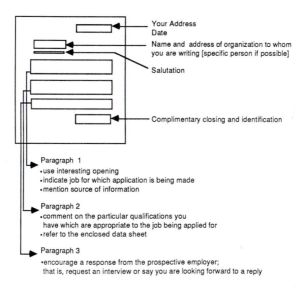

Figure 10.1 Outline of Application Letter

Here are some guidelines in preparing the application letter:

- Use good quality business stationery.
- Use correct letter format and center your letter attractively on the page (see E66-E67).
- Carefully check all spelling, grammatical points, and factual information (see Unit 7, *Grammar, Usage, and Style*).
- Type the letter and submit the original copy. Never submit a photocopy or duplicated letter of application.
- Limit your letter to one page if at all possible.
- Indicate your source of information about the job opening.
- Personalize the letter by addressing it to one specific individual if at all possible.

Job Search and Application

- Convince the prospective employer that you have something to offer the company. Describe yourself from the employer's perspective.
- Concentrate on your positive qualities. Be honest, confident, and enthusiastic.
- Write your cover letter so that it serves as an invitation to read your data sheet. This can be accomplished through statements such as:

    My involvement in extra-curricular activites shows that I am able to work both with and through others. . . .

    My work experience record shows that I have accepted greater responsibilities with each new position. . . .

    As my data sheet shows, even my hobbies complement my keen interest in obtaining employment in a sports-related field. . . .

- Proofread the letter more than once—at separate times if possible—to be certain that it is technically accurate and that it presents you in a favorable light (Figure 10.2).
- Keep a record of letters mailed, and of your follow-up telephone calls and interview results (see J17).
- Ask for some action on the part of the reader, such as a phone call or a written reply. A good strategy is to tell the reader how you will follow up to obtain an interview, rather than to request an interview and leave the follow-up to the reader.

J5 The Data Sheet

The data sheet, also known as the resume, is rarely read thoroughly; therefore, it should be short, easy to read, and organized so that it will draw attention to your most significant achievements and skills. Ideally, every data sheet should be tailored to the job being sought. But many people find a well-thought-out data sheet useful for various positions, and the cover letter sufficient to zero in on the specific job being sought.

Information on a data sheet can be presented in the sequence shown in Figure 10.3; however, no one sequence is correct. An important guideline to use when deciding on the placement of items on a data sheet is to place the items that will be most meaningful to the potential employer first. If you have an excellent work experience record, for example, place that before your education.

J5 The Data Sheet

```
                               63 Marshall Avenue
                               West New York, NJ 07093-4480
                               January 12, 19--

Ms. Vivian Palmer
Personnel Director
ABC Corporation
11 Queen Court
Secaucus, NJ 07087

Dear Ms Palmer:

Please consider my application for the Personal Computer
Trainer position you advertised in last night's Hudson
Observer.  I believe I have the skills, experience, and
personal qualities that you are seeking.

As the enclosed data sheet reveals, I have had more than
three years of diversified experience in using personal
computers.  I have used them to input data; I have learned
and evaluated commercial software packages; and I have
assisted in conducting computer orientation sessions.

As a recent graduate of Hudson View College, I hold a degree
in Office Systems Administration.  While at college, I was a
Dean's List student each semester.  My academic experience
and my work experience complement each other.  I believe
that they have provided me with theoretical and hands-on
experience, and opportunities to work with others in a
variety of office settings.

I would welcome the opportunity to discuss my application
with you further in the hope that you would agree that I
would be the right person for the Personal Computer Trainer
position you have available.  I will telephone you within
the next few days to obtain an appointment.

                               Sincerely,

                               Ms. Robin Alvarez
                               Ms. Robin Alvarez

Enclosure
```

Figure 10.2 Application Letter

```
                          PERSONAL DATA SHEET

PERSONAL INFORMATION:   Ms. Robin Alvarez
                        63 Marshall Avenue
                        West New York, NJ 07093-4480
                        Telephone Number:  (201) 889-4736

EDUCATION:              Hudson View College
                            Earned B.S. degree in Office Systems
                            Administration, December 19--

                        Stevens Junior College
                            Earned A.A degree in Liberal Arts, June 19--

                        North Hudson Regional High School
                            College preparatory subjects, Graduated
                            June 19--

WORK EXPERIENCE:        June 19-- to Present
                        Laboratory Assistant and Trainer
                            Bridge Pharmaceutical Company, North Bergen, NJ
                            Part-time position involving the maintenance of
                                a computer software library and one-to-one
                                instruction for new users on word processing,
                                spreadsheet, and data base software
                                applications

                        July 19-- to June 19--
                        Microcomputer Laboratory Assistant
                            Bridge Pharmaceutical Company, North Bergen, NJ
                            Part-time position involving the study and
                                evaluation of new software packages in word
                                processing, spreadsheet, and data base
                                applications

                        September 19-- to June 19--
                        Inventory Clerk
                            Willard Electrical Supply Company
                            Part-time cooperative education position
                                involving inventory maintenance and word
                                processing on a personal computer

SPECIAL ACHIEVEMENTS:   Vice-President, Student Chapter of the
                            Administrative Management Society, Hudson View
                            College
                        Dean's List, 19-- to 19--

REFERENCES:             Available on request
```

Figure 10.3 Data Sheet

J6 Personal Information

Provide your name, address, and telephone number. Any other information you provide is voluntary. The law prohibits discrimination in employment based on grounds of sex, race, religion, marital status, age, or nationality. This information is not relevant to any job.

J7 Job Objective (Optional)

This section provides the reader with instant knowledge about the type of job you are seeking. It can be specific, such as:

To obtain employment as an administrative assistant.

Or it might be stated in such a way as to identify long-range career goals as well:

To obtain an administrative assistant position with opportunities to display initiative, analyze and write reports, and assume supervisory responsibility.

Seeking an administrative assistant position that offers the potential for growth into supervison.

Obviously, if a resume is to be used to apply for a broad range of job categories, or is to be used for a variety of purposes, it would be more practical to omit the job objective statement.

J8 Education

- Include the name of the institution(s) you attended; your major concentration; certificates or degrees earned; dates and any honors, scholarships, or special awards you received.
- Note any work-related training—evening courses, professional workshops, special training courses, etc.
- Do not include elementary school information.

J9 Work Experience

- List your previous jobs, starting with the most recent one.
- Provide approximate starting and ending dates.
- Indicate your areas of responsibility in previous jobs. Do no simply list the titles of those jobs.
- Do not mention salaries.

J10 Achievements, Interests or Hobbies

Information in this section can provide useful insights for prospective employers. Cite honors earned, membership in organizations, leadership experiences, involvement with volunteer work and youth groups, and other experiences that illustrate your leadership potential.

J11 References

- Ask permission from people you quote as references before you use their names.
- Do not use relatives as references.

Here are some guidelines for preparing the Data Sheet.

- There is no one correct format; however, the arrangement selected should be consistent, uncluttered, attractive to the eye, and parallel in arrangement and wording.
- Aim to keep the data sheet to one page.
- Put key information such as personal data, education, and work experience at the top of the page, with work experience and achievements before your educational background if they are the strengths of your application.
- Put the most recent experiences at the top of each section.
- Keep in mind that the only personal information you *must* supply is your name, address, and telephone number. Any other information is supplied voluntarily.
- Avoid abbreviations for academic terms or any other terms that the reader might not know.
- It is possible to organize your data sheet by function rather than by time spent in various endeavors. Sometimes this kind of organization can help a potential employer see your qualifications more easily. For example, if a position calls for someone with proven writing, speaking, organizational, and clerical skills, you might use these headings in your *work experience* section and match your experiences to the headings.
- If you indicate that references are available on request, be sure that you have gotten *prior permission* from at least three people—not relatives—whose names, addresses, and telephone numbers you could supply if asked.
- It is acceptable to send a duplicate of your data sheet, but an original copy—even if prepared on word processing equipment—makes a better impression than a photocopied data sheet.
- Proofread your data sheet carefully to be certain that it is accurate in every respect.

J12 The Application Form

Although you have provided an extensive data sheet, you will still be required by most organizations to complete an application form. In doing so:

- Try to get some practice in filling out application forms before you have to do it in an actual interview situation.
- Examine the entire form first before starting to answer the questions line by line.
- Follow directions; *print* if the directions say to print, *write* if the form says to write. (This might be the only handwritten document the interviewer has on which to judge your writing skills.)
- If a section does not apply, write *N/A*, meaning *not applicable*. Writing *N/A* indicates that you haven't overlooked answering this section.
- Have a copy of your data sheet with you, since much of the information requested on the application form will already be on your data sheet. The data sheet will also make it easier to remember dates and other facts.
- Complete the form neatly. Take your time and try to avoid crossouts and corrections. There is usually some degree of pressure as you fill out the application form, so being prepared is the best way to approach the situation.
- Be truthful, but not unnecessarily modest. You will be asked to sign the application form and indicate that all the information you present is true.
- Remember that the application form will become part of your permanent record with the company if you are hired. Let it reflect you favorably.

J13 The Interview

A successful interview is a major factor in landing a job, it is important to prepare ahead of time so that you can put forth your best effort at the interview itself.

J14 Preparing for the Interview

Learn about the company. Get as much information as you can about a company before the interview. To do this, you can:

- Telephone to find out the personnel manager's name.
- Try to obtain further information about the company from friends, family, teachers, and acquaintances.
- Obtain a copy of the company's Annual Report from your local library and study the information in it. Read the president's message carefully and make note of the company's future growth plans.
- Check library reference materials to learn more about the company, its organization, and its products (see Q13).
- Be alert to the company's advertising and public relations efforts.
- Consider preparing a *Company Fact Sheet* for each firm with whom you interview. Here are some questions you might want to explore.
    - What does the company do?
    - What are the company's primary products or services?
    - What are its primary market areas?
    - What is its form of organization (sole owner, family-owned, partnership, corporation)?
    - How long has the company been in business?
    - What is the company's reputation? in the marketplace? as an employer?
    - Where are its plants, stores, branches, or corporate offices?
    - What is its growth record? Its prospects for the future?
    - Who are its competitors? How many are there?
    - What are the company's financial prospects?
    - What makes this company distinctive in the field?
    - What kinds of jobs does the company have that you can fill? Is there a career ladder of job opportunities?
    - What type of promotion plan is currently in effect?
    - What type of training is available for new and/or promoted personnel?
    - What is the approximate entry-level salary for the position you are interested in?
    - What are the special skills and/or requirements of the position you are interested in?
    - What fringe benefits, if any, are available to employees?
    - What is the average employee turnover rate?

Job Search and Application

Prepare yourself to answer questions. Reflect on some of the questions that you might be asked at the interview and practice answering these questions aloud. Of course, the questions will vary from job to job, but here are some of the typical ones that you would be well-advised to review.

- Why are you interested in this particular job?
- What experience do you have that qualifies you for this position?
- What do you think are your best personal qualities?
- What do you recognize as your limitations or weaknesses?
- What did you like most/least about your last job?
- What do you know about our organization?
- Describe what you have learned from previous jobs.
- Describe your long range career objectives.
- What specific goals other than those related to your career have you established for yourself?
- How would you describe yourself?
- How do you think a friend, instructor, or previous employer would describe you?
- What motivates you to put forth your greatest effort?
- Why should I hire you?
- What special skills besides technical skills can you bring to this job?
- What qualities do you have that make you think you will be a success in business?
- In what ways do you think you can make a contribution to our company?
- What subjects do you like best? least?
- Do you have plans for continuing your education?
- Do you think your grades are a good reflection of your academic achievement?
- How well do you work under pressure? Give examples.
- If you had to describe your greatest achievement to date, what would it be?
- Tell me a humorous story. (The range of questions at an interview is limitless, so be prepared.)

Be Prepared to Ask Questions. Typically, during the course of an interview you will be invited to ask questions. Again, be prepared. Even if your interviewer seems to have dealt with all the information you require, try to ask at least one sensible question when you are invited to do so. Questions you might consider are:

- What are the opportunities for advancement and development with the company if I perform well?

- What will my exact responsibilities be?
- What type of equipment will I be working with?

> **Note:** The applicant who asks good questions appears to be more interested in the position, and that interest could be the deciding factor leading to a job offer; however, you must choose these questions carefully. Putting too much emphasis on questions concerning vacations, fringe benefits, and time off will undermine your chances for success.

Prepare Yourself Physically. The interview will require that you be at your best. Plan your wardrobe ahead of time. Make sure your clothes are clean, well pressed, and professional-looking. Get enough sleep the night before. Make the necessary arrangements to arrive at the interview on time. Organize the materials you will need for the interview: your social security card, a pen, a copy of your data sheet, and any other materials you wish to take along.

J15 Presenting Yourself at the Interview

The interview is designed to provide information for both the employer and the applicant; however, no two interviews will be the same. Most interviews follow a pattern, and being aware of this pattern will make you a more confident interviewee.

Stand to greet the interviewer and, if a hand is extended, shake hands with a firm grip. At the outset, you can expect a few minutes of introductory small talk. This might be followed by a short introduction to the firm, its activities, and its products. Next, the interviewer will ask you questions about your education, your work experience, or for clarification of any information on your data sheet. Other probing questions such as those suggested earlier will be asked of you. Details of the vacancy will then be provided, and you might be asked additional questions about how your qualifications would fulfill the job requirements. Finally, you will be asked if, after hearing about the job firsthand, you are still interested or have any other questions. At this point, try to ask at least one question to demonstrate your interest and enthusiasm for the position. You might also ask when a decision will be made regarding the position if this was not made clear earlier in the interview. Sense that the interview is coming to a close, thank the interviewer, respond to a handshake if offered, and leave promptly.

Job Search and Application

Here are some important points to note in successfully presenting yourself at an interview.

- Do the preliminary planning suggested; it will help you feel more comfortable (see J14).
- Have a positive attitude; strive to be cheerful.
- Coordinate your wardrobe so that you will look your best but will also be comfortable.
- Stress similarities between you and the interviewer's ideas or life experiences if possible.
- Expect to fill out an application form; and, for some positions, expect to be tested.
- Go alone to the interview.
- Arrive in plenty of time. (As you travel to the interview site, consider the cost and convenience of the travel as a factor to determine whether or not you really want the job.)
- Let the interviewer guide the interview. Wait for an offer to shake hands and an indication of where you should sit.
- Remember your interviewer's name and use it during the course of the interview to personalize the conversation.
- Avoid *yes* and *no* responses. Expand on your answers and give examples of your experience, your positive attitude, and your initiative whenever you can.
- Look at the interviewer. Direct eye contact demonstrates self-confidence.
- Smile when appropriate.
- Demonstrate positive body language—do not sit with arms crossed, tap your foot, or use too many hand gestures, as these will detract from your effectiveness.
- Keep the discussion to the job only. Home or social concerns have no place in the interview.
- Do not smoke even if you are invited to do so.
- Be honest about your capabilities, but don't be too modest.
- If you are being interviewed by more than one person, make sure you direct your answers to all the people in the group.
- Speak clearly and distinctly. Don't talk too fast.
- Use correct grammar and avoid the use of slang.
- Capitalize on *cues* given to you by the interviewer; pay attention to the interviewer's body language and use it to your advantage when you can.

Note: You may find it informative to refer to Unit 14 on the subject of *How to Conduct an Interview* so that you are aware of what an employer is trying to find out about you (see P9).

J16 Follow-Up

After the interview is over, go home and review what took place.

- Make a note of what you felt were your strong points.
- Be aware of those areas in which you might need improvement.
- Reflect on the job itself and evaluate your interest in accepting the position should it be offered to you.

If you have a real interest in obtaining the position, you may want to write a thank you letter to the interviewer. The letter should be written immediately following the interview and should indicate that you are looking forward to a reply (Figure 10.4). If there were unanswered questions, or if new relevant material has come to mind, include this information.

If you have not heard anything from the company within approximately ten days, you should feel free to place a tactful call to learn the status of the job opening.

```
                              63 Marshall Avenue
                              West New York, NJ 07093-4480
                              January 23, 19--

Ms. Vivian Palmer
Personnel Director
ABC Corporation
11 Queen Court
Secaucus, NJ 07087

Dear Ms. Palmer

Thank you for the time you spent with me at
the interview today.  After talking with you
and Mr. Ferraro, I feel more certain than
ever about my interest in working with the ABC
Corporation as a Personal Computer Trainer.

I look forward to hearing from you to learn
your decision.

                              Sincerely,

                              Ms. Robin Alvarez
                              Ms. Robin Alvarez
```

Figure 10.4   Thank You Letter

J17 Resume Log

As you conduct your job search, it may be helpful to keep a written record of resumes sent, responses received, follow-up made and other pertinent details for later reference. A log such as the one illustrated in

Job Search and Application

Date	Company Contacted	Person Contacted	Type of Contact	Documents Sent	Comments	Follow-Up Needed	Date For Follow-Up
9/10	ABC Co.	Sue Jones	letter	Cover letter resume		phone call	9/20
9/20	ABC Co.	Sue Jones	phone call	—	made interview appt.	interview	9/21 10 a.m.

JOB SEARCH LOG

Figure 10.5 Job Search Log
Reprinted from the *Business Education Forum*, Vol. 40, Number 7, April 1986. Courtesy of Dr. Lena M. Cunningham Smith and the National Business Education Association.

Figure 10.5, and a well-organized filing system of all documents sent out and received will help keep you organized as your quest for employment continues.

J18 Final Thoughts

If you are offered the job, congratulations! If you are unsuccessful, try not to be discouraged. Most firms do not provide a reason for rejecting candidates. It is possible you may have been passed over because you were *over* qualified for the job and it was felt that you would not have remained in the position very long—who knows?

Remember that the three key qualities of a prospective employee are:

- genuine interest
- the ability to perform the job well
- willingness to learn

If you have demonstrated these, and follow the job search hints given here, it will not be long before you secure the job that is just right for you.

UNIT 11

LETTER AND MESSAGE DELIVERY

L

Mail Techniques	**L1-L4**
Handling Incoming Mail	
Handling Outgoing Mail	
The Mail Register or Mail Log	
Mailroom Facilities and Equipment	**L5-L10**
Mailroom Functions	
Mailroom Design	
Mail-Handling Equipment	
Ways to Ensure Efficient Mail-Handling	**L11**
Services and Products of the United States Postal Service	**L12**
Types of Mail	
Classes of Mail	
Standard Letter Dimensions/Nonstandard Mail	
Selected Mail Services and Products	
Alternatives to Postal Services	**L49**
Checklist for Controlling Mailing Costs	**L50**
Stay Current	**L51**

Letter and Message Delivery

Advances in office technology permit information to be exchanged between organizations by many means; however, the sending and receiving of *original* documents and other items is still a vital part of a company's operation. Mailing costs are a significant expense of any business. Controlling these costs should be the concern of each employee. Efficient mail handling can increase business yet also decrease the cost of doing business.

In this unit, you are given suggestions for handling incoming and outgoing mail, an introduction to mailroom techniques and equipment, and a summary of the major services and products of the United States Postal Service.

L1 Mail Techniques

L2 Handling Incoming Mail

You might be required to open mail for one person or for all employees of a department. You might also be in a position where you need to open your own mail. Regardless of the situation, you should follow a system in handling this procedure. Here are the key steps involved in opening mail.

Open the Mail
Use a standard letter opener or an electric letter opening machine. Never open mail marked *Personal* or *Confidential* unless it is addressed to you. Be sure that you extract the entire contents from an envelope before discarding it.

Sort the Mail
Divide the mail into separate stacks as follows:

Mail requiring special handling—mailgrams, letters marked *Personal or Confidential*, certified letters, and express mail

First-class mail—letters, orders, bills

Interoffice mail—memos, copies to be filed, directives

Third-class mail—advertisements, circulars, and catalogs

Second-class mail—periodicals and newspapers

Fourth-class mail—packages

L1-L2 Mail Techniques

Log Documents Requiring Special Handling
It is good practice to keep a separate, chronologically-arranged record book or mail register of all correspondence and packages received that were delivered by special services (see L4).

Examine the Mail
Some employers require that envelopes be fastened to the correspondence; others do not. Determine your employer's preference. Usually, however, if there is no return address in the letter or if the postmark is critical, such as in the payment of a bill with a discount, you should save the envelope.

Date Stamp the Mail
Date each piece of mail using a rubber stamp; or if equipment is available, date and time stamp each piece of mail.

Once again at this point, you must be alert to the preferences of your employer regarding the amount of annotating you should do and how the mail should be arranged for final presentation. You might be responsible for all or some of the following steps.

Read and Annotate the Mail
Read each piece of mail and annotate it—that is, use a colored pen or highlighter pen to call attention to key information in documents. You may also be asked to locate related documents in the file or attach a note to documents with pertinent information that might be helpful to your employer in decision making or in composing a reply.

Route the Mail
If a piece of correspondence is to be read by a number of people and the timeliness of distribution is important, you can make copies of the document and distribute a copy to each person. If time is not a critical factor, you can attach a routing slip as shown in Figure 11.1.

```
                    ROUTING SLIP

    FROM: H.A. Elliot         Date _____
          Office Manager

    Please initial after reading and pass on.

    TO:    Adams, L. _____
           Giles, P.  _____
           Welsh, R.  _____
           Zimmer, K. _____

    Return to H.A. Elliot
```

Figure 11.1 Routing Slip

Letter and Message Delivery

Arrange the Mail for Presentation

If you open the mail for a particular person, you will need to arrange the mail according to your supervisor's preference. Usually the mail is arranged in a folder with *MAIL* written across the front. One method of arrangement might be:

Mail requiring special handling first—letters marked *Personal*, mailgrams, certified letters; followed by

Documents to be answered or requiring action; followed by

Documents to be answered by the secretary/administrative assistant as routine; followed by

Documents to be answered by someone else or referred to someone else; followed by

Documents to be read for information.

Another approach is to present mail in the same order as you sorted the mail: special handling mail first, followed by first-class, interoffice, third-class, and second-class mail.

L3 Handling Outgoing Mail

Whether you handle your own outgoing mail or whether you handle it for someone else, make sure that you verify each of the following items prior to releasing a piece of mail.

- Be certain that the correct size envelope is used.
- Be certain that signatures are in place.
- Be certain that a file copy has been retained.
- Be certain that all enclosures have been inserted.
- Verify the envelope address with the correspondent's address in the letter or document.
- Be certain that the envelope address has been prepared in the correct format (see E52).
- Determine the type of postal service to be used. If special handling is required, prepare appropriate forms and/or give specific instructions to the mail room.
- Log outgoing mail requiring special handling in an *Outgoing Mail Log*. Entries in this outgoing mail register might contain information such as the date, the complete address of the recipient, the contents, the method of transmittal, the name or initials of the person dispatching the mail, and other related information (see L4).

L3-L4   Handling Outgoing Mail

- Be certain that the return address is included.
- Secure the contents of packages carefully and wrap the package in accordance with shipping regulations (see L41).
- Be certain that items that must be mailed by a certain time are ready for the scheduled mail pickups at your office.
- Place the mail in an outbox for pickup and delivery to the mailroom.
- If there is no mailroom, be certain that the appropriate postage is attached.

L4 The Mail Register or Mail Log

The mail register or mail log (Figure 11.2) is a record of all incoming and outgoing mail. It provides for the effective management and organization of mail. An accurate log can often identify mail-handling problems and suggests quick solutions. A good system can also document mail costs, mail flow, and mail distribution.

Separate incoming and outgoing registers or logs can be used depending on the needs of a particular department or organization. A log may be a composite record (lists all items), or a specific record for certain items, which may include:

special handling items in the incoming mail

incoming packages

all outgoing packages

special handling items in the outgoing mail

a summary of items, quantities, and costs of the incoming and outgoing mail

Date	To/From	Incoming	Outgoing	Item	Contents	BY
3/1	Allied Insurance	✓		Reg. Mail	Policy #269842	JL
3/1	Barker Office Supp		✓	Parcel Post	Package	JL
3/2	Lyons & Clark	✓		Cert. Letter	Deposition	JL
3/4	Robert Akers		✓	Exp. Mail	Report	AA

INCOMING/OUTGOING MAIL REGISTER   For the month of March 19--

Figure 11.2   Mail Register

Letter and Message Delivery

Some companies keep a list of all incoming and outgoing documents and packages. This, however, is a very time consuming procedure. The day to day record of correspondence placed in the interoffice mail or the outgoing mail can be documented if a reading or correspondence file is kept (see F67).

L5 Mailroom Facilities and Equipment

L6 Mailroom Functions

The basic mailroom functions are receiving and sending mail.

- *Receiving* functions include:

    date stamping—marking the date received on incoming correspondence

    sorting—separating incoming correspondence for systematic delivery

    distributing—delivering correspondence to its proper destination within the organization

- *Sending* functions include:

    metering—tracking the volume of outgoing correspondence

    weighing—assuring that proper postage is applied according to weight and destination.

    mailing—sorting and routing items for most efficient delivery

L7 Mailroom Design

For greatest efficiency, the larger mail-handling areas—where mail is opened, sorted, and read prior to distribution—should be designed in two loops, one for incoming mail and one for outgoing mail (Figure 11.3).

L8 Mail-Handling Equipment

The use of specialized equipment facilitates the handling of incoming and outgoing mail. The following items are merely suggestive of some of the equipment available. Combination units, electronic units, and even units that are interfaced with copiers or data processing equipment are becoming more and more prevalent.

L5-L9 Mailroom Facilities and Equipment

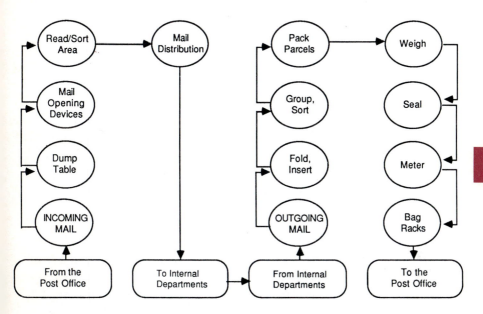

Figure 11.3 Typical Mailroom Design

L9 For Incoming Mail

- Dump Tables and/or Work Tables

    U-shape, L-shape, or rectangular work tables provide compact work areas and can often be placed so as to reduce the steps needed in sorting the mail. Tables on casters and tables with storage space underneath provide additional advantages.

- Sorting Bins

    Sorting bins are important pieces of equipment in a mail room. Each compartment should be large enough to handle various sized documents. Modular equipment with adjustable shelves is best to accommodate the various sizes and shapes of documents.

- Mail Openers

    Equipment to open envelopes ranges from hand-operated models to electronic models that feed, transport, remove envelope edges, and count the mail in a single operation.

Letter and Message Delivery

- Mail Delivery Carts

    Delivery carts are used to deliver mail to departments and offices throughout the company and to bring outgoing mail to the mailroom on prescribed routes and at specific times during the day.

- Mailmobiles

    A mailmobile is a robot-type mail delivery cart that travels on a chemically treated route placed on the flooring. It provides for the distribution and collection of the mail without human assistance.

L10 For Outgoing Mail

- Addresser/Printers

    Equipment used to affix mailing list labels to envelopes. Data may be pre-recorded on a plastic or metal plate or generated from a computer data base.

- Folding Equipment

    Automatic units can be set to fold single folds, letter folds, and other special folds. They can be separate pieces of equipment or they can be interfaced with high-speed copiers and duplicators.

- Mail Inserters and Presorters

    This semi-automatic or fully automatic equipment is designed to insert mailing pieces into envelopes. It is most often used with computer-generated billings, statements, and letters. Some advanced equipment is capable of inserting and pre-sorting mail according to USPS regulations.

- Postage Scales

    Newer electronic models and can be programmed to compute the least expensive and most efficient rates for letters and parcel mail. They help cut costs because the precise weighing of items and the accurate calculation of rates by zones provide cost-saving advantages.

- Postage Meter

    Ensures accurate postage, provides a quality stamp image, reduces visits to the post office, and speeds mail delivery since letters are pre-canceled. Postage meters can be set for any stamp value designed, so there is no need to stock a wide range of stamps of various denominations. Postage meters protect against unauthorized or non-business use of the postage budget, and also reduce the amount of time spent in manually separating and affixing individual stamps.

The metering machine may be purchased or leased from various vendors for a relatively small fee. The meter itself, however, can be leased only from USPS vendors. The meter measures the amount of postage actually used. It is set according to a prepaid amount and must be reset and again prepaid when the value approaches zero.

L11 Ways to Ensure Efficient Mail-Handling

A properly organized and managed mail room can serve as an organization's communication center and can promote cost-cutting if efficient alternatives to traditional mail service are considered and used whenever possible. Here are some suggestions for handling the mail economically and effectively.

- Periodically delete obsolete names and addresses from mailing lists.
- Address envelopes carefully by following the latest USPS guidelines for addressing envelopes (see L40).
- Always use a return address.
- Standardize mailing pieces to conform to USPS size restrictions.
- Select the correct form of postal service and clearly identify the type of service selected on the face of the document.
- Provide specially marked envelopes, or rubber stamps for identifying the appropriate class of service.
- Plan to mail documents in a timely manner; avoid waiting until the last minute.
- Wrap packages according to USPS instructions (see L41).
- Purchase specialized mail-handling equipment if the volume of mail justifies it.
- Use a postage meter to affix postage instead of using loose stamps.
- Be certain that the meter is reset before the prepaid balance reaches zero.
- Consider the cost-saving advantages offered by Bulk Mailing (see L24) and Presort First-Class Mail (see L43) if you have large volume mailings.

Letter and Message Delivery

L12 Services and Products of the United States Postal Service

The United States Postal Service offers a wide variety of helpful services. The following list summarizes some of the major services and products available. For more specific information, contact the Customer Service Department of your local post office or:

Consumer Advocate

U.S. Postal Service

Washington, DC 20260-6320

Telephone: (202) 245-4514

L13 Types of Mail

L14 Domestic Mail

Mail sent to addresses within the United States, its territories and possessions (Puerto Rico), and to military Post Offices (APO and FPO) and the United Nations, is referred to as *domestic* mail. Domestic rates also apply to mail sent to Canada and Mexico.

L15 International Mail

For letter mail sent to other foreign countries, the rates are higher, and there are different rates and weight limits depending on destination. Your local post office can supply you with more specific rates, regulations, and types of service. Packages sent overseas can be sent air parcel post or surface parcel post. Air parcel post may take ten days or less, while surface parcel post could possibly take up to two months for delivery. Customs declarations must be included with packages (see D25, D29, D30).

L16 Classes of Mail

L17 First-Class

Mail in this category consists of written or typed matter—letters, printed business forms, receipts, documents, and post cards up to 12 ounces. Most first-class mail is dispatched airmail unless surface transportation is more efficient.

L12-L19 Service and Products of the United States Postal Service

Parcels weighing from 12 ounces to 70 pounds, whose maximum size is 108 inches in combined length and girth (distance around at thickest part of package), can be sent by first-class *Priority Mail* (see L44). These parcels receive priority air service and are usually delivered in from two to four days, but cost more than fourth-class parcels (see L20).

Properly addressed first-class domestic mail will generally be delivered locally overnight, by the second day to major population centers, and by the third day to outlying areas. To help assure one-and two-day delivery, mail should be deposited in time for a 5 p.m. collection by the USPS.

L18 Second-Class

This service may be used only by printers, publishers, and registered news agents who meet certain post office requirements for mailing printed matter. Second-class may not be used by the general public. Special forms must be filed to qualify and the mailing must be in bulk lots. No handwritten messages may be included with second-class mail. The cost and speed of USPS mail delivery usually depends on the class of service selected. The following entries define the various classes now available. All mail, regardless of class, must meet minimum size standards in order to be processed. Pieces that are 1/4 of an inch or less in thickness will be mailable only if they are:

1. rectangular in shape.
2. at least 3 1/2 inches high.
3. at least 5 inches long.
4. at least .007 of an inch thick (about thickness of a postal card).

Any mail not meeting these standards will be returned to the sender. (See L21.)

L19 Third-Class

Third-class mail is sometimes called *advertising mail*. It consists of printed matter mailed by individuals or companies other than publishers. This material must be of a non-personal nature. It includes printed material and merchandise parcels weighing less than 16 ounces. Rate structures are available for single pieces or bulk mail. Third-class mail has a lower priority but is less expensive than first-class mail service.

Letter and Message Delivery

L20 Fourth-Class (Parcel Post)

Items weighing 16 ounces or more are often sent parcel post or fourth-class mail. Size, weight, and distance from sender to receiver determine costs. Packages that are 16 ounces or more and that are not marked *Priority Mail* are considered fourth-class mail. There may be reduced rates for books or catalogs. Fourth-class mail may take three to ten days for delivery, but it is the least expensive mailing service.

L21 Standard Letter Dimensions/Nonstandard Mail

The United States Postal Service is rapdily modernizing thorugh automation systems that use high technology equipment. In order for these systems to operate efficiently, it is essential that first-class letter-size mail meet the criteria for processing by this equipment. The USPS standards for letter dimensions are:

	Letters	Post Cards
Minimum size	3 1/2" x 5"	3 1/2" x 5"
Maximum size	6 1/8" x 11 1/2"	4 1/4" x 6"
Minimum thickness	0.007 of an inch	0.007 of an inch
Maximum thickness	1/4 of an inch	0.0095 of an inch

The *aspect ratio* (ratio of length to height) must also be considered. To determine the aspect ratio, divide the length of an item by its height. If the result is between 1.3 and 2.5, the item is within the standard aspect ratio.

Nonstandard mail includes first-class mail weighing one ounce or less, and single-piece third-class mail weighing two ounces or less that exceeds *any* of the following:

- 6 1/8" in height
- 11 1/2" in length
- 1/4" in thickness

If the aspect ratio is below 1.3 or above 2.5, the item is considered nonstandard. A surcharge (additional fee) is added to the regular postage for each piece of nonstandard mail. To control costs and assure efficiency, be certain that all first- and third-class mail meets USPS standards.

L20-L27   Fourth-Class (Parcel Post)

L22 Selected Mail Services and Products

L23 Aerogrammes

Lightweight stationery that folds into a mailing envelope is available for purchase from the post office. Called *aerogrammes*, these mailers are used most often for letters sent overseas.

L24 Bulk Mail

For quantity mailings, organizations or individuals can save money by using bulk mail. To qualify, a minimum of 200 identical pieces must be mailed at one time. There is an annual charge for a bulk mailing permit, and a one-time charge for the permit imprint, which must be affixed to the mailing. The user must count, sort, and bundle the mail according to ZIP Codes. Bulk Mail is sent third-class so advance planning is necessary if specific delivery dates are to be met. There are different third-class rates for business and non-profit organizations. Recognized and authorized non-profit organizations can usually send third-class mail at a lower rate than for profit businesses.

L25 Caller Service

Caller pickup service is available during regular post office hours. It is a service designed for those who receive a large volume of mail or those who need a box number address when no boxes are available. Users of this service must pick up mail at the post office. It is not delivered to a specific address.

L26 Cash Receipts

Upon request, you can obtain a receipt to verify the amount of a purchase of stamps or other postal supplies.

L27 Certificate of Mailing

For a fee, you can obtain a certificate of mailing receipt that will provide you with evidence of mailing. No record of the receipt is kept at the post office and no insurance for loss or damage is provided.

L28 Certified Mail

Certified mail is available for domestic mail only. It provides you with a mailing receipt, and a record of delivery is kept at the post office. This service is intended for items with no intrinsic value. Ordinary mail handling is used. For an additional fee, a return receipt may be requested to provide the sender with proof of delivery.

L29 Claims

A claim requests payment for damage or reimbursement for certain postal fees. Claims are usually filed for insured, registered, C.O.D., or express mail items that are lost or damaged in delivery. Special claim procedures must be followed. USPS personnel will provide the correct form and explain claim procedures.

L30 C.O.D. (Collect on Delivery)

If you wish to have the post office collect payment for merchandise when it is delivered to an address, C.O.D. service may be used. The maximum value is limited to $500, the items must have been ordered by the addressee, and the fee charged includes insurance protection against loss or damage. This service is not available for international mail.

L31 Customs

Mail to and from foreign countries is subject to U.S. Customs Service examination. Imported goods are subject to U.S. Customs duty. When goods enter the country by mail, a duty fee and a customs clearance and delivery fee are collected (see L15).

L32 Delivery Service

Mail is delivered on a regular basis to any location with a recognized address and on a regular mail route. Generally, the delivery point must be easily accessible, and provide an approved mailbox and displayed address. Businesses may prefer to pick up their mail at a post office box or use caller service (see L25 and L42).

L33 Express Mail

The fastest, and most expensive, regular mail service offered by the USPS. Express mail guarantees overnight delivery service if certain conditions are met. The service may not be available at all post office stations and overnight delivery may not be possible to all destinations. Check with your local post office branch for guarantees and delivery areas served.

Classes of Service
A-label service provides delivery from one post office to another for pickup by the receiver by 10 a.m. the next *business* day. *B-label* service provides attempted delivery from a post office to a specific address or individual by 3 p.m. the next day—weekends and holidays included. A-label service is less expensive than B-label service.

Qualifications
To guarantee overnight service, express mail packages must be accepted by a sending station by 5 p.m. (or an earlier time if designated by the postmaster). In some areas, prepaid packages may be deposited in specially marked collection boxes prior to collection time. All express mail packages must have a properly completed label attached and should be enclosed in specially marked envelopes or cartons provided by the USPS. Packages are limited to no more than 70 pounds in weight and 108 inches in combined length and girth.

Fees
Flat rate fees, regardless of destination, apply to packages up to two pounds and packages in excess of two pounds but less than five pounds. Packages in excess of five pounds are assigned a fee based on weight and distance to delivery point. On location pickup service, same day airport service, custom designed service, proof of delivery, and international service are available at extra cost. All fees include a proof of mailing receipt and insurance up to a $500 maximum. If delivery is not *attempted* by the guaranteed time, the fee is reimbursed through application to the sending post office.

L34 Insurance
Up to $500 worth of insurance can be purchased on first-, third-, and fourth- class mail. The insurance fee (plus regular postage) is based on the value of the article. Items valued over $500 should be sent by Registered Mail. Only items sent by domestic mail may be insured. It is important to save the insurance receipt; in case of loss, reimbursement will be made for the actual value of the item less depreciation—not necessarily the amount of the insurance purchased.

Letter and Message Delivery

L35 Intelpost

Intelpost is a facsimile transmission service that permits rapid transmission of documents via satellite. You can send (or receive) a high-quality black and white facsimile of any written material, document, or graphic. The sender must take the document to the Intelpost center at the main post office in certain key cities—New York, Washington, D.C., Vancouver, Amsterdam, Berne, and London are some examples. Within minutes, the copy will be available for pickup by a correspondent at one of the other remote locations.

L36 Mail Fraud

If you have difficulty with a mail order company or if you suspect that you are a victim of fraud, contact your local postmaster, local postal inspector, or the Consumer Advocate Department.

L37 Mailgram Service

Mailgram is an electronic message service that enables you to send one or many messages to any address in the United States. Delivery is normally made with the next business day's mail. Mailgrams can be sent by calling Western Union's toll-free number, or you can use your office Telex or TWX equipment. The cost for sending 50 words is approximately $5, and more words can be sent at an additional cost. Mailgram is a cooperative effort of the USPS and Western Union Corporation.

L38 Merchandise Return Service

Merchandise return service is available to *business shippers* through a special permit. A receiver can return a parcel and have the return postage paid by the shipper if special labels provided by the merchants are affixed. Merely apply the label to the package and deposit it at the post office or other designated mailing point.

L39 Money Orders

Money orders offer a safe way to send money. They can be cashed at no cost at the recipient's post office, and can be replaced, upon proof of purchase, if lost. You can buy domestic money orders at all post offices in amounts up to $700. The larger the amount, the higher the fee. Copies of paid money orders are retained for two years after the date they are paid.

L40 OCR (Optical Character Reader) Mail Processing

The post office now uses sophisticated optical character readers that can read ZIP Codes and sort the mail more accurately and efficiently than manual processing. OCR's read the actual address or special bar codes provided by the USPS. To be certain that your mail will meet the requirements for this electronic sorting, try to meet the following standards:

- Type or machine print all addresses.
- Be certain that addresses in window envelopes have at least a 1/2 inch margin on all sides.
- Avoid any printing other than the address on or below the delivery address (the line containing the street address).
- Leave the bottom right corner of the envelope blank. The OCR will automatically print bar codes in this space to speed sorting.
- Use black printing on white envelopes.
- Use standard typefaces.
- Be certain that affixed computer labels are straight.
- Type the envelope address in uppercase characters, single-spaced, with no marks of punctuation (see E52). Single-space between address elements and between lines.
- Use the two-letter state abbreviation and a thirteen-letter maximum city abbreviation (see inside front cover).
- Always include ZIP Codes on the city/state line. Do not divide ZIP Code numbers.
- Place the address so that the top of the city, state, and ZIP Code line is no further than 2 1/4" from the bottom of the envelope nor any closer than 5/8" to the bottom of the envelope.
- Separate hand-addressed mail from typed mail when bundling it.
- Be certain that the typeface and pitch are complementary, because letters typed too closely together will be rejected by the scanning equipment.

L41 Packaging and Addressing Parcels

Proper packaging and accurate addressing of packages are the best ways to prevent parcel damage and loss. Use a strong container, cushion the contents to make sure they do not move within the container, and print the address information carefully. It is also a good idea to place the addressee's name and address inside the package. Pressure-sensitive filament or reinforced tape is recommended for closing flaps and seams. *Do not use wrapping paper and string.*

Letter and Message Delivery

L42 Post Office Boxes

Post office boxes are rented by businesses and individuals who do not wish to use a full address, or who do not have letter carrier service. The renter pays an annual fee, is assigned a box number, and is given a key. The contents of the post office box are accessible only by the renter, and mail can be obtained any time the post office lobby is open.

L43 Presort First-Class Mail

A service that provides first-class delivery at discounted rates. To be eligible for special pre-sort postage rates, 500 pieces of mail or more must be mailed at one time. The mail must be sorted according to ZIP Codes by the sender. You can save three cents on each letter sorted according to five-digit ZIP Codes, and four cents when sorted according to nine-digit ZIP Codes.

L44 Priority Mail

Priority mail is a form of first-class mail for items weighing more than 12 ounces but not more than 70 pounds. The maximum size cannot exceed 108 inches in combined length and girth. Items sent by Priority Mail must be marked as such; otherwise they will be delivered as fourth-class mail. Free Priority Mail stickers are available from the post office. Delivery is usually made in two to three days.

L45 Registered Mail

All first-class and priority mail may be registered. Registered mail is designed for irreplaceable items, such as extremely important papers, documents, and high-value items. Articles to be registered must be taken to the post office. On payment of a postage fee plus a registration fee (based on the value of the article), the sender is given a numbered receipt. The receipt (registration) number is stamped on the registered package and is recorded by the postal clerk. When the package is delivered, the addressee must sign for it. If a registered item does not arrive at its destination, the registration number enables the package to be traced. Three important regulations must be observed when preparing registered mail: do not use self-sealing envelopes, do not use masking or transparent tape to seal items, and do not use padded bags. For an additional fee you may purchase up to $25,000 of postal insurance on registered mail items. Reimbursement is limited to the actual value of the item at the time of mailing. Whether the mailing is insured or not, the full value of the mailing must be declared at the time the item is sent.

L42–L49 Post Office Boxes

L46 Special Handling

Special handling service is available for third- and fourth-class mail only, including insured mail. It speeds delivery through preferential handling in dispatch and transport, but does not include special delivery.

L47 Special Delivery

Special delivery service may be purchased on all classes of mail except third-class. It provides delivery separate from regularly scheduled route delivery, including weekends. Delivery is not always by special messenger. Items must be mailed from a post office. The sender pays first-class postage plus an additional fee. Items should be clearly marked: *Special Delivery*. Delivery is usually made within two days.

L48 ZIP + 4 Code

The five-digit ZIP Code designates a particular geographic region. Once the sorting equipment with its OCR reader *reads* the ZIP Code, the mail is automatically transferred to the next step in the processing until the mail reaches its destination.

The four added digits in ZIP + 4 represent an even smaller geographic region than the five-digit code. For example, the first two numbers represent sectors such as several blocks or a group of streets. The last two numbers represent segments of these sectors, such as one side of a city block, one floor of a large building, a cluster of mail boxes or other similar geographic locations.

Use of the ZIP + 4 Codes is voluntary, but by complying you will be rewarded in the form of more stable postal rates. ZIP + 4 mailers who meet quantity minimums and who pre-sort their mail can qualify for additional savings using the ZIP + 4 Codes (see I30 and L43). A national ZIP + 4 directory is available. If you send your regular five-digit ZIP Code mailing list to the customer service department of the USPS, they will add the correct final four digits to each addres at no cost and return the list to you.

L49 Alternatives to Postal Services

For alternatives to the USPS delivery services, see Unit 4 on Delivery and Shipping Services and Unit 17 on Telephone and Telecommunication Systems.

Letter and Message Delivery

L50 Checklist for Controlling Mailing Costs

Efficient and cost-effective mail service is essential in any business. The following list suggests ways of controlling mailing costs.

1. Mail early to get lower rates and premium service.
2. If an in-house scale is used, be certain it is accurate.
3. Consult with the United States Postal Service for the most efficient and least expensive method before mailing.
4. Use the *group mail* method when mailing many letters to the same address.
5. Consider bulk mailings or pre-sort mailings if quantity of outgoing mail meets qualifications.
6. Consider printing on both sides of the paper when possible to reduce the weight of the mailing (when mailing multiple-page documents, for example).
7. Keep mailing lists accurate and current.
8. Prepare packages properly; address them accurately and seal them securely.
9. Use ZIP Codes in both mailing and return addresses.
10. Use *Third-Class* for mass mailings.

L51 Stay Current

Postal rates, requirements, and available services change frequently. The USPS issues many free publications detailing current practices. They also offer free consulting services for many mailing problems. Contact your local post office customer service representative (listed in the white or blue pages of your local telephone directory under "U.S. Government Offices—Postal Service") whenever you have questions or need help in improving your mail operations.

UNIT 12

MATHEMATICS IN BUSINESS

Fractions	M1
Decimals	M2
Percentages	M3
Common Equivalents	M4
Algebraic Equations	M5
Business Formulas	M6-M12
Accounting Equation	
Amortization Formula	
Interest	
Selling Price	
Taxes (Property)	
True Interest Rate	
Pricing Goods for Sale	M13-M18
Retail and Wholesale Prices	
Discounts	
Break Even Point	
Statistical Data	M19-M23
Averages	
Ratio	
Proportion	
Charts and Graphs	
Foreign Currency Exchange	M24
Electronic Calculators	M25-M30
Touch Indexing	
Machine Logic	
Factors to Consider When Purchasing an Electronic Calculator	
Basic Electronic Calculator Function Keys	
Desktop Calculator Features	

Mathematics in Business

Dealing with business problems involving commissions, taxes, statistics, and billing demand mathematical skill. To solve business problems, you must be able to work with fractions, decimals, and percentages. Calculators are often used to perform routine computations; however, to use the calculator efficiently, you must know the mathematical steps by which to get the correct result. This unit summarizes commonly used mathematic applications in business, and suggests some ways you can select and use electronic calculator features for best results.

M1 Fractions

M

A *fraction* is any number with a numerator and a denominator.

Terms: $\frac{1}{15} \quad \frac{\text{numerator}}{\text{denominator}}$

An understanding of fractions, their functions and uses is helpful in working with decimal fractions. Having a knowledge of fractions is also useful in dealing with algebraic expressions.

There are several types of fractions.

Improper Fraction (numerator larger than denominator): $\frac{4}{3}$

Proper Fraction (numerator smaller than denominator): $\frac{1}{2}$

Mixed Number (combination of whole number and fraction): $7\frac{2}{5}$

Equivalent Fractions (fractions of the same value but different numerators and denominators): $\frac{1}{4}$ and $\frac{2}{8}$

Product (result of two numbers multiplied by each other): $2 \times 3 = 6$ (6 is the product)

To Add and Subtract Fractions

1. Find the lowest common denominator (i.e., the smallest amount into which each denominator can be evenly divided).

$\frac{1}{3} + \frac{3}{5}$ —lowest common denominator is 15

M1 Fractions

2. Rewrite each fraction as an equivalent fraction using the lowest common denominator.

$$\frac{1}{3} + \frac{3}{5} = \frac{5}{15} + \frac{9}{15}$$

3. Add or subtract the numerators.

$$\frac{1}{3} + \frac{3}{5} = \frac{5}{15} + \frac{9}{15} = \frac{14}{15}$$

To Add and Subtract Mixed Numbers

1. Add or subtract the whole numbers.
2. Add or subtract the fractions.
3. Add or subtract the results.

$$6\frac{1}{2} + 3\frac{5}{8} + 3\frac{3}{4} - 2\frac{1}{6}$$

Step 1: $6 + 3 + 3 - 2 = 10$

Step 2: $\frac{1}{2} + \frac{5}{8} + \frac{3}{4} - \frac{1}{16} = \frac{(8 + 10 + 12 - 1)}{16}$

$$= \frac{29}{16} = 1\frac{13}{16}$$

(To express an improper fraction as a mixed number, divide the numerator by the denominator.)

Step 3: $10 + 1\frac{13}{16} = 11\frac{13}{16}$

To Multiply Fractions
Multiply numerator by numerator and denominator by denominator and reduce to the lowest common denominator.

$$\frac{1}{3} \times \frac{3}{5} = \frac{1 \times 3}{3 \times 5} = \frac{3}{15} = \frac{1}{5}$$

Mathematics in Business

To Multiply Mixed Numbers Express the mixed numbers as improper fractions and multiply as you would proper fractions. To express a mixed number as an improper fraction, rewrite the whole number as a fraction with the same denominator as the other fraction and add the two:

$$1\frac{1}{2} = \frac{2}{2} + \frac{1}{2} = \frac{3}{2}$$

$$1\frac{1}{2} \times 3\frac{4}{5} = \frac{3}{2} \times \frac{19}{5} = \frac{15}{10} \times \frac{38}{10} =$$

$$\frac{570}{100} = 5\frac{70}{100} = 5\frac{7}{10}$$

To Multiply a Fraction by a Whole Number Rewrite the whole number as a fraction with a denominator of 1 and multiply as you would proper fractions. Reduce your answer to its lowest value.

$$\frac{5}{8} \times 2 = \frac{5}{8} \times \frac{2}{1} = \frac{10}{8} = 1\frac{2}{8} = 1\frac{1}{4}$$

To Divide by a Fraction Invert (interchange) the numerator and denominator of the second fraction and multiply.

$$\frac{5}{6} \div \frac{2}{5} = \frac{5}{6} \times \frac{5}{2} = \frac{25}{12} = 2\frac{1}{12}$$

M2 Decimals

Decimals are more meaningful to the user than fractions because they are easier to work with when making comparisons. Additionally, calculators cannot work with fractions unless they are decimal fractions; therefore it is important to understand and be able to work with decimal fractions effectively.

A decimal fraction may be written .55 or 0.55 for amounts less than 1. In business, the .55 is often used. In the statistical and scientific areas, the 0.55 style is most frequently used.

The following examples will describe how to convert fractions to decimals as well as how to work with decimals.

M2 Decimals

To Change Fractions to Decimals To express a fraction as a decimal, divide the numerator by the denominator.

$$\frac{3}{5} = 3 \div 5 = 0.6$$

$$\frac{2}{3} = 2 \div 3 = 0.6667 \text{ to 4 places}$$

$$= 0.667 \text{ to 3 places}$$

To Change Decimals to Fractions To change a decimal to a fraction, write the decimal figure as the numerator and the denominator as a power of ten (the number of digits to the right of the decimal point is the number of zeros after the 1 in the denominator).

$$0.1 = \frac{1}{10}: \quad 0.01 = \frac{1}{100}: \quad 0.001 = \frac{1}{1000}$$

$$0.6 = \frac{6}{10} = \frac{3}{5} \text{ (reduced to its lowest value)}$$

$$0.06 = \frac{6}{100} = \frac{3}{50}$$

$$0.43 = \frac{43}{100}$$

To Add or Subtract Decimals Write the numbers so that the decimal points are in line and add or subtract in the normal way.

```
 0.07
21.314
 2.6183
───────
24.0023
```

To Multiply With Decimals Multiply the numbers as though the decimals did not exist. To arrive at the number of decimal places in the product (total), *add* the number of decimal places being multiplied and insert the decimal that number of places to the left of the final digit.

Multiply 4.54 by 2.2.

$$4.54 \times 2.2 = 9.988$$
$$2 + 1 = 3 \text{ decimal places}$$

Mathematics in Business

To Divide With Decimals Divide as though the decimals did not exist. To arrive at the number of decimal places in the quotient (final result), *subtract* the number of decimal places in the divisor from the number of decimal places in the number to be divided and insert the decimal point that number of places to the left of the final digit.

Divide 15.625 by 2.5.

$$\underset{3}{15.625} \div \underset{1}{2.5} = \underset{2}{6.25} \text{ decimal places}$$

Rounding Off Decimal Numbers When dealing with money amounts or statistical data, rounding off decimal numbers is commonplace. The procedure is as follows:

1. Decide how many decimal places you want to have in the answer. For most business data and monetary transactions, calculations are made to the second decimal place.
2. Once you have decided on the number of desired decimal places, carry out the calculation to one more decimal place than the number desired. If two decimal places are required, carry out the answer to three places.
3. Look at the number in the additional decimal place (i.e. the third place digit if a two-digit decimal answer is desired). If the number is 5 or more, add one to the digit to the left; if the number is 4 or less, let the digits to the left stand.
EXAMPLES:

   Rounding $429.333 to 2 places = $429.33

   Rounding $565.855 to 2 places = $565.86

   Rounding 21.66344 to 4 places = 21.6634

   Rounding 1264.00518 to 4 places = 1264.0052

M3 Percentages

A percent of a number is a hundredth of that number. Therefore, 5% of a number is 5 hundredths of a number and may be expressed as $\frac{5}{100}$, or 0.05, or 5%.

M3 Percentages

To Change a Percent to a Decimal Divide the rate percent by 100; that is, move the decimal marker two places to the left.

$$35\% = \frac{35}{100} = 0.35$$

Note: When a calculator is used, a percent must be expressed as a decimal.

To Change a Decimal to a Percent Multiply the decimal by 100%; that is, move the decimal marker two places to the right.

1.34 as a percent is $1.34 \times 100\% = 134\%$

To Change (Convert) a Percent to a Fraction Remove the percent sign; divide the percent number by 100, and reduce to the lowest terms.

$$30\% = \frac{30}{100} = \frac{3}{10}$$

To Change (Convert) a Fraction to a Percent Divide the numerator by the denominator, and multiply the answer (quotient) by 100.

$$\frac{4}{5} = 4 \div 5 = .80 \times 100 = 80\%$$

To Find What Percent One Number is of Another Divide the number that has *of* in front of it into the other number and multiply by 100.

What percentage is 15 of 75?

$15 \div 75 = .20$

$.20 \times 100 = 20\%$

To Find the Full Number of Which a Percentage is Already Known Divide the number known by the percentage known and multiply by 100.

35% of a number is 56. Find the number.

$$\frac{56}{35} \times 100 = \frac{5600}{35} = 160$$

Mathematics in Business

To Find the Percentage Increase of One Number Over Another
Subtract the base number from the increased number to find the amount of the increase. Divide the base number into the amount of the increase and multiply by 100.

Sales rose from $4000 (base number) to $5000 (increased number). What is the percentage increase? Sales increased by $1000.

$$\frac{1000}{4000} \times 100 = 25\%$$

To Find the Amount of Increase or Decrease When the Base Number and Percentage Increase or Decrease are Known
Add the percentage rate of increase to 100, divide the result by 100, and multiply by the base figure.

$4000 increased by 25% of itself equals what?

$$\frac{125}{100} \times 4000 = 5000$$

That is, $4000 increased by 25% of itself equals $5000.

To find a decreased rate, subtract the percentage rate decrease from 100.

$4000 decreased by 25% of itself equals what?

$$\frac{75}{100} \times 4000 = \$3000$$

M4 Common Equivalents

Certain percentages and their decimal and fractional equivalents are used so frequently that knowing them can save a great deal of unnecessary calculation time. Figure 12.1 gives a listing of these equivalents.

Percent	Decimal Fraction	Common Fraction	Percent	Decimal Fraction	Common Fraction
1%	0.01	1/100	37 1/2%	0.375	3/8
5%	0.05	1/20	40%	0.40	2/5
6 1/4%	0.625	1/16	50%	0.50	1/2
8 1/3%	0.083	1/12	60%	0.60	3/5
10%	0.10	1/10	62 1/2%	0.625	5/8
12 1/2%	0.125	1/8	66 2/3%	0.666	2/3
16 2/3%	0.1666	1/6	70%	0.70	7/10
20%	0.20	1/5	75%	0.75	3/4
25%	0.25	1/4	80%	0.80	4/5
30%	0.30	3/10	87 1/2%	0.875	7/8
33 1/3	0.333	1/3	90%	0.90	9/10
			100%	1.00	

Figure 12.1 Table of Common Equivalents

M5 Algebraic Equations

Business formulas are frequently expressed as algebraic equations. Algebra means working with one or more unknown variables; an equation is a sentence of two expressions connected by an equal sign.

I = Prt [Interest (I) equals principal (P) multiplied by rate (r) multiplied by time (t).]

As you work with an equation, it must be kept constantly in balance; that is, if you add, subtract, divide, or multiply on one side, you must do the same thing on the other side.

Rearranging Formula Terms
Where one numerical value in a formula is not known, it is necessary to isolate the unknown quantity. To do this, keep the equation in balance.

The simple interest formula is I = Prt

Find P when I = $18, r = 9%, t = 2 years.

Since P is the unknown, it must be isolated; that is, both sides must be divided by rt.

P = I/rt

$$P = \frac{18}{0.09 \times 2}$$

P = $100

Rules to Observe in Reducing Algebraic Expressions to Their Simplest Form

- To multiply powers having the same base, add the indexes

    a × a × a is a^3

    Unless otherwise indicated, the index of any base number is 1; the sum of the indexes in this case is 3. Similarly,

    $a^3 \times a^2 = a^5$

- To divide a power by a power having the same base, subtract the indexes

    $a^3 \div a^2 = a$

Mathematics in Business

- Only like terms may be added or subtracted:

  $3a + 3a = 6a$, but $3a + 3b = 3a + 3b$

- The order of operations used to reduce an algebraic expression to its simplest form is:

  1. Simplify any expressions inside brackets.
  2. Remove brackets.
  3. If the word "of" is used, replace it with a multiplication sign.
  4. Divide and multiply next. Do these operations in the order given, working from left to right.
  5. Add and subtract last. Do these operations in the order given, working from left to right.

The true interest rate formula is $r = \dfrac{2Nc}{A(n+1)}$

r = annual interest rate
c = cost of borrowing
n = number of payments needed to pay the loan in full
N = number of payments in one year
A = amount borrowed

What is the true interest rate on a loan of $2500 to be repaid in monthly installments in 18 months at 13 1/2%? The cost of borrowing is quoted as $275.60.

$$r = \frac{2 \times 12 \times 275.60}{2500(18+1)}$$

$$r = \frac{2 \times 12 \times 275.60}{2500 \times 19}$$

$$r = \frac{6614.4}{47{,}500}$$

$r = 0.1392$

Expressed as a percentage, the true interest rate is 13.92%.

M6 Business Formulas

M7 Accounting Equation

$A = L + OE$

A = assets, L = liabilites, OE = Owner's Equity

M8 Amortization Formula

$$p = \frac{Pi(1+i)^n}{(1+i)^n - 1}$$

p = amount to be paid per payment period
i = interest rate per time period
n = total number of payment periods
P = principal

M9 Interest

There are two types of interest:

- **Simple:** interest is calculated only on the original principal.

    $I = Prt$

    I = interest, t = time in years, r = annual rate, and P = principal

- **Compound:** interest is calculated periodically and added to the principal so that for succeeding periods both the original principal and the accumulated interest earn interest.

$A = P(1+i)^n$

A = amount that the principal (P) will accumulate to at i rate of interest per interest period for n interest periods. (If time is expressed in days, express as, for example, $\frac{30}{365}$; if time is one year show as 1.)

Mathematics in Business

M10 Selling Price

$S = C + M$

S = selling price, C = cost, M = markup

M11 Taxes (Property)

$T = Ar$

T = taxes, A = assessment, r = rate (mills)

($1 = 1000 mills)

M12 True Interest Rate

$$r = \frac{2Nc}{A(n+1)}$$

r = annual interest rate
c = cost of borrowing
n = number of payments to pay the loan in full
N = number of payments in one year
A = amount borrowed

M13 Pricing Goods for Sale

Pricing means establishing the price at which goods can be sold. Pricing takes into consideration discounts and allowances to be given, transportation costs, pricing legislation, demand, type of business, competition, and level of profit sought (e.g., a certain percentage return on sales or on investment).

M14 Retail and Wholesale Prices

M15 Markup and Margin

Most retail and wholesale prices are established by using markups; that is, adding a set percentage to the price at which the goods were purchased that the seller feels will cover operating expenses and provide a reasonable net profit.

If the owner of a business seeks a net profit of, for example, 12% of sales, and the operating expenses of the business are expected to be 27% of sales, he must establish his selling price to produce a gross profit (or margin) of 39%. The cost price of each article should, therefore, be 61% of its selling price.

Sales (100%) − Cost Price (61%) = Gross Profit or Margin (39%)

Gross Profit (39%) − Expenses (27%) = Net Profit (12%)

If cost price = $56,

61% of the selling price is $56,

and selling price = $56 \times \dfrac{100}{61}$ = $91.80

Therefore, markup = $91.80 − $56.00 = $35.80

> **Note:** Margin and markup are the same in amount but different in percentage because margin is related to selling price and markup is related to cost price.
>
> If selling price is known to be $91.80, then margin is $35.80, or 39% of the selling price; if cost price is known to be $56, then markup is $35.80, or 64%.

M16 Markdown

A markdown is often called a discount. It means a reduction in the regular marked price and is usually offered by the seller to attract customers and increase sales.

M17 Discounts

Discounts in the form of percentages off list prices are offered as incentives to buy.

Trade discounts: given by manufacturers to wholesalers or retailers and by wholesalers to retailers. When a series of discounts is quoted, this is known as a *chain discount*. The first discount is always taken off the

Mathematics in Business

list price. The second discount is taken off the remainder and so on. Successive discounts cannot be added together.

```
List price    $ 1000
          -    200   1st trade discount 20%
               800
          -     80   2nd trade discount 10%
               720
          -     36   3rd trade discount 5%
             $ 684
```

Cash discounts: sometimes offered as an incentive to pay a bill quickly. For example, if the expression 2/10, n/30 is shown on an invoice, it means that if the invoice is paid within 10 days a 2% discount may be deducted from the net (total) amount. If the invoice is not paid within 10 days, the 2% may not be deducted and the net amount is due in 30 days. The 2% discount may not, of course, be deducted from any shipping charges shown.

M18 Break Even Point

For a business to be worthwhile, income must exceed expenses. The point at which income and expenses intersect is known as the *break even point* (BEP). (Anything above the BEP equals profit; anything below the BEP equals loss.) The break even point is calculated to determine the minimum output or sales necessary for income to cover costs. The break even point analysis is particularly useful for comparing pricing alternatives.

$$\text{Break even point} = \frac{\text{Total fixed costs (costs that cannot be changed)}}{\text{Suggested selling price per unit} - \text{variable costs per unit (costs that can be changed)}}$$

Total fixed costs for a small book are $32,000, variable costs per unit $0.75, and suggested selling price is $1.25.

$$BEP = \frac{32{,}000}{1.25 - 0.75} = \frac{32{,}000}{0.50} = 64{,}000 \text{ units}$$

Therefore, 64,000 copies of the book must be sold before a profit is achieved. To improve this position, the selling price might be raised, or some way of cutting variable costs (e.g., using less expensive paper) might be sought.

M19 Statistical Data

Frequently, business information is presented in the form of averages and ratios to indicate comparisons and trends.

M20 Averages

Mean

A *mean* (or average) is a single number that represents a central value in a group of numbers. Averages (means) may be simple or weighted.

Simple average. Find a simple average by dividing the sum of a series of numbers by the total number of members of the series.

T-shirts sold for $4.90 in the spring sale, $6.25 at regular price, and $5.44 in the fall sale. Average selling price was

$$\frac{4.90 + 6.25 + 5.44}{3} = \frac{16.59}{3} = \$5.53$$

Weighted average. The simple average is based on only one unit of each number being added and then being divided by the sum of the units. However, in some situations this may not provide a true average. Find a weighted average by multiplying each quantity by its unit value, add the products, and then divide by the sum of the quantities.

120 T-shirts were sold at $4.90 in the spring sale, 230 at $6.25, and 90 at $5.44 in the fall sale. Average (weighted) selling price was

$$\frac{(4.90 \times 120) + (6.25 \times 230) + (5.44 \times 90)}{120 + 230 + 90} =$$

$$\frac{588 + 1437.50 + 489.60}{440} = \frac{2515.10}{440} = \$5.72$$

Compare with $5.53 as the simple average.

Mathematics in Business

Mode
Mode is the figure occurring most frequently in a list of numbers.

6, 7, 9, 6, 7, 8, 7, 8. The mode is 7 (occurs 3 times).

This type of statistical information is most interesting to a shoe retailer, for example, who wishes to know the most common selling shoe size.

Median
The *median* (middle value) in a series of numbers arranged in numerical order is the quantity that appears at the mid point of the list. One half the quantities have a higher value and one half have a lower value. Find the median figure by arranging the series of numbers in order of size or value and then selecting the middle one.

Seven students earned these marks: 24, 76, 10, 73, 74, 70, 66. Arrange in order: 10, 24, 66, 70, 73, 74, 76. The median mark is 70. There are three numbers higher than 70 and three lower. (When the number of items is even, the median is the average of the two middle numbers.)

M21 Ratio

The *ratio* of two numbers compares the size or value of one number with the size or value of another number.

There are 20 females and 10 males in the office. The ratio of females to males is 20:10 or 2:1 (reduced to the lowest form).

M22 Proportion

The term "proportion" is used to indicate that two ratios are equal.

1:4 is proportional to 2:8.

When two ratios are equal, their cross products are also equal.

If three terms in a proportion are known, the fourth is easily found.

x:16 is proportional to 3:12

$$\frac{x}{16} \diagup \frac{3}{12} \qquad \begin{aligned} 12x &= 48 \\ x &= \frac{48}{12} \\ x &= 4 \end{aligned}$$

4:16 is proportional to 3:12

M23 Charts and Graphs

Suggestions for presenting statistical data in pictorial form are in Unit 5, E44-E49.

M24 Foreign Currency Exchange

The rate at which one country's currency can be exchanged for that of another at a bank is called the *foreign currency exchange rate*. Newspapers frequently publish lists of exchange rates, but the bank rate may vary from these because of the constant fluctuations caused by economic and political factors. Most currencies are now expressed as decimals and conversions are simple.

Change $25 U.S. to Canadian dollars where $1 U.S. = $1.15 Canadian.

$25 U.S. = 25 × 1.15 = $28.75 Canadian

Therefore $25 U.S. = $28.75 Canadian

Change $25 Canadian to U.S. dollars where $1 Canadian = 85¢ U.S.

$25 Canadian = 0.85 × 25 = $21.25 U.S.

Therefore $25 Canadian = $21.25 U.S.

Mathematics in Business

The same method of calculation works with currency expressed in terms other than dollars. For example, the British use the pound (£) as their currency base.

Change $25 U.S. to British pounds where $1 U.S. = .7307 in British pounds.

$25 U.S. = 25 × .7307 = £18.27 British pounds

Therefore, $25 U.S. = £18.27 British

Change £25 British to U.S. dollars where £1 British = $1.3685 U.S.

£25 British = 1.3685 × 25 = $34.21 U.S.

Therefore, £25 British = $34.21 U.S.

M25 Electronic Calculators

M26 Touch Indexing

To operate a desktop calculator efficiently, proper *touch indexing* or *touch fingering* should be used. Figure 12.2, shows the correct hand placement. Notice that the right index finger strikes the *1, 4,* and *7* keys; the third finger strikes the *2, 5,* and *8* keys; the fourth finger strikes the *3, 6,* and *9* keys; and the thumb strikes the *0* key. If a decimal point needs to be entered, the fourth finger of the right hand or *6* key finger is used. The *4, 5,* and *6* keys are referred to as the *home keys.* The little finger of the right hand strikes the *plus.*

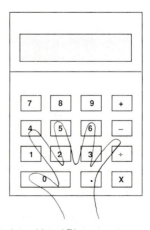

Figure 12.2 Calculator Hand Placement

M27 Machine Logic

Most electronic calculators operate with *adding machine logic*, which means that the function key ($\times$, $+$, $-$, or $\div$) is pressed after the number is indexed. For example, to perform the problem, $3 - 4 + 2 =$, the following sequence is followed:

Depress 3, depress $+$, depress 4, depress $-$, depress 2, depress $+$, depress total key. The answer should be 1.

M28 Factors to Consider When Purchasing an Electronic Calculator

- Cost—Varies with equipment capacity and features.
- Memory—Machine can have one or more memories; each memory will retain data that has been specifically input.
- Power Source—Selection can be made from AC line powered, battery powered, solar powered, electric light powered, or a combination of these through the use of adapters.
- Display Only, Print Only, or Print/Display Option—The latter is the most popular and permits the operator to change from one mode to another with a flick of a switch or the tap of a key. A printed tape helps verify the entered material.
- Screen Displays—The two basic types are LED (light emitting diode) and LCD (liquid crystal display). The LED is the most widely used.
- Printer Type—Dot matrix printers and thermal printers are the most popular, although some models still have impact printers.
- Special Functions—Special function keys can be purchased according to specific needs. Usually the more special functions included, the greater the cost.
- Warranty—A statement by the seller to the buyer that promises what the seller or manufacturer will do to repair or replace defective equipment.
- Capacity—The number of digits that can be displayed at one time; desktop calculators usually read to 12 or more places.
- Size—Calculators range in size from desktop models, to hand-held models, to those the size of a wristwatch. Many hand-held calculators have the same features as desktop models; however, for heavy-duty use, desktop models are usually more durable.

Mathematics in Business

 Basic Electronic Calculator Function Keys

Figure 12.3 shows some of the common features on a hand-held calculator. These are similar to those found on desktop calculators.

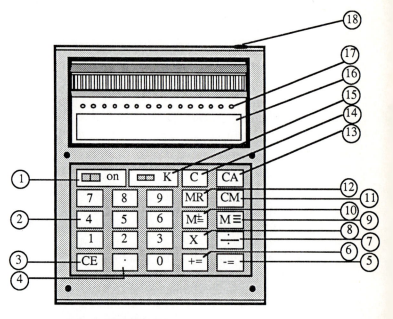

1. Power ON-OFF Switch
2. Number Keys
3. Error correction Key
4. Decimal entry Key
5. Minus-Equals Key
6. Plus-Equals Key
7. Division Key
8. Multiplication Key
9. Memory Minus-Equals Key
10. Memory Plus-Equals Key
11. Clear Memory Key
12. Memory Recall Key
13. Clear All Key
14. Clear Key
15. Constant Control
16. Number Display
17. Sign Display
18. AC Adapter Jack

Figure 12.3 Common Calculator Features

M29-M30 Basic Electronic Calculator Function Keys

M30 Desktop Calculator Features

The following features, if used properly by an operator, can make the use of a calculator more efficient.

- **Add Mode**

    This special feature allows the entry of numbers to two decimal places without the need to enter the decimal point. It is a handy feature when working with dollar amounts and the feature can usually be turned on or off with a switch.

- **Constant Multiplier/Divider**

    This feature can be an automatic feature or one that is turned on and off by the operator. If multiplying or dividing a series of numbers by one number, the operator can do the operation without constantly re-entering the multiplier or divisor.

    Example: 5 × 4 =
               5 × 2 =
               5 × 7 =

    Be sure the constant key is engaged, then:

    Depress 5, depress ×, depress = (20 is displayed as answer)
                 depress 2, depress = (10 is displayed as answer)
                 depress 7, depress = (35 is displayed as answer)

- **Decimal Indicator**

    A *fixed* decimal setting restricts the number of decimal places in the answer to a prescribed number of places; a *floating* decimal setting puts no restriction on the number of decimal places in the answer.

Example: 1.56 × 2.335	F 1 2 3 4 5 ▲	FIXED DECIMAL SETTING answer would show as 3.64
1.56 × 2.335	F 1 2 3 4 5 ▲	FLOATING DECIMAL SETTING answer would show as 3.6426

Mathematics in Business

- **Round-off Keys**
  (Feature works in conjunction with the fixed decimal setting)

 ROUND OFF—The last digit displayed in an answer is increased by one if the following digit is 5 or greater

Example: 2.665, if set to round off to two decimal places, would show 2.67 on the display as the answer.

 ROUND UP—The last decimal digit displayed in an answer is increased by one if the following digit is 1 or greater.

Example: 2.6601, if set to round to 2 places, would read as an answer of 2.66.
but
2.6611, if set to round to 2 places, would read as an answer of 2.67.

 TRUNCATE—No change occurs in the last decimal digit. If a machine does not have this position, every answer that contains decimals will be rounded whether or not it is desired.

Example: 2.6601, if set to round to 2 places, would read 2.66.

Example: 2.6668, if set to round to 2 places, would read 2.66.

- **Memory**

Numbers placed in memory areas will be retained until they are cleared with a special *memory clear* key. Usually some indicator signals that numbers reside in a memory bank.

M30 Desktop Calculator Features

$\boxed{M+}$ Add to memory

$\boxed{M-}$ Subtract from memory

$\boxed{CM}$ Clear memory

$\boxed{RM}$ Read memory

Consult the operating machine manual that accompanies your calculator to learn about other special function keys that might be available on your calculator. Using special function keys can save time in indexing and reading answers.

UNIT 13

ORGANIZING MEETINGS AND CONFERENCES

Planning the Meeting	O1-O5
Advance Planning	
Announcing the Meeting	
The Agenda	
Last-Minute Preparations	
Conducting the Meeting	O6-O11
The Chairperson's Role	
Parliamentary Procedure (Formal Rules of Debate)	
Minutes (Record) of the Meeting	O12-O16
Minutes	
Taking Notes for the Minutes	
Tape Recording the Minutes	
Producing the Minutes	
Follow-Up After the Meeting	O17

Meetings and conferences are a regular and important part of business activities. Most meetings are *informal* and are held to enable participants to share ideas about new procedures, products, or strategies. However, some meetings are *formal* and must be conducted strictly according to procedures stated in the constitution and bylaws (i.e., the governing rules of conduct of the corporation or organization). Examples of formal meetings are regular meetings of the Board of Directors, Annual Shareholders' Meetings, and Annual General Meetings. These are held to obtain authority to take a specific action, such as to distribute profits, to amend the constitution, or to receive reports.

Although there are variations of purpose, size, and degrees of formality, the planning, announcing, conducting, and recording of meetings have many similarities. Advance plans must be carefully made, meetings must be conducted efficiently, and the points raised and decisions made must be accurately recorded. This unit suggests the steps needed to conduct successful meetings, regardless of type or purpose.

O1 Planning the Meeting

O2 Advance Planning

If the meeting is held on the company's premises, reserve the room needed well in advance. Make a list of the things to be dealt with before the required date. Be sure to do each job on this list in sufficient time to guarantee that everything is available for the meeting.

- Reserve the meeting room and double check the reservation at a later time.
- Order refreshments, if necessary.
- Plan and confirm coffee break, lunch, and/or dinner needs—cost, time, menu, number of persons, and other necessary information.
- Make and confirm hotel accommodations for out-of-town participants, or do the necessary research to provide participants with the information with which to make their own hotel arrangements.
- Get written confirmation of all reservations or bookings.
- Verify in writing each speaker or presenter's role in the meeting or conference, and obtain a statement from each person regarding any audiovisual aids he or she will need.
- Order audiovisual equipment or any other special equipment needed.

- Determine how the meeting will be publicized or how participants will be reminded of the meeting.
- Plan to obtain and/or prepare an agenda for the meeting and distribute it to the participants ahead of time.
- Request that guest speakers supply a biographical sketch if they will be introduced to the group at a formal session.
- Be certain that you fully understand the extent of your responsibilities for making the arrangements for the meeting or conference.

O3 Announcing the Meeting

Determine the best method to invite or inform participants about a meeting. The following list provides some guidelines for preparing a meeting announcement:

- Be sure to include the time, date, location, and purpose of the meeting in the notice.
- Send out a formal notice far enough in advance so that people can fit the meeting into their plans, but not so early that it can be forgotten.
- For formal meetings, provide the necessary length of time for advance notices (usually specified in the organization's constitution or bylaws).
- For conferences involving outside participation, prepare an attractive flyer that includes a registration form.
- If appropriate, announce the conference through professional organizations and other possible communication channels, such as newsletters and bulletins.
- A formal notice of the meeting may be sent out on letterhead or on a postcard as shown in Figure 13.1.

```
ATLANTIC TRADING COMPANY
437 Atlantic Road, Norwalk, CT 06856

April 5, 19--

NOTICE OF MEETING
A meeting of the Office Automation Committee will be held
at 1 p.m. on Wednesday, April 25, in the Russ Lounge of
the Atlantic Trading Company at 437 Atlantic Road,
Norwalk, Connecticut.  An agenda will follow.

Linda Sue Jamieson, Secretary
Administrative Assistant
```

Figure 13.1   Post Card Notice of Meeting

O4 The Agenda

The agenda is the *plan* for the meeting. It lists the place, date, and time of the meeting, as well as the items of business and the order in which they are scheduled. Although there is no fixed format that needs to be followed in preparing an agenda, the preparation of an agenda is a must.

For small informal meetings, an interoffice memo indicating the discussion topics usually serves as an effective agenda (Figure 13.2). A detailed program indicating discussion topics and length of discussion times may be advantageous for large gatherings with many discussion topics. In all cases, the agenda should be sent out *in advance* of the meeting so that participants may be properly prepared.

```
              OFFICE AUTOMATION COMMITTEE MEETING

       1 p.m. to 2 p.m, Russ Lounge, Wednesday, April 25, 19--
     Atlantic Trading Company, 437 Atlantic Road, Norwalk, Connecticut

1.   Call to order                  Marion Wolentz, Chair

2.   Reading of the minutes         Bob Ruether, Recorder

3.   Committee Reports:

          Personnel Survey          Warren Frankel (10 minutes)

          File Room Inventory       Amy Chen (5 minutes)

          Vendor Investigations     Lisa Market (10 minutes)

4.   Training Needs

          Background                Vic Butler (5 minutes)
          Suggestions, ideas,
             discussion             Committee (20 minutes)

5.   Summary, Identify Next         Marion Wolentz (5 minutes)
        Meeting Date
```

Figure 13.2 Agenda for Small Group Meeting

Agendas for formal meetings contain discussion topics that come within the scope of the organization as outlined in the constitution and bylaws. A typical formal agenda might include some or all of the following: call to order, roll call, minutes (reading and approval), committee reports, old business, new business, nominations and elections, date of the next meeting, adjournment (Figure 13.3).

Organizing Meetings and Conferences

```
                MEETING OF THE BOARD OF DIRECTORS
                           BOARD ROOM A
                      February 17, 19--, 2 p.m.


                              A G E N D A

        2:00    Call to order, reading and approval of January 11 minutes

        2:10    Discussion of matters arising from the minutes

        2:15    Reports

                (a) Report from Mr. Glover on the progress of the
                    proposed plant move
                (b) Report from Ms. Alexander on the developments
                    regarding in-house training programs

        2:40    New business

        2:55    Date and time of the next meeting

        3:00    Adjournment
```

Figure 13.3 Agenda for Formal Meeting

O5 Last-Minute Preparations

- Conduct a last-minute check of all details. Use a checklist similar to the one in Figure 13.4.
- Have available:

    extra agendas

    extra copies of the minutes of the last meeting

    the minute book or file

    copies of the constitution and bylaws

    any previously submitted motions

    copies of reports to be presented

    name plates or name tags of participants (if appropriate)

    cassette recorder and extra recording supplies

- Check on the meeting room temperature.
- Check the meeting room arrangement.
- Distribute any handouts or materials at each participant's place, if appropriate.
- Try out audiovisual equipment, and check to see that chalk or felt pens are available for chalkboard, overhead equipment, or flip chart use.

O5-O7 Last-Minute Preparations

```
                    CHECKLIST FOR MEETING ARRANGEMENTS
   Name of Meeting _____
   Date _____              Time_____
   Place_____

   ITEM                                            Arrangements  Confirmed
                                                       Made

   Facilities

        Room                                        _____    _____
        Room arrangement                            _____    _____
        Audiovisual Equipment                       _____    _____
        Other special equipment--telephones, facsimile
             lecturn, podium, microphones, etc.     _____    _____
        Registration table                          _____    _____
        Placement of banners, signs or other
             specialized demonstration materials    _____    _____
        Pads, pencils, or other supplies needed     _____    _____

   Speakers

        Confirmation letters sent                   _____    _____
        Request for biographical sketch made        _____    _____
        Request for audiovisual equipment made      _____    _____
        Announcement flyer or meeting notice sent   _____    _____
        Name tags prepared                          _____    _____
        Luncheon or dinner arrangements made        _____    _____
        Hotel arrangements made                     _____    _____

   Public Relations

        Flyers or notices sent out                  _____    _____
        Programs prepared                           _____    _____
        Handouts coordinated                        _____    _____
        Name tags prepared                          _____    _____

   Refreshments

        Refreshments ordered                        _____    _____
        Time schedule for the delivery of the
             refreshments made clear                _____    _____
        Special arrangements for table setup,
             water, smoking/no smoking sections     _____    _____

   Last Minute Arrangements

        Room set up correctly                       _____    _____
        Room temperature satisfactory               _____    _____
        Registration table name tags and materials
             available                              _____    _____
        Audiovisual aids working properly           _____    _____
        Special equipment delivered and positioned
             correctly                              _____    _____
        Handouts or programs available              _____    _____

                                                 Administrative Assistant
```

Figure 13.4 Checklist for Meeting Arrangements

O6 Conducting the Meeting

O7 The Chairperson's Role

The meeting is conducted by the chairperson. With informal meetings, the chairperson's role is simply to maintain order, to ensure that the meeting follows the agenda, and to ensure that the proper communication of ideas and dissemination of information takes place.

Organizing Meetings and Conferences

In formal meetings, it is customary to employ parliamentary procedures (formal rules of debate), and it is the chairperson's task to see that these rules are followed. While the rules might seem cumbersome, they do give everyone an equal right to be heard, have his or her point of view considered, and to vote on an issue.

In particular, the chairperson:

- ensures that there is a quorum present (i.e., the legally required number of participants in a formal meeting that is stated in the constitution or bylaws)
- calls the meeting to order (i.e., makes sure that it starts on time)
- maintains order
- explains and decides all questions of procedure (unless a Parliamentarian has been assigned this function)
- announces and clarifies all business under consideration
- states motions and resolutions
- conducts the votes
- announces the final decisions of the votes
- decides on tie votes

O8 Parliamentary Procedure (Formal Rules of Debate)

O9 Presenting a Motion

When a proposal is made at a formal meeting, it is referred to as a *motion* and must have the support of another person, who is referred to as the *seconder*.

The participant making the motion should rise and be recognized (acknowledged) by the presiding officer (usually the chairperson).

A typical motion begins, "I move that . . ."

A typical motion support begins, "I second the motion . . ."

Discussion and, perhaps, amendment of the motion follows.

Note: While motions to amend a motion may be made, only *one* main motion at a time may be discussed. Motions to amend must be discussed and voted upon so that the main motion is properly amended before it is finally discussed and voted upon. For example:

Main Motion   I move that the staff receive a bonus this year.
                    seconded Jill Brown

O8-O11 Parliamentary Procedure (Formal Rules of Debate)

Amendment	I move that the motion be amended . . . that the staff receive a bonus this year only if the company earns a profit in excess of 10 percent. seconded John Whiteside. Discussion. Vote carried.
Amended Main Motion	That the staff receive a bonus this year provided the company earns a profit in excess of 10 percent.

The chairperson finally conducts the voting (by ballot or show of hands) on the motion and announces the result of the vote. If more than half the participants vote in favor, the motion is adopted (carried). If a motion is not voted on, the procedure for disposing of it is to *table the motion*. A motion can be tabled until the next meeting, until a particular event takes place, or indefinitely.

O10 Point of Order

Should a member feel that a debating rule has been broken, that member may interrupt the person speaking and address the chairperson directly, without waiting for recognition. Points of order must be made immediately after the alleged violation. They are not debatable, and the member who was interrupted must yield until the matter is clarified.

Note: Only a brief outline of the commonly used aspects of parliamentary debating procedures has been included here. Full details are contained in *Roberts Rules of Order,* available in paperback or hard copy editions. Anyone who is required to conduct or take notes at an important formal meeting should become familiar with Robert's rules.

O11 Proxies

The constitution and bylaws of most organizations permit a person who cannot attend important meetings to be represented by *proxy*. A proxy may be either:

- another person who can attend the meeting with authority to vote and make decisions on behalf of the absent person
- a ballot (voting) card that has been sent before the meeting and has been completed and returned by the absent person

Organizing Meetings and Conferences

O12 Minutes (Record) of the Meeting

O13 Minutes

Minutes are designed to record, first of all, that a meeting was held; and secondly, the decisions that were made at the meeting. In addition, some minutes record proposals that were made and rejected, as well as a summary of the discussion. They should provide sufficient information for those not present to have a clear understanding of what took place. Figure 13.5 is an example of meeting minutes.

```
                     ATLANTIC TRADING COMPANY
                        BOARD OF DIRECTORS
              Minutes of Meeting, February 17, 19--, 2 p.m.

TIME AND PLACE       The monthly meeting of the Board of Directors of the
                     Atlantic Trading Company was held at 2 p.m., Tuesday,
                     February 17, 19--, in Board Room A, conducted by the
                     Chairperson, John A. Morrell.

ATTENDANCE           Present: Mr. Lee Marinovich; Ms. Thelma Chalmers; Mr.
                     Frank Remsen; Mr. William Hamilton; Ms. Helene
                     Ostrowski; Mr. Michael Hernandez; Mr. Robert Venino; Ms.
                     Pat Alexander; Mr. Arthur Glover.

                     Absent: Ms. Linda Reeves.

APPROVAL OF MINUTES  Mr. Robert Venino moved that the minutes of the meeting
                     held on January 11, 19--, be approved as read. Ms.
                     Ostrowski seconded the motion. CARRIED.

MATTERS ARISING      Since there were no matters arising from the previous
                     minutes, Chairman Morrell proceeded with the next order
                     of business.

REPORTS              Mr. Glover, the Production Manager, reported that
                     construction of the new plant site was progressing
                     slightly ahead of schedule. Unseasonably warm weather
                     enabled more outside work to be completed than
                     anticipated. As a result, Mr. Glover was confident that
                     the move would be completed before the end of the summer
                     as planned.

                     Ms. Alexander, Training Director, reported that 256
                     employees had taken part in training programs offered
                     through her department in the last quarter of 19--.
                     This represented a 10 percent increase over the previous
                     quarter. She also reported on a new evaluation method
                     that her department was planning to use. Suggestions
                     were made by board members. A revised evaluation
                     procedure will be presented at the next board meeting.

NEW BUSINESS         The advantages of having an Employee Suggestion Plan
                     were outlined by Mr. Marinovich, Human Resources
                     Director. Mr. Marinovich agreed to head a committee to
                     suggest an Employee Suggestion Plan that would be
                     appropriate for our company. Ms. Ostrowski, Mr.
                     Hernandez, and Mr. Hamilton will serve on the committee,
                     which plans to have a report ready for the April meeting.

NEXT MEETING         The next meeting of the Board will be on March 15, 19--.

ADJOURNMENT          On a motion by Mr. Hamilton, and seconded by Mr.
                     Hernandez, the meeting was adjourned at 3:15 p.m.


                          CHAIRPERSON _____

          DATE_____ SECRETARY _____
```

Figure 13.5 Minutes

O12-O14 Minutes (Record) of the Meeting

Properly prepared minutes:

- clearly state the name, purpose, time, and place of the meeting
- note who was present (and sometimes even those who were absent)
- are accurate, concise, and unbiased
- provide a summary of the results, not a complete description of the proceedings
- contain exact statements of motions and the names of the individuals who made the motions and seconded them
- state the terms of any resolutions adopted
- provide a statement regarding the method of voting used and the outcome of the voting
- note appointments made
- are signed by the individual who prepared them

O14 Taking Notes for the Minutes

- Sit close enough to the chairperson so that you can get his or her attention if you miss a detail.
- Study the agenda in advance and read over any specified documents prior to the meeting so that you are familiar with the names and terms.
- Go over the minutes of the previous meeting to familiarize yourself with previous discussion topics.
- Prepare—in advance—a list of people who *should* be in attendance so that only a checkmark is needed to designate their absence or attendance.
- Make a seating plan and assign a number to each person present. Try to identify each person by some feature that would help recall names.
- Plan to take your notes so that you have room for names and discussion topics. Organize your notes so that all discussion on any one subject is kept together. Note the name of each person introducing a topic, and the names of people who made motions and seconds.
- Take more notes than necessary; they can be condensed later.
- For formal meetings, a preprinted notetaking sheet would be useful. It is especially helpful for motions because they must be recorded *verbatim* (word for word). Record whether a motion was adopted, lost, referred to a committee, or tabled.
- Note anything that demands action after the meeting.
- Do not hesitate to interrupt discreetly to ask for a restatement of a motion, clarification of a point, or identification of a speaker.

O15 Tape Recording the Minutes

Before planning to use a tape recorder, remember these possible disadvantages:

- objections by some people
- can be technically difficult to set up so voices of all members are audible
- can be time consuming in playing back and transcribing
- difficulty of identifying speakers

If you *do* use a tape recorder:

- Change tapes during pauses in meetings, or use two recorders and start the recording on the next tape while the previous one is ending.
- Number and identify each tape.

O16 Producing the Minutes

- Produce a rough draft while the information is still fresh in your mind.
- Follow the sequence of topics established in the agenda.
- Refer to previously prepared minutes and use the same style.
- Make resolutions stand out in some way; use capitals, for example.
- Be objective; do not include personal opinions.
- Reports, depending on their importance, may be:

    summarized and attached

    attached in their entirety

    referred to in the body of the minutes

- Submit the final draft to the chairperson of the meeting for approval.
- Produce sufficient copies for participants, others on the distribution list, the file (or official minute book), as well as extras for use at the next meeting.

O17 Follow-Up After the Meeting

- Distribute the minutes promptly.
- Handle any requests that may have arisen at the meeting (for additional information, for information from previous minutes, etc.).
- Send reminders, if necessary, about action to be taken.
- If possible, circulate the minutes with the notice and agenda of the *next* meeting so that participants can check items in advance for accuracy, and so that absentees can be kept informed.
- Send out appropriate thank you notes.
- If you maintain someone's calendar, note the next meeting date as well as any other significant dates suggested by the minutes of the meeting.

UNIT 14

PERSONNEL PLANNING: STAFFING THE OFFICE

Personnel Planning	P1
Job Analysis	P2
Recruitment	P3-P12
Sources of Personnel	
Advertisements	
Hints for Effective Advertising	
The Application Form	
The Interview	
How to Conduct an Interview	
Tests	
Follow-Up to the Interview	
A Summary of Recruitment Strategies	
Orientation of New Employees	P13
Evaluation of Employees	P14-P16
New Employee Evaluations	
Regular Performance Reviews	
Promotion Policy	P17

Leaving a Job   P18-P20
   Dismissal
   Resignation

Records   P21

Payment Policy   P22-P24
   Job Evaluation
   Fringe Benefits

Temporary Help   P25-P28
   Finding Temporary Help
   Making the Best Use of Temporary Help
   Other Ways to Control Fluctuations in the Work Force

Channeling Employee Motivation   P29

Personnel Planning: Staffing The Office

The office is the hub of organizational activities. Office activities are performed *by* and *for* people; therefore, people are the most critical resource in the performance and maintenance of the information workflow. Since the operation of any business organization, large or small, is strongly influenced by its office employees, it is important that a firm have a fair and consistent personnel policy.

The personnel policies that are summarized in this unit—planning, job analysis, recruitment, orientation, evaluation, and motivation—are applicable to most firms regardless of their size or business function.

P1 Personnel Planning

What are the firm's needs for office staff and how are these needs to be met? Most organizations favor the type of systematic procedure that follows.

1. Study the existing use of staff to see if greater efficiency can be obtained.
2. Forecast the future volume of work based on the firm's long-range plans.
3. Forecast the future number and types of employees needed to deal with the anticipated work volume.
4. Consider the present staff so that their anticipated contribution to future needs is known.
5. Plan the recruitment of the right number of appropriately qualified personnel.

P2 Job Analysis

People involved in the hiring process must be properly prepared; therefore, an analysis of the vacancy must be done and a job description drawn up if one is not already available.

A typical job description generally consists of five key sections: (1) job title; (2) job summary; (3) reporting relationship; (4) qualifications; and (5) typical duties and responsibilities. Normally, this information can be adequately expressed in one or two typed pages. Some guidelines for preparing each of the above sections of a job description are:

- Job title—Provide a brief one- or two-word name and avoid designating the gender of the employee.

- Job summary—A concise one- or two-sentence description of the basic functions of the job.
- Reporting relationships—Identify the position with supervisory responsibility over the job being described; identify, too, any subordinates who will report to the person holding this job.
- Qualifications—In realistic terms, list the skills, experience, and educational qualifications necessary for the position.
- Typical duties and responsibilities—Summarize the work performed by identifying each key job function in descending order of priority. Start each item on the list with an action verb. For example: "transcribes business correspondence from machine dictation equipment"; "operates office equipment, such as the telex unit, the photocopier, and the electronic typewriter."

P3 Recruitment

Anyone involved in the hiring of personnel must be aware that legislation exists that prohibits discrimination as to race, color, nationality, age, sex, and religion. Advertisements, application forms, or questions pertaining to hiring may not express nor imply qualifications or references based on the above characteristics. Some jobs may have Bona Fide Occupational Qualifications (BOQ), such as physical characteristics, gender, or age. Be certain, though, that any stated BOQ's are justified and not based on personal preference.

P4 Sources of Personnel

- state employment centers
- advertisements placed in local newspapers or national newspapers and periodicals
- recruitment efforts at high schools, colleges, universities, and private business schools
- employment agencies
- local union offices
- professional associations
- applications already on file
- recommendations from other employees
- personnel already employed (promotion from within)
- participating in cooperative education programs with high schools, post-secondary vocational schools, and colleges
- temporary help agencies

Personnel Planning: Staffing The Office

P5 Advertisements

The job description may serve as the basis for an advertisement placed in local or national newspapers. A well-written advertisement provides a complete, clear description of the job, and a suitable balance between overselling and underselling the position (Figure 14.1).

Advertising

Classified Ad Assistant

National business publication seeks conscientious individual able to work independently to price and place classified advertising for clients and follow-up billing. Accurate typing (45—50 wpm) and good math skills required. 6 months—1 year similar experience is desirable. Salary to mid-teens. For appointment call after 9 am.

616-244-1212

Equal Opportunity Employer m/f

ADMINISTRATIVE ASSISTANT/ SECRETARY

Exciting opportunity in our Corporate Tax Department. If you're an aggressive, self starter who is accurate, can work independently and enjoys a fast —paced environment, come grow with us at TELEMEDIA, Inc.

We are seeking an Administrative Assistant /Secretary with a minimum of 3 years experience to report directly to our Assistant Treasurer and also assist the tax department staff. Qualified applicant must have excellent typing/dictaphone, organizational skills and a pleasant telephone manner. Prior word processing and personal computer experience preferred.

For prompt consideration send resume including salary history to: Human Resource Dept./TDS

TELEMEDIA, Inc.
2 Plaza Rd
Secaucus, NJ 07094

Figure 14.1 Concisely Worded Advertisements

P5-P7 Advertisements

P6 Hints for Effective Advertising

- Be specific. Avoid vague expressions such as "good wages, nice working conditions, good personality needed," and "large, progressive, and leading company."
- Confine each advertisement to one job only.
- Aim to attract the most suitable people for the job, not just to obtain a large response.

  Choose your newspaper with care. Some papers are best for management positions and others for clerical positions.

  Advertise toward the end of the week, as there is a larger readership at that time.

  Be cautious about mentioning salary. It can attract unqualified people interested solely in the money; or it can discourage qualified people who may require a higher salary and who may think salary is not negotiable.

- Follow affirmative action guidelines set forth by federal and state legislation.
- Provide factual information. Do not hide the truth if the job has many routine aspects. (Applicants do not want to waste their time and the employer does not want to screen a lot of unsuitable applicants.)

P7 The Application Form

The application form must provide a full, yet pertinent, description of the candidate. Care must be paid to its design so that the form:

- obtains sufficient relevant information.
- provides enough writing space for full responses.
- adheres to the law on what may or may not be asked. (No questions pertaining to the applicant's race, color, religion, nationality, age, sex, marital status, or handicap(s) may be asked.)
- is worded so that the purpose of each question is clearly understood.

The information requested in the typical application form is divided into five sections: *personal, education, work experience, recreational pursuits,* and space for any *additional information* the candidate may wish to provide.

Personnel Planning: Staffing The Office

Since the application form may be the *only* source of information for applicants, be certain that it includes space for all needed background information, skills, and previous education and employment experience, including gaps in either.

P8 The Interview

The interview is designed to:

- obtain relevant facts not provided by the completed application form and/or application letter and data sheet (e.g., appearance, attitudes, ambitions, skills) so that an objective assessment can be made.
- provide the prospective employee with information not contained in the advertisement, such as salary, working conditions, promotion possibilities, and fringe benefits.

P9 How to Conduct an Interview

Be Properly Prepared

- Prepare in advance a list of the essential characteristics of the person being sought; for example, qualifications and experience, personality and attitudes, general intelligence, special aptitudes, interests, and career goals.
- Be familiar with the details of the job and the special skills needed.
- Review the information already provided by the applicant (letter, resume, application form).

Make the Applicant Comfortable

- Provide for privacy during the interview.
- Make an appointment for the interview, leaving enough time between interviews for evaluation purposes.
- If appropriate, involve other supervisory employees in the interview, or schedule follow-up interviews with the candidates you have selected as the best possibilities.
- Do not keep the applicant waiting.
- Be the first to offer a handshake.
- Indicate clearly where the applicant is to sit.
- Provide a comfortable chair and be sure not to put the candidate at a disadvantage; for example, ensure that the chair height is not lower than the interviewer's or that the sun is not shining in the applicant's eyes.

P8-P9 The Interview

- Use an appropriate language level. Do not talk down to the candidate nor use vocabulary he or she will not understand.
- Be warm and friendly and give the candidate your full attention so that he or she feels at ease.
- Lead the discussion at first.
- Avoid interruptions such as telephone calls.
- Do not take notes.
- As much as possible, keep the interview style and the interview questions the same for each candidate.

Give the Applicant a Turn

- Be a good listener (see W18).
- Word questions so that they require more than a *yes* or *no* answer.
- Provide sufficient talking time so that you can find out about each applicant's confidence level, oral communication skills, and attitudes.
- Invite questions.
- Ask applicants to tell you their specific interests and goals and why they feel suited to the position.
- Tactfully seek explanations for any vague answers, gaps, tendencies to change jobs, or personality conflicts.
- Remember that according to the Equal Employment Opportunity Commission, you should not ask questions pertaining to the applicant's race, religion, nationality, age, or marital status. Questions about the applicant's children, physical condition, and military or police records, should also be avoided.

Provide All the Details of the Job

- Offer a full description of the position.
- Outline company policy, fringe benefits, promotion possibilities, and any other pertinent information.

Try to Establish Your Short List (Likely/Unlikely Candidates)

- If the person is obviously unsuitable, try to explain this gently at the interview.
- If the person is a likely candidate, try to provide some definite date by which you will be in touch again. He or she may be considering other jobs.
- Find out when the applicant could start if the job were offered.

Personnel Planning: Staffing The Office

Record Your Reaction

- Before you go on to the next interview, write a full impression of the applicant who has just left.

P10 Tests

- Don't test just for the sake of it. A folder of job samples (typed reports, complex tabulations) might serve just as well.
- Test only skills relevant to the job being applied for.
- Where specific skills and knowledge are required for the position (such as a medical or legal background), these skills should be included in the testing.
- Make allowance for nervousness.
- Provide a comfortable setting and adequate equipment and supplies.
- Make reasonable demands; for example, five minutes of typing and three minutes of dictation are sufficient.
- Make your testing realistic; for example, ask a secretary to produce a letter rather than type a five-minute speed test.
- Use testing material that is free of language and terms peculiar to your particular firm or organization.

P11 Follow-Up to the Interview

The interview may be followed up, depending on the firm's policy, by:

- checking a candidate's references
- a medical examination
- a second interview with the candidate's prospective superior

P12 A Summary of Recruitment Strategies

1. Define the job realistically. Job descriptions clarify the qualifications for employment, the reporting relationships, and the activities to be performed.
2. Use the right recruiting sources. Consider the success of previous recruitment efforts in selecting these sources.
3. Conduct interviews professionally and promptly. Some pitfalls to avoid are:

    letting first impressions count too heavily

    talking too much yourself during the interview

    making a false assumption based on a candidate's previous record with a prestigious firm letting a few outstanding qualities of the candidate overshadow other limitations

relying too much on *what if* questions instead of getting the facts about the interviewee's record and experiences

comparing candidates too much with each other rather than to the job to be performed

looking for a candidate who is a mirror image of the person now performing the job

4. Check references carefully.
5. Stay in touch with the candidate after an offer has been accepted and after the starting date of employment.
6. Help the new employee get the first few days and weeks of employment off to a good start.

In general, prospective employers are entitled to contact an applicant's former employers to verify information given during the application process and to request any *job-related* information or opinions. Some states have laws restricting the disclosure of information about a present or former employee to a prospective employer. It is a good idea to be aware of the laws in your state in order to avoid possible legal ramifications. It may be easier to obtain information if you have the applicant sign a statement authorizing former employers to supply information and if you promise the employer that the data will be kept strictly confidential. Most schools and colleges will not provide information about a former student without his or her written permission.

P13 Orientation of New Employees

A good orientation plan is the first step toward developing a successful employee. Learn what the representatives from your personnel department will cover and then build your orientation strategies to follow up on their efforts. Here are some guidelines to follow.

- Spread the orientation over a period of time rather than trying to accomplish everything in several days or a week.
- Recognize that shorter orientation sessions are better than longer ones.
- Prepare a written orientation plan or checklist; identify those responsible for each phase of the plan and a timeframe for carrying out the responsibilities; give the new employee a copy of the checklist.

Personnel Planning: Staffing The Office

- Provide for the sharing of information and knowledge between the new employee and those employees with more expertise and experience.
- Cover topics according to priority. The most important topics regarding critical rules and policies, company benefits, job procedures, location of employee facilities, introduction to departmental employees, and hours of work, rest periods, and expected behaviors should be covered first. In later orientation sessions, the new employee might be involved in a tour of the other departments in the organization, a session with the personnel office for an explanation of career path opportunities, promotion practices, and an overview of other company locations and practices.
- Enlist the help of other experienced employees by having them serve as mentors for the new worker.
- Provide new employees with relevant written materials to help them better understand the firm and their role in it. Reviewing important sections of an employee handbook with a new worker is an important activity in the early days on the job.
- Describe the performance appraisal criteria and process in the first week of employment, then conduct a follow-up discussion about the third week of employment.
- Maintain a positive attitude throughout the orientation period. Encourage the new worker to ask questions and answer them patiently and carefully.
- Provide the new worker with frequent feedback; make positive comments when they are appropriate and comment supportively and promptly on errors or undesired behavior.
- Realize that the first three to six weeks are critical for the new employee and for you, so be prepared to be as involved in the orientation process as you were in the recruitment and hiring process.

P14 Evaluation of Employees

P15 New Employee Evaluations

Personnel policies vary, but most firms usually provide for the evaluation of a new employee at regular intervals, normally at the end of the first 30, 60, and 90 days of employment. It is important that the new employee receive feedback so that job expectations can be clarified and goals for improvement can be established.

P16 Regular Performance Reviews

Recognition of an employee's contributions and efforts is an important factor in maintaining good employee relations, high morale, and low turnover. The regular performance appraisal can be one of the best ways to maintain a positive and constructive dialogue between employee and supervisor. Periodic reviews—conducted at six-month or annual intervals—are intended to identify employees who are ready for salary increases, bonuses or promotions. They can also be used to help employees set goals, plan for transfer, or obtain other supportive assistance.

To keep the evaluation as unbiased as possible, a carefully designed rating sheet (Figure 14.2) should be used.

CONFIDENTIAL CONFIDENTIAL

PERFORMANCE APPRAISAL

NAME ____________ DATE ____________

DEPARTMENT ____________ HIRE DATE ____________

POSITION ____________ LAST REVIEW DATE ____________

PERFORMANCE CHECKLIST

CATEGORIES	RATING P	F	G	S	E
QUANTITY OF WORK					
QUALITY OF WORK					
ABILITY TO WORK WITH OTHERS					
ADAPTABILITY					
INITIATIVE					
COMMUNICATION SKILLS					
PERSISTENCE					
DEPENDABILITY					
OVERALL PERFORMANCE ASSESSMENT					

LEGEND:

P = POOR: NEEDS MAJOR IMPROVEMENT.

F = FAIR: BARELY ACCEPTABLE - NEEDS IMPROVEMENT

G = GOOD: SATISFACTORY-MINOR IMPROVEMENT COULD BE MADE

S = SUPERIOR: ALWAYS MORE THAN SATISFACTORY AND OCCASIONALLY OUTSTANDING

E = EXCEPTIONAL: CONSISTENTLY OUTSTANDING

SUPERVISOR'S COMMENTS ON OVERALL PERFORMANCE ____________

AREAS NEEDING IMMEDIATE IMPROVEMENT ____________

PLANS FOR PERFORMANCE IMPROVEMENT ____________

EMPLOYEE'S COMMENTS ON RATING ____________

EMPLOYEE'S SIGNATURE ____________ DATE ____________

SUPERVISOR'S SIGNATURE ____________ DATE ____________

Figure 14.2 Employee Evaluation Form

Personnel Planning: Staffing The Office

The evaluation can be based on quality of work, quantity of work, initiative shown, relationship with others, attitude and cooperativeness, punctuality and attendance, or any other appropriate factors.

Several approaches can be used in the evaluation process.

- The supervisor can complete the evaluation form, then discuss it with the employee and invite reaction.
- The employee can be invited to fill out the evaluation form for discussion with his or her supervisor.
- The evaluation can be kept entirely confidential. (This is not recommended, however, because it provides no learning experience for the employee, and the objectivity of the evaluator might be questioned.)

P17 Promotion Policy

Every business should strive to promote workers from within its present staff. To encourage fairness, a firm's policy might encompass *equality of opportunity* (any suitably qualified employee is invited to apply); *merit* (the ability to do a job well); and *seniority* (length of service).

Promotion based solely upon merit or soley upon seniority has definite disadvantages.

- Merit alone may cause poor morale in very experienced senior, but less able, employees.
- Seniority alone may prevent the best candidate from getting the job and can be discouraging to newer, ambitious, and able staff members.

A fair promotion policy, therefore, is one that uses a mix of merit and seniority. If there is a union contract, compliance with contract terms is imperative.

P18 Leaving a Job

P19 Dismissal

The dismissal or termination of an employee may be unavoidable because of loss of business, automation, take over, or closure. It may arise because of problems of incompetence, personality conflicts, dis-

P17-P21   Promotion Policy

honesty, or failure to comply with company policy. Whatever the cause, dismissal is a very serious matter and should be the subject of a clearly defined policy.

- All dismissals should be based on careful documentation. Employees should first be warned and given a probation period in which to improve performance.
- Care should be taken not to negatively influence a person's chances for employment elsewhere.

Except in rare circumstances, such as discovery of a criminal act, notice of dismissal must be given in writing. The length of notice will depend on the nature of the job, the length of employment, and the contractual arrangement with the company. Verifying the proper procedure with the Department of Labor in your state will clarify the legal requirements.

P20 Resignation

Resignations should be treated with the greatest seriousness. A reason for every resignation should be obtained so that:

- a valued employee might be encouraged to stay
- an underlying problem, if any, might be discovered and resolved

P21 Records

A confidential file on each employee should be maintained. The file might contain:

- application form and correspondence (including references from previous employers, if appropriate)
- periodic evaluation reports
- attendance records
- salary record
- courses and additional training taken
- job description of the position presently held

This file will be consulted in the event of promotion opportunities. Therefore, in the employee's best interest, it must be complete and up-to-date. Upon termination, the employee should have access to the material in the file.

Personnel Planning: Staffing The Office

P22 Payment Policy

A firm's payment policy will be based on these considerations:

- legally prescribed minimum rates
- the need to attract and keep the right kind of employee
- the need to keep employees contented and properly motivated

A payment policy must be competitive with that of other firms in the area and with similar businesses, and provide for regular pay increases to cover:

- increases in cost of living
- rewards for length of service
- merit recognition for job performance

When a labor union is involved, payments will also be influenced by the union contract.

P23 Job Evaluation

The salary that each employee receives is determined by an accurate and fair evaluation of each job. Most frequently, available jobs within an organization are classified according to difficulty, skills required, education requirements, and degree of responsibility. Each classification is then given a job level rating, and a salary range is established for each rating.

P24 Fringe Benefits

Fringe benefits are supplements to salary or wage payments. They are designed to encourage more and better work and to keep employees contented. The benefits will vary with the size and success of the business. Paid annual vacations, paid sick leave, and some insurance payments are mandatory. Other benefits that might be offered are profit-sharing plans, bonuses, flexible working hours, supplementary pension plans, supplementary health insurance schemes, dental plans, group life insurance, staff discounts, payment of education fees, subsidized recreational facilities, and Christmas gifts.

P22-P27 Payment Policy

P25 Temporary Help

P26 Finding Temporary Help

If the need arises for additional help for short periods of time (e.g., to cover vacations or inventory time), temporary workers may be obtained from a number of sources. Some of these are:

- Agencies that specialize in providing skilled help of all kinds. The employer pays the agency and the agency pays the temporary employee.

  Be sure to:

  Investigate more than one agency (check the Yellow Pages for a list of local agencies).

  Find out how each agency operates.

  Are employees bonded (insured as to their honesty)?

  Have employees been tested?

  Does the agency handle *all* payment details?

  Is satisfaction and a fast replacement guaranteed?

  Can the agency handle requests on short notice?

- Advertisements.
- Local high schools, post-secondary vocational schools, and colleges.

P27 Making the Best Use of Temporary Help

To get the best value for your temporary help dollar, organize the temporary helper's work in advance.

- Have a properly equipped work place ready.
- Have all necessary supplies available.
- Provide as many written instructions as possible; for example, a style manual, job models, or a procedures handbook.
- Keep your expectations reasonable.
- Be available to answer questions.

Personnel Planning: Staffing The Office

P28 Other Ways to Control Fluctuations in the Work Force

Peaks and valleys in volume of work are common phenomena. To compensate for heavy work loads at periodic intervals, the following alternatives might be considered in addition to the use of temporary help.

- Part-Time Help

Having some part-time workers available on an *as needed* basis can be helpful. Former employees, retired employees, and students in colleges, post-secondary vocational schools, high schools, and cooperative education programs might be interested in this form of employment.

- Service Bureaus

If work gets bogged down in specialized areas, outside agencies can be used effectively. Commercial printers, micrographics service bureaus, and computer time-sharing facilities are examples of types of service bureaus available.

- Cross-training of Workers

Each employee should be provided with training in another job within the same department. This training can prove to be a valuable resource in the case of vacation coverage, unexpected absence, and peak work periods at certain workstations.

- Hire Contract Employees

If there is need for a worker with special skills or if regular employees are not available, contract or free-lance workers who work for a company on a fee basis can be hired. These workers are paid a predetermined fee (hourly, by project, or by volume of work), and they receive no fringe benefits. They may be helpful in data entry, word processing, programming, or other areas of specialization. Contract employees often work from their own homes.

- Maintain a Permanent Squad of Workers Who Move With Work Load Demands

Hire a number of employees who are made available throughout the firm on an *as needed* basis. These employees might be sent to various

P28-P29 Other Ways to Control Fluctuations in the Work Force

departments to help handle peak and valley work loads, to cover daily or prolonged absence, to fill in while regular employees are away for training, and to take part in one-time jobs, as in the case of reorganizing a department or doing a records inventory.

P29 Channeling Employee Motivation

The effective supervisor knows how to channel motivation effectively. Here are some effective practices.

1. Be a role model. By being enthusiastic about your work and by displaying mastery in getting the work done, your employees will most likely imitate your attitude and practices.
2. Set up an open and supportive communication environment. Be a good listener and request and use employee feedback regularly.
3. Develop a predictable style of behavior. Employees need to know that you will be consistent in your policies, practices, and temperament.
4. Define every employee's role clearly. Every employee must have a clear understanding of the job to be done and the expected results.
5. Treat each employee as an individual. Work with each employee to set challenging work goals that combine personal goals with departmental and organizational goals.
6. Encourage employee self-development. Help employees obtain further training and new skills.
7. Seek employee participation and involvement in work decisions. Delegate work and involve employees on committees, task forces, and other team projects in which they can assume greater responsibility for their own productivity.
8. Use rewards—not punishment—to direct employee motivation. There are many types of rewards, and the supervisor needs to select the appropriate one. Praise, new work opportunities, titles, and increased salary are some examples.
9. Use the physical environment as a motivator. An attractive and organized work environment encourages employee performance.
10. Provide immediate reinforcement whenever possible. Feedback or acknowledgement of results lets workers know where they stand so they can recognize their accomplishments or learn what needs to be done to improve.

UNIT 15

QUERIES: LOCATING INFORMATION

Almanacs and Yearbooks	Q1
Atlases	Q2
Biographical Dictionaries (Who's Who)	Q3
Dictionaries	Q4-Q5
Specialized Dictionaries	
Encyclopedias	Q6
English Usage Books	Q7
Form and Style Books	Q8
Government References	Q9
Indexes to Periodicals	Q10-Q12
Newspapers	
Magazines	
Information About Business Organizations	Q13-Q17
Annual Reports	
City Directories	
Classified Telephone Directory	
General Industry Surveys	
Postal Information	Q18
Specialized References	Q19

How to Use a Library	Q20-Q23
Book Retrieval	
Periodical Retrieval	
Interlibrary Loans	
Computerized Reference Searches	Q24
Company Library	Q25
Related Vocabulary	Q26

Queries: Locating Information

Efficient office workers must be able to find business-related information quickly. The reference books that are available in your particular office will, of course, depend on the type of business in which you are involved. There are many sources of information that will not be used often, but you should know of their availability in case you do need to use them. It takes ingenuity to match the type of information needed to the right source of that information.

This unit should be helpful to you because it is organized around the sources of information most frequently used by the business person. The references cited are generally considered to be the most authoritative. For those situations in which more specialized information is required, you will find the reference section of your local library an invaluable aid. A growing trend is to search for information on-line by using computerized retrieval services that often can be accessed by your own office's computer equipment or that are available through a local library.

Sections on reference books, how to find information in a library, a brief introduction to computerized reference searches, and library-related terms are included in this unit.

Q1 Almanacs and Yearbooks

Almanacs and yearbooks are annual publications that are one-volume sources of general information of all kinds. They are crammed with statistics and short factual statements on topics like trade and transportation; religion; educational institutions; noted personalities; history; geography, science; and data on state, national, and international governments including population, structures, and other statistics.

Two examples are:

Information Please Almanac, Atlas and Yearbook.
New York: Simon and Schuster

The World Almanac and Book of Facts.
New York: Newspaper Enterprise Association, Inc.

Q2 Atlases

Atlases contain statistical and descriptive data about various regions and countries of the world, as well as detailed maps and indexes.

Two examples are:

Rand McNally Cosmopolitan World Atlas, New Census Edition.
Chicago: Rand McNally

Rand McNally Atlas of the United States
Chicago: Rand McNally

Q3 Biographical Dictionaries (Who's Who)

Biographical dictionaries supply factual data on prominent people. Entries include information about their background, age, parentage, education, degrees earned, occupation or profession, affiliation, achievements, and honors. The dictionaries are often biennial (every two years) publications.

Some of these dictionaries are:

Who's Who in America
Chicago: Marquis Who's Who, Inc.

Who's Who in the World
Chicago: Marquis Who's Who, Inc.

Who's Who in Finance and Industry
Chicago: Marquis Who's Who, Inc.

Who's Who of American Women
Chicago: Marquis Who's Who, Inc.

Many specialized Who's Who references in different subject areas are also available. For example:

Who's Who in the United Nations
New York: Arno Press

Who's Who in American Art
New York: R. R. Bowker

Who's Who in Economics
Cambridge, Massachusetts: MIT Press

Note: For information about notable people no longer alive, refer to encyclopedias or *Who Was Who*, Chicago: Marquis Who's Who, Inc.

Queries: Locating Information

Q4 Dictionaries

Dictionaries contain words that are listed alphabetically, usually with the following information:

- meanings and definitions.
- preferred form of spelling, if more than one is acceptable.
- syllabic division shown by a heavy accent, light accent, centered period, or hyphen.
- correct pronunciation indicated by accent marks—a heavy mark indicates major stress; a lighter mark denotes less stress.
- part of speech—if more than one is indicated, any change in pronunciation will also be shown.
- derivation of words (their origins) in square brackets at the end of an entry.
- synonyms and antonyms indicated by *syn* and *ant* at the end of an entry.
- usage examples in phrases and clauses to complement the common definition and clarify usage.
- prefixes and suffixes with their definitions.

Consult the front of the dictionary for greater details on etymology (word origins), pronunciation, and abbreviations used in the dictionary. The alphabetic list of words is usually followed by an appendix of words with special uses, a section on abbreviations, and foreign words and phrases. Some dictionaries also supply information on international currencies, scientific and technical terms, titles of address, and weights and measures.

Two examples are:

The American College Dictionary
New York: Random House

Webster's New World Dictionary of the American Language
New York: Simon and Schuster

Q5 Specialized Dictionaries

Thesaurus
A *thesaurus* (directory of synonyms and antonyms) is useful when you have an idea of what you want to say but need a particular word to convey the exact meaning; or when you need a variation for a frequently

454

repeated word. A thesaurus comes in two forms: the words are either arranged alphabetically as in a dictionary, or they are listed according to the ideas they express.

Here are two examples:

Roget's Thesaurus of English Words and Phrases
New York: St. Martin Press

Roget's II: The New Thesaurus
Boston: Houghton Mifflin

Other Handy References
20,000 Words
New York: Gregg Division, McGraw-Hill Book Company, Inc.
A dictionary of words spelled and divided for quick reference. No definitions are provided.

The Business Dictionary
Englewood Cliffs, New Jersey: Prentice-Hall, Inc.
A simple, up-to-date, alphabetic list of business terms with definitions.

The Word Book
Encino, California: Glencoe Publishing Company
A handy, pocket-size reference guide to the correct spelling and division of more than 23,000 words commonly used in business.

Note: Most professions and scientific, technical, and trade specialization areas have their own specialized dictionaries. Examples include dictionaries in sociology, psychology, business, and computers.

Q6 Encyclopedias

Encyclopedias provide general information on the arts, sciences, history, and technological fields; domestic and foreign political and economic developments; and brief biographical information on prominent persons. Some examples of encyclopedias are:

Columbia Encyclopedia
New York: Columbia University Press
Information of a general nature is presented in non-technical form in one volume.

Queries: Locating Information

Encyclopedia Americana
New York: Grolier, Inc.
Multi-volume set containing condensed narratives describing topics in American history. The sciences and biographies are highlighted.

Encyclopedia Britannica
Chicago: Encyclopedia Britannica, Inc.
Top authorities in many fields contribute to articles in this long-standing reference source.

Q7 English Usage Books

Office handbooks such as this one indicate fundamental rules of grammar, usage, style, and office procedures. Other sources include:

The Gregg Reference Manual, 6th edition
Gregg Division, McGraw-Hill Book Company

The Handbook of Executive Communication,
Illinois: Dow-Jones-Irwin

English Usage
Rowley, Massachusetts: Newbury House

Reference Manual for Office Workers, 2d ed.
Encino, California: Glencoe Publishing Company

Q8 Form and Style Books

Form and style books render assistance to students and other writers in the preparation of technical reports. They often cover all aspects of writing from choosing a topic through researching and writing the final report. Sample finished report pages are often included and these illustrations are helpful to the writer and to the typist. Some examples of form and style books include:

The Elements of Style, 3d ed., New York: Macmillan. (Strunk and White)

The Chicago Manual of Style, 13th ed.
Chicago: University of Chicago Press

Form and Style: Theses, Reports, Term Papers, 6th ed. (Campbell, Ballou and Slade)
Boston: Houghton Mifflin Company

A Manual for Writers of Term Papers, Theses, and Dissertations, 4th ed. (Turabian)
Chicago: University of Chicago Press

The Business Writer's Handbook, 2d ed., (Brusaw, Alred and Oliu)
New York: St. Martin's Press

Q9 Government References

Government publications are available through the Superintendent of Documents (United States Government Printing Office, North Capitol and H Streets, NW, Washington, D.C., 20401) on a wide variety of topics. Consumer publications may be obtained free or for a minimal fee. Public libraries often subscribe to monthly, quarterly, or annual government publications. Technical publications, which are updated frequently, can be obtained on a subscription basis.

Many libraries throughout the United States are designated as Official U.S. Government Depository Libraries. The following publications, as well as many others, will be available in these designated libraries. Your local librarian should be able to identify the nearest depository library for you.

The Congressional Record. A daily record of the proceedings and debates in Congress. Texts of the bills themselves are not included. A complete history of all legislation in one Congressional year is provided through the final index to a volume that lists names and subjects of bills and a history of each bill under its respective numbers.

The Congressional Directory. An annual publication that contains names and geographical data on all members of Congress as well as maps of Congressional districts.

Monthly Catalog of U.S. Government Publications. A comprehensive listing of all publications issued by various government departments and agencies.

Queries: Locating Information

United States Government Manual. An annual publication containing information on the agencies of the United States Government. Information includes the address, a list of principal officials, a brief history, and the role and purpose of the agency.

Selected U.S. Government Publications. Upon request, the Superintendent of Documents provides subscribers with a semi-monthly listing of selected publications in a variety of fields.

Standard Industrial Classification Manual. The authoritative source for the four-digit SIC (Standard Industrial Code) numbers. Major business activities are assigned a specific three-digit code number. Subdivisions of the major activity are assigned the fourth digit. For example, the apparel industry's major code number is 560; men's apparel is assigned the fourth digit of 1; therefore, the SIC Code for men's apparel is 5601. These SIC code numbers organize information related to a particular industry into common categories for statistical and comparison purposes.

Statistical Abstract of the United States. An annual publication compiled by the Bureau of the Census, Department of Commerce. It contains summary statistics about area and population, education, climate, employment, social security, military affairs, transportation, manufacturing, forestry, and many other topics.

Q10 Indexes to Periodicals

Periodical indexes are useful reference works that are issued frequently and then collected into annual volumes, each of which lists articles published the previous year. The entries are classified by subject.

Newspapers

New York Times Index. Presents a condensed and classified history of the world as it is recorded in daily issues of the *Times*. Contains abstracts of news under subject headings and references to the location of the specific articles. Back-dated copies of the newspaper are often available in microfilm format.

Wall Street Journal. A daily business newspaper. Each entry begins with a brief abstract of the article. A citation by which to locate the article is also given. The index is arranged in two parts: one part gives the news arranged by company name, the other gives the news arranged by general topics. Back-dated copies of the newspaper are often available in microfilm format. This index is also available in a computerized version.

> **Note:** Some libraries have indexes available to other papers—namely, the *Christian Science Monitor,* the *Washington Post,* and the *Los Angeles Times.* In addition, libraries often index local newspapers for which no commercial indexes are available.

Q12 Magazines

Readers Guide to Periodical Literature. A cumulative author and subject index to popular and general interest periodicals.

Business Periodicals Index. A reference that provides a cumulative subject index to articles from a large number of business periodicals. It includes many topics such as management, labor, accounting, banking, advertising, general business, insurance, and real estate.

Q13 Information About Business Organizations

The following sources will help you locate information relating to business, trade, and industry; to people, organizational structures, and products; and to finance, marketing, and other business-related subjects.

Q14 Annual Reports

Annual reports to shareholders are prepared by most large corporations as a public relations tool. They are required by companies listed on the stock exchange. Annual reports of companies listed on the major stock exchanges can usually be found in microfiche formats in large libraries. Reports vary in content but often contain statistical, financial and non-financial news about the company and its future programs and plans. Annual reports are a helpful reference for job-seekers interested in learning more about a company prior to an interview (see J14).

Queries: Locating Information

Q15 City Directories

City directories are published annually by commercial enterprises in large communities. They may contain some or all of the following information about residents and companies in a particular geographic area: alphabetic listing of residents, businesses, and telephone numbers; alphabetic listing by street names; miscellaneous information including population statistics, municipal officials, and other community-oriented information.

Q16 Classified Telephone Directory

The *Yellow Pages* section of the telephone directory lists names, addresses, and telephone numbers of businesses in a particular area classified by type.

Q17 General Industry Surveys

America's Corporate Families—The Billion Dollar Directory
Parsippany, New Jersey: Dun's Marketing Services
A reference that identifies the major United States parent companies. It displays corporate family connections of subdivisions and divisions. A separate volume is also available showing international affiliates.

Directory of Corporate Affiliations—Who Owns Whom
Parsippany, New Jersey: Dun's Marketing Services
A reference that provides a compilation of the major United States companies and their corporate structure, divisions, subsidiaries, and affiliates.

Dun & Bradstreet's Million Dollar Directory
New York: Dun & Bradstreet, Inc.
A three-volume directory that lists selected United States companies by alphabetic, geographic, and product categories. It includes brief information about each company, such as address, principal officers, number of employees, product lines, and other facts.

MacRae's Industrial Directory
New York: MacRae's Blue Book
Available for most states, this directory contains a list of manufacturers in the state with alphabetic, geographic, and classified indexes. Brief information about the company is given in the geographic section.

Q15-Q17 City Directories

Moody's Manuals
New York: Moody's Investors Service, Inc.
Seven manuals, each devoted to a specific area (public utilities, transportation, banking and finance, industrial, international, municipal and government, and OTC industrial) comprise this resource. Background information is given on specific companies, such as the history, management, location of offices and plants, subsidiaries, products and statistics on sales, and earnings and profits. The manuals are issued annually and are kept up-to-date with news reports issued twice a week.

Standard & Poor's Industry Surveys
New York: Standard & Poor's Corporation
A quarterly publication, this resource contains sections covering major industries such as apparel, cosmetics, and computers. The coverage in each section includes background material, statistics, trends, and outlook for leading companies in each field.

Standard and Poor's Register of Corporations, Directors, and Executives
New York: Standard & Poor's Corporation
Contains three volumes. Volume 1 gives the name and address of the corporation, officers and products, sales, and number of employees. Volume 2 contains brief biographies of principal directors and executives. Volume 3 has a geographic index and an index by SIC numbers (see Q9).

Thomas Register of American Manufacturers
New York: Thomas Publishing Company
A multi-volume work issued annually. The main section lists manufacturers by specific products. Other volumes contain a list of addresses and trade names. Catalogs of some companies are also provided.

U.S. Industrial Outlook
Washington, DC: Superintendent of Documents
An annual overview of the nation's industries. This resource is divided into broad categories such as transportation, consumer goods, and communication. Each chapter gives a description of the industry with statistics and growth projections.

Queries: Locating Information

Q18 Postal Information

For information about postal fees and services, the authoritative source is the *United States Postal Manual*. This comprehensive resource is often found in the large mail room. For information about postal fees and rates, or for advice in unusual mailing situations, it is best to contact your local post office. A handy reference, however, for most offices and a must reference for the mail room is:

National ZIP Code Directory
U.S. Government Printing Office, Washington, D.C.
A comprehensive volume containing ZIP Code prefixes, state post office numbers and ZIP Codes by cities, towns, and major street locations for larger cities. All fifty states are included.

Another helpful postal reference is:
National ZIP + 4 Code Directory
U.S. Government Printing Office, Washington, D.C.
Expands upon the standard ZIP Code Directory by listing the newer 9-digit codes referred to as ZIP + 4. Also explains how to use ZIP + 4 for business mailings.

Q19 Specialized References

The following list of sources is a suggestion of references available for special situations.
Bartlett's Familiar Quotations
Boston, MA: Little, Brown & Co.

Emily Post's Etiquette, 14th Edition
New York: Harper & Row

Roberts Rules of Order, Revised
New York: Scott, Foresman and Company
Contains rules of parliamentary law and explains methods of organizing and conducting meetings, conventions, and other formal business meetings (see Unit 13, *Organizing Meetings and Conferences*).

Hotel and Motel Red Book
New York: American Hotel Association Directory Corporation
Published annually, this resource lists hotels and motels alphabetically by city and state. Includes information on the number of rooms, services, rates, and locations (see A23).

Official Airline Guide
Oak Brook, IL: The Official Airline Guide, Inc.
Provides a listing of direct flights between cities, ground transportation information, and instructions on how to arrange connecting flights (see A3).

Datapro Directory of Microcomputer Software
Datapro Directory of Minicomputers
Datapro Directory of Office Automation
Datapro Directory of Personal Computers
Delran, New Jersey: Datapro Reports, Inc.
Separate looseleaf volumes. Users subscribe to periodic updates that provide comprehensive information about equipment, supplies, and technolgical developments.

Books in Print
Chicago, IL: R. R. Bowker Company
Published annually, this resource lists books in separate indexes by author, book title, and subject. This is also a good reference for addresses and telephone numbers of publishers.

Q20 How to Use a Library

Q21 Book Retrieval

Most libraries, regardless of size or specialization, provide *card catalogues* that list which books the library owns. There are usually three card index files—author, title, and subject, each alphabetically arranged. If you know the title or author, check one of these files; if not, look in the subject file. The reference numbers on the card (Figure 15.1) will direct you to the shelf location of the book.

All libraries use a classification system to catalogue and shelve their holdings. The two most widely used systems are the *Dewey- Decimal System* and the *Library of Congress* (LC) system.

Queries: Locating Information

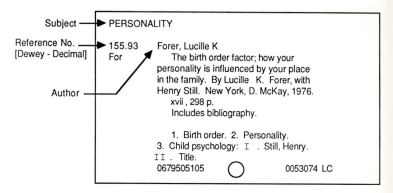

Figure 15.1 Library Reference Card

The Dewey Decimal System establishes ten broad topic categories that are further divided into specific topic subcategories. Each category is identified numerically and books are shelved in numeric order.

The LC system establishes 21 major categories that are further divided into more specific topic subcategories. Each category is identified with an alphabetic letter.

The sample catalog card shown is in the Dewey Decimal System, thus the first three digits (155) tell you that the book falls under the *Philosphy* classification.

Many large libraries no longer maintain card catalogs. Their holdings are listed in catalogs or on-line computer programs. Written, audio, or video instructions are always available to help you use these tools.

Periodical Retrieval

Most libraries have a list of periodicals to which they subscribe. In addition, *union lists* of periodicals are often available that include the periodical holdings of several libraries. The periodicals list usually indicates whether the material is available in hard copy, microfilm, or microfiche formats. The librarian normally obtains the items you request. Policies for borrowing printed copies vary according to library policy; however, coin-operated copiers are usually available to make copies of needed articles. Microfilm or microfiche readers require that you read the microfilm using the library's equipment. If microfilm or microfiche reader-printers are available, you will be able to make a hard copy of the desired pages for a fee.

Q23 Interlibrary Loans

When a library does not have a book or periodical article that you need, you might request that the library obtain the desired item through interlibrary loan from another library. Libraries often have reciprocal borrowing agreements with other libraries and will share books and periodicals on an *as needed* basis. There will, of course, be a time lag in obtaining the material. This service is usually provided without a fee to the patron, but library policies do vary.

Q24 Computerized Reference Searches

The printed indexes and references that fill up a library's reference shelves are often available as on-line data bases to any office with a computer (see I48).

Anyone with a communicating word processor or computer terminal, a modem, and a telephone can—as a subscriber—access electronic libraries that contain a wealth of up-to-date information. The information in the electronic files or data bases is even more timely than the printed volumes on library shelves because it is being kept current through weekly or monthly updating.

Depending on the data base accessed, the computer-search requests can be made by author, title, subject, or keyword. The researcher may retrieve the information in the form of a *bibliographic citation*, an *abstract*, or *full-text*, depending on the capability of the data base used and the parameters identified by the researcher (see Q26).

Simply stated, the procedure to do a computerized reference search involves the following:

The researcher places a telephone call to the telephone number of the desired mainframe's data base. When the desired data base service acknowledges the telephone call, the researcher logs onto the data base by keying in a user number and/or a password. Using specific commands, the special index or file to be used in the search is entered. Again, using desired commands and keywords, the researcher logs onto the data base by keying in a user number and/or a password. Using specific commands, the special index or file to be used in the search is entered. Again, using desired commands and keywords, the researcher defines the parameters and the configuration of the information desired. As the researcher keyboards commands and interacts with the electronic file, responses are observed on the screen. Printed data can also be obtained in accessing some data bases.

Determining the commands and the keywords that will lead the researcher to the desired information is a special skill that takes time to learn. College and university librarians are often called upon to do computer searches. There is a charge for the service and fees vary from institution to institution.

With the growing number of personal computers in today's offices, more and more firms are taking advantage of computerized reference searches. It provides offices with one more advantageous use of the computer and, even more importantly, it provides desired information in minutes rather than in days or weeks. Software programs are being developed to simplify the search process; therefore, future trends indicate that doing computer searches will become an important function of the office worker.

Q25 Company Library

In most offices there are certain reference works that are frequently consulted. These books may be general reference sources such as dictionaries, style manuals, wordbooks, and office manuals; or they may be specific to the particular business conducted in an office such as tax guides and law books. The maintenance of an organized, easily accessible company library can be a useful tool to all office personnel. A specified location should be established for these reference books, and an effort made to keep the latest editions on hand.

Q26 Related Vocabulary

Abstract A summary of the contents of an article or book.

Bibliographic Citation A specific source of information. For a book, this includes the author, the book title, the publisher, and the copyright date. For an article in a periodical it includes the author and title of the article, its page numbers, and the name, volume, and month of the publication.

Bibliography A list of sources on a specific subject. This could include books, articles in periodicals, pamphlets, government documents, and conference proceedings.

Q25-Q26 Company Library

Biography A written account of a person's life.

Call Number The letters and numbers that identify a particular book and indicate both its location on the shelves and its position relative to other books. The call number is usually marked on the lower part of the spine of a book and it appears at the upper left corner of catalog cards.

Card Catalog Card files found in the library to let a patron know what books a library owns.

Circulation Desk The desk or counter where books are charged out for loan and where they are returned after the loan period is over.

Classification Number The number found in the upper left-hand corner of a card in the card catalog. This number serves as a location device telling where to find a book on the library's shelves.

Closed Stacks Section of a library in which materials are accessible only to library personnel. Readers must request the material at the desk or counter. Sometimes periodicals are kept in closed stacks.

Dewey Decimal System The classification system that uses numerals divisible by ten and divides fields of knowledge into 10 general categories.

Dictionary Card Catalogs Cards representing authors, titles, and subjects organized in one alphabetical arrangement.

Divided Card Catalogs Author and title cards arranged in one card catalog and subject cards arranged in another card catalog.

Excerpt A word for word extract from a book, article, or piece of music.

Full Text Being able to view an entire article word-for-word in a computerized reference search.

Interlibrary loan The procedure by which one libary can obtain a book or periodical from another library on special request.

Journal A periodical usually issued by a society or institution.

Library of Congress Classification The classification system that uses the alphabet and divides the world of knowledge into 21 parts (some letters have been reserved for future use). Books classified by the Library of Congress system have a letter or combination of letters, such as A, AE, G, GV, on the top line of the call number.

Queries: Locating Information

Keywords Related terms and synonyms used in a computerized reference search to describe a topic for which information is sought. To get further information on *women in business in the United States* for example, the data base would need to be searched by at least three keywords and a combination of each: *women and business,* and *women and business and the United States.*

Microfiche A flat sheet of photographic film bearing micro-images of the text of a publication or document in horizontal and vertical rows. One sheet of microfiche can hold many pages of text depending on the reduction ratio. Machines are necessary for reading microfiche.

Microfilm A microphotograph on a reel of cellulose film. It may be negative or positive. Machines are necessary for reading microfilm.

Microfilm or Microfiche Reader A machine used for reading micro-images. It produces an enlarged image on an opaque or transparent screen.

Microform A term indicating any form of micro-image, whether on film, microfiche or other form (see F72).

Non-Print Media A term used to describe library holdings such as filmstrips, audio cassettes, records, slides, and videotapes.

Periodical A broad term including magazines, newspapers, and journals.

Reference Books Books kept for reference use only, such as dictionaries, indexes, bibliographies, and atlases. These books are not allowed to be taken outside the library.

Subject Heading The word or group of words under which books and other material on a topic are entered in a card catalog.

Ultrafiche A microfiche with very small images. One thousand pages can be accommodated on one 3" x 5" fiche. Machines are necessary for reading ultrafiche.

UNIT 16

REPROGRAPHICS

Definition of Terms	R1
The Reprographic Process	R2
Reprographic Options	R3
Considerations in Selecting a Copying or Duplicating Process	R4
Copying Processes	R5-R20
Machine Copying Equipment	
A Comparison of Copying Processes	
Economical Use of the Copier	
Carbon Copying	
The Cut and Paste Technique	
Guidelines for the Fair and Reasonable Use of Copiers	
The Duplicating Processes	R21-R23
The Offset Process	
Comparison of Duplicating Processes	
Choosing Reprographic Equipment	R24-R27
Copier Selection Guidelines	
Additional Copier Features to Consider	
Duplicator Selection Guidelines	
Auxiliary Reprographic Equipment	R28
Photocomposition	R29
Photocomposition Terms	R30
Computer Graphics	R31
Intelligent Copiers	R32
Paper Terms	R33
Controlling Reprographic Costs	R34

Reprographics

Even with computer memories, micrographics, and magnetic media, there continues to be a demand for reproducing one or multiple copies of original documents in a timely manner. This unit describes various alternatives used to produce paper copies.

As an office worker, your responsibilities involving copying and duplicating will vary depending on your particular office. It is wise, however, to have an understanding of some of the basic copying and duplicating methods. Knowing how to select the appropriate process and being able to use equipment features correctly will make you a more valuable employee. Finally, knowing some facts about the legality of copying, the characteristics of paper, some terms used in photocomposition, and some special purpose auxiliary reprographic equipment will enhance your ability to make better decisions when producing one copy or many copies.

R1 Definition of Terms

Copying is a direct production process whereby one or many copies can be prepared on a photocopy machine. The original can be the output of a typewriter, a printer, or some previously duplicated or copied work. The original can also be a *pasteup*, which is a composite made by cutting and pasting from several different sources.

Duplicating is an indirect reproduction process because a medium such as a stencil, a spirit master, or an offset mat must first be prepared from an original. The medium can be prepared by retyping or by the use of special purpose equipment that has the ability to electronically prepare a medium from an original. Once the medium is prepared, it is then *run* on a piece of equipment such as a fluid duplicator, a mimeograph machine, or an offset machine in order to produce quantity or *multicopies*.

Reprographics is a broad term used to describe an overall knowledge of all the various reproduction methods and processes. A knowledge of reprographics implies knowing the *ins and outs* of the various methods of making copies. It presumes a knowledge of all phases of preparing a finished piece of work from the selection of a process to formatting the final result (Figure 16.1). A knowledge of reprographics also implies knowing all the advantages and disadvantages of the processes and equipment so that effective decisions can be made at each step in the reprographics process.

Figure 16.1 The Reprographics Process

R2 The Reprographic Process

Factors to consider in the reprographic process are:

- How many copies are needed?
- How quickly are they needed?
- How professional-looking must the finished result be?
- Does provision need to be made for special paper, photographs, use of color, or two-sided printing?
- What are the advantages of the processes available?
- What are the disadvantages of the processes available?
- What is the potential cost of each option in terms of supplies, type of output, employee productivity, and time?
- Is the original usable as is?
- Can the cut and paste technique be used?
- What alternatives are available by which I can prepare a medium?

Reprographics

- What can be done to make the finished result look as professional and attractive as possible?
- How easy is the equipment to operate?
- What special features of the equipment should I use to enhance the final presentation?
- How easy is the equipment to set up?
- How easy is the equipment to maintain?
- May I run special paper on the equipment?
- How can collating be provided for?
- Should the information be bound?
- How should copies be organized for distribution?

R3 Reprographic Options

You face three possible situations with respect to copying and duplicating.

- **Do it yourself.** In many instances, you will be required to handle the copying or duplicating yourself. To do this, you must be knowledgeable about how the original should look, how to prepare a medium for a duplicating process, if necessary, and how to produce the desired number of copies.
- **Prepare a work order for the Reprographics Department.** If there is a centralized reprographics department in your company, you will be required to prepare a work order or requisition for duplicating jobs. On the work order, you will be asked to state the type, size, and color of the paper to be used; the department to be charged; the number of copies desired; the date you want the finished work; and whether any other special features are desired, such as collating, folding, stapling, and two-sided printing.
- **Place an order with an outside vendor.** For certain jobs that require quality reproduction, you may have to make arrangements to have special printing done at a quick-copy shop or by a commercial printer. You will be required to give clear and complete job specifications in making these arrangements. You may also have to do comparative shopping to get the job done economically.

R3-R7   Reprographic Options

R4 Considerations in Selecting a Copying or Duplicating Process

For the greatest efficiency at the lowest cost, you need to select a reprographic process with care. There are several basic considerations to keep in mind when making the selection.

- speed
- number of copies required
- quality required
- ease of equipment operation
- availability of supplies
- time required for and ease of preparing a medium
- color requirements
- photo requirements
- compatibility with other available equipment
- special options necessary such as enlarging, reducing, two-sided copying, special size paper
- type style and composition of the original
- length of the document

R5 Copying Processes

R6 Machine Copying Equipment

The easiest way to obtain quick copies is to use a photocopy machine, most often called a *copier*. While there are many makes and models of copiers available, three basic types will be discussed here: the *plain paper copier*, the *coated paper* copier, and the *thermal* copier.

R7 The Plain Paper Copier

The prevailing trend is toward the use of the plain paper copier. As its name implies, the user can print copies on any office paper (letterhead, bond paper, duplicating paper, and even colored paper). The *Xerographic* process is used to prepare copies, and this process is similar to

473

Reprographics

taking a picture with a camera. A two-component toner/developer combination followed by a heat and pressure fusing process (known as *fixing*) is the prevailing method found on the lowest to highest volume models.

Plain paper copiers give fine quality reproduction and the most expensive copiers can even reproduce color photographs. When these machines are used in high volume operations, the cost per copy is low.

R8 The Coated Paper Copier

Copiers that print only on specially-treated paper are less expensive to purchase initially; however, the need to stock special supplies, the inconsistent copy quality, and the noticeable background and slick finish of the copies are limitations. For monthly copying volumes under 500 copies, this machine might still be selected; however, the use of coated paper copiers is diminishing.

Note: To make copies on plain paper and coated paper copiers, the basic steps are as follows: lift the protective cover, place the original face down on the glass, replace the cover, and press the start button.

R9 The Thermal Copier

Thermal or thermographic copiers make copies directly from the original using a heat process and special copy paper. For the processing to work, the image on the original copy must have a high carbon content such as an image made with a pencil, typewriter ribbon, or carbon paper. Images made with a ball point pen or colored pencils often will not show up on the copies. The process is used primarily for making transparencies (or viewgraphs) for the overhead projector. Transparencies are transparent sheets containing images that are projected onto a screen to help the audience understand key points of a presentation. With the proper supplies, the thermal copier can also be used to prepare media such as spirit masters for the fluid duplicator and stencils for the mimeograph machine.

Note: To operate a thermal copier, place a sheet of specially-treated paper (or a piece of blank transparency film) on top of the original and pass the two sheets into the machine with the original face up.

R10 A Comparison of Copying Processes

To help you select the appropriate copying method for your particular needs, consult Table 16.1 (pp. 476–477) for a comparison of copying processes.

R8-R12 The Coated Paper Copier

R11 Economical Use of the Copier

Copying machines are simple to operate and require little special instruction. However, while the convenience factor is high, be sure to avoid such wasteful jobs as:

- producing copies for distribution to staff members when circulation of the original document would do
- producing copies when carbon copies might be typed
- using a copier when a cheaper process would suffice
- using a copier to reproduce forms

When the copier is the best choice, use it as efficiently and economically as possible.

- Save your copying until you have several items.
- Put the counter back to *1* when you are through so that the next user does not risk making unnecessary copies.
- Use the right size paper for the job.
- Make only the exact number of copies needed.
- Use the clean side of copies that did not reproduce well or are no longer needed as scrap paper.
- Keep close track of the device assigned to you to monitor copying.
- Plan to use the copier first thing in the morning or at the end of the day; often it is less busy at these times.

R12 Carbon Copying

The least expensive method of producing copies for documents that are yet to be typed is to use carbon paper and carbon copy paper, known as *onion skin*. Depending on the typewriter used and the quality of the carbon paper, it is often possible to prepare up to eight good copies using carbon paper.

Although carbon paper is economical and reusable, it is not used in many offices where there is easy access to a convenience copier. However, if the office copier is in a busy location or available only at a substantial distance from the workstation, carbon copies can effectively be used for documents requiring only a limited number of copies or only an office file copy.

Reprographics

Table 16.1 A Comparison of Copying Processes

Process	Quality of Reproduction	Number of Copies	Advantages
Plain Paper Copier	Excellent. Will produce an exact black and white copy of the original.	Unlimited	speed; quality usually consistent; accepts single or 3-dimensional objects; many special features available on equipment; easy to operate; can prepare transparencies with special supplies; no special paper needed
Coated Paper Copier	Good. Will produce an exact black and white copy of the orginal.	Unlimited	speed; accepts 3-dimensional objects; many special features available on equipment; easy to operate; can prepare transparencies with special supplies
Thermal Copier	Good if original is clear and has a high carbon content.	Unlimited	speed; ease of use; copier can produce thermal spirit masters, thermal stencils, transparencies for the overhead projector, and single copies easily
Carbon Copies	Fair. Copies diminish in quality as a greater number of copies are made simultaneously.	Up to 8 copies on an electric or electronic typewriter	low cost

A Comparison of Copying Processes

Limitations	Relative Costs	Most Appropriate Uses
copying in color; copies are black and white only; sometimes photographs do not reproduce well	Equipment is expensive to purchase at the outset. Cost per copy becomes less expensive as equipment for large volume copying is obtained.	. . . where quality and speed are important. Copies are excellent for the needs of most organizations for internal and external use.
inconsistent copy quality; copies must be made on special paper; copying in color; copies are black and white only; sometimes photographs do not reproduce well	Equipment is compact and comparatively inexpensive to purchase. Cost per copy is higher than plain paper copier.	. . . where speed is important and quality is not imperative. Copies are good but not always consistent in quality. Best for low-volume copying needs.
copies will fade; will not copy colors or most ballpoint pen images; accepts only single sheets	Equipment is multifunctional, easy to operate, and comparatively inexpensive to purchase.	. . . where copies for internal distribution are the primary need. Copy quality effective only with carbon based originals. Mostly for internal use.
messy; takes long to correct errors; good for only a few copies; image not always clear	Least expensive in terms of equipment and supplies.	. . . where very few copies are needed; generally for internal use only.

Reprographics

R13 Assembling the Carbon Pack

1. Place a piece of copy paper on the desk.
2. Place a piece of carbon paper (shiny, carbon-coated side down, Figure 16.2) on the copy paper with the precut corner of the carbon at the top left corner. Repeat steps 1 and 2 as many times as the number of copies you require.

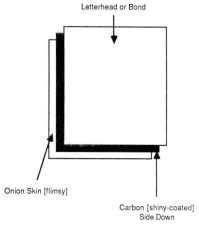

Figure 16.2   Carbon Pack

3. Place the top sheet (letterhead or other bond stationery) on top of the final carbon sheet, printed side up.
4. Pick up the pack, tap it at the top end to line up all the edges, and insert it into the typewriter (Figure 16.3). Be sure to keep the shiny (coated) side of the carbon away from you. *Do not permit the carbon paper to crease.*

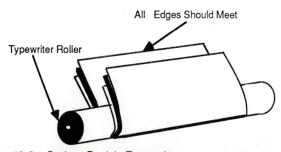

Figure 16.3   Carbon Pack in Typewriter

Note: An envelope or folded sheet placed over the top edge of the pack makes it easier to insert the pack into the typewriter and keep all the

R13-R16   Assembling the Carbon Pack

sheets straight. Roll the pack into the machine and then remove the envelope or folded sheet.

R14   Correcting Errors on Carbons

The process of correcting errors on carbons is a time-consuming one. Many offices that use carbon paper for file copies correct only the errors in key items in a document such as dates, places, and names. Other typographical errors are corrected on the original copy only; therefore, they show up as strike over on the office file copy. The process by which to correct an error on carbons is as follows:

1. Place a piece of card or paper in front of the first sheet of carbon behind the error.
2. Erase the error or use a tape cover-up.
3. Move the card or paper in front of the next sheet of carbon.
4. Remove the error using a pencil eraser or correction aids designed for correcting carbon copies.
5. Continue erasing or correcting until all the copies have been fixed.
6. Type the correct character on the top copy.

Note: This process works equally well if you start from the back of the pack and work forward.

R15   Trends in the Use of Carbons

- Some offices use continuous form carbon paper in word processing equipment to produce originals and carbons simultaneously.
- Some offices use carbon sets of specially-treated paper that takes the place of inserting and handling the carbon paper itself.
- Some offices use carbon paper sets (carbon film and onion paper fastened together) when only an office copy is needed. In such cases, too, only key items in a document are erased and corrected on the carbon copy which remains in the file.

R16   The Cut and Paste Technique

Often, a master is prepared using the cut and paste technique. Usually the better the original, the better the potential for good quality output from a copier. Here are some guidelines to keep in mind when preparing an original or pasteup for quick copies.

- Use opaque *white* paper as the basis of the original.
- Use paper cement or rubber cement sparingly to affix material added to the page.

- Use line drawings rather than photographs because line drawings reproduce better.
- Draw, write, or trace, but keep in mind that an instrument that writes black is best.
- Consider using special lettering to add to the attractiveness of your finished document. Some sources include dry transfer letters; peel off plastic letters; special elements or font typestyles; template lettering; and lettering, headlines, and drawings cut from magazines, brochures, and other eye-catching sources.
- Use a scissor or an *x-acto* knife for cutting and trimming.
- Consider *reducing* typewritten copy to obtain special effects or to save on reproduction costs in long runs.
- Consider *enlarging* typewritten copy to obtain special eye-catching effects, or in the preparation of pasteups for transparencies.
- Use a black pen or a felt tip pen that writes black to sharpen line drawings and headlines as necessary.
- Leave sufficient white space in between the copy and in the margins to enhance readability.
- Consider producing the lettering using graphics software and printing the output on a dot-matrix printer, a laser printer, or a plotter.
- Design an effective layout to provide for eye appeal and to promote and maintain the reader's interest.
- Use a soft eraser to erase guidelines or make them with a non-reproducing pencil.

R17 Guidelines for the Fair and Reasonable Use of Copiers

Office employees need to be aware that there are certain documents that should not be copied and that copying large amounts of material from books and other printed sources requires permission from the copyright holder and possibly the payment of fees.

R18 Items That Should Not Be Copied

Congress, by statute, has forbidden the copying of certain documents. Under certain circumstances, penalties of fines or imprisonment may be imposed on those guilty of making copies of the documents for unlawful purposes. These restricted documents are:

> obligations or securities of the United States Government—such as treasury bonds, paper money, Federal Reserve Bank notes, postage stamps, and postal money orders

certificates of citizenship or naturalization

passports, immigration papers, and visas

draft registration cards or selective service induction papers that bear confidential information about the registrant

automobile licenses and automobile title certificates

badges, identification cards, and passes carried by military personnel

obligations or securities of any foreign government, bank, or corporation

R19 Impact of the Copyright Laws

Effective January 1, 1978, the Copyright Revision Act was made law. The act recognizes the prime ownership of a work that has been *copyrighted*. A copyright gives the author exclusive right to the ownership of a specific work (poem, song, music, book, etc.) for the lifetime of the author plus an additional 50 years. When a work is copyrighted, no one may modify the work or use it in any way without the permission of the owner.

The *fair use* concept introduced into this law enables an individual to copy material without permission from or payment to the publisher when the use is *reasonable*; that is, when it does not detract from the rights of the publisher or author. Teachers and trainers often need to duplicate material for instructional purposes. They need to be particularly aware of their rights and responsibilities with respect to the *fair and reasonable use* guidelines. Some of the guidelines are:

- Single copies of a chapter from a book, an article, a cartoon, a graph, or other copyrighted material may be made for scholarly research or for teaching or preparing to teach a class.
- Not more than one copy of the above may be made for a student. To make multiple copies you must include a notice of copyright. This should be done only if you don't have time to wait for permission. There should be no more than nine instances of multiple copies for one course during one term.
- Copying should not be used as a substitute for buying books, publisher's reprints, or periodicals.
- You may not repeatedly copy the same material from term to term.
- You may not charge students beyond the actual cost of the photocopying.
- You may not copy *consumable works*, such as workbooks, exercises, standardized tests, or test booklets and answer sheets.

R20 Requesting Publisher Permission

To request permission from a publisher if the *fair use* guidelines are to be exceeded, simply write a letter providing the following information:

1. Exact title, author and/or editor, and edition of material to be duplicated.
2. Amount of material to be copied, page numbers, and a photocopy of the material.
3. Number of copies to be made.
4. Use to be made of the duplicated material.
5. Explanation of the form of distribution—classroom, newsletter, mailing.
6. Whether or not the material is to be sold and the fee to be charged, if applicable.
7. Type of reprint to be used—exact reproduction, stencil, copy, etc.

R21 The Duplicating Processes

There are three basic duplicating processes: the *fluid process*, the *mimeograph process*, and the *offset process*. The fluid process and the mimeograph process are rarely used in business today and so will not be discussed in detail here (see Table 16.2 for major features).

R22 The Offset Process

The offset process produces high-quality copies. Offset duplicators range from desktop models to sophisticated pieces of equipment that vary in size, capability, and need for operator training and maintenance. Offset duplicators are used by commercial printers and can also be found in reprographic centers of businesses that frequently require a high volume of quality copies. Organizations with their own reprographic centers often produce their own forms, stationery, and other publication materials. The medium for the offset process is the offset mat, or plate, which is usually either paper or metal. Typists can type on direct image paper masters; or machines similar to copiers are available that can produce paper masters directly from an original or pasteup. If many copies are needed or if subsequent runs will be necessary, metal masters are prepared. Due to the special skill needed to operate offset equipment, most office workers will not become directly involved with the offset equipment. Office workers should, however, be aware of those situations when the offset process should be used in order to get desired results.

R23 Comparison of Duplicating Processes

Table 16.2 Comparison of Duplicating Processes

	Fluid Process	Mimeograph Process	Offset Process
MEDIUM	Masterset	Stencil	Offset Mat
MEDIUM DESCRIPTION	A two-part set containing a white page and a carbon backing sheet	Special fiber paper with a backing sheet	A special sheet of paper or aluminum
MEDIUM TYPE	Direct Impression Master—type, write, or draw directly on the masterset	Direct Impression Stencil—type directly on the stencil or draw and write on it with a stylus	Direct Image Paper Master—type with a high carbon content ribbon or write or draw with a high carbon content pencil
	Thermal Master—prepare an original or pasteup and feed it through a thermal copier with a thermal master	Thermal Stencil—prepare an original or pasteup and feed it through a thermal stencil	Electrostatic Master—Prepare an original or pasteup and process it on an electrostatic platemaker
		Electronic Stencil—prepare an original or pasteup and place it on a special piece of equipment called an electrostatic stencil maker or scanner	Aluminum Master—same as above but processed on a special piece of equipment that etches the image into the aluminum

Reprographics

Table 16.2 Continued

ERROR CORRECTION (For *Direct Impression* Methods Only)	Scrape off unwanted carbon image; replenish area with new carbon; retype	Cover with a special correction fluid; let area dry; retype	Erase to a ghost image with a soft eraser; retype
EASE OF MACHINE OPERATION	Easy	Easy but can be messy	Training and skill necessary
CARE OF EQUIPMENT	Very little	Limited	Much care and maintenance necessary
COPY QUALITY	Not satisfactory or professional. Usually purple because this dye color provides the most copies	Good but not printing press quality	High Quality
REUSE OF MEDIUM	Possible, but quality deteriorates	Yes	Metal and plastic mats may be reused; masters cannot be reused

R24 Choosing Reprographic Equipment

For the greatest efficiency at the lowest cost, obtain the right equipment for the job. Table 16.2 gives a good comparison of reprographic equipment. There are several basic considerations to keep in mind.

- Cost: Which is best—buying, leasing, or renting?
- Speed: How important is speed? Is the extra cost involved in faster copying or duplicating justified for your needs?
- Space: How much space do you have available in an area that is accessible yet isolated enough that noise is not a problem?
- Monthly needs: How much copying or duplicating do you need? The system should be the right size: not so powerful that its capability is wasted; not so small that overuse poses a problem of frequent breakdown.
- Quality of copy produced: Will the copy quality meet all the firm's requirements?

R24-R26 Choosing Reprographic Equipment

- Type of material to be copied: Is the system capable of handling all your needs for both in-house and outside use?
- Needs for the future: Will the system fit in with future expansion possibilities?

R25 Copier Selection Guidelines

Considerable care must go into the selection of the office copier because many types and makes are available. Compare copiers on at least the following basic points:

- copy volume to be handled
- quality of the copies
- warranty details and lengths of time covered
- speed of producing copies per minute
- trade-in value of existing equipment
- availability and cost of service contracts
- any special wiring or power supply changes necessary
- compatibility with existing equipment
- potential for upgrading, expansion, or integration with other equipment
- cost of supplies and other maintenance products
- rating of the equipment by independent agencies
- recommendations from others with needs similar to yours
- whether or not the repair technicians are factory-trained
- whether the vendor is an authorized dealer with a full line of products
- cost and cost-benefit computations
- the result of comparison shopping efforts
- the result of an on-site demonstration or trial period
- ease of restocking the machine with paper and toner (ink)
- amount of space needed to stock necessary supplies
- noise level of the equipment
- warm-up time needed
- control devices available so that machine use can be measured
- optional features available

R26 Additional Copier Features to Consider

The basic copier reproduces sheets in standard and legal size from written, typed, or printed copy. Copiers are also available with a variety of features but these usually add to the cost. Before you select a

Reprographics

copier, identify the additional features you need from the list below and resist obtaining a more sophisticated machine than necessary.

- collating, stapling, and stacking
- copying colors
- copying large documents
- producing projection transparencies
- handling unusual widths and/or lengths
- duplexing (copying on two sides)
- reducing originals to various sizes
- enlarging the original to various sizes
- using regular stationery
- using stationery in rolls or sheets of legal or letter size
- copying from bound materials, brochures, magazines
- producing cardweight copies
- printing on colored paper
- automatically feeding originals
- reproducing from three-dimensional objects
- making offset plate masters
- copying photographs (half tones)
- offering hookup to communications lines so that copies may be sent to other locations
- a self-diagnostic device to indicate problems with the machine
- a security lock feature that prevents unauthorized use of the equipment
- edge-to-edge copying capability
- automatic exposure feature by which the copier electronically selects the proper exposure for variable documents
- interrupt-pause-resume capability that permits a long run to be interrupted for rush copies with the ability to resume the run without losing count
- computer forms feeder that permits copying directly from printouts without bursting the stack
- energy-saving feature that permits the machine to use less electricity when it is on but not making copies

R27 Duplicator Selection Guidelines

Stencil and fluid duplicators are less expensive than copiers, and a duplicator may be useful in your office as a complement to the copier. Consider the following points:

- cost
- ease of operation

- the need for multiple copies
- the quality of the reproduction
- how well this system will meet the future needs of the business
- how well this sytem will interface with existing copying or duplicating facilities

R28 Auxiliary Reprographic Equipment

- **Collating Equipment.** Collating equipment comes in automatic and semiautomatic models. Models are available in 10-bin to 50-bin sizes. By placing pages of a document in sequential bins, collating equipment will produce composite copies of a document.
- **Sorting Equipment.** Sorting equipment usually operates on-line with a copier or offset press. As pages are printed, a copy of each page is distributed to a specific number of sorting bins which, at the end of a run, contain complete sets of a document.
- **Binding Equipment.** A variety of formats are available by which to bind multi-page documents. Some of these methods include stapling, punching and spiral plastic binding, thermal tape binding, and other variations of bindings that permanently fuse the document's pages.
- **Joggers.** Jogging equipment serves as a vibrator to line up the pages in a document before the document is bound. Joggers can be purchased as a separate unit or attached to collating and sorting units.
- **Lettering Machines.** To add a professional touch to the preparation of documents that are to be printed or copied, lettering machines can be used to prepare titles and headline information. The operator dials the headline letter by letter and the desired word or words are printed in black letters on a transparent tape. The taped heading is then fastened to the original. Various typestyles and spaces between letters can be obtained. Some lettering machines can also serve as peripherals for computer-generated output.
- **Electronic Stencil Scanners.** This equipment enables you to prepare a stencil directly from a pasteup. The original is fastened on one side of a drum and a special blank stencil is fastened to the other side of the drum. By means of a vertical scanning process, the image on the original is burned into the electronic stencil medium. The process takes about five minutes and eliminates the need to retype from the original onto the stencil.

Reprographics

R29 Photocomposition

Photocomposition is rapidly becoming an important part of a company's reprographics system. It involves a method of preparing original documents that are formatted with proportional lettering, variable spacing, and typeface variety. As a result of photocomposition or phototypesetting, the finished result will look better, be more readable and, because of its compactness, be less costly if quantity copies are produced.

Advances in electronic technology are leading to greater in-house typesetting installations. It is possible to electronically transmit information captured on a word processor, microcomputer, or data processing system to a photocomposition unit. OCR (see I30) equipment can also transmit information to a photocomposition unit. Desktop or electronic publishing is an emerging technology combining personal computers and laser printers to produce quality publications in-house.

Through a special command language and codes, the size and shape of the type to be produced is controlled. The ability to interface the photocomposition unit with other equipment to obtain higher-quality documents, to use less paper, and to eliminate the need for rekeyboarding information supports the concept of photocompositon as a logical extension of information processing systems in the future.

R30 Photocomposition Terms

Bullet A large dot or symbol used in typesetting to emphasize or indicate an area.

Cold Type Composition that is produced by direct impression or a strike-on method, such as copy produced on a typewriter.

Format A combination of commands that can be stored in memory and recalled to quickly restore a set of parameters (margins, spacing, typefaces).

Galley A proof of typeset material usually arranged in long columns of text.

Gutter The two inner margins of facing pages of a book.

Justification Spacing a line of type to fill the selected line measures. The ultimate effect is flush, or even, left and right margins.

Kerning The reduction of white space between individual characters to produce a better fit of letters.

Leaders Rows of dots or dashes used to guide the eye to another area within the line.

Leading The amount of space between lines.

Letterspacing Additional amounts of space placed between characters to justify a line.

Mark-Up Written typographic specifications for a manuscript including line measure.

Pica Printer's unit of measure. There are six picas to one inch.

Point A division of the pica. There are 12 points to a pica with 72 points to the inch.

Ragged Right A composition style in which all lines end at various points near the right margin (the opposite of a justified margin).

RC Paper A resin-coated photographic paper providing high quality and stability.

Typography The art of selecting, arranging, and using type.

Widow A single word or part of a word in a line by itself. An extremely short last line in a paragraph. Widows are regarded as poor typography.

R31 Computer Graphics

The old axiom that "a picture is worth a thousand words" is as important today as ever. Today desktop computers with graphics capability are providing a popular method by which to convert data into meaningful charts, graphs, and tables. The right combination of hardware and software makes it possible to produce computer graphics in black and white or in color, as well as to print hard copies or transparencies in black and white or in color. The market for desktop pen plotters and color printers and plotters is expected to grow substantially in the years to come.

Reprographics

R32 Intelligent Copiers

The intelligent copier is a sophisticated computer-based piece of equipment that merges the optical system of the copier world with the digital system of the computer world. With conventional copier technology, electronic information from a typewriter, word processor, or computer is first put on paper using some form of printing device. The printed page is then put on a copier to be duplicated for distribution.

With the new laser technology, electronic information is translated directly from computer memory into a printed page in copier quality at laser copier speeds. Intelligent copying allows the computer or other information source to be linked directly to electronic printers at many locations to disseminate printed information with no need for mail, messenger, or hard copy. The intelligent copier has the added advantage that some models can also be used as simple convenience copiers.

R33 Paper Terms

If you know some background information about paper, you can make better decisions about paper selection. Here are some common terms associated with paper to help you make better selections when planning duplicating jobs.

Antique Finish A descriptive term representing paper that has a rough finish.

Weight The weight in pounds of a ream of 500 sheets of paper cut to a given standard size for that paper. The higher the weight, the thicker the paper. Most paper is 16 or 20 pounds; onion skin paper used for carbon copies is 9 pounds and paper for brochures and covers can be as high as 72 pounds.

Bond Paper The type of paper usually used for letterheads. It is used when durability, strength, and permanence are important.

Cover Stock Heavier weight paper usually used for report covers, catalogs and brochures.

Deckle Edge Paper with an untrimmed or uneven edge. Used in programs and invitations to create a special effect.

Grain The direction in which the paper fibers lie. Long grain paper is best for duplicating equipment, while short grain paper is best for typing paper.

Matte Finish A paper finish that is dull. It has no gloss or luster.

Opacity A property of paper that minimizes the *bleed through* of the print in two-sided printing.

Watermark Logo or other design or name that appears in a sheet of paper if it is held up to the light. Usually found on bond paper and reflects quality.

R34 Controlling Reprographic Costs

The effective management of reprographic systems and services requires the following considerations:

- Careful equipment selection so that the optional features purchased are appropriate for the organization's needs.
- Consideration of ease of use, required maintenance, and cost of materials when choosing equipment.
- Negotiation for the most favorable leasing plans and purchase prices for equipment.
- Consideration of anticipated volume—number of copies per month and number of copies per original—when selecting equipment.
- Efficient operator orientation and training.
- Availability of a procedures manual with guidelines on how various types of jobs will be produced.
- A security control system to discourage unauthorized copier use.
- Clearly establishing and enforcing a policy controlling personal copies made by employees.
- Some type of charge-back or logging system to keep track of costs.
- Careful storing of paper and supplies so as to minimize their effect on equipment repairs. For example, paper stored in a damp place will promote feed problems.
- Proper monitoring of the shelf life (expiration dates) of inks, toners, and other supplies.
- Purchasing supplies in bulk.

Reprographics

- Assuring effective maintenance through the use of service agreements with preventive maintenance provisions.
- Reducing hand labor by using automatic collators and other specialized equipment if applications warrant (see R28).
- Periodic review of needs and equipment to monitor the effectiveness of the copying process being used.
- Standardizing equipment throughout the organization.
- Having equipment properly allocated in centralized or decentralized work areas.
- Assigning someone the responsiblity for reprographics management.

UNIT 17

TELEPHONE AND TELECOMMUNICATION SYSTEMS

The Telephone   T1-T34

    Telephone Technique
    Directory Assistance
    Long-Distance Calling
    Direct Dialing Options
    Special Assistance Calls
    Overseas Calling
    Special Types of Calls
    Business Telephone Equipment and Services
    Private Telephone Answering Services
    Money-Saving Telephone Tips

Telecommunication Systems   T35-T47

    Electronic Mail and Message Transmission
    Data Transmission

Controlling Telecommunication Costs   T48

Telephone and Telecommunication Systems

Every office worker knows that the telephone is a vital communications tool in the office. It can be a fast and convenient way to communicate information if you are aware of the types of telephone services available and how to use them correctly. You must also be able to handle both incoming and outgoing calls correctly.

There are times, however, when written messages need to be sent and, for this type of transaction, a telephone call is not adequate. To transmit written documents and messages immediately, telecommunication processes are used. *Telecommunications* is a relatively new word in our vocabulary. It is a broad term that represents the process of transmitting all forms of information—voice, written, and image—over a distance by electronic or electromagnetic systems.

This unit highlights valuable information for using the telephone efficiently. It will also orient you to the latest developments in telecommunication fundamentals.

T1 The Telephone

T2 Telephone Technique

T3 Taking Calls

- Answer promptly—on the first or second ring is preferred.
- Identify yourself. Suggested telephone answering methods are:

for a firm:	"Campbell Company. May I help you?"
your own phone:	"Mary Barnes" *or* "Ms. Barnes."
department phone:	"Accounting Department, Mrs. Meyers."
	"Accounting Department, Amy speaking."
	"Accounting Department, this is Amy."
another's phone:	"Dr. Richardson's office, Ms. Wilson."

- Speak distinctly and cheerfully. Do not smoke, chew, or conduct another conversation at the same time you are on the telephone.

T1-T3 The Telephone

- Phrase questions and requests courteously and tactfully.

  to find out who is calling: "May I ask who is calling?"
  "May I tell Ms. Richards who is calling?"

  to offer to be of help: "May I help you?"
  "I'm sorry, Ms. Richards is not in at the moment. May I take a message?"

  to get information repeated: "Would you repeat that please?"
  "I'm sorry, I'm not sure I understood you, Mr. West, would you please repeat the street name?"
  "I'm sorry, our connection does not seem to be clear. Could you speak a little louder please?"

- Keep a note pad or a message pad (Figure 17.1) and pen near the telephone.

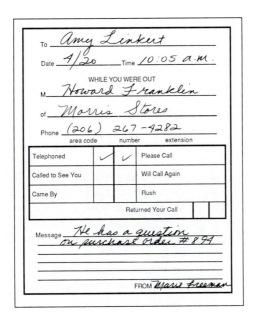

Figure 17.1   Telephone Message Form

Telephone and Telecommunication Systems

- Take accurate telephone messages by:

  verifying doubtful spelling

  getting the caller's telephone number and reading it back to verify its accuracy

  reading back and verifying any other dates, numbers, and times that might be a part of the message

  writing legibly

  jotting down the date and time the message came in and signing the message

  placing the message so that the recipient will see it upon return to the workstation

- If you must leave your desk, arrange to have your telephone answered by forwarding calls (see T32), or by leaving word when you will be back and having someone else take your calls.
- Personalize telephone conversations by using the caller's name.
- Avoid keeping callers on the line. Offer to call back if you need to obtain information. If you must leave the line, place the caller *on hold* but return to the line periodically to provide progress reports. When you return to the line, use such phrases as "Thank you for waiting" or "Sorry for the delay."
- Treat every call as an important one.
- Terminate your call in a polite and businesslike manner (the caller should terminate the call first).

T4 Transferring Calls

- Transfer calls only when it is essential and only if the caller agrees.
- If you do not know who should handle the call, note the caller's name and telephone number, offer to locate the right person, and have that person call back.
- If you do know who should handle the call, make sure that the person is available and give a brief explanation of the call before you transfer it.
- Give the caller the number of the party to whom you are transferring the call so that it can be used for future reference or in the event that you get cut off.

T5 Making Calls

- Plan ahead: have questions ready, make notes if necessary, have files available, and think through the conversation and the purpose(s) of the call before dialing.
- Identify yourself and your affiliation.
- Use the most appropriate type of telephone service and dial direct if possible.
- Consider time zones when making long-distance calls (see Appendix, page A8).
- Take advantage of any special rates or discounts (see front section of your telephone directory).
- If a wrong long-distance number is contacted, call the operator to have the charge cancelled.
- As the caller, you should conclude the conversation.
- Return all calls promptly.
- Hang up gently.

T6 Directory Assistance

T7 Using the Telephone Directory

The telephone company directory has two parts: alphabetic subscriber listings (white pages) and classified subscriber listings (yellow pages). In some areas, telephone directories also contain a section of blue pages that list federal, state, city, and county offices.

Alphabetic Directory (White Pages). Names, addresses, and telephone numbers of individuals and organizations are listed alphabetically by name. Names of subscribers are automatically listed free of charge, but a monthly charge is levied against subscribers wanting unlisted numbers.

The introductory pages list worldwide area codes, the types and rates of calls, telephone services available, and other useful facts.

Classified Directory (Yellow Pages). Organizations subscribe to the yellow pages if they wish to be listed alphabetically by category or want to advertise their service or product. A charge is made for each listing and each advertisement.

Telephone and Telecommunication Systems

Personal Directory. Frequently used telephone numbers can be assembled in a personal directory for quick reference. This may be a list, a card index file, or an indexed desktop accessory or container. The list should be organized alphabetically and should show the area code, the number, and the extension number, if appropriate. Frequently used telephone numbers can be stored using an automatic dialing feature (see T32).

T8 How to Find Numbers in the Telephone Directory

When you cannot find a number for which you are looking in a directory:

- Check alternate listings. Names may be listed in different ways: *John Jones Company* might appear as *Jones, John Company*.
- Check different spellings. *Sherrer* might be spelled *Cherrer, Scherrer* or *Shirrer*.
- Be aware of the filing rules used in preparing the telephone directory.
  - Initials precede first names. For example, *Jones A.* comes before *Jones, Albert*.
  - Abbreviations are listed as if the word were spelled out. For example, *St. James Hospital* is alphabetized as *Saint James Hospital*.
  - Numbers are spelled out if used as names. For example, to find *21 Cleaners*, look under *Twenty-One Cleaners*.
  - Names consisting of all capital letters, such as radio and television stations, are listed at the beginning of their related alphabetic section. For example, *WXYZ Radio* should be among the first listings in the *W* section.
  - United States Government and state, city, county and township offices may be listed in a variety of ways. They may appear in the "blue pages" of the directory (see T7), in a special section at either the front or at the back of the directory, or in the regular alpha listings in the white pages. Agencies of the federal government are listed under *United States Government*.

T9 How to Call Directory Assistance

- Local Directory Assistance

  For numbers within your area code, dial *1 + 411*.

T8-T10 How to Find Numbers in the Telephone Directory

There is usually a charge for each call in excess of a given number of calls per line per month. You may request two numbers each time you call Directory Assistance. From coin telephones, calls placed from qualified hospitals or hotel guest lines, or from mobile units, there is no charge. Special exemptions and services are available for qualified disabled persons.

- Long-Distance Assistance

    For long-distance numbers within your area code, dial *1 + 555-1212*.

    For numbers outside your area code, dial *1 + area code + 555-1212*.

    Charges vary, depending on your long-distance company; some companies have other procedures by which to obtain directory assistance.

- Toll-Free Numbers

    For toll-free numbers of businesses and individuals, dial *1 + 800 + 555-1212*.

- Dial-It Service

    For Dial-It Service numbers in your area, call *1 + 900 + 555-1212*.

T10 Long-Distance Calling (Calls Outside Your Local Dialing Area)

Prior to 1984, one company, American Telephone and Telegraph (AT&T), owned or controlled most of the equipment and services required to complete long-distance calling. A United States Justice Department decision in 1982, however, forced changes in this "monopoly" control. Simply stated, the decision required AT&T to, by 1984, divest itself (give up ownership) of the many companies and services it controlled, thus allowing open competition for both long-distance service and equipment.

Today a number of companies provide long-distance calling service for calls outside your service area. Not all companies may serve your area, however, so you should contact the long-distance company of

Telephone and Telecommunication Systems

your choice to determine if they serve your area and if they provide services to the places you wish to call. Some long-distance companies are AT&T, MCI Communications, GTE Sprint, Allnet, ITT Longer Distance, and Western Union. Consult the yellow pages of your telephone directory under *Telephone Companies* to locate the long-distance companies serving your area.

In many areas of the country, these "alternative" long-distance systems enjoy *equal access* telephone service. This means that any long-distance company approved in your area can provide *Dial 1* service. Regardless of primary carrier, then, you merely dial *1* plus the area code (if applicable) and the desired 7-digit telephone number to complete a call. Additionally, if you wish to subscribe to service other than your primary long-distance carrier for some of your calls, you may. After establishing an account, the company assigns you a code number that must be dialed before accessing the long-distance lines.

Dial 1 calls are automatically billed by your primary long-distance carrier. Special code calls are billed directly by the company that services your account. Multiple system service may result in multiple, but not duplicate, long-distance billings each month.

T11 Direct Dialing Options

T12 Station-to-Station

A direct call with possible operator intervention for the particulars of billing. The charge begins when the called telephone is picked up.

To call *within your area* (between places with the same area code), dial *1* + the desired seven-digit number.

To call *another area code*, dial *1* + area code + desired seven-digit number.

T13 Calling Card Calls

Calling cards can usually be obtained from the company servicing your account. They enable you to place calls from any location and have them charged to your home or business account.

From touch-tone phones with touch-tone service, dial *0* + area code + desired seven-digit number (wait for tone) + calling card number. (Do *not* use the *1* prefix as you would with station-to-station calls.)

Take special precautions as you key in the numbers of the calling card, and as you store your calling card so that others cannot fraudulently use the numbers and charge calls to your account. Restricted calling cards are also available; they enable you to take advantage of lower rates charged on your account to one telephone number only.

T14 Special Assistance Calls

To place special assistance calls, dial 0 + area code + desired seven-digit number. (Do not use the 1 prefix as you would with direct dial calls.) Special assistance calls include collect calls, third number calls, and person-to-person calls.

T15 Collect Calls

You may call collect if the person or firm agrees to pay the charges. Dial 0 + area code (if necessary) + desired seven-digit number. When the operator answers, say that you are placing a collect call and give your name. The operator will leave the line when the person you have called agrees to accept the charges.

T16 Third Number Calls

You can make a long-distance call from another telephone and bill it to your own telephone number or another number if that party agrees to pay for the call. Dial 0 + area code + seven-digit number. When the operator comes on the line, say that you would like to charge your call to a third party number and give that number including the area code. The operator may verify the third number charge before advancing your call.

When making a third number call from a coin telephone, the operator must verify the third number charge by calling the third number and confirming that the charges will be accepted. If there is no confirmation, the operator cannot complete the call unless you make other billing arrangements, pay the coin rate, use your calling card, or make a collect call.

T17 Time and Charges

When placing a long-distance call, you can ask the operator to tell you the length of time you talked and how much it cost. Dial the call, and when the operator comes on the line, say that you will want time and charges when the call is completed. The operator will ask you to stay on the line at the end of the conversation.

Telephone and Telecommunication Systems

T18 Person-to-Person Calls

This is the most expensive type of call. Use this type of service when you wish to reach a particular person or extension number. Dial the call; when the operator comes on the line, give the name of the person to whom you wish to speak. The operator will leave the line and the charge begins when the person you are calling has answered the phone. There is no charge if the requested person is not available to accept the call.

T19 Overseas Calling

T20 Obtaining a Telephone Number

To obtain the telephone number of an overseas party, dial your operator and give the name and address of the party you wish to contact. The operator will contact the specific country's information operator and obtain the number for you.

T21 Making an Overseas Call

Station-to-Station. A station-to-station call is the least expensive of all overseas calls. Not all parts of the country can dial direct at this time, so consult your telephone directory or operator for up-to-date information. Direct dialing, if available, involves dialing an access code, a country code, a routing code, and a local telephone number.

Collect, Calling Card, Third Party, and Person-to-Person Calls. All of these telephone options require the overseas operator's assistance and may be requested at an additional charge. Contact your local operator for the procedures to be used in your area.

T22 Special Types of Calls

Conference. A conference call is made when several people at different locations wish to confer at the same time. Dial 0 for operator and ask for a conference call to be arranged. You will then be given the Conference Operator who will take the information regarding the parties you wish to call. When all parties are on the line, you will be called back. Charges begin when you start to speak with all parties. This service is available for both long-distance calls and overseas calls.

Marine. To communicate with ships equipped with radio-telephone service, first dial 0 for operator. The operator will put you in touch with the Marine Operator who will be able to place your call or provide you with information assistance.

T18-T25 Person-to-Person Calls

Mobile. To contact cars, trucks, trains, or aircraft with radio-telephone service, first dial 0 for operator. The operator will put you in touch with the Mobile Operator who will be able to place your call or provide you with information assistance.

WATS (Wide Area Transmission Service)

Inwats (Incoming Wats—Code 800)
Inwats service is used by businesses and service companies to encourage customers to call long-distance free of charge within a certain radius. Dial *1 + 800 + special Inwats number.*

Outwats (Outgoing WATS)
Outwats service is available to companies that make wide-area calls. The charge is lower than for regular long-distance calls because customers usually pay on a flat-rate basis.

The WATS subscriber pays according to the zone coverage desired. In addition, a choice of rate structures based on hours of usage is possible.

900 Dial-It Service. Dial-It service does not provide the toll-free calling privileges of the *800* numbers, but it does enable callers to place calls for a flat fee which is usually substantially lower than the normal calling rate. Information about the Dial-It Service Directories available in your local area may be obtained by dialing *1 + 900 + 555-1212.* By using the *900* number provided, you may be able to obtain stock reports, sports reports, travel bargain hotline information, as well as any other services that may be available on a local basis. Part of the cost for this service is paid by the organization providing the hotline information service.

T23 Business Telephone Equipment and Services

T24 Centralized Answering

The type of central answering service an organization has will be determined by the number of trunk (in/out) lines, extension lines, and services it requires. All calls coming into an organization are dealt with through some type of switchboard, telephone set, or telephone exchange.

T25 PBX (Private Branch Exchange)

The connections for all incoming, outgoing, and interoffice calls are completed by PBX equipment, a switching system usually located on the customer's premises. It can be operated manually or automatically.

T26 PABX (Private Automatic Branch Exchange)

PABX equipment usually handles only incoming calls. Outgoing and interoffice calls are dialed directly from the employees' workstation. As the name suggests, all switching is automatic.

T27 Call Director (Desktop Switchboard)

Call Director equipment is available with up to ten trunk lines and up to sixty local lines. It can provide central answering services for a company or within a department. The operator handles only incoming calls.

T28 Centrex

This is a large central switchboard in one location that has its own exchange number. Each employee has his or her own telephone and telephone number and can make and receive direct and interoffice calls.

T29 Electronic Telephone Systems

Systems such as Horizon, Dimension, and Centrex ESS are electronically operated telephone systems. The number of outside lines and features vary from one installation to another. These systems appear to the user like large cordless switchboards. They require training for effective operation.

T30 Personal Paging Systems

Paging systems are often referred to as *beeper* systems. They are helpful to people who need to stay in touch with the office, yet must move around in a building, organization, or nearby geographic location.

Some systems allow one-way voice communication in which the person in the office can be heard but the person out of the office cannot answer through the system. The person paged must locate a telephone and call the office. In other systems, the person contacts the individual in the field by dialing a special telephone number. This causes an audible tone to sound on a radio receiver carried by the user. Personal paging systems might also provide a feature that enables the user to dial a specific telephone number and, by means of the paging device, trigger the telephone answering machine to play back any information recorded on it.

T26-T32 PABX (Private Automatic Branch Exchange)

T31 Computer-Based Telephone Systems

Computerized telephone systems are available for any size installation. They can provide all the services of PABX or Centrex, plus integrated voice and data communications, and many of the features listed below under *Additional Features*. A computer-based telephone system is an integrated voice and data telephone set. It consists of a telephone set, a screen, and a keyboard. It provides access to information from data bases, simultaneous voice and data communications, electronic mail capabilities, and interface capability with peripheral equipment. Microprocessor-controlled software, call timing, clock, calculator, reminder service, auto dialing, handsfree capability, and last number redial are some of the features available with a computer-based system.

T32 Additional Features

The equipment described under *Centralized Answering* usually includes both standard and optional features.

Automatic Dialing. Many telephone numbers can be stored and automatically dialed by push-button direction. If a line is busy, it can be redialed at the press of a button.

Automatic Ring Again. When a busy station or outside line is free, the phone automatically rings again signaling that the line is now clear.

Call Forwarding (Call Transfer). Calls are automatically forwarded from one extension to another by entering specified codes or numbers.

Call Switching. If an extension is to be left unattended, incoming calls may be automatically switched to another extension for answering.

Call Waiting. A person already on a call receives a *beep* tone periodically to indicate that another call is waiting.

Camp On. If a number called is busy, the caller can wait without hanging up and will be automatically connected when the line is free.

Conference Calling (Three-Way Calling). A third person (on some equipment, up to *three* additional people) can be brought in on a two-way conversation.

Telephone and Telecommunication Systems

Control Features. Some systems prevent unauthorized telephone use or provide for the built-in monitoring of costs. Such systems include:

Station restriction—Telephones may be installed so that the user has limitations, such as no outside calls, no calls outside the local dialing area, and possibly even the monitoring of calls and billing.

Locks—Locks can be purchased to prevent the rotary dial from moving on a rotary phone and to lock the switchhook (switch activated by the removal or replacement of the handset or receiver) on a touch tone phone.

Call Accounting Systems—Large organizations keep records of calls made on all telephones for charge-back (assigning costs to a specific person or department) accounting purposes. Updated records are available periodically to determine specific charges to customers, clients, departments, or personnel.

Data Transmission. (See this unit, T41-T47.)

Dial Access to Central Dictating Systems. The caller can dial and dictate into the telephone. For more detail, see E145.

Group Listening. A speaker in the handset is switched on to enable those present to hear both sides of a telephone conversation.

Handsfree—Listen on Hold. If you are placed on hold, you may hang up and a built-in speaker will monitor the line for you, allowing you to pick up the handset again when the other party returns.

Handsfree Speakerphone. Permits the user to move about the room and even hold conferences with several people present.

Interoffice Communications. Provides a direct-dial communication link between offices and departments. A *selective conference* feature is also available that permits conferences using up to five lines at one time.

Last Number Redial. The last number the caller tried to reach is automatically redialed.

Multiple-Line Conferencing. (See *Conference Calling*.)

On-Hook Dialing. Receiver may be left in place until dialing is complete.

Paging Access. Provides dial access to a loudspeaker or personal beeper paging system.

Saved Number Redial. With this feature you can *store* a number while you make or receive other calls and then redial automatically.

Speed Calling. Numbers frequently called can be programmed and dialed automatically by push-button command.

Tie-Trunks. Provide direct system-to-system links for multiple location businesses.

Video Conference Calls (Speakerphone). By means of satellite hookup, participants can see as well as speak to each other.

Telephone companies are constantly adding new developments to their range of services. A call to your telephone company will inform you about specific services or equipment to suit your company's needs.

T33 Private Telephone Answering Services

Organizations exist which will, for a fee, answer telephone calls on a subscriber's behalf. Such services are available on a 24-hour basis, if needed. The telephone can be answered in the name of an individual, the name of a company, or any other identification requested. Some organizations simply take messages; others offer paging services. Consult the yellow pages of your telephone directory for a list of the answering service organizations in your area.

In addition, equipment may be purchased or rented that permits the telephone to be answered in the subscriber's absence. The subscriber makes a recording of his or her voice, which the caller will hear. The recording invites the caller to leave a message and his or her name and number so that the call may be returned.

T34 Money-Saving Telephone Tips

- Always plan your phone calls before dialing to make effective use of calling time.
- Avoid directory assistance charges by maintaining a file of frequently called numbers and by getting telephone numbers from a directory whenever possible.
- If you dial long-distance and reach a wrong number, dial the operator immediately, explain your error, and request that the operator arrange for proper credit to your account.
- Be aware of time differences when placing calls to other parts of the United States and overseas (see Appendix, page A8).

Telephone and Telecommunication Systems

- Place calls during low-priority calling hours whenever possible; keep in mind that the highest rates are charged for calls placed between 8 a.m. and 5 p.m. local time on Monday through Friday.
- Dial direct whenever possible and avoid person-to-person calls.
- Use *800* toll-free numbers when they are available.
- Take advantage of credit card calling when you are away from the office to avoid calling collect.
- If you have a poor connection, both parties should hang up immediately; contact the operator and ask to be reconnected. There will be a rate adjustment for the period of the bad connection.
- Compare costs of long-distance companies and place calls based on each carrier's advantage to you. Some telephone equipment automatically directs outgoing calls to provide this cost advantage.

T35 Telecommunication Systems

The marriage of communications technology and computers has enlarged both fields, making possible the immediate accessing of a wide array of enhanced telephone and telecommunication services. Two characteristics of a telecommunication system are:

- communication over a distance
- transmission by telephone lines, cables, microwaves, satellites, and light beams

Four major types of telecommunication systems are available today: voice, message, data, and image.

The first section of this unit discussed voice telecommunication systems; the following portion of the unit discusses the other areas.

T36 Electronic Mail and Message Transmission

Business communication often requires the timely delivery of written information and messages. Postal service delivery is sometimes too slow, and a telephone call does not provide the necessary written documentation. Electronic mail refers to messages that are sent and received in the form of electronic signals that are translated into readable messages by a receiving unit. Descriptions of the major categories of electronic mail follow.

T37 Facsimile Transmission (Fax)

Facsimile transmission permits the electronic transmission of an exact copy of any document from one location to another using telephone lines. The material transmitted may be typed, handwritten, or drawn, and may include extremely detailed graphics and photographs. Two compatible units are needed—one for sending and one for receiving. An *acoustic coupler* is attached to the facsimile unit and the document is inserted. The sender dials a telephone number and is connected with a compatible facsimile unit. The handset is plugged into the coupler, a switch is pushed, and the material is transmitted. The acoustic coupler converts outgoing electronic signals from the digital device into analog sounds and transmits them to the microphone of the telephone handset. At the earpiece end of the receiving phone, the coupler reconverts the analog sounds into digital electronic signals and transmits them to the attached digital device. Most acoustic couplers link telephones to computer terminals and facsimile machines. Transmission cost is related to the speed of transmission. Facsimile transmission units are available with speed ranges from four minutes to twenty seconds per page and in varying degrees of automation. The equipment may be purchased or leased from major equipment manufacturers.

T38 Mailgram

Mailgram messages were introduced in the 1970's as an economical way to deliver written messages with the next day's mail. The service is provided through Western Union and the United States Postal Service and is effective when there is a need to send brief, important messages quickly.

A mailgram message is transmitted over Western Union's microwave or satellite communications network to the United States Post Office nearest the recipient. At the post office, the message receives preferential treatment. It is typed by high-speed printing equipment and inserted into a distinctive blue and white envelope for mail delivery. A mailgram message can be sent by Telex, certain communicating typewriters or data terminals, and computers. Mailgram messages can be sent 24 hours a day, seven days a week by simply telephoning Western Union. The cost depends on the length of the message (approximately $5 for 50 words or less). The sender can receive a copy of the mailgram sent for an additional minimum charge. Usually a mailgram message sent to Western Union by 7 p.m. will reach the recipient with the next day's mail.

Telephone and Telecommunication Systems

T39 Telegrams and Cables

Telegrams can be sent by calling Western Union. When Telex is not suitable or available, and when long-distance telephoning is too expensive, telegrams (in North America) and cables (overseas) can be an effective means of dealing with rush orders or urgent messages. They may be sent prepaid or collect. Telegram and cable messages are generally delivered by telephone and are followed by a written confirmation.

Telegraphic Service. Full-rate telegrams receive immediate attention, and have a minimum charge for 15 words with an additional charge for extra words. Overnight telegrams are usually delivered by 2 p.m. the following day, and have a minimum charge for 35 words with an additional charge for every 2 extra words.

Telegraphic Money Orders. Money orders may be used to send money almost anywhere in the world. The sender takes the appropriate currency to a Western Union Office and gives the message and the name and address of the recipient. Western Union will transmit the message and instructions of payment to the destination telegraph office. The receiving office will notify the recipient who must present identification before collecting the money.

Cable Service. There are three classes of overseas cable service: The *urgent* cable message receives priority attention. The minimum charge is for seven words, and the delivery is made as soon after transmission as possible. The *full-rate* cable provides a minimum charge for seven words, and delivery is made within hours the transmission. The *letter telegram* has a minimum charge for 22 words and an extra charge for additional words. Delivery is made the next morning.

T40 Teletypewriter Networks (Telex/TWX)

The teletypewriter transmits and receives written messages and can be a fast and efficient means of communication when an immediate written record is necessary. There are various kinds of teletypewriters with different capabilities. Western Union's Telex is one of the most widely used. It provides for the sending of messages anywhere within the United States, Canada, Mexico, and Alaska, as well as 250,000 terminals overseas. TWX (Teletypewriter Exchange) is also provided through Western Union, but many of its features differ from Telex.

As a worldwide, direct-dial teleprinter exchange service, Telex units provide for the instantaneous delivery of alphanumeric information 24 hours a day, seven days a week. Messages can be received when a terminal is unattended. This is especially useful when communicating to different time zones and it allows the user to take advantage of lower sending rates.

A Telex terminal is as easy to operate as a typewriter and errors can be corrected before transmission. Both the sending and receiving terminals get exact copies of the printed record. After dialing another Telex unit, you can get automatic confirmation that you have reached the desired party. There is even the capability of holding written *conversations* from Telex to Telex. One message can also be sent to any number of people in different locations. A Western Union directory called *InfoMaster* provides the name, location and Telex identification number of all subscribers.

T41 Data Transmission

Large, highly computerized companies use telecommunications services for other than verbal or visual transmission. Data such as credit verification, inventory control, reservation requests, sales reporting, and financial transactions may be communicated by wire to microwave links by public or private companies. The cost of transmission is dependent upon the type of service. Private networks are more costly because the user pays for the connecting line whether or not it is in use; shared networks (pay as you use) are more economical.

This is an area of rapid and constant change in office technology, and the processes that follow merely suggest some systems presently being used.

T42 Carrier-Based Message Systems

Data transmission is also available to the general public through *carrier-based message systems*. Services differ from carrier to carrier (Figure 17.2). In some instances the services are fully electronic. In other instances, the electronic transmission is supplemented by United States Post Office delivery or messenger delivery. Examples of such systems include Western Union's *EasyLink, MCI Mail,* and Federal Express *ZapMail.* Consult your telephone directory to call companies directly for further information.

Telephone and Telecommunication Systems

	TYPE		USE		FEATURES					COST		
	CAN SEND ALPHANUMERIC DATA	CAN SEND GRAPHS AND CHARTS	INTRACOMPANY	INTERCOMPANY	COMPANY TO CUSTOMER	EQUIPMENT COMPATABILITY IS A FACTOR	HAS DELIVERY IMPACT	CAN TAKE ADVANTAGE OF DELAYED DELIVERY	CAN PROVIDE MULTIPLE DELIVERY	PROVIDES SPEED DELIVERY	CAN SEND DATA OVERSEAS	RELATIVELY INEXPENSIVE	MODERATE COST	EXPENSIVE
FACSIMILE	x	x	x	x	x	x		x			x	
MAILGRAM	x		x	x		x	x				x	
TELEGRAM	x		x	x		x						x
TELETYPEWRITER NETWORKS [TELEX/TWX]	x		x	x		x	x	x	x		x	

Figure 17.2 User Choice Comparisons for Electronic Message Transmission

T43 Message Switching

A process of routing messages to several locations using circuit switching or computer techniques is known as *message switching*. Carriers such as Western Union, GTE, Telenet Corporation, and SBN provide public networks for message switching purposes. International carriers include International ITT, World Com, RCA Globecom, and Western Union International.

T44 Voice Mail

Voice mail differs from electronic mail in that the transmitted voice is stored and retrieved at a later time by a recipient who listens to the message rather than reading it in hard copy or on a video display. Each user has a *mailbox* that records and stores voice messages. The mailbox holder may respond to the message and have the response automatically delivered, may selectively listen to the messages in the mailbox, or may have the message forwarded to one or more individuals—all by pressing keys on a touch-tone phone.

T45 Teleconferencing

Teleconferencing allows groups of individuals gathered at two or more different locations to exchange ideas and information instead of meeting in person. It reduces the cost and inconvenience of travel, and can take the form of written, audio, and video media.

Written teleconferencing can take place through facsimile transmission, interactive Telex transmission, and communicating visual displays. The *Electronic Bulletin Board* enables participants at two different locations to read writing placed on a screen or monitor. *Computer Conferencing* enables members of a working group at different locations to send and receive information swiftly.

Audio teleconferencing involves only the transmission of sound, and permits meetings to be held with individuals at remote locations.

Videoconferencing permits groups of people to see and hear each other.

Full-Motion Video is like cable television. It provides for signals to be carried over a coaxial cable (group of insulated copper and aluminum wires; see I55) distribution system through special lines connecting the points of transmittal. *Fixed-Frame Video* transmits a picture several times per minute in black and white or color at a much lower cost than full-motion video. When satellite transmission is more commonplace, videoconferencing will become more commonplace.

T46 Communicating Visual Displays

Some word processors, data terminals, and microcomputers have the ability to send documents from one location to another over telephone lines or other telecommunication channels. Compatibility of the operating systems is an important factor in enabling various units to *talk* or communicate with each other.

T47 Networks

The ultimate aim of an integrated office environment is to interconnect all the technologies and equipment. The most dramatic recent advance in office automation technology has been the development of equipment and software to *network* a wide range of information processing equipment and technologies through a single computer. The computer operates independently, yet has direct access to all other equipment in the network. Linking units in a limited geographic area, such as within a building or several buildings in a small geographic area, is known as a *local area network* (LAN). Linking two local area networks at remote locations is referred to as a *global network* (see I60).

Telephone and Telecommunication Systems

T48 Controlling Telecommunication Costs

Efficient management of a telephone/telecommunication system requires providing the best possible service at the least possible cost. The following list suggests ways of controlling and monitoring costs:

1. Obtain comprehensive, up-to-date information about equipment, services, vendors, and prices.
2. Evaluate the various service and equipment offerings and match them with your particular needs to determine the most economical configuration for your office.
3. Train all employees in the most efficient use of equipment.
4. Establish ongoing system controls:

    a. Devise a method for monitoring phone calls, such as keeping a phone call log, or requiring all charged calls to be placed through an operator.

    b. Learn to read and understand the monthly telephone bill and verify charges each month.

    c. When possible, allocate charges to the department responsible for them; perhaps prorate charges on the basis of the equipment in each department.

    d. Monitor the system's capacity to control system waste or overload.

    e. Periodically evaluate the usefulness of all equipment.

5. Set standards against which to measure system performance.

UNIT 18

WORKSTATION AND PERSONAL ORGANIZATION

Workstation Organization   W1-W15
    Creating Procedures Manuals
    Having the Right Equipment Available
    Organizing Your Work Area
    Organizing Supplies Properly
    Providing for Office Safety
    Recognizing Work Space Organization Factors

Personal Organization   W16-W30
    Avoiding Stress
    Becoming a Better Listener
    Establishing Yourself Assertively
    Handling Correspondence Efficiently
    Improving Your Reading Skill
    Maintaining Appointments Effectively
    Managing Time Effectively
    Taking Notes
    Using the Appropriate Calendar or Appointment Book

Workstation and Personal Organization

Accomplishing all that is required of you in a day, retaining your composure, and maintaining a high level of energy and efficiency is a difficult juggling act. Maintaining an organized workplace also takes some skill which, when mastered, is very helpful in accomplishing daily goals. In this unit are some ideas on how to become a successful *juggler* in order to get more out of your workday and your work environment—without taking too much out of yourself.

W1 Workstation Organization

W2 Creating Procedures Manuals

Repeated verbal explanations of procedures can waste valuable time. A procedures manual eliminates this problem. The key elements of a good procedures manual are easy reading, easy reference, and easy revision.

To provide for easy reading:
- Have the manual typed.
- Use a consistent format throughout.
- Present the details in an accurate but concise format.
- Apply the principles of good business communication and English usage skills (see Units 3 and 7).

To provide for easy reference:
- Use frequent subheadings.
- Provide a comprehensive table of contents.
- Use terminology that best describes the operations and procedures to be performed.
- Include samples and illustrations for clarity.

To provide for easy revision:
- Use a looseleaf notebook format.
- Have written material on only one side of a page.
- Try to include only one activity or task per page to facilitate revision and change.

W3 Types of Procedures Manuals

Often, more than one procedures manual can be helpful in an office environment. Some typical types of manuals are:

- **Form Letter Manual**

    A book containing all the form letters used in a company or department. Form paragraphs might also be included in this manual.

- **Company Style Manual**

    A collection of the correspondence, report, and table styles preferred by a company (or a particular individual).

- **Task Performance Manual**

    A collection of procedures for tasks not handled by the same person all the time. This manual might also include tasks not performed frequently or those requiring a number of step-by-step procedures in a specific sequence for proper performance.

- **Workstation Manual**

    Detailed information on a particular job or workstation including a description of how to perform the tasks related to that job. This manual can be helpful in training new employees.

- **Operations Manual**

    A filing system including indexing, coding, cross-referencing, and charge-out procedures could be the subject of an operations manual. The flow of work in a specific office or department might also be the subject of this type of manual.

- **Equipment Usage Manual**

    A manual describing specific operational procedures such as how to power up a microcomputer; how to enter the appropriate software; how to respond to specific prompts; troubleshooting suggestions; hot line numbers; or the location of supplies.

- **Contact Manual**

    A listing of names, addresses, telephone numbers, specific preferences of individuals, and other pertinent information related to individuals within or outside the firm.

Workstation and Personal Organization

W4 Having the Right Equipment Available

Having the right working tools and equipment available can save time, money and your personal energy as well.

- Where ownership is not possible, consider renting or leasing equipment. In some cases, having tasks performed by service bureaus or by outside commercial businesses might be effective alternatives. A service bureau can be used to produce and develop microfilm, for example, or a quick-copy shop or commercial printer can be used to print a flyer or brochure if a reprographics department is not available.

- Consider the advantages of information processing equipment (see I12), special mail-handling equipment (see L8-L10), appropriate telephone features (see T23-T33), and carefully selected reprographic equipment (see R24-R28).

- In addition to having the obvious small equipment items available, consider the advantage of purchasing specialized items such as:

Forms separator	separates carbon and carbonless continuous forms into stacks
Burster	separates continuous forms and checks into individual sheets
Special Purpose Stapler	for heavy-duty stapling needs or for bulletin board tacking needs
Paper Punch	for two- or three-hole punching needs
Numbering Machine	for the consecutive numbering of documents
Postage Meter	substitutes for stamps and eliminates the need to keep stamps on hand and to attach them to envelopes
Postage Scale	weighs letters and packages to indicate the exact amount of postage, thereby saving money by helping avoid putting too much postage on an item
Electric Wastebasket	shreds paper and preserves the confidentiality of documents that are to be destroyed.

W4-W6 Having the Right Equipment Available

W5 Organizing Your Work Area
W6 Desk Organization

One desk arrangement cannot be suggested for all office jobs. To determine the best arrangement for you, you will need to carefully study your work style and your work demands. Consider the equipment and supplies you use frequently, whether you are left- or right-handed, and what tasks you perform most often—writing, typing, filing, telephoning. The answers to these questions should help you tailor your work arrangement to your job needs.

Some considerations are:

>**Desk layout.** Save time by keeping frequently used supplies and equipment within easy reach (Figures 18.1 and 18.2).

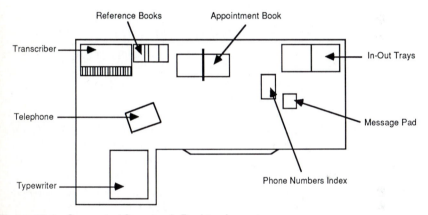

Figure 18.1 Suggested Secretary's Desktop Layout

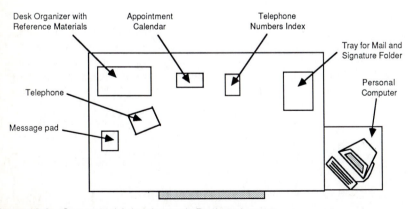

Figure 18.2 Suggested Administrator's Desktop Layout

Workstation and Personal Organization

Telephone location. Place it on the same side of your desk as your non-writing hand so that you pick up the receiver with that hand and leave your writing hand free for note-taking.

Files and reference sources. Locate close to the work station. If they are in constant use, position them directly beside or behind your desk so that you can reach them from your chair.

Center (shallow) drawer. Use for small items such as paper clips, pencils, pens, erasers, elastic bands, rulers, scissors, staples, tape, stamp pads, steno pad, moisteners, and other similar items.

Stationery drawers. Position stationery in the order in which you make up a carbon pack: letterheads first, carbon next, onionskin in the third, continuation next, and, so on.

W7 Other Suggestions

- If you use a stapler and writing instruments frequently, leave them on the desk during the working day for easy accessibility.
- Keep pencils and pens in a container on the desk top.
- Keep only a limited number of file folders in a desk organizer that holds folders in an desktop file holder.
- Keep frequently used reference items—telephone directory, time tables, schedules, and price lists in a desk organizer; keep less frequently used references on a nearby shelf or in a file or desk drawer.
- Keep only a week's inventory of supplies in your desk; too many accumulated supplies get in the way.
- Inventory your desk supplies weekly and throw away broken, torn or unusable items.

W8 Organizing Supplies Properly

The following suggestions are helpful if you need to organize a supply room or supply cabinet:

- Keep the area neat and orderly.
- Store frequently used items at eye level.
- Store heavy items on lower shelves.
- Avoid having the closet so full that supplies are difficult to see and remove.
- Store all supplies of one type together.
- Label the items on each shelf.

W7-W9 Other Suggestions

- Open boxes or packages carefully and leave unopened packages beneath opened ones.
- Tag or mark the last box to indicate that reordering is necessary.
- Keep a pad and pencil in the cabinet to write down items to be reordered.
- Put someone in charge of keeping the closet organized and inventorying supplies periodically—weekly or monthly, depending on use. Giving this assignment to employees on a rotating basis sometimes makes everyone more conscious of having supplies available.
- Be certain that the procedures for ordering and obtaining the supplies are understood, including time needed for ordering both within your company and from outside vendors.
- Recognize that some supplies have *shelf life* (expiration dates). Don't overstock items that will dry up or lose their chemical potency, such as ink pads or copier supplies.
- Label the contents of any unmarked boxes.
- Leave envelopes and other hard-to-store supplies in their boxes.

W9 Commonly Used Office Supplies

The following supplies are most often found in an office worker's desk:

- transparent tape dispenser
- small scratch pads
- desk calendar
- appointment book
- staple remover
- file folder labels
- mailing labels for large envelopes
- letterhead stationery
- interoffice stationery
- plain paper to match stationery
- envelopes to match stationery
- interoffice envelopes
- stapler
- file folders
- plain white paper
- routing slips
- rubber bands
- correction tapes, lift-off tabs, or cover-up tabs
- paper cement
- letter opener
- stamp pad
- date stamp
- paper clips
- thumbtacks
- removable, self-stick tabs
- scissors
- ruler
- pencils
- pens
- felt tip pens
- highlighter pen

Workstation and Personal Organization

transparent tape dispenser
small scratch pads
desk calendar
appointment book
staple remover
file folder labels
mailing labels for large envelopes
letterhead stationery

interoffice stationery
plain paper to match stationery
envelopes to match stationery
interoffice envelopes
stapler
file folders
plain white paper

W10 Providing for Office Safety

Many accidents occur in the office even though we often consider an office a safe place. Be safety conscious and act within the following guidelines:

- Do not leave desk drawers and file cabinets open.
- Repair tears in carpeting.
- Wipe up liquid spills immediately.
- Be careful with hot beverages.
- Do not permit obstructions—such as wastebaskets, extension cords, and telephone lines—to block or be located in aisles or walkways.
- Do not overcrowd equipment on work surfaces, and make sure equipment is securely in place on a desk or table.
- Be careful when lifting or moving equipment or furniture.
- Carry sharp objects (scissors, letter openers) with the points down.
- Know where the first aid kit is located.
- Know where fire extinguishers are located and be sure that they are routinely checked.
- Know the location of fire exits.
- Provide for the security of personal computers by bolting them in place or through the use of other security devices.
- Lock your purse and/or other personal belongings in a drawer or store them in some other place for safekeeping.
- If working late,
    — notify the guard or personnel department if you are working alone;
    — work near a telephone and have emergency numbers handy;
    — lock doors leading to your work area.

W11 Recognizing Work Space Organization Factors

Work areas must be organized for the performance of tasks and with consideration for the individual's need for privacy, quiet, and security.

W12 Space Planning Concepts

Space planning concepts vary. The following are the most prevalent:

- **Conventional**

    The conventional arrangement employs solid walls to separate workspace into distinct and unchangeable work areas. Minimal furnishings include a desk, a bookcase, and two chairs.

- **Modular**

    Modular space planning arrangements are offices equipped with movable partitions that can be changed as needed. Typical furnishings include modular shelves, desktops, and filing cabinets that are adjustable and are attached to the partitions.

- **Combination**

    Many offices depict a mixture of the conventional and modular design. In such offices, the administrative personnel might be housed in solid wall offices around the perimeter of the building while the support staff occupies interior spaces separated by modular partitions.

W13 General Factors to Consider in Office Design

Ergonomics is the science of work and workplace design. It integrates the concern for physiological as well as psychological factors in an effort to create an effective and productive work environment. Research has shown that the surroundings have an effect on how workers feel about their job and on the amount of work they actually do. The following factors need to be considered when planning the use of office space:

- floor plan layout
- electrical needs
- heat and air-conditioning needs
- noise factors
- lighting
- furniture and workstation components

Workstation and Personal Organization

- equipment space needed
- environmental factors—dust, smoke, magnetic and static electricity
- workflow patterns
- inside and outside traffic
- security concerns
- need for privacy and confidentiality
- the effects of color
- demands on energy and utilities

W14 Office Furnishings

Studies on furniture, furniture arrangement, light, and sound reveal these to be significant factors in office efficiency. Consider these points.

- **Desks**

    L-shaped desks provide 80 percent more work space than conventional desks. Choose light or medium tan or gray for the desk top because these colors are less tiring on the eyes than dark wood colors. Executive desks measure 76" x 36"; general office workers' desks measure 60" x 34" or 42" x 30"; and clerical workers' desks measure 50" x 30".

- **Systems Furniture**

    Systems furniture creates the most efficient work station as far as space and employee productivity are concerned. With systems furniture, the work station consists of pre-wired movable panels of varying heights, plus such added components as work surfaces, files, and individual lighting in whatever configuration is best suited to the task to be accomplished.

- **Lighting**

    Desk or task lighting is better for productivity than overhead (ambient) lighting.

- **Noise Control**

    Sounds from office machines bounce off walls, ceiling, and other surfaces and cause noise disturbance. Sound-absorbing materials in a room, in dividing panels, and in ceilings can help alleviate this problem. Carpeting and drapes are also useful in absorbing sound.

- **Terminals**

    Ergonomically designed terminals have separate keyboards with appropriate spacing between keys, screens that tilt and rotate and have anti-glare surfaces, and other special features that permit the brightening and dimming of screen images.

- **Chairs**

    Chairs on casters or gliders that can be adjusted vertically and backward to provide back support are preferred.

W15   Office Layout Considerations

Office layout has considerable influence on efficiency and productivity levels. Here are some considerations in planning the office layout.

- Give preference to dominant workflow and communication needs.
- Place related departments and workstations for jobs of a similar nature near each other.
- Put departments with frequent traffic from outside visitors nearest the outside entrance.
- Place vending machines, copiers, fountains, and bulletin boards where they will cause the least traffic and interference.
- Position shared equipment (copiers) so that the area does not serve as the office socializing spot.
- Move the work to the employees rather than the employees to the work whenever possible.
- Provide soundproofing for noisy equipment and work areas.
- Locate supervisors so that they can easily observe their work areas and personnel.
- Consider using modular furniture because the mix and match features of desk tops, desk pedestals (drawers), and filing units and shelves provide flexibility for later use when there might be need for change or modification.
- Consider a modular arrangement or open plan of design, which means that 80 percent of available space is used; the conventional plan permits only 40 percent of the space to be used.
- Match the positioning of desk and workstations to the work flow, thereby permitting a minimum of interruptions and backtracking.

Workstation and Personal Organization

- Provide enough space for people to move around freely.
- Choose filing cabinets or shelves to suit the amount of space and types of records to be stored (see F54-F61).
- Group employees together who are using the same equipment or records.
- Locate service areas (mail room, reprographics, file room) near the departments that use them most.
- Consider adjustable shelves or bookcases to fit odd-size items. You may wish to choose a credenza (enclosed cabinet) instead of open shelves.
- Consider rollaway cabinets for files requiring shared use, vaulting, or portablility.

W16 Personal Organization

Keeping yourself organized is just as important to the efficient functioning of an office as maintaining an organized workstation. The last section of this unit suggests methods of personal organization.

W17 Avoiding Stress

Pace yourself throughout the day so that you eliminate periods of fatigue and stress.

- Plan the toughest jobs or appointments for the start of the day when you are freshest.
- Don't cram too many activities into a short time span. Plan for a breathing space in between appointments.
- If you must leave the office or building for any reason, allow yourself sufficient time to arrive at your destination and return for your next appointment without rushing.
- Resist lunch and evening appointments.
- Allow for rest periods when planning long business trips. Jet lag is a serious problem.
- Delegate as many routine tasks as possible.
- Find things you like about your job and do them at least once a day.
- Write yourself notes to keep yourself organized and to minimize nagging worries.

- Don't skip meals.
- Get adequate sleep.
- Take notes and make lists; don't use valuable short-term memory capacity.
- Be alert to ways to alleviate tension from prolonged work at a desk or workstation; use good posture.
- Do short exercises on breaks or during lunch. Here are two examples:

    Shoulder exercise: Stand with arms at sides, bring shoulders up as high as possible and then as low as possible. Do this several times.

    Leg circulation: Lean forward, hands on knees, lift both heels off the floor while contracting calf muscles; lower heels and lift toes high toward shin. Do this several times.

W18 Becoming a Better Listener

Listening is more than hearing; it involves comprehension and retention. Effective listening leads to greater understanding, better human relationships, and greater personal efficiency. Since you listen faster than the speaker can speak, you must force yourself to concentrate so that you accurately comprehend what is being said. Aim to improve your listening skill by:

- **Preparing**

    Be an active listener. Keep quiet and listen to what is being said. Know your power and responsibility as a listener.

- **Perceiving**

    Know your emotional biases and try to correct them so they don't work against your ability to honestly hear and interpret what has been said. Listen without judging, and give the speaker's message an opportunity to reach you without the interference of your previous biases. Listen to what is actually said instead of to what you think it means.

- **Participating**

    Give the speaker steady, sincere eye contact and verbal and nonverbal feedback (as appropriate) so that he or she knows that you understand. Give the speaker your undivided attention.

- **Processing**

    Think about the ideas given by the speaker. Restate the ideas in your own words and think through what they mean. As you do this, judge the words, not the speaker. Don't allow yourself to be distracted from thinking through the ideas suggested by the speaker.

- **Probing**

    Formulate questions as you concentrate on what is being said. Have a notepad ready; listen and then write down key facts. Ask questions for clarification or restate the speaker's ideas to provide feedback.

- **Personalizing**

    Consider the speaker's information with respect to your own circumstances. Think of how you can apply the ideas given to your situation.

W19 Establishing Yourself Assertively

To perform effectively as a professional, you should demonstrate sensitivity and awareness in your daily relationships. You also need to have a sense of self-worth to make the most of your potential. Knowing what to do and knowing how to do it are two very different things. *Assertiveness* is expressing what you believe, feel, and want in direct, honest, and appropriate ways that respect the rights of other persons. Ignoring your feelings and desires and succumbing to the demands and feelings of others is *non-assertive* behavior. Using sarcasm, intimidation, and coersion to get what you want is *aggressive* behavior.

To act assertively, non-assertively, or aggressively is a decision that *you* make. Since your behavior is your choice, it is affected by your perceptions of yourself in your relationships with others. To make the most of your potential, you need to accept both the *rights* and *responsibilities* of acting assertively.

Some positive first steps in establishing yourself assertively are:

- Make eye contact when you are with other people.
- Don't be apologetic in your manner by preceding statements with "I think," or ending statements with "Do you agree?" Instead of saying "I'm sorry to bother you but . . .," say "I'd like to talk with you about . . ."

W19-W20   Establishing Yourself Assertively

- Don't end too many sentences by raising your voice as if you are asking a question. Keep remarks such as "I did it right, didn't I?" to a minimum.
- Keep your composure when you say "no" so as not to weaken your position.
- Refuse requests for favors politely but firmly. Say: "I'm sorry, but I just can't do it."

W20 Handling Correspondence Efficiently

- Don't procrastinate. Whenever possible, handle each piece of correspondence only once and make decisions now. You will probably not know anything more about the subject three days later.
- Have incoming mail opened, screened, and sorted if possible. Divide the mail into four categories: immediate action, low priority, pending action, and reading material. Immediately discard any unnecessary mail.
- Use as many form letters or form paragraphs as possible.
- Use previously written letters for similar circumstances rather than writing new letters.
- Use dictation equipment (see C45 and E143-E145) if it is available.
- Write responses on incoming letters or memos, photocopy them for your file, and send the original back to the writer, if circumstances permit.
- Use preprinted routing slips or other preprinted stickers (Figure 18.3) to route correspondence to others.
- Carry a pocket size dictation unit to record information when you are out of the office. Be sure, however, that the recording medium is compatible with the transcribing unit in the office.
- Write brief, easy-to-understand letters (see Unit 3, *Communication in Business*).
- Use rubber stamps (see H28).
- Use informal notes rather than letters, if appropriate.
- Don't clutter your own files with unnecessary copies of correspondence.

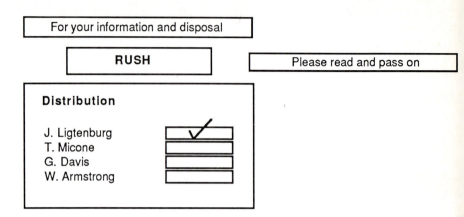

Figure 18.3 Preprinted Stickers

 Improving Your Reading Skill

Research has shown that the faster you read, the more you concentrate and retain. Most people read average material at the rate of 250 wpm; efficient readers read average material at 1000 wpm. Efficient readers do not *word* read, pause, skip back, or silently mouth the words; they skim the page while concentrating on the words.

To encourage efficient reading, first determine your present rate and then aim to increase it. Figure 18.4 provideds a quick guide to determining your reading speed.

To develop your reading skill, follow these steps:

- Set up a good reading environment. Make sure the area is quiet and comfortable with respect to lighting and temperature.
- Preview the material before starting to read. Skim the introduction, table of contents, headings, and summary to get a mental outline of the content and organization of what is to be read.
- Decide why you are reading. Read slowly when you are reading something technical or trying to understand explanations or instructions; read faster if you are reading for some particular fact of information or for pleasure.
- Concentrate on what you are reading by blocking out distractions.
- Strive to improve your comprehension by constantly building your vocabulary, taking notes, and reviewing or recalling the main points of the material as you are reading.

W21-W23 Improving Your Reading Skill

> - Start a stopwatch.
> - Read a two-page non-fiction article.
> - Stop the watch. Calculate the amount of time [in seconds] it took you to read the two pages.
> - Count the number of words in the article by adding the number in one line and multiplying this by the total number of lines in the article.
> - Divide the words by the number of seconds.
> - Now multiply the answer by 60 to get your score in minutes.

▶ **Figure 18.4** Determine Your Reading Speed

W22 Maintaining Appointments Effectively

Being at the right place at the right time demonstrates that you are alert and businesslike. To keep track of your long-range and short-range commitments, personal planning calendars are essential tools. They can be used as reminders and, in some types of work, for billing purposes.

W23 For the Administrator

Establish a policy on who can make appointments for you. Clearly specify special preferences you may have about the scheduling of appointments. Some of them may include:

- Recording all appointments on an appointment calendar or an appointment book.
- Placing a telephone number after each name in case it is necessary to change an appointment.
- Determining the reason for the appointment and writing the reason on the appointment calendar so that advance preparation can be made if necessary.
- Scheduling enough time for each appointment.
- Writing neatly in the appointment book or on the calendar.
- Coordinating appointments. If appointments are made in your absence, have them listed separately for you to see when you return. If you schedule an appointment when out of the office, be sure to record it in your appointment book as soon as you return to the office.

Workstation and Personal Organization

- Being certain to leave time before and after meetings to provide for travel time.
- Recording future-date items as soon as they are known—conventions, staff meetings, budget due dates, long-range reports. Place a reminder of these critical due dates on your calendar by making a notation a week or two in advance.
- Recording recurring events as soon as a new calendar is started.
- Having the administrator and the support person review the day's calendar each morning to monitor the day's activites.
- Looking over the next day's appointments to determine if any special arrangements need to be made.
- Retaining calendars with end-of-year file materials.

W24 For the Administrative Support Person

When scheduling appointments, follow these general suggestions:

- Consider your employer's desires first; ask if there are any special preferences.
- Avoid scheduling appointments before 10 a.m. and after 4 p.m. whenever possible.
- If possible, keep the appointments light a week before and a week after a planned business trip or vacation.
- Do not schedule an appointment between 12 p.m. and 2 p.m. unless it is specifically a luncheon appointment or unless your employer has no objection.
- Allow enough time if there is a luncheon appointment.
- Allow ample time between appointments.
- Avoid scheduling too many appointments at busy times of the month or at times when reports are due.
- Schedule appointments in blocks, whenever possible, rather than scattered throughout the day.
- Do not schedule an appointment if you are unsure of your supervisor's willingness to meet with the person. Do this tactfully by saying, "I'm only scheduling appointments at Mr. Warren's request in the next few days because he is involved in a major project right now."

W25 Managing Time Effectively

W26 Assessing Your Use of Time

Find out what you are presently doing with your time by keeping a log of each day's activities for several weeks. Analyze your log and try to determine which time periods are most productive in your typical day

W24-W27　For the Administrative Support Person

and which are the least. Try to schedule difficult jobs at productive times and easier jobs during hectic times of the day. Here are some other suggestions to help you make better use of your time.

W27　Controlling Time Wasters

Recognize time wasters and take steps to minimize them.

Time Waster	Means of Control
lack of planning	Set goals; identify activities that will help you achieve your goals; establish priorities among goals.
too many meetings	Streamline meetings that you conduct by having an agenda, starting on time, staying on the topics, and ending on time (see Unit 13, *Organizing Meetings and Conferences*).
interruptions	Try to allocate a stated daily period for them but realize that this is not always possible; try to defer interruptions with "I'm really busy now, but let's get together at 3:30 and resolve this problem."
excessive telephoning	Make sure all points are covered by making notes before you place the phone call. Batch telephone calls and make them early in the day so that your call can be returned to you later or so that you can determine when the other party will be available for a later callback. Have your incoming phone calls screened. Have a calendar, pad, and pencil available for notes and messages. Have those taking messages for you take complete messages including the caller's telephone number and the reason they are calling.
lack of delegation	Realize that you can't do everything yourself. Let those who are involved with the facts use good judgment to decide and act on issues whenever possible.

repetitive inquiries

Communicate effectively by informing people ahead of time instead of having them interrupt you to ask questions. Give your support staff answers to frequently asked questions and have them respond to such inquiries.

W28 Planning Your Day

- Make a work schedule (Figure 18.5) for yourself listing exactly what you must accomplish in a day.

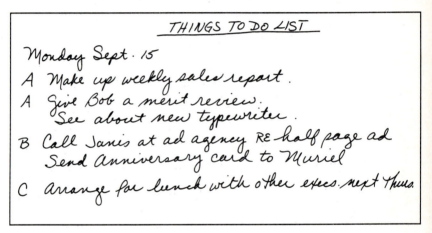

Figure 18.5 Things To Do List

- Assess each task on your *To Do* list with an *A* (high priority; handle first), *B*, or *C* (do as time permits) priority and establish deadlines.
- Delegate all *C* jobs (and as many others as you can). For example, permit an administrative support person to open and sort the mail; screen visitors and callers; make copies as necessary; and annotate magazine articles.
- Tackle complex and hardest tasks when you are freshest and in uninterrupted blocks of time, if at all possible.
- Do tasks correctly the first time.
- Finish one job before you start another.
- Check off jobs on your *To Do* list as you complete them. This will serve as a psychological reward for your efforts.

W28-W29   Planning Your Day

- Maintain a long-term calendar as well as a daily one and use these tools efficiently (see W30).
- Resist an *open door policy* all the time by having your desk positioned so that your back or side is facing the door.
- Keep breaks short, but take them.
- Try to get everything done in the shortest time with the fewest wasted motions. Think through each activity and reduce it to a series of mechanical routines.
- At the end of the day, analyze why each unfinished job was not completed.
- Develop and use good procedures manuals (see W2 and W3).
- Group related jobs together. For example:

    Save copying jobs until you have several so that you walk to the copier just once.

    Do all mailing jobs at one time.

    Do one batch of filing a day, if possible.

    Use a follow-up system (see F65).

    Keep a filing system that is easy to use and clean it out frequently.

    Have an easy-to-read phone number list or contact list handy.

    Plan ahead and make preliminary preparations to meet peak workload demands—prepare envelopes ahead, requisition needed supplies, have enclosures reproduced ahead of time, and partially complete forms ahead of time whenever possible.

W29   Taking Notes

Effective note-taking can be an effective organizational tool.

- Place the date and meeting time on your notes.
- Keep related notes together in one notebook.
- Use an established shorthand system or create your own system by abbreviating, dropping silent letters, writing key phrases rather than complete sentences—or using any other shortcuts of your own.
- Highlight key ideas by underlining, circling, writing in caps or leaving blank space before and after the idea.
- Leave ample white space as you take notes so that you can easily locate key sections or add additional thoughts at a later time.

Workstation and Personal Organization

- Use asterisks (*) to signal follow-up activities that you might be responsible for in between meetings.
- Record vital information such as direct quotes, names, dates and amounts.
- Read your notes immediately after the meeting to clarify gaps and fill in missing information.
- Read the last set of notes before going to the next meeting.

W30 Using the Appropriate Calendar or Appointment Book

Stationery stores offer a wide variety of calendars and appointment books. Take time to carefully select the types that best meet your personal needs and preferences. Some of the popular types are:

- **Monthly Calendar**

    Used for long-range and at-a-glance planning. This type of calendar is helpful in getting an overview of the workflow, and can be helpful in balancing assignments, projects, and scheduling.

- **Weekly Calendar**

    Provides you with the option of looking at one week at a time; gives more room to record daily activites than monthly calendars; is helpful for a short-range overview of commitments.

- **Daily Calendar, Appointment Book or Desk Diary**

    Provides a day by day listing. Each day may be divided into intervals of 5-, 15-, or 30-minute segments to provide for the recording of appointments or to serve as a record-keeper for billing purposes, as in the case of lawyers who bill clients based on time spent on a case.

- **Pocket Calendar**

    A monthly or weekly calendar for scheduling personal appointments.

APPENDIX

A PPENDIX

Abbreviations — A2
  Official Postal Service Abbreviations
  Standard Business Abbreviations

Commonly Used Foreign Words and Phrases — A2

Holidays — A3
  United States National Holidays
  Candian National Holidays

Metric System — A4
  Metric Units
  Common Metric Prefixes
  Most Frequently Used Metric Measurements
  Common Unit Conversion (to three decimal places)

Roman Numerals — A7

Time Zones — A8
  United States
  Canada

Weights and Measures — A9
  Cubic Measure
  Avoirdupois Weight
  Liquid Measure
  Long Measure
  Dry Measure
  Metric Equivalents

Other — A11

Appendix

Abbreviations

Official Postal Service Abbreviations

(See inside front cover for two-letter state and territory abbreviations.)

Street Addresses

Apartment	APT	Avenue	AVE
Boulevard	BLVD	Box	BX
Broadway	BDWY	Circle	CIR
Court	CT	Drive	DR
East	E	Fort	FT
Garden	GDNS	Headquarters	HQ
Heights	HTS	Highway	HWY
Lake	LK	Lane	LN
Mount	MT	Mountain	MTN
North	N	Parkway	PKY
Place	PL	Point	PT
Port	PRT	Road	RD
Route	RT	South	S
Street	ST	Terrace	TER
Trail	TRL	Trailer	TRLR
Turnpike	TPKE	West	W

Standard Business Abbreviations

(See G56.)

Commonly Used Foreign Words and Phrases

ad hoc	temporary; for a specific purpose
ad infinitum	without limit or end
ad nauseam	to the point of disgust
ad valorem	according to value
bona fide	in good faith
caveat emptor	let the buyer beware
carte blanche	full discretionary powers

Appendix

circa	about
coup d'état	a sudden and decisive political measure
cum laude	with honor, praise
esprit de corps	team spirit, team work, cooperation
ex-officio	by virtue of an office
fait accompli	something already done
faux pas	false step, error
incognito	in disguise
in toto	altogether, entirely
kudos	praise
laissez faire	the principle of letting people do as they please
modus operandi	method of operating
modus vivendi	way of life
ne plus ultra	the highest degree
nom de plume	pen name, pseudonym
non seqitur	does not follow, irrelevant
per annum	each year
per capita	each person
per diem	each day
per se	itself
persona non grata	an unacceptable person
pièce de résistance	an outstanding item or event
prix fixe	set price for a complete meal
pro forma	for the record, matter of form
pro rata	in proportion to
raison d'être	reason for being
répondez s'il vous plait	please reply (RSVP)
sine qua non	something essential
status quo	current state of affairs
terra firma	solid earth, dry land
verbatim	word for word

Holidays

United States National Holidays

New Year's Day	January 1
Martin Luther King Day	January 20
Washington's Birthday	third Monday in February

Appendix

Good Friday	Friday before Easter Sunday
Easter Monday	day after Easter Sunday
Memorial Day	last Monday in May
Independence Day	July 4
Labor Day	first Monday in September
Columbus Day	second Monday in October
Veteran's Day	November 11
Thanksgiving Day	fourth Thursday in November
Christmas Day	December 25

Canadian National Holidays*

New Year's Day	January 1
Good Friday	Friday before Easter Sunday
Victoria Day	Monday prior and closest to May 21
Canada Day	July 1
Labour Day	first Monday in September
Thanksgiving Day	second Monday in October
Christmas Day	December 25

Government offices are also closed on Easter Monday and Remembrance Day (November 11).

Banks are also closed on Remembrance day.

*Provincial Holidays are observed in addition to national holidays.

Metric System

Metric Units

Name	Unit of	Symbol
meter	length	m
liter	volume	L (or *l* when handwritten)
gram	mass	g
second	time	s
degree Celsius	temperature	°C

Appendix

Common Metric Prefixes

Prefix	Meaning	Factor (Multiplier)	Symbol
mega	1 million	10^6 (1,000,000)	M
*kilo	1 thousand	10^4 (1,000)	k
hecto	1 hundred	10^2 (100)	h
deca	ten	10 (10)	da
deci	one tenth of a	10^1 (0.1)	d
*centi	one hundredth of a	10^2 (0.01)	c
*milli	one thousandth of a	10^3 (0.001)	m
micro	one millionth of a	10^6 (0.000 001)	u

*most frequently used

Most Frequently Used Metric Measurements

Quantity	Unit	Symbol
Length	millimeter	mm
	centimeter	cm
	meter	m
	kilometer	km
	(1 m = 100 cm or 1,000 mm)	
Area	square centimeter	cm^2
	square meter	m^2
	square kilometer	km^2
	hectare	ha
Volume	cubic centimeter	cm^3
	cubic meter	m^3
	(1 m^3 = 1,000,000 cm^3)	
	milliliter	mL
	liter	L (or *l* when handwritten)
	(1 L = 1,000 mL)	
Mass	milligram	mg
	gram	g
	kilogram	kg
	ton	t
	(1 kg = 1,000 g)	

Appendix

Time	second	s
	minute	min
	hour	h
Speed	meters per second	m/s
	kilometers per hour	km/h
Temperature	degree Celsius	°C

Common Unit Conversion (to 3 decimal places)

Length	1 inch	= 0.025 m (2.54 cm or 25.4 mm)
	1 foot	= 0.305 m (30.48 cm)
	1 yard	= 0.914 m
	1 mile	= 1.609 km
Area	1 square inch	= 6.452 cm^2
	1 square foot	= 0.093 m^2
	1 square yard	= 0.836 m^2
	1 acre	= 0.405 ha (hectare)
	1 square mile	= 2.590 km^2 (259 ha)
Volume	1 fluid ounce	= 28.413 cm^3 (28.4 mL)
	1 pint (imperial)	= 0.568 dm^3 (0.57 L)
	1 quart	= 1.137 dm^3 (1.14 L)
	1 gallon	= 4.546 dm^3 (4.546 L)
	1 cubic inch	= 16.387 cm^3
	1 cubic foot	= 28.317 dm^3 (28.32L)
	1 cubic yard	= 0.765 m^3
Mass	1 ounce	= 28.350 g
	1 pound	= 0.454 kg
	1 ton (short 2000 lb.)	= 907.185 kg
Speed	1 mile per hour	= 0.447 m/s
		= 1.609 km/h
Temperature	5/9 x No. of degrees Fahrenheit − 32	= degrees Celsius

Appendix

Roman Numerals

- Use upper case numerals for major divisions in outlines and in literary publications, such as volumes, books, chapters, and appendixes.
- Use lower case numerals for preliminary pages in reports and subsections.

ARABIC	ROMAN	ARABIC	ROMAN
1	I	30	XXX
2	II	40	XL
3	III	50	L
4	IV	60	LX
5	V	70	LXX
6	VI	80	LXXX
7	VII	90	XC
8	VIII	100	C
9	IX	300	CCC
10	X	400	CD
11	XI	500	D
12	XII	600	DC
13	XIII	900	CM
14	XIV	1,000	M
15	XV	5,000	$\overline{V}$*
16	XVI	8,000	$\overline{VIII}$*
17	XVII	10,000	$\overline{X}$*
18	XVIII	30,000	$\overline{XXX}$*
19	XIX	50,000	$\overline{L}$*
20	XX		

*Note: A horizontal line placed over a number multiplies its value by 1000.

Build combinations of Roman numerals by prefixing or annexing letters. A letter prefixed to another is substracted from it; a letter annexed is added.

$$49 = \overset{40}{\overbrace{L - X}} + IX = XLIX$$

$$62 = \overset{60}{\overbrace{L + X}} + II = LXII$$

Do not repeat a Roman numeral more than three times.

337 = CCCXXXVII
(437 = CDXXXVII not CCCCXXXVIII)
1985 = MCMLXXXV

Appendix

Time Zones

United States

The continental United States is divided into four time zones. There is one hour's difference between each zone as you move across the country. The map in Figure A1 shows the different time zones and telephone area codes.

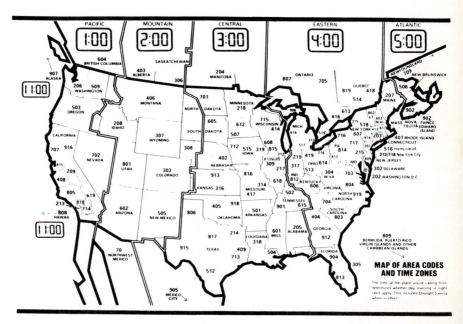

Figure A1 Time Zones and Area Codes of the United States
(Courtesy of GTE Directories Corporation)

Canada

Canada is divided into seven time zones. There is one hour's difference between each zone as you move across the country. Newfoundland time, however, is only one-half hour different from Atlantic time. (See Figure A2.)

Appendix

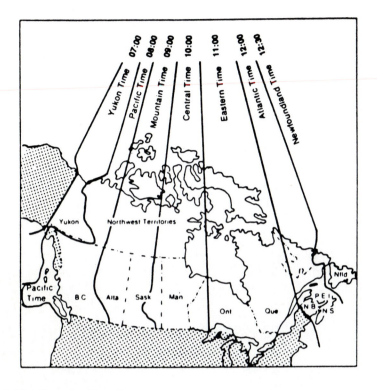

Figure A2 Canadian Time Zones

Weights and Measures

Cubic Measure

1,728 cubic inches	= 1 cubic foot
27 cubic feet	= 1 cubic yard
128 cubic feet	= 1 cord (wood)
40 cubic feet	= 1 ton (shipping)
231 cubic inches	= 1 U.S. standard gallon

Appendix

Avoirdupois Weight

27 11/32 grams	= 1 dram
16 drams	= 1 ounce
16 ounces	= 1 pound
25 pounds	= 1 quarter
4 quarters	= 1 cwt. (hundred weight)
2,000 lbs.	= 1 short ton
2,240 lbs.	= 1 long ton

Liquid Measure

4 gills	= 1 pint
2 pints	= 1 quart
4 quarts	= 1 gallon
31 1/2 gallons	= 1 barrel

Long Measure

12 inches	= 1 foot
3 feet	= 1 yard
5 1/2 yards	= 1 rod

Dry Measure

2 pints	= 1 quart
8 quarts	= 1 peck
4 pecks	= 1 bushel
36 bushels	= 1 chaldron

Appendix

Metric Equivalents

1 centimeter	= 0.3937 inch
1 inch	= 2.54 centimeters
1 meter	= 1.0936 yards
1 yard	= 0.9144 meter
1 kilogram	= 2.2016 lbs.
1 pound	= 0.4536 kilograms

THERMOMETER: 100° Centigrade equals 212° Fahrenheit
0° Centigrade equals 32° Fahrenheit

Other

Use this space to add any other information that you need to access frequently.

Index

NOTE: The **boldface** letter/number combinations in this index refer to *sections* of the handbook; the lightface numbers refer to *page numbers*. Appendix references are to page numbers and are numbered A1–A11.

Abbreviations, **A**2
  addresses, **E**52-152
  alphabetizing, **F**24-223
  compass points, **G**60-305
  date and time, **G**57-304
  frequently used, **G**56-300
  measurements, **G**58-305, **A**5-A6
  places, **G**59-305, inside front cover
  plurals, **G**84-313
  publication terms, **G**61-305
  style, **G**54-299
  titles, **G**62-305
Abstract, report, **E**96-182
Academic fields, capitalization, **G**65-306
Accounting, **B**75-52
  account, **B**79-55
  equation, **M**7-407
  financial statements, **B**81-57
  journals, **B**77-53
  ledger, **B**78-54
  sample documents, **B**86-65, **B**87-66
  source documents, **B**76-52
  trial balance, **B**80-56
  vocabulary, **B**84-60
Accounts payable, **H**24-329
Account types, banking, **B**2-23
Accuracy ratio, filing, **F**68-251
Acknowledgment letter, **C**7-74
Activity ratio, filing, **F**68-251
Addressee notation, **E**87-175
Addresses, **C**24-85
  abbreviations, **A**2
  envelopes, **E**52-152
  inside, **C**25-86, **E**70-166
  style, **G**55-299, **A**2
Adjectives
  commas between, **G**14-274
  compound, hyphen, **G**26-279
Administrative work, cf.clerical, **I**1-335
Adverbs, conjunctive, **G**40-283
Advertisements, classified, **P**5-436
Aerogrammes, **L**23-389
Agenda, meetings, **O**4-423
Airbill, **D**4-109
  preparing, **D**6-111
Air express, **D**2-108
Air travel, **A**2-3
  baggage, **A**9-6
  confirmation and cancellation, **A**4-5
  fares, **A**5-5
  getting to and from airport, **A**10-6
  OAG, **A**3-4
Algebraic equations, **M**5-405
Almanacs, **Q**1-452
Alphabetic filing, **F**43-230
Alphabetizing, **F**17-220
  abbreviations, **F**24-223
  board names, **F**38-228
  company names, titles in, **F**32-226
  compound words, **F**35-227
  geographic terms, **F**33-226
  government names, **F**39-228
  identical names, **F**40-228
  names, **F**20-222
  numbers, **F**41-229
  seniority terms, **F**31-226
  sequencing, **F**18-221
  special situations, **F**36-227
  titles and degrees, **F**30-225
  units, identifying, **F**19-221
  see also Filing
Amortization formula, **M**8-407
Annual reports, **Q**14-459

Index

Answering services, **T**33-507
Anthologies, **E**126-193
Apology letter, **C**8-74
Apostrophe
  alphabetizing, **F**25-224
  contractions, **G**7-272
  plurals, **G**8-272, **G**84-313
  possessives, **G**9-272
Applications, job, form, **P**7-437; *see also* Job search
Appointments
  book, **W**30-536
  maintaining, **W**22-531
Area codes, **A**8
Arithmetic. *See* Mathematics
Astronomical bodies, capitalization, **G**67-306
Atlases, **Q**2-452
Attention line, **E**71-167
Author, unknown, **E**129-194
Automatic tellers, **B**36-39
Automation, office. *See* Information processing
Automobile travel, **A**11-7
  recording mileage, **A**12-7
  rental cars, **A**13-8
  travel aids, **A**14-8
Averages, **M**20-411

Baggage
  air travel, **A**9-6
  insurance, **A**28-14
  train travel, **A**19-9
Balance sheet, **B**83-58
  sample, **B**87-66
Banking, **B**1-23
  account types, **B**2-23
  automatic tellers, **B**36-39
  certificates of deposit, **B**8-26
  checks, **B**16-30
  deposits, **B**13-28
  IRAs, **B**11-27
  Keogh Plan, **B**12-28
  money market accounts, **B**9-27
  passbook savings, **B**3-24
  reconciling statement, **B**32-37

  reminders, **B**85-64
  special services, **B**35-39
  statement savings, **B**4-24
  tax-sheltered pension trust accounts, **B**10-27
  withdrawals, **B**15-29
Bar graph, **E**46, **E**49-150
Bibliography, **C**40-98, **E**134-196
Billing forms, **H**19-327
Bill of lading, **D**10-112
  export, **D**19-114
  form, **H**18-327
Biographical dictionaries, **Q**3-453
Blind carbon, **E**87-175
Block style, **E**66-163
Board names, alphabetizing, **F**38-228
Boilerplate, **C**13-78
Books, references to, **E**127-193
Brackets, **G**32-280
Break even point, **M**18-410
Bubble storage, magnetic, **I**36-349
Bulk mail, **L**24-389
Bus
  delivery services, **D**3-108
  travel, **A**15-8

Cables, **T**39-510
Calculators, electronic, **M**25-414
  desktop, **M**30-417
  keys, basic functions, **M**29-416
  machine logic, **M**27-415
  purchase considerations, **M**28-415
Calendar, **W**30-536
Call director, **T**27-504
Caller mail, **L**25-389
Calling card calls, **T**13-500
Canada
  holidays, **A**4
  time zones, **A**8
Capitalization, **G**64-306
Carbon copy notations, **E**84-173
  blind, **E**87-175
Carbon paper, **R**12-475
Cellular radio, **I**59-354
Centering, typing, **E**6-121, **E**9-122
Centrex, **T**28-504

Index

Certificates of deposit, **B8**-26
Certified checks, **B25**-35
Certified mail, **L28**-390
Chairperson, meeting, **O7**-425
Charge-out, files, **F63**-247
Charts, typing, **E44**-149
Checking accounts, **B5**-24
   noninterest-bearing, **B6**-24
Checks
   bank, **B24**-34
   canceled, **B30**-36
   certified, **B25**-35
   dishonored, **B31**-36
   endorsing, **B19**-32
   NSF, **B29**-36
   parts of, **B16**-30
   payroll, **B68**-50
   post-dated, **B27**-35
   preparing, **B18**-31
   reconciling statement, **B32**-37
   stale-dated, **B28**-36
   stopped, **B26**-35
   stub/register entries, **B17**-30
City directories, **Q15**-460
Claims, mail, **L29**-390
Classified ads, **P5**-436; *see also* Job search
Clauses, nonrestrictive, **G17**-276
Clerical work, cf. administrative, **I1**-335
Closing, company name in, **E79**-171
Coated paper copier, **R8**-474
Coaxial cables, **I55**-353
Coding, filing, **F13**-217
C.O.D. mail, **L30**-390
Collect calls, **T15**-501
Collection, **E126**-193
   bank services, **B37**-39
   forms, **H22**-328
   letter, **C9**-75
Colon, **G10**-274
Color coding, files, **F64**-248
Commas, **G13**-274
   adjectives, **G14**-274
   compound sentences, **G15**-275
   correspondence, **G16**-275
   introductory, **G20**-277
   nonrestrictive clauses, **G17**-276

   parenthetical expressions, **G19**-277
   series, **G22**-278
   within a sentence, **G21**-277
   words, omission of, **G18**-277
Commercial drafts, **B38**-39
Communications, oral, **C42**-100
   dictation, machine, **C45**-101
   in person, **C44**-101
   speakers, **C47**-104
   speeches, **C48**-104
   voice qualities, **C43**-100
Communications, written, **C1**-68
   checklist, **C41**-99
   interoffice memos, **C28**-89
   model, **C2**-68
   news releases, **C29**-90
   reports, **C30**-92
   verbal/nonverbal, **C3**-70
   written correspondence, **C4**-71
   see also Correspondence; Reports
Communication satellites, **I57**-353
Company name
   alphabetizing, **F22**-222, **F37**-227
   in closing, **E79**-171
Compass terms, alphabetizing, **F33**-226
Complaint letter, **C10**-76
Complimentary close, **C24**-85, **C26**-88, **E78**-170
   capitalization, **G73**-308
Compound sentences, semicolon in, **G39**-282
Compound words
   alphabetizing, **F35**-227
   hyphen, **G26**-279
Computerized reference searches, **Q24**-465
Computer(s)
   assisted retrieval, **I48**-352
   CPU, **I8**-340
   graphics, **R31**-489
   languages, **I10**-342
   output
      devices, **I40**-350
      microfilm, **I47**-351
   processing devices, **I39**-350
   programming, **I9**-341

Index

references, Q19-462
software packages, I11-342
storage devices, I32-348
telephone systems, T31-505
types, I7-339
with word processing, E25-137
see also Information processing; Telecommunications; Telephone; Text editors
Condolence letter, C23-85
Conference calls, T22-502
Conferences. *See* Meetings
Congratulatory letter, C11-77
Conjunctive adverbs, semicolon, G40-283
Contents, table of, reports, E97-182
numbering pages, E106-187
Contractions, apostrophe, G7-272
Copiers
economical use, R11-475
intelligent, I43-351, R32-490
selection guidelines, R25-485
types, R6-473
see also Reprographics
Copy notation, correspondence, E84-173
blind, E87-175
Copyright guidelines, R17-480
Corrections
text editor, E31-139
typing, E27-137
Correspondence, C4-71
acknowledgment, C7-74
addressee notation, E87-175
address, C24-85
apology, C8-74
attention line, E71-167
basic letter-writing tips, C5-71
blind carbons, E87-175
body, E74-168
capitalization, G73-308
collection letter, C9-75
commas in, G16-275
complaint letter, C10-76
complimentary close, C24-85, C26-88, E78-170
company name in, E79-171
congratulatory letter, C11-77

copy notation, E84-173
date, E69-166
displayed information, E75-168
donation request response, C21-83
effective handling, W20-529
enclosure notation, E83-173
files, F6-213
folding, E57-155
form letters, C13-78, E89-177
gratitude/thank you letter, C14-80
headings, multiple page letters, E86-174
identification line, E81-172
inquiry letter, C12-77
inside address, C25-86, E70-166
introduction letter, C15-81
job application
letter, J4-365
response, C20-83
mailing notations, E68-165
meeting announcements, O3-422
memos, E92-179
order letter, C16-81
parts, E65-162
payment letter, C17-82
post cards, E93-180
postcript, E85-174
proofreading, E36-144
quoted or inset information, E76-170
rapid production, E91-178
recommendation, C18-82
reference initials, E82-172
reservation, C19-82
sales letter, C22-84
salutation, C24-85, C25-86, E72-167
sample letters, C6-74
signature, E80-171
small stationery, E90-178
styles, E66-163
styles, additional, E88-176
subject line, E73-168
sympathy or condolence, C23-85
tabulated information, E77-170
see also Mail
Courier services, D4-108
choosing, D5-110
Credit cards, A26-12, B40-40

Index

Credit invoice, **H21**-328
Cross-referencing, filing, **F14**-217
Crowding (squeezing), typing, **E30**-138
CRT display, **I41**-350
Customs, **A35**-15
  imports, **D25**-115
  mail, **L31**-390

Dash, **G23**-278
Databases, **Q24**-465
Data transmission, **T41**-511
Data vs. information, **F1**-210
Dates
  abbreviations, **G57**-304
  capitalization, **G68**-306
Decimals
  equivalents, **M4**-404
  mathematics, **M2**-400
Decorative devices, typing, **E10**-123
Deductions, payroll, **B61**-48
  legal obligations, **B71**-51
Degrees
  in addresses, **E70**-166
  alphabetizing, **F30**-225
Delivery and shipping services
  air express, **D2**-108
  bus, **D3**-108
  courier, **D4**-108, **D5**-110
  domestic, **D9**-112
  export, **D12**-113
  imports, **D24**-115
  log, **D34**-117
  terms, **D33**-116
  UPS, **D7**-111
Deposits, bank, **B13**-28
Desk organization, **W6**-519
Desktop calculators, **M30**-417
Desktop switchboard, **T27**-504
Destruction, file, **F53**-241
Dictation equipment, **C45**-101, **E143**-203
  centralized devices, **E145**-203
  sample text, **C46**-103
  types, **E144**-203
Dictionaries, **Q4**-454
  biographical, **Q3**-453
Die plate stamps, **H28**-330

Digest, reports, **E96**-182
Digitizers, **I26**-347
Direct deposit, **B41**-40
Directory assistance, **T9**-498
Directory, telephone, **T7**-497
Disbursing forms, **H24**-329
Discounted notes, **B39**-39
Discount formula, **M17**-409
Diskettes, floppy, **I15**-345, **I34**-349
  filing, **F75**-257
  hardware, **I33**-348
Dismissal, job, **P19**-444
Displayed information, correspondence, **E75**-168
Distribution, information, **I53**-353
Domestic mail, **L14**-386
Donation, response letter, **C21**-83
Drafts, bank, **B42**-40
Duplicators. *See* Reprographics; labels, continuous, **E54**-154

Earnings
  gross, **B57**-45
  record, **B60**-47
  see also Payroll
Editing. *See* Typewriting; Word processing
Editions, text, in references, **E128**-194
Education in resume, **J8**-368
Electric typewriters, **E21**-134
Electronic mail, **T36**-508, **T42**-511
Electronic typewriters, **E23**-134; *see also* Text editors
Employees. *See* Payroll; Personnel
Enclosure notation, correspondence, **E83**-173
Encyclopedias, **Q6**-455
Endnotes
  reports, **E118**-190
  typing, **E124**-192
Enumeration, typing, **E11**-123
Envelopes, **E50**-151
  chain feeding, **E55**-154
  dimensions, postal service regulations, **L18**-386, **L21**-388
  interoffice, **E56**-154

Index

sealing and stamping, **E58**-157
window, **E57**-156
Ergonomics, **W13**-523
Essays. *See* Reports
Exclamation mark, **G24**-278
Executive absence, office worker's role, **A38**-18
Expense reports
  form, **A40**-20
  travel, **A36**-16
Export, **D12**-113
  documentation, **D13**-113
  services, **D23**-114
Express mail, **L33**-390

Facsimile transmission, **I50**-352, **T37**-509
  equipment, **I28**-347
Fair use, **R17**-480
Family relationships, capitalization, **G69**-307
Fax. *See* Facsimile transmission
Fiber optics, **I58**-354
File cabinets, **F55**, **F56**-242
Filing
  alphabetic, **F43**-230
  charge-out, **F63**-247
  coding, **F13**-217
    color, **F64**-248
  correspondence, parts, **F6**-213
  cross-referencing, **F14**-217
  data vs. information, **F1**-210
  destruction, **F53**-241
  diskettes, **F75**-257
  electronic, **F74**-257
  electronic power, **F61**-246
  elements of comprehensive system, **F69**-252
  equipment, **F54**-242
  folders, **F8**-213
  fundamentals, **F9**-214
  geographic, **F44**-231
  guides, **F7**-213
  high density movable, **F59**-244
  indexing, **F12**-217, **F17**-220; *see also* Alphabetizing
  inspecting, **F11**-216

insurance records, **F80**-260
mechanical, **F60**-245
microforms/micrographics, **F72**-254, **F71**-253
numeric, **F47**-235
open shelf, **F58**-244
procedures manual, **F66**-250
ratios, **F68**-251
reading file, **F67**-250
records cycle, **F2**-210
retention, **F51**-238
skip numbering, **F49**-238
sorting, **F15**-219
steps, **F10**-216
storing, **F16**-220
subject, **F45**-232
summary, **F70**-252
systems, **F42**-230
  control, **F62**-247
  creation, **F3**-212
  elements of, **F5**-212
  maintenance and use, **F4**-212
terminal digit, **F50**-238
tickler (follow-up) systems, **F65**-248
transfer, **F52**-240
visible files, **F57**-242
vocabulary, **F81**-261
Financial advice, banks, **B43**-40
Financial statements, **B81**-57
  balance sheet, **B83**-58
  income, **B82**-57
  typing, **E59**-158
First-class mail, **L17**-387
  presort, **L43**-394
Flowcharts, **H1**-318
Footnotes, **C39**-98, **E118**-190
  formatting, **E125**-193
  typing, **E123**-191
Foreign currency, **B44**-40, **M24**-413
Foreign words, **A2**
  plurals, **G87**-314
Foreword, reports, **E96**-182
Formatting. *See* Typewriting; Word processing
Form letters, **C13**-78, **E89**-177

Index

Forms
  basic, H3-319, H26-329
  billing, H19-327
  books, Q8-456
  collection, H22-328
  credit invoice, H21-328
  definition, H2-319
  design, H29-331
  flowcharts, H1-318
  job application, P7-437
  legal, E62-160
  performance review, P16-443
  preprinted, H25-329
  production, H12-324
  purchase, H4-321
  receiving, H7-322
  rubber stamps, H28-330
  selling, H14-325
  shipping, H16-326
  stockkeeping, H9-323
  typing, E60-159
Fourth-class mail, L20-388
Fractions
  equivalents, M4-404
  hyphen, G27-279
  mathematics, M1-398
  typing, E16-125
Fraud, mail, L36-392
Fringe benefits, P24-446
Furniture, office, W14-524

Geographic filing, F44-231
Geographic terms
  alphabetizing, F33-226
  capitalization, G70-307
Gift checks, B45-41
Government names, alphabetizing, F39-228
Government references, Q9-457
  capitalization, G71-307
Grammar, usage, and style
  apostrophe, G6-272
  colon, G10-274
  comma, G13-274
  dash, G23-278
  exclamation mark, G24-278
  hyphen, G25-279
  nonrestrictive clauses, G17-276
  numbers, G82-311
  parentheses and brackets, G30-280
  parenthetical expressions, G19-277
  period, G33-280
  plurals, G83-313
  prefixes, G29-280
  punctuation, G5-272
  question mark, G34-281
  quotation marks, G35-281
  references, Q7-456
  semicolon, G38-282
  sentences
    compound, G15-275
    construction, G3-268
    flaws, G4-270
    structure, G2-268
  series, G22-278
  spelling, G49-295
  terms, G1-265
  titles, G37-282
  underscore, G42-283
  word choice, G43-283
  word division, G88-315
  words, omission of, G18-277
  see also Abbreviations; Spelling
Graphics, computer, R31-489
Graphs
  typing, E44-149
Gratitude letter, C14-80
Gross earnings, B57-45

Headings
  multiple page letters, E86-174
  reports, E100-184
  typing, E12-124
Health requirements, international travel, A34-15
High density movable files, F59-244
Hobbies on resume, J10-369
Holidays, A3
  capitalization, G68-306
Homonyms, G45-285
Hotel/motel accommodations, A21-10
  Red Book, A23-10, Q19-462

17

Index

requesting, **A22**-10
terms, **A24**-12
Hyphenated names, alphabetizing, **F26**-224
Hyphens
   plurals, **G85**-313
   prefixes, **G29**-280

Identification line, correspondence, **E81**-172
Illustrations, reports, **E112**-188
Imports, **D24**-115
   customs, **D25**-115
   documents, **D28**-115
   permits, **D18**-114
Indentation, paragraph, **E66**-163
Indexes
   periodicals, **Q10**-458
   reports, **E135**-199
Indexing
   electronic filing, **F76**-258
   filing, **F12**-217
Industry surveys, **Q17**-460
Information processing
   automated office, **I1**-335
   computer role, **I4**-338
   criteria, **I2**-337
   cycle, steps in, **I5**-338
   devices, **I12**-344
   distribution devices, **I53**-353
   history, **I3**-337
   input devices, **I13**-344
   integrated office, **I61**-354
   terms, **I62**-355
   see also Computer(s)
Information vs. data, **F1**-210
Initials, alphabetizing, **F27**-224
Input devices, computer, **I13**-344
Inquiry letter, **C12**-77
Inset information, correspondence, **E76**-170
Inside address, **E70**-166
Inspecting files, **F11**-216
Institutions, capitalization, **G72**-308
Insurance, **A27**-14
   life and baggage, **A28**-14

mail, **L34**-391
travel, **A29**-14
Intelpost, **L35**-392
Interest rates, formulas, **M9**-407, **M12**-408
Interlibrary loans, **Q23**-465
International mail, **L15**-386
Interoffice memoranda, **C28**-89
Interview, job, **J13**-370, **P8**-438
   follow-up, **P11**-440
Introduction letter, **C15**-81
Introduction, reports, **E96**-182
   numbering pages, **E106**-187
Inventory control forms, **H9**-323
Invoices, **H20**-327
   export, **D15**-113
   import, **D30**-115
   services, **D32**-116
IRAs, **B11**-27
Itinerary, **A25**-12
   form, **A39**-19

Job analysis, **P2**-434
Job application, response letter, **C20**-83
Job search, **J1**-363
   application, **J3**-364
      form, **J12**-370
      letter, **J4**-365
   data sheet (resume), **J5**-366
   interview, **J13**-370
      follow-up, **J16**-375
   leads, **J2**-363
   log, **J17**-375
   summary, **J18**-376
   see also Personnel
Journals, accounting, **B77**-53
Joystick, **I23**-346
Justification, typing, **E13**-124

Keyboarding equipment, types of
   machine, **E20**-134; *see also* Text editors; Typewriting; Word processing

Languages, capitalization, **G75**-309
Lateral file cabinet, **F56**-242
Leaders, typing, **E14**-124
Ledger, accounting, **B78**-54

Index

Legal documents, typing, E61-159
Letters. *See* Correspondence; Mail
Letters (of alphabet), plurals, G84-313
Letters of credit, B46-41
Libraries, Q20-463
   company, Q25-466
   depository, U.S., Q9-457
Life insurance, A28-14
Light pen, I24-347
Line graph, E45-150
Listening, better, W18-527
Loans, B47-41
Local area networks (LANs), I60-354, T47-513
Long-distance calling, T10-499
   area codes, A8

Machine logic, electronic calculators, M27-415
Magazines, indexes, Q12-459
Magnetic ink character recognition, I14-345
Magnetic tape/disk, I15-345, I33-348; *see also* Diskettes, floppy
Mail
   abbreviations, A2
   aerogrammes, L23-389
   alternatives to postal services, L49-395
   bulk mail, L24-389
   caller service, L25-389
   certificate, L27-389
   certified, L28-390
   claims, L29-390
   C.O.D., L30-390
   cost control, L50-396
   customs, L31-390
   delivery service, L32-390
   electronic, T36-508, T42-511
   express, L33-390
   first-class, presort, L43-394
   fraud, L36-392
   guidelines, L11-385
   incoming, L2-378
   insurance, L34-391
   Intelpost, L35-392
   log, L4-381
   mailgrams, L37-392
   merchandise return, L38-392
   money orders, L39-392
   OCR service, L40-393
   outgoing, L3-380
   packaging, L41-393
   postal service, types of service, L12-386
   post office boxes, L42-394
   priority mail, L44-394
   receipts, L26-389
   references, Q18-462
   registered, L45-394
   special delivery, L47-395
   special handling, L46-395
   standard dimensions, L21-388
   staying current, L51-396
   voice, T44-512
   ZIP+4, L48-395
Mailgrams, L37-392, T38-509
Mailing notations, E68-165
Mailroom, L5-382
   design, L7-382
   equipment, L8-382
   functions, L6-382
   incoming mail, L9-383
   outgoing mail, L10-384
Mainframe computer, I7-339
Manuals, procedures, W2-516
Manuscripts. *See* Reports
Margin, formula, M15-408
Margins
   reports, E98-183
   typing, E7-122
Marine calls, T22-502
Markdown, M16-409
Markup, formula, M10-408, M15-408
Mathematics, M1-398
   accounting equation, M7-407
   algebraic equations, M5-405
   amortization, M8-407
   averages, M20-411
   business formulas, M6-407
   decimals, M2-400
   electronic calculators, M25-414
   equivalents, percent-decimal-fraction, M4-404

Index

foreign currency exchange, M24-413
fractions, M1-398
interest, M9-407, M12-408
percentages, M3-402
pricing, M13-408
property taxes, M11-408
proportion, M22-412
ratio, M21-412
Roman numerals, A7
selling price, M10-408
statistical data, M19-411
Mean, M20-411
Measurements, A9
abbreviations, G58-305
conversion, A6
Mechanical files, F60-245
Median, M20-412
Meetings, O1-421
agenda, O4-423
announcements, O3-422
chairperson's role, O7-425
conducting, O6-425
follow-up, O17-431
last minute preparations, O5-424
minutes, O12-428
motions, presenting, O9-426
parliamentary procedure, O8-426
planning, O2-421
point of order, O10-427
proxies, O11-427
Memoranda, C28-89, E92-179
Merchandise return service, L38-392
Message switching, T43-512
Metric system, E39-146, A4
abbreviations, G58-305
Microcomputer, I7-340
Microforms (microfilm, microfiche, etc.)
computer input, I31-348
files, F71-253, F72-254
output, I47-351
Microwave transmission, I56-353
Minicomputer, I7-340
Minutes, meeting, O12-428
Misspelled words, G52-297
Misused words, G46-290

Mixed numbers, M1-398
Money market accounts, B9-27
Money orders, B48-41, L39-392
telegraphic, T39-510
Monuments, capitalization, G74-309
Motivation, employee, P29-449
Mouse, electronic, I22-346

Names
alphabetizing, F20-222
hyphenated, F26-224
capitalization, G64-306
Nationalities, capitalization, G75-309
Networks, T47-513
local area (LANs), I60-354, T47-513
Newspapers
indexes, Q11-458
references to, E130-194
News release, C29-90
Nonrestrictive clauses, G17-276
Notary service, B49-41
Note taking, W29-535
Nouns, plurals, G86-314
Numbered lists, reports, E110-188
Numbering systems, reports, E101-185
Numbers
alphabetizing, F41-229
figures cf. words, G82-311
hyphen, G28-279
plurals, G84-313
typing, E41-147
Numeric filing, F47-235

Office automation. *See* Information processing
design, W13-523
furniture, W14-525
layout, W15-525
safety, W10-522
supplies, W8-520
Official Airline Guide, A3-4, Q19-462
Offset duplicators, R22-482
Optical character recognition (OCR), I30-348
mail processing, L40-393

Index

Optical disks, I38-349
Optical mark reading, I16-345
Order letter, C16-81
Organizations, capitalization, G76-309
Orientation, new employee, P13-441
Overseas calls, T19-502

PABX, T26-504
Packaging, mail, L41-393
Packing list, export, D22-114
Paging systems, T30-504
Paper tape, I17-345
Paper, terms, R33-490
Paragraphs, indentation, E66-163
Parcel post, L20-388
Parentheses, G31-280
Parks, capitalization, G74-309
Parliamentary procedure, O8-426
Passbook savings, B3-24
Passport, A32-14
Pay by phone, B50-42
Payment letter, C17-82
Payment policy, P22-446
Payroll, B56-45
  deductions, B61-48
  employee earnings record, B60-47
  forms, H24-329
  gross earnings, B57-45
  legal obligations, B71-51
  payment methods, B67-49
  register, B59-46
  vacation, holiday, severance pay, B66-49
PBX, T25-503
Percentages, M3-402
  equivalents, M4-404
Performance reviews, employee, P16-443
Period, G33-280
Periodicals
  library, Q22-464
  references to, E130-194
Permissions, copyright, R20-482
Permits, export, D17-114
Personal computer. *See* Computer(s); Information processing

Personal organization, W16-526
  appointment book/calendar, W30-536
  appointments, W22-531
  better listening, W18-527
  correspondence, handling, W20-529
  note taking, W29-535
  planning day, W28-534
  reading skill, W21-530
  self-assertiveness, W19-528
  stress avoidance, W17-526
  time management, W25-532
  see also Workstation organization
Personnel, P1-434
  advertisements, P5-436
  application forms, P7-437
  dismissals, P19-444
  evaluations, P14-442
  fluctuations, coping with, P28-448
  fringe benefits, P24-446
  interview, P8-438
    follow-up, P11-440
  job analysis, P2-434
  job evaluation, P23-446
  motivation guidelines, P29-449
  new employees
    evaluation, P15-442
    orientation, P13-441
  payment policies, P22-446
  performance reviews, P16-443
  records, P21-445
  recruitment, P3-435, P12-440
  resignation, P20-445
  sources of, P4-435
  temporary, P25-447
  tests, P10-440
Person-to-person calls, T18-502
Petty cash fund, B55-43
  sample record, B86-65
Photocomposition, I49-352, R29-488
  terms, R30-488
  see also Reprographics
Pictogram, E48-151
Pie chart, E49-151
Pivoting, typing, E15-125
Placement, reports, E98-183

I11

Index

Place names
  abbreviations, G59-305
  capitalization, G77-309
Plain paper copier, R7-473
Planning day, W28-534
Plotters, computer, I45-351
Plurals, G84-313
  apostrophe, G8-272
Point of order, O10-427
Political references, capitalization, G71-307
Possessives, apostrophe, G9-272
Post cards, E93-180
Post-dated checks, B27-35
Post office boxes, L42-394; *see also* Delivery and shipping services; Mail
Postscript, E85-174
Preface, reports, E96-182
  numbering pages, E106-187
Prefixes
  alphabetizing, F21-222
  hyphens in, G29-280
Preprinted forms, H25-329
Presort first-class mail, L43-394
Pricing
  break even, M18-410
  formula, M13-408, M17-409
Printers, computer
  impact, I42-350
  nonimpact, I44-351
Printing. *See* Reprographics
Priority mail, L44-394
Procedures manuals, W2-516
  filing, F66-250
Production order, H13-324
Promotion policy, P17-444
Proofreading, E34-143
  guidelines, E37-145
  pointers, E36-144
  steps, E35-143
  symbols, inside back cover
Proportion, M22-412
Proxies, O11-427
Publications, capitalization, G78-310
Punched cards, I18-345

Punctuation, G5-272
  capitalization after, G79-310
  apostrophe, G6-272
  styles, E66-164
  see also Grammar, usage, and style
Purchasing, H4-321
  purchase order, H6-321
  purchase requisition, H5-321

Queries
  almanacs and yearbooks, Q1-452
  annual reports, Q14-459
  atlases, Q2-452
  biographical dictionaries, Q3-453
  business organizations, information on Q13-459
  city directories, Q15-460
  computerized searches, Q24-465
  dictionaries, Q4-454
  encyclopedias, Q6-455
  form and style books, Q8-456
  government references, Q9-457
  industry surveys, Q17-460
  library, Q20-463
    company, Q25-466
  periodical indexes, Q10-458
  postal information, Q18-462
  specialized, Q19-462
  specialized references, Q19-462
  thesauruses and word division, Q5-454
  usage guides, Q7-456
  vocabulary, Q26-466
  Yellow Pages, Q16-460
Question mark, G34-281
Quotation marks, G35-281
Quotations
  colon, G11-274
  correspondence, E76-170
  references, Q19-462
  reports, E113-189

Races, capitalization, G75-309
Ratios
  filing, F68-251
  mathematics, M21-412

Index

Reading file, F67-250
Reading improvement, W21-530
Realignment, typing, E28-137
Receipts, mail, L26-389
Recommendation letter, C18-82
Recording minutes, O15-430
Records, personnel, P21-445; see also Filing
Recruitment, P3-435
Reference books. See Queries
Reference initials, correspondence, E82-172
References on resume, J11-369
Registered mail, L45-394
Religious references, capitalization, G80-311
Reports, C31-92, E94-181
  back matter, C40-98
  bibliography, E134-196
  body, C39-98
  drafting, C35-96
  ending pages, E104-187
  finalizing, C36-97
  footnotes and endnotes, E118-190
  front matter, C38-97
  headings, E100-184
  illustrations, E112-188
  index, E135-199
  investigating, C23-94
  numbered lists, E100-188
  numbering pages, E105-187
  numbering sections, E101-185
  oral, C48-104
  outlining, C34-94
  parts, C37-97
  placement, E98-183
  planning, C32-92
  preface, E96-182
  quoted material, E113-189
  receiving, H8-322
  spacing, E99-184
  table of contents, E97-182
  tabulated material, E111-188
  textnotes, E133-195
  title page, E95-181
  typing guide sheet, E136-200

Reprographics
  auxiliary equipment, R28-487
  carbon paper, R12-475
  computer graphics, R31-489
  copiers, intelligent, R32-490; see also Copiers
  copying machines, R5-473
  cost control, R34-491
  cut and paste, R16-479
  duplicating processes compared, R23-483
  equipment choice, R24-484
  fair use guidelines, R17-480
  offset process, R22-482
  options, R3-472
  paper terms, R33-490
  photocomposition, R29-488
  process, R2-471
    selection, R4-473
  terms, R1-470
Research. See Queries
Reservations letter, C19-82
Resignation, P20-445
Restaurant terms, A24-12
Resume, J5-366
Retail price, formula, M14-408
Retention, file, F51-238
Roberts Rules of Order, O10-427, Q19-462
Roman numerals, A7
Rubber stamps, H28-330

Safety deposit boxes, B51-42
Safety, office, W10-522
Sales confirmation, export, D14-113
Sales letter, C22-84
Sales order, H15-325
Salutations, C24-85, C25-86, E72-167
  capitalization, G73-308
Sea travel, A20-9
Second-class mail, L18-387
Self-assertiveness, W19-528
Self-correcting typewriters, E22-134
Selling forms, H14-325
Selling price, formula, M10-408
Semiconductor secondary storage, I37-349

Index

Seniority designations, alphabetizing, F31-226
Sentences
  compound, G15-275, G39-282
  construction hints, G3-268
  flaws, G4-270
  structure, G2-268
Series
  commas, G22-278
  semicolons in, G41-283
Shipping
  forms, H16-326
  order, H15-325
  see also Delivery and shipping services
Signature, correspondence, E80-171
Skip numbering, F49-238
Software, computer, I11-342
Sorting, filing, F15-219
Space planning, W12-523
Spacing, typewriting, E42-148
  reports, E99-184
Special delivery, mail, L47-395
Special handling, mail, L46-395
Speeches, C48-104
Spelling, G49-295
  guidelines, G50-295
  misspelled words, G52-297
  rules, G51-296
  see also Grammar, usage, and style
Spreading, typing, E29-138
Squeezing (crowding), typing, E30-138
Staffing. See Personnel
Stamping envelopes, E58-157
Statement savings, B4-24
States, abbreviations, G59-305, inside front cover
Stationery, small, E90-178
Station-to-station calls, T12-500
Statistical data, M19-411
Stopped checks, B26-35
Stress avoidance, W17-526
Style
  abbreviations, G54-299
  addresses, G55-299
  mechanics, G53-299
  references, Q8-456

Subject filing, F45-232
Subject line, correspondence, E73-168
Summary, reports, E96-182
Symbols, typing, E16-125
Sympathy letter, C23-85
Synopsis, reports, E96-182

Table of contents, reports, E97-182
Tabulated material
  correspondence, E77-170
  reports, E111-188
  typing, E17-127
Tape, magnetic, I35-349, I46-351
Taxes
  payroll, B63-48
    legal obligations, B72-51
  property, formula, M11-408
Tax-sheltered pension trust accounts, B10-27
Telecommunications, T35-508
  cost control, T48-514
  data transmission, T41-511
  electronic mail, T36-508
  facsimile transmission, T37-509
  mailgram, T38-509
  message switching, T43-512
  networks, T47-513
  teleconferencing, T45-513
  telegrams and cables, T39-510
  Telex/TWX, T40-510
  visual displays, T46-513
  voice mail, T44-512
  see also Computer(s); Telephone
Teleconferencing, T45-513
Telegrams, T39-510
Telephone, T1-494
  answering services, T33-507
  area codes, A8
  calling card, T13-500
  collect calls, T15-501
  directory, Q16-460
    assistance, T6-497, T9-498
    using, T7-497
  equipment, T23-503
    features, T32-505
  and information processing, I54-353

Index

long-distance calls, T10-499
making calls, T5-497
money-saving tips, T34-507
overseas calls, T19-502
pay by phone, B50-42
person-to-person calls, T18-502
special calls, T22-502
station-to-station calls, T12-500
taking calls, T3-494
third number calls, T16-501
time and charges, T17-501
transferring calls, T4-496
see also Telecommunications
Telex, I50-352, T40-510
equipment, I29-347
Temporary personnel, P25-447
Terminal digit filing, F50-238
Terminals, computer, I20-346
Tests, personnel, P10-440
Text editors
common features, E32-139, E33-143
corrections, E31-139
Textnotes, E133-195
Thank you letter, C14-80
Thermal copier, R9-474
Thesaurus, Q5-454
Third-class mail, L19-387
Third number calls, T16-501
Tickler systems, F65-248
Time
capitalization, G81-311
and charges, telephone, T17-501
management, W25-532
zones, A8
Title page, E95-181
Titles
abbreviations, G62-305
alphabetizing, F29-225
company names, F32-226
quoted, G37-282
Touch indexing, electronic calculators, M26-414
Touch-sensitive screen, I25-347
Trademarks, capitalization, G66-306
Train travel, A16-8
classes, A18-9

fares, A17-9
luggage, A19-9
Transaction terminals, I21-346
Transfer, file, F52-240
Transportation terms, D33-116
Travel
agents, A1-3
air, A2-3
automobile, A11-7
bus, A15-8
expense reports, A36-16
form, A40-20
foreign currency, B44-40
funds, A26-12
hotel/motel accommodations, A21-10
insurance, A27-14
international, A30-14
itinerary, A25-12
form, A39-19
office worker's role in executive absence, A38-18
planning, A37-16
references, Q19-462
reservations letter, C19-82
sea, A20-9
train, A16-8
Traveler's checks, B52-42, A26-12
Trial balance, B80-56
TWX, T40-510
Typesetting, I49-352, R29-488
terms, R30-488
see also Reprographics
Typewriting, E1-120
centering, E6-121, E9-122
charts and graphs, E44-149
corrections, E27-137
decorative devices, E10-123
enumerations, E11-123
envelopes, E50-151
chain feeding, E55-154
financial statements, E59-158
footnotes and endnotes, E123-191
forms, E60-159
heading styles, E12-124
justification, E13-124
labels, continuous form, E54-154

Index

leaders, E14-124
legal documents, E61-159
margins, E7-122
metric expressions, E39-146
pivoting, E15-125
placement, E2-120
realigning, E28-137
spacing rules, E42-148
special characters, E16-125
spreading, E29-138
squeezing/crowding, E30-138
style, E38-146
tabulation, E17-127
types of machine, E20-134
see also Proofreading; Text editors; Word processing

Underscore, G42-283
United Parcel Service, D7-111
Usage, English, Q8-456
U.S. Savings Bonds, B53-42

Vertical file cabinet, F55-242
Videoconferencing, T45-513
Visa, A33-15
Visible files, F57-242
Visual displays, communicating, T46-513
Voice
  input devices, I27-347
  mail, T44-512
  messaging, I52-352
  output, I51-352
  qualities, C43-100

WATS, T22-503
Weighted average, M20-411
Weights and measures, A9
W-2 form, B74-51
White Pages, T7-497
Wholesale price, M14-408
Who's Who, Q3-453

Wire transfers, B54-43
Withdrawals, bank, B15-29
Word choice, G43-283
  confused words, G45-285
  misused words, G46-290
  trite expressions, G44-284
  see also Grammar, usage, and style
Word division, G88-315, Q5-454
Word processing, E24-135
  centralized, E138-201
  configurations, E137-201
  cycle, E142-202
  decentralized, E139-202
  dictation equipment, E143-203
  log, E138-201
  satellite, E140-202
  single-unit workstation, E141-202
  terms, E146-204
  see also Computer(s); Information processing; Text editors; Typewriting
Words, compound, hyphen, G26-279; see also Grammar, usage, and style
Work experience, resume, J9-368
Work order, H13-324
Workstation organization, W1-516
  desk organization, W6-519
  equipment, W4-518
  furniture, W14-524
  layout, W15-525
  office design, W13-523
  office safety, W10-522
  procedures manuals, W2-516
  space planning, W12-523
  supplies, W8-520
  see also Personal organization

Yearbooks, Q1-452
Yellow Pages, Q16-460, T7-497

ZIP Codes, Q18-462
ZIP + 4 mail, L48-395